Student Guide with Map
to Accompany

THE ENDURING VISION

A History of the American People
Third Edition

by

Paul S. Boyer • Clifford E. Clark, Jr. • Joseph F. Kett
Neal Salisbury • Harvard Sitkoff • Nancy Woloch

Barbara Blumberg
Pace University

D. C. Heath and Company
Lexington, Massachusetts   Toronto

Address editorial correspondence to:

D. C. Heath and Company
125 Spring Street
Lexington, MA 02173

Preface

The *Student Guide with Map Exercises to Accompany The Enduring Vision,* Third Edition, is intended to help you master the history presented in *The Enduring Vision: A History of the American People.* It is *not* a substitute for reading the textbook. However, used properly as a *supplement* to the text, it should assist you in focusing on the important events, issues, and concepts in American history, as well as on the well-known figures and ordinary people alike whose ideas and actions help us to understand the past. It is also designed to build your vocabulary, improve your knowledge of geography, and enhance your understanding of how the historian learns about the past.

Each chapter in the *Student Guide* corresponds to a chapter in *The Enduring Vision* and is divided into the following sections:

- *Outline and Summary.* This follows the outline of the textbook chapter and summarizes the material discussed under each text heading. You should read it quickly before reading the textbook chapter to give yourself an overview of the contents. Then carefully read the text chapter. After completing the text chapter, reread the outline and summary as a review.

- *Vocabulary.* In this section social-science terms and other words used in the text chapter that may be new to you are defined. Look over the list before you read the textbook chapter. Familiarize yourself with any words that you do not already know.

- *Identifications.* Here you will find the important persons, laws, terms, groups, and events covered in *The Enduring Vision.* After reading the text chapter, test yourself by identifying who or what each item was and how this person or thing fits into the overall story. That is, what is its historical significance?

- *Skill Building.* In most of the chapters of the *Student Guide,* you will find either (a) a section designed to help you interpret charts and tables in the textbook or (b) a map exercise, asking you to locate places mentioned in the text chapter and to explain the historical significance of those geographical places. Some chapters contain both.

- *Historical Sources.* Too often we simply accept what we see in print as true and memorize it without stopping to ask how the author obtained the information and whether we should believe it. The purpose of the Historical Sources section found in most chapters is to explain where the historian gets his or her facts, and to assist you in evaluating the reliability of those sources and the conclusions based on them.

- *Multiple-Choice Questions, Short-Answer Questions, Essay Questions, and Answers to Multiple-Choice Questions.* After reading the corresponding chapter in *The Enduring Vision,* you should try to answer these questions. They are designed to help you review the significant material in the chapter; they will probably be similar to the kinds of questions and essays that your professor will give you to write on in papers, quizzes, and exams. Answers to the multiple-choice questions appear at the end of the *Student Guide*.

The last *Student Guide* chapter is intended to aid you in preparing for the final examination in your history course. It contains hints on studying, as well as multiple-choice and essay questions that ask you to consider and pull together the material presented in *all* of the chapters of *The Enduring Vision*.

For help in preparing the *Student Guide,* I would first like to thank the authors of *The Enduring Vision* for writing a lucid, informative political, social, and cultural history of the United States that is a pleasure to read and to write about. Second, I appreciate the help of the editors at D. C. Heath who made valuable suggestions. I am grateful to my husband, Alan Krumholz, and to my son, Mark, for their patience and support while I worked on this project.

Barbara Blumberg

Contents

PROLOGUE

Enduring Vision, Enduring Land

OUTLINE AND SUMMARY

I. Introduction

America's "enduring vision" has constituted (1) a vision of the land itself in which the land offers a "haven for new beginnings" and opportunities, and (2) a search for a just social order that has constantly sought to balance individual freedom with obligations to the social group, or "community." Many times in our past we have not lived up to our ideals of freedom and social responsibility, but those who have tried to bring us back to the vision, along with most other Americans, have shared a hopefulness about progress.

II. An Ancient Heritage

The oldest rocks on the North American continent are 3 billion years old. By the Paleozoic era (around 250 million years ago), forests covered much of what would eventually be the United States, and the organic matter of these ancient forests was to provide America with its abundant coal deposits. About 180 million years ago, earth's one big landmass, Pangaea, began to split apart into separate continents. Millions of years later, violent movements of the earth's crust created the Pacific Coastal, Sierra Nevada, and Cascade mountain ranges on the western edge of the continent. Between 65 and 70 million years ago the shallow sea that covered much of west-central North America disappeared and was replaced by the Rocky Mountains. The decay and fossilization of plant and animal organisms in these regions had already started to form America's oil deposits.

The four glaciations of the Ice Age, between 2 million and 10,000 years ago, reshaped much of Canada, New England, New York, and the Midwest. Only as those glaciers began their last retreat northward did human beings arrive in North America.

III. The Continent and Its Regions

A. Introduction

As the ice retreated, North America slowly warmed. The geological, geographical, and climatic diversity that followed has contributed to the regional cultural differences that have developed and to America's physical beauty, wealth of resources, and political preeminence.

B. The West

Lands in Alaska and Canada ranged from the treeless tundra of the Arctic to the heavily forested taiga of the subarctic. Farther south the Pacific Northwest had a temperate, rainy climate and many resources, while the southern California coast offered a drier, warmer, Mediterranean climate. To the east of the fertile intermountain range valleys and the Sierra Nevada lay the Great Basin, an arid, formidable desert. The backbone of western North America is formed by the Rocky Mountains. Beyond the Rockies' front range is the Continental Divide, the watershed separating rivers flowing eastward into the Atlantic from those draining westward into the Pacific. In the hot southwestern deserts of Arizona, southern Utah, western New Mexico, and southeastern California, Native Americans cultivated the first crops in what is now the United States.

C. The Heartland

North America's heartland extends from the Rocky Mountains to the Appalachians. Over the millennia, the Mississippi-Missouri-Ohio river system that drains it has carried so much silt down to the Gulf of Mexico that a fertile delta capable of providing food for a large population has been built up. Most of the eastern and northern sections of the heartland were once covered with thick forests. To the west the trees give way gradually to grass-covered prairies. Beyond the Missouri River, these prairies become the Great Plains—treeless, an endless sea of grass, bitter cold in winter, blazing hot in summer, and often dry. In the nineteenth century, white settlers displaced the Indians in the American heartland—felled the trees, plowed up the grasses, and turned the Midwest into a breadbasket for the world, except during periodic droughts when it was subjected to severe dust storms.

D. The Atlantic Seaboard

East of the Appalachians lies the upland area known as the piedmont, extending from Alabama to Maryland. Once blessed with rich, red soil, its fertility in modern times has been ruined by excessive cotton and tobacco farming. The northward extension of the piedmont runs from Pennsylvania to southern New England. In contrast, the terrain of upstate New York and most of New England was sculpted by glaciation. Strewn with the rocks and boulders left behind by retreating ice, New England's soil is difficult to plow.

The fall line, a series of rapids in the rivers that block navigation upstream from the coast, separates the Atlantic coastal plain, or tidewater, from the interior. In the south the tidewater is cut by numerous small rivers. To the north it narrows and flattens to form the New Jersey Pine Barrens, Long Island, and Cape Cod. North of Massachusetts Bay, the shoreline becomes mountainous. North America's true eastern edge, the continental shelf, is an area of relatively shallow water that extends as much as 250 miles into the Atlantic.

Some ten thousand years ago, Indians followed a warming climate eastward over the Appalachians to the coast. They found the waters of the Grand Banks and Cape Cod teeming with fish, and the hardwood forests abundant with berries and game. Carrying Woodland culture with them, they also engaged in agriculture.

IV. A Legacy and a Challenge

Geographical isolation and ecological variety characterized the New World before the arrival of Europeans. Until the early twentieth century Americans hoped that separation would isolate them from Europe and its problems. Modern technology has killed that dream and posed another challenge—how to stop destruction of the very environment that has sustained us. Here we could well draw on the legacy of the Native Americans and reestablish a sense of historical and cultural continuity with our predecessors on the land. In this way we might recapture the Indians' sense "that the land—its life-sustaining bounty and its soul-sustaining beauty—is itself of inestimable value and not merely a means to the end of material growth."

VOCABULARY

The following terms are used in the Prologue. To understand it fully, it is important that you know what each of them means.

eon   an indefinitely long period of time; an age; the largest division of geologic time, composing two or more eras

ephemeral   fleeting, impermanent, short-lived

geology   the scientific study of the earth, rocks, and the changes that the earth has undergone or is undergoing

exploitation   unfair or reckless use of people, animals, and/or the environment to profit materially from them

tundra   nearly level, treeless plain with sparse, stunted vegetation of the kind found in the arctic regions of Europe, Asia, and North America

taiga   the evergreen forests of subarctic lands covering vast areas of northern North America and Eurasia

anchorage   harbor

steppe   dry, grassy land or plains

delta   a nearly flat plain of river-deposited silt and soil between diverging branches of the mouth of a river

bayou   a sluggish tributary or a swampy arm of a lake or river

millennium (plural: millennia)   a period of a thousand years

pristine   of or pertaining to the earliest period or state; original, primitive, or having its original purity

ecologist   one who studies the interaction between plants and animals and their environment

IDENTIFICATIONS

After reading the Prologue, you should be able to identify and explain the historical significance of each of the following:

New World

Pangaea and continental drift

Precambrian era

Paleozoic era

Mesozoic era

Ice Age

Continental Divide

breadbasket

fall line

continental shelf

Grand Banks

SKILL BUILDING: MAPS

1. On the map of North America, locate each of the following and explain its geologic origins:

   continental shelf

   Appalachians

   Pacific Coastal, Sierra Nevada, and Cascade mountain ranges

   Rocky Mountains and Continental Divide

   Great Lakes

   Great Basin and Utah's Great Salt Lake

   southwestern desert, Colorado River, and Grand Canyon

   Mississippi Delta

   Great Plains

   tidewater region and fall line

   piedmont

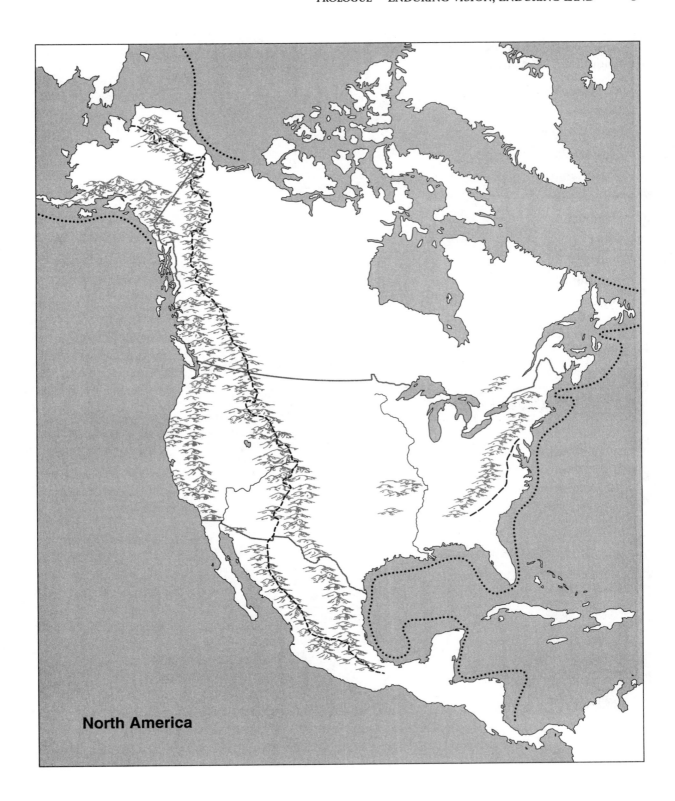

North America

2. On the map below locate each of these major North American rivers, showing its point of origin and its mouth:

St. Lawrence

Hudson

Susquehanna

Potomac

Savannah

Mississippi

Missouri

Ohio

Snake

Columbia

Rio Grande

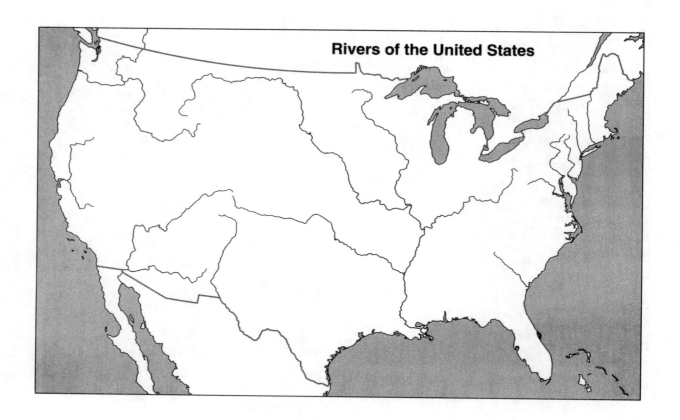

Rivers of the United States

MULTIPLE-CHOICE QUESTIONS

Circle the letter of the item that best completes each statement or answers the question.

1. The fall line is
    a. the edge of the continental shelf where the Atlantic Ocean suddenly becomes much deeper.
    b. the mountain ranges of California over which Pacific air masses drop their moisture in the form of heavy rainfall.
    c. the divide between the treeless Great Plains and the more forested Mississippi-Ohio Valley.
    d. the series of rapids in rivers where hard continental rock meets the sedimentary plains along the Atlantic.

2. About how long ago did the last glacial expansion in North America occur?
    a. no one knows
    b. 50,000 years
    c. 10,000 years
    d. 2 million years

3. Agriculture was first practiced by the Indians of the
    a. Pacific Northwest.
    b. desert Southwest.
    c. midwestern heartland.
    d. Atlantic seaboard.

4. The Continental Divide is found in the
    a. Sierra Nevada.
    b. fall line.
    c. Ohio Valley.
    d. Rocky Mountains.

5. All of the following were created by glaciation *except*
    a. the Great Lakes.
    b. New England's rocky soil.
    c. the Grand Canyon.
    d. the coastline of Alaska.

6. Because of its geological and ecological history, North America has to this day the world's largest deposits of
    a. bauxite.
    b. coal.
    c. iron ore.
    d. oil.

7. Since the nineteenth century the geographical region that has become America's breadbasket is
   a. the Midwest.
   b. the Far West.
   c. the Atlantic seaboard.
   d. the Great Basin.

8. The region with the greatest annual temperature range in the United States is
   a. New England.
   b. the Southeast.
   c. the Pacific Northwest and Alaskan panhandle.
   d. the Great Plains.

9. An environmental historian has stated, "The ancestors of American buffalos, Eurasian cattle, and Australian kangaroos shambled and hopped down diverging paths of evolution." Why did that happen?
   a. The plants and animals on each continent were virtually isolated from those on other continents for 180 million years.
   b. Agriculture and hunting patterns brought great changes to the plant and animal kingdoms.
   c. It was so cold in the northern hemisphere that the animals which survived there were very different from those of the southern hemisphere.
   d. No one knows the reasons for this diversity.

10. All of the following states have a portion of the piedmont running through them *except*
    a. Alabama.
    b. Pennsylvania.
    c. Rhode Island.
    d. North Carolina.

SHORT-ANSWER QUESTIONS

1. What was Pangaea? What happened to it about 180 million years ago? What were the consequences?

2. Describe the climate and terrain of each of the following regions: the West, the heartland, the Atlantic seaboard.

3. How was the fertile Mississippi Delta created?

4. Why was much of New England's soil rocky and difficult to plow?

ESSAY QUESTIONS

1. According to the Prologue, what has been the enduring vision of Americans? What have been some of the problems and contradictions within that vision?

2. "Geology, geography, and environment are among the fundamental building blocks of human history." Explain the meaning of this statement, and illustrate it with as many specific examples from the Prologue as possible.

1

America Begins

OUTLINE AND SUMMARY

I. Introduction

American history began more than ten thousand years before Columbus's first voyage. Here Native Americans developed cultures quite different from those of the Eastern Hemisphere and richly varied from one region to another.

II. The First Americans

A. *Introduction*

Between forty thousand and fifteen thousand years ago bands of hunters from Siberia crossed the then existing land bridge into Alaska. Most Native Americans descended from these first migrants.

B. *The Peopling of North America*

As the Ice Age ended about 10,000 B.C. and the land bridge submerged under the sea, the Alaskan hunters journeyed southward and spread over the plains in pursuit of mammoths, mastodons, horses, camels, bison, and moose, all of which roamed the continent. These Paleo-Indians (early hunters) lived in small groups and devised "fluted" points with which they hunted very effectively. About 9000 B.C. the mammoths and mastodons became extinct because of climatic warming and relentless hunting.

C. *Archaic Societies*

As the earth's atmosphere warmed, a tremendous range of plants and animals flourished on the North American continent and in its waters. This enabled archaic peoples (North Americans of the period 8000 B.C. to 1500 B.C.) to broaden their diets to include small mammals, fish, and wild plants. This abundance was especially apparent in parts of the East and Midwest, allowing larger groups of people to live in a smaller area and establish permanent villages. Archaic peoples learned how to make tools, weapons, and utensils from materials such as stone, bone, shell, clay, and leather. They also started extensive trade networks to obtain items not available in their own area. Ideas and religious beliefs, as well as material goods, spread along these networks. Although these peoples did not have class structures or centralized political power, they did distinguish sharply between men's and women's roles: men hunted and fished; women harvested and prepared wild plants.

III. The Indians' Continent

A. *The Northern and Western Perimeters*

By 1500 B.C. in western Alaska a new arctic way of life was emerging. The Eskimos and Aleuts were making and using the first bows and arrows, ceramic pottery, and pit houses. The Eskimos spread across the tundra regions as far east as Greenland. They received some metal tools from trade with Siberia and the Norsemen in Newfoundland.

Along the Pacific coast, from southern Alaska to northern California, Indians fished for salmon and learned to dry and store their catch year-round, making possible the establishment of permanent villages of several hundred people. Farther south California Indians also resided in permanent villages and sustained themselves by collecting and grinding acorns into meal. Both groups engaged in trade and warfare and, as a result, united under the leadership of chiefs. Because the climate of the Great Basin was so warm and dry, Indians of that area could not settle in one region but continued to roam, hunting small mammals and foraging for wild seeds and nuts.

B. *The Southwest*

In the Southwest, Indians turned slowly to farming, creating sophisticated systems of irrigation. Farming in the Western Hemisphere began in about 5000 B.C. in central Mexico, and the techniques of plant domestication spread to western New Mexico. By the third century B.C. the Hohokam people of southern Arizona had built extensive canal systems for irrigation that allowed them to harvest two crops a year. They also resided in permanent villages of several hundred people. The Anasazi people of the Southwest lived primarily by farming, too. These ancestors of the modern Pueblo Indians dominated the Southwest for almost 600 years, founding villages such as Chaco Canyon, New Mexico, inhabited by about fifteen thousand persons. By the thirteenth century, however, the Anasazi and Hohokam cultures declined, and these peoples abandoned their large settlements because of prolonged periods of drought. At roughly the same time the foraging Apaches and Navajos arrived in the Southwest.

C. *The Eastern Woodlands*

Many tribes in the Eastern Woodlands (the area from the Mississippi Valley to the Atlantic coast) experimented with village life and political centralization even before they started farming. As early as 1200 B.C. five thousand people lived at Poverty Point on the shore of the Mississippi River in Louisiana. As Poverty Point declined in importance, a new mound-building culture, the Adena, emerged. Adena mounds, often containing graves and playing an essential role in the people's religion, were built all over the Mississippi Valley and Northeast. In the first century B.C. Adena culture evolved into the more complex and widespread Hopewell civilization, which built more elaborate mounds.

Agriculture did not become the primary source of food for Eastern Woodlands peoples until after the seventh century A.D. The first full-time farmers in the East lived on the floodplains of the Mississippi River, where, incorporating elements of Hopewell culture, they evolved into the still more sophisticated Mississippian civilization. Mississippian towns grew to have thousands of inhabitants. The most important town was Cahokia, near present-day St. Louis. Mississippian artists produced works of clay, stone, shell, and copper. Their religion was based on sun worship, and their political system was centralized and hierarchical. By the thirteenth century, Mississippian culture had declined and most Eastern Woodlands Indians had abandoned large settlements and centralized political power. However, they continued to engage in agriculture, using the ecologically sound slash-and-burn method of land clearing to grow their corn, beans, and pumpkins. They practiced other resource conservation measures as well, which later European settlers neither understood nor followed.

Many different Indian cultures existed on the North American continent by 1500, but most shared certain characteristics: use of bows and arrows and ceramic pottery, belief in some common religious practices and rituals, preference for small kin-based communities, and rejection of political centralization.

IV. New World Peoples on the Eve of European Contact

A. *Introduction*

By 1492 about 75 million people lived in the Western Hemisphere. Of these, 7 million to 10 million inhabited land north of Mexico. These peoples were divided into several hundred nations and tribes and spoke diverse languages. The most important social groupings were the family, the village, and, for many of the tribes, the clan.

B. *Family and Community*

Kinship held Indian societies together. The kinship group, or extended family, was far more important than the nuclear family of husband, wife, and young children. The men hunted, fished, traded, negotiated, and fought; the women did the farming (except among the tribes of the Southwest, where both sexes were cultivators).

C. *Indian Religion and Social Values*

Native Americans found all nature, including humanity, interrelated and suffused with spiritual powers or, in the language of the Algonquian, *manitou*. Indians sought to placate and be in tune with these spiritual forces. They did this through dreaming; altering their state of consciousness by acts of physical endurance and self-torture, such as the Sun Dance of the Plains Indians; and following the advice of shamans. To smooth relations between persons of unequal status and power and hold their societies together, Indians relied on reciprocity, which included the giving of gifts and trading of goods in return for receiving prestige, deference, and authority. Indian communities generally demanded conformity and close cooperation of their members.

V. Conclusion

Isolation from the Eastern Hemisphere and the great climatic and geographical diversity of the North American continent shaped Indian cultures. Human history in the Western Hemisphere did not begin with the arrival of Columbus. For thousands of years before 1492 Native Americans hunted; gathered; farmed; built communities, roads, and trails; and created complex societies.

VOCABULARY

The following terms are used in Chapter 1. To understand the chapter fully, it is important that you know what each of them means.

archaeological   of or pertaining to the scientific study of any prehistoric culture by excavation and description of its remains

indigenous   native to a particular region

shaman   a medicine man; a worker with the supernatural

kiva   a large chamber, often wholly or partially underground, in a Pueblo Indian village; used for religious ceremonies and other purposes

deference   submission or yielding to the judgment, opinion, and/or will of another; respectful or courteous regard

clan   a group of families or households whose heads claim descent from a common ancestor

hierarchy   a system of placing persons or things in a graded order, from lower to higher, in wealth, power, status, and so on

reciprocity   a system of mutual give-and-take, allowing individuals or social groups of unequal power, wealth, or status to get along while preserving unequal power relationships; also, a system by which human beings can coexist with nature and the powerful supernatural forces in which they believe

consensus   agreement in opinion; collective opinion

IDENTIFICATIONS

After reading Chapter 1, you should be able to identify and explain the historical significance of each of the following:

League of the Iroquois

Paleo-Indians

Archaic peoples

pit houses

Hohokam culture

Anasazi and Pueblo cultures

Chaco Canyon

Poverty Point, mound-building culture, and Adena culture

Hopewell and Mississippian cultures

Eastern Woodlands peoples

Cahokia

nuclear families versus extended families

manitou and the Sun Dance

potlatch ceremony

SKILL BUILDING: MAPS

On the map of North America on the following page, locate the regions where these Indian cultures and the sites associated with them existed:

Aleuts, Eskimos, and Arctic culture

Northwest Coast Indians

California Indians

hunting bands of the Great Basin

Hohokam culture

Anasazi and Pueblo cultures

Poverty Point

Adena culture

Hopewell and Mississippian cultures (Cahokia)

Eastern Woodlands culture (Iroquois Confederacy)

North America

HISTORICAL SOURCES

In learning about the past, historians have generally depended on written records as their major source. But written documents do not always exist for all places, groups, and times. For most of history the world's peoples were preliterate or illiterate and therefore left no written communication. The Indians inhabiting the present-day United States had not developed written languages before the Europeans arrived. How can historians attempt to reconstruct the lives and experiences of these peoples? As the author of Chapter 1 tells us on page 1, "archaeological evidence and oral traditions, examined critically, are our principal sources. . . ." Archaeologists can detect much about a long-lost way of life by uncovering the artifacts and remains left by the people who shared a past culture. For example, on page 8 the author refers to evidence found at an archaeological dig at Bat Cave in western New Mexico. What does that evidence indicate? In "A Place in Time: Cahokia in 1200" there is a description of a grave mound uncovered in another dig. What was found at that site? What does the historian surmise from the contents of this mound and of other grave mounds in the same area?

Many tribes had special storytellers who handed down the history and myths of their people from generation to generation. The Hiawatha legend that opens Chapter 1 is one example. Find other references to Indian myths in the chapter.

In addition to these sources, historians have turned to the writings of early European explorers and settlers. In the capsule history of Cahokia the author refers to French explorers' accounts of Natchez Indian society in the 1600s and La Salle's description of Cahokia in 1682. What does the historian learn from these? At other places in Chapter 1 Roger Williams, Puritan minister and founder of Rhode Island, is quoted on Indian religious beliefs, and another seventeenth-century English colonist describes warfare among the Indians. Although such written records can be very helpful, scholars have to be aware of the biases and the class and cultural points of view that can distort the writers' accounts. How might a person's cultural or class background color his or her perceptions?

MULTIPLE-CHOICE QUESTIONS

Circle the letter of the item that best completes each statement or answers the question.

1. The first inhabitants of the Americas reached the New World by
    a. giant outrigger canoes from the western coast of Africa.
    b. swift sailing vessels crossing from northern Europe to Iceland to New England.
    c. migrating from Asia across the then existing Alaska-Siberia land bridge.
    d. migrating in outrigger canoes from Polynesia to the Isthmus of Panama and Central America.

2. The densest Indian populations in what would later be the United States were found in
    a. the Great Basin.
    b. the Great Plains.
    c. California and the Pacific Northwest.
    d. the southwestern desert.

3. Which one of these Indian cultures is *not* correctly matched to the geographical area in which it flourished?
    a. Pueblo—Arizona and New Mexico
    b. Woodlands—the Pacific Northwest and California
    c. Hopewell—the Midwest
    d. Hohokam—Arizona

4. All of the following helped shape Native Americans' social and cultural development before 1500 *except*
    a. geographical isolation.
    b. great climatic and geographical variations across America.
    c. contact with Asian and African cultures, from which they adopted many practices.
    d. long-term changes or cycles in weather, such as warming trends and extended droughts.

5. Which of the following tribes was the ancestor of the modern Pueblo Indians?
    a. Adenas
    b. Anasazis
    c. Aleuts
    d. Apaches

6. At the time of Columbus's first voyage to the New World, about how many native Americans lived on the continent north of present-day Mexico?
    a. 7 million to 10 million
    b. 75 million
    c. 50,000 to 100,000
    d. 1 million to 2 million

7. All of these were characteristics of Native American culture before contact with the Eastern Hemisphere *except*
    a. strong kinship or extended family ties.
    b. the belief that all nature was infused with spiritual power.
    c. the belief that property ownership gave the owner perpetual and exclusive control over the land.
    d. strong oral traditions but no written languages.

8. The purpose of the potlatch ceremony of the Pacific Northwest Indians was to
    a. demonstrate personal physical bravery.
    b. impress rival tribes with their military prowess.
    c. convince a woman's father to give her in marriage to a particular man.
    d. win prestige for the giver of gifts.

9. Among North American Indians women alone did the farming *except* for in tribes in the
    a. Northeast.
    b. Great Basin.
    c. Southwest.
    d. Mississippi Valley.

10. The term *Archaic peoples* refers to
    a. native North Americans from about 8000 to 1500 B.C.
    b. the first nomadic hunters to reach North America.
    c. the mound builders of the Mississippi Valley.
    d. all Native Americans living here at the time of Columbus's voyage.

SHORT-ANSWER QUESTIONS

1. Where and when did the earliest direct contact between Europeans and Americans probably occur? What, if anything, resulted from the contact?

2. Where and how was agriculture first practiced in what is now the United States?

ESSAY QUESTIONS

1. Compare and contrast the development and later decline of each of these major Indian cultures: Hohokam and Anasazi; Adena, Hopewell, and Mississippian.

2. Discuss the differing ways of life of the Native Americans living in the Arctic, the Pacific Northwest, California, the Great Basin, the Southwest, the Mississippi Valley, and the Eastern Woodlands. Explain how the physical environment influenced each way of life.

3. Because the Indian peoples of the present-day United States had not developed written languages before the coming of Europeans, how have historians attempted to reconstruct Native American history? Give as many specific examples from Chapter 1 as possible.

4. Compare and contrast the descriptions of Native American culture presented in Chapter 1 with the impressions offered in movies and television.

2

Transatlantic Encounters and Colonial Beginnings, 1492–1630

OUTLINE AND SUMMARY

I. African and European Peoples

A. West Africa and Its Peoples

In the grasslands south of the Sahara Desert and east of the West African coast, several empires rose and declined—Ghana, Mali, and Songhai. Islam spread to the upper classes of these kingdoms, and by 1492 the last of them, Songhai, was at the height of its glory. Its major city, Timbuktu, boasted a leading Islamic university and was an important trading center. Its large army and bureaucracy dominated much of the African interior. In the fifteenth century, the small states on the Guinea and Senegambian coast grew in population and importance because of foreign demand for the gold that the Africans mined and traded. In the mid-1400s the Portuguese arrived on the coast, too, looking for gold and slaves. West African leaders ranged from powerful emperors, who claimed demigod status, to heads of small states, who ruled mainly by persuasion. Kinship groups formed the most important unit holding people together. Polygyny was permitted, allowing high-status men to establish kinship networks with other important families through their several wives. Africans did not regard land as a commodity to be bought and sold. Rather, one honored one's ancestors and their spirits by proper land cultivation. Agriculture was difficult in Africa and required the labor of both men and women, who grew yams, rice, and other grains. Polytheistic religion and belief in magic permeated African culture and inspired artistic endeavors. West Africans developed sophisticated art and music, on which much of twentieth-century art and jazz are based. By the 1500s Islam was starting to spread to the common people of the grasslands. Christianity, introduced by the Portuguese in the 1400s and 1500s, made little headway until the nineteenth century.

B. European Culture and Society

At the time of Columbus's first voyage to America, Europe was at the height of a great cultural revival, the Renaissance. Scholars were trying to map the world and to understand natural science, including astronomy. European society was hierarchical; at the top were the kings who governed most states and had been consolidating their power for a century. Their authority depended on the cooperation of the aristocracy, to whom they made certain concessions. At the bottom were the peasants, who accounted for 70 percent to 80 percent of the people. Population increases in the sixteenth and seventeenth centuries made land in Europe scarce and valuable. That encouraged the upper classes to enclose more and more of the common fields, converting them to their private property, while displaced country people drifted to the small towns, which were crowded, dirty, and disease-ridden. Traditional European society, which like Native American and African cultures had been based on extended families and social reciprocity, was starting to change. Nuclear families were slowly replacing kinship networks. New business enterprises and organizations, like joint stock companies, broke the bonds of social reciprocity. Emerging entrepreneurs favored "unimpeded acquisition of wealth" and unregulated competition. They "insisted that individuals owed one another nothing but the money necessary to settle each market transaction." Most Europeans regarded democracy as mob rule and feared it would lead to the destruction of social distinctions and order. They also feared rule by women.

C. Europeans and Their God

Except for small Jewish and Muslim minorities, all Europeans in 1492 were Christians. The Roman Catholic church was headed by a pope whose authority was acknowledged everywhere except in Russia and the Balkan Peninsula, and it was administered by a hierarchy of clergy who did not marry. By the fifteenth century this powerful institution was selling indulgences (blessings that would shorten the repentant sinner's time in purgatory) for donations to the church.

In 1517 a German friar, Martin Luther, denounced indulgences and other corrupt practices, broke with the pope, and initiated the Protestant Reformation. Luther and other Protestants preached that one could not buy or earn salvation by good works (or donations to the church) and that priests had no special powers of intervention. God alone decided who was saved and who was damned, and Christians must have faith in his love and justice. French Protestant leader John Calvin and his followers went a step further, emphasizing the doctrine of predestination—that is, God's foreknowledge of who was saved and who was damned.

The Protestant challenge led to the Counter-Reformation, in which the modern Roman Catholic church was born. The renewed church cleaned out corruption, stimulated religious zeal, and attempted to suppress Protestantism. Thereafter, European countries divided into rival Protestant and Catholic camps and engaged in religious wars from the mid-sixteenth to the mid-seventeenth century. Meanwhile the Tudor king Henry VIII feared that England would revert to civil wars after his death unless he could pass the throne to a male heir. Because his wife had borne no sons, Henry asked the pope to annul his marriage and allow him to take another queen. When the pontiff refused, Henry broke with the pope, seized monastic lands in England, sold them to the gentry to raise money for the royal treasury, and declared himself supreme head of the Church of England, or Anglican church.

D. The Rise of Puritanism in England

Religious strife continued in England for more than one hundred years after Henry's split with the Catholic church. Henry's son and successor, Edward VII, leaned toward Protestantism during his brief reign. He was followed by "Bloody Mary," who tried to restore Catholicism by burning Protestants at the stake. This persecution turned her successor and half-sister, Elizabeth I (1558–1603), and the majority of English people against Catholicism. But the English differed on how Protestant the Church of England should be. Those who wanted to remove all vestiges of Catholicism were called Puritans. These Calvinistic Puritans believed in predestination and felt that only the saved should belong to the church. They wanted each congregation to be self-governing and free from interference from bishops and a church hierarchy. Puritanism, with its message of righteousness and self-discipline, appealed particularly to England's landowning gentry, small farmers, university-educated clergy, intellectuals, merchants, shopkeepers, and artisans.

Elizabeth managed to satisfy most English Protestants (Puritan and Anglican), but her successor, James I (1603–1625) made clear his dislike of Puritans and his intentions to crack down on them. Charles I, who became king in 1625, increased the campaign to root Puritanism out of the Church of England. Under this repression, some Puritans lost hope of reforming Anglicanism and became Separatists. A group of Separatists moved to Holland, and some of them later founded Plymouth in New England. Economic hard times (unemployment, depressions, falling wages) also persuaded many Puritans, both Separatists and Non-Separatists, to leave England. Non-Separatist Puritans established the Massachusetts Bay and Connecticut colonies.

II. European Expansion

A. Seaborne Expansion

Portugal led the way in Europe's seaborne expansion. Because of advances in maritime technology, Prince Henry the Navigator was able to send Portuguese sailors farther and farther down the coast of Africa to fight Muslims and seek opportunities for profitable trade. Portugal established a slave station at Arguin, rounded Africa's Cape of Good Hope, and developed valuable commercial links with India. These Portuguese voyages brought Europeans face to face with black-skinned Africans for the first time and demonstrated the wealth that could be acquired from slave trading.

B. The "New Slavery" and Racism

Slavery existed in West African life before the arrival of Europeans, but it was not based on racial differences between masters and slaves, and the slaves were often absorbed eventually into the owners' families. First Muslims from North Africa, then Europeans turned African slavery into an "intercontinental business." Generally, European slavers bought war captives from African slave-trading kings, which encouraged those rulers to engage in constant warfare with their neighbors. Nearly 12 million Africans would be shipped across the Atlantic under terrible conditions to labor in the Western Hemisphere before the international slave trade finally ended, centuries later. The tremendous profits made in the trade would fuel the commercial expansion of Europe, and the new slavery based on race would further dehumanize black Africans in the eyes of white Europeans.

C. Europeans Reach America

Christopher Columbus, like other educated men of the fifteenth century, believed that the world was round. Unlike others, however, he insisted that Europeans could reach Asia and its rich trading opportunities by sailing westward across the Atlantic. He convinced the king and queen of Spain, who were anxious to break Portugal's monopoly of trade via the route around Africa, to finance his voyages of discovery. On his 1492 trip he landed on the island of San Salvador, in the West Indies, which was located about where he calculated Japan should be. On subsequent voyages he reached Hispaniola and the American mainland. He died never realizing he had discovered a new world. Others, however, soon suspected it, and most of the later explorers were bent on discovering a water route through or around the landmasses of the Americas to the beckoning trade of Asia. Balboa crossed the Isthmus of Panama and reached the Pacific in that quest. Magellan sailed around the tip of South America, getting as far as the Philippines before being killed. Verrazano explored the coast of North America, and Jacques Cartier sailed up the St. Lawrence, each looking for the supposed Northwest Passage to Asia.

D. The Conquerors

The early Spanish explorers soon became conquerors as well. Columbus exported Indian slaves from Hispaniola and gave grants to Spaniards to extract labor and other tribute from the native population there. In 1519 Hernán Cortés landed in Mexico and subjugated the mighty Aztec empire. During the rest of the sixteenth century, Spanish conquerors fanned out over the Caribbean and the Americas from Mexico to Chile, subduing and enslaving the native peoples and enriching themselves and Spain with fabulous finds of gold and silver. In their wake came 100,000 to 300,000 Spanish settlers, who developed West Indian sugar plantations, Mexican sheep and cattle ranches, and gold and silver mines, all worked with slave labor. The Indian population was nearly decimated by forced labor, warfare, starvation, and, above all, alien diseases to which the Indians lacked immunity. When shortages of Indian slaves developed, the Portuguese delivered African substitutes. The riches flowing to Spain enticed other Europeans to challenge her in the Americas.

III. Footholds in North America

A. New Spain's Northern Frontier

In the 1500s a number of Spaniards, searching for gold, silver, and slaves, penetrated areas that would one day be the United States. Cabeza de Vaca and Estevanico traveled from Florida to Texas to New Mexico; de Soto's party went from Tampa Bay to the Appalachians and then to Texas. Although they found no gold, these and other expeditions spread European diseases that wiped out most of the surviving Mississippian communities. Coronado plundered pueblos and searched for riches from the Grand Canyon to Kansas. In 1598 Juan de Oñate proclaimed the royal colony of New Mexico, which barely survived repeated Indian attacks and uprisings.

B. France: Initial Failures and Canadian Success

In 1534 Jacques Cartier explored the St. Lawrence River for France. But French attempts at planting permanent colonies in the St. Lawrence Valley in 1541, South Carolina in 1562, and Florida in 1564 all ended in failure. However, the French carried on lucrative fur trading with the Indians from Newfoundland to Maine and along the St. Lawrence. In 1608, Samuel de Champlain founded Quebec, the first permanent French settlement in Canada, and allied it with the Hurons.

C. The Enterprising Dutch

After Henry Hudson, in the employ of the Dutch, explored the river that bears his name, Hollanders erected Fort Nassau, at present-day Albany, and established New Netherlands. In 1626, the colony's director-general, Peter Minuit, purchased Manhattan Island from local Indians and started the city of New Amsterdam. Most of the settlers lived by the fur trade. They dealt primarily with the Iroquois, the enemies of the French-backed Hurons.

D. Elizabethan England and the Wider World

By the late 1500s England was also becoming interested in the Western Hemisphere. Overseas colonies seemed like an ideal place to ship the unemployed. Restless, disinherited younger sons of the gentry saw adventure and a chance to make their fortunes in exploration and conquest. With the encouragement of Queen Elizabeth, English "sea dogs" like Francis Drake, John Hawkins, Humphrey Gilbert, and Walter Raleigh raided Spanish treasure ships and ports, searched for the Northwest Passage, and scoured the Western Hemisphere for colony sites. In 1578 Gilbert attempted to found a settlement in Newfoundland, but it soon disbanded. His half-brother Raleigh sponsored the ill-fated colony on Roanoke Island.

E. The Beginnings of English Colonization: Virginia

In May 1607 a party of 105 English people landed in Virginia and began the settlement of Jamestown. The venture was organized and financed by an English joint-stock company, the Virginia Company of London. The only role of the English government was to grant a charter to the company giving it the right to land anywhere from Cape Fear to the Hudson River. Many of the early arrivals were "gentlemen" who refused to farm, hoping instead to find gold and quickly return to England. Because the company had given them inadequate supplies, they were soon starving. During the first years, or "starving time," the majority of the settlers died, and the survivors were on the verge of leaving several times. The discipline and forced work imposed for a while by Captain John Smith helped save the colony. Settler John Rolfe's development of a tobacco palatable to Europeans gave the colony the profitable export that ensured its financial success.

At first the stockholders in England treated the settlers as company employees, denying them any say in the colony's government or ownership of any of its land. To attract additional settlers and capital, the company started awarding land to people who paid their own and other people's passage to Virginia. This "headrights" system enabled planters who imported many indentured servants to acquire large estates. In 1619 the company also granted inhabitants the right to elect delegates to a legislative assembly, thus marking the beginnings of representative government in North America. An Indian attack in 1622 killed many of the English settlers. Charges of company mismanagement led King James I to revoke the charter in 1624, and Virginia became a royal colony.

F. The Origins of New England: Plymouth Plantation

In the winter of 1620, the *Mayflower* landed 102 English men and women at Plymouth Bay, where they founded Plymouth Plantation. The settlement was financed by some London merchants headed by Thomas Weston, who had received a patent from the Virginia Company of London to establish a colony. Weston had entered into an agreement with a group of English Separatists who had been living in Holland to escape Anglican persecution. The Separatists and other non-Puritan Englishmen who joined the expedition promised to send lumber, furs, and fish back to Weston for seven years in return for his investment.

Winter storms, however, blew the *Mayflower* off course, and the colonists landed outside the boundaries of Virginia and the jurisdiction of its government. Therefore, the adult males signed the Mayflower Compact, creating their own civil government and pledging to abide by its laws. Half the Pilgrims, as they came to be called, died during the first winter in Plymouth. Those still alive in the spring of 1621 were greatly helped by two friendly Indians, Squanto and Samoset, who taught them how to plant corn and arranged treaties with neighboring tribes. While Plymouth Plantation never grew wealthy or large, it was the vanguard of a mighty Puritan migration to New England in the 1630s and has shaped our image of the sturdy, freedom-seeking English colonists.

IV. Conclusion

By 1630 European settlement of North America was well under way. The Spanish had advanced as far into Florida and New Mexico as they thought necessary to protect their Mexican and Caribbean possessions. The English were planting tobacco in the Chesapeake region of Virginia and farming at Plymouth. Dutch and French colonies engaged in brisk commerce in furs. This European expansion into the Western Hemisphere had taken a tremendous toll, however, in lives lost, native peoples displaced and decimated, and Africans transported and enslaved.

VOCABULARY

The following terms are used in Chapter 2. To understand the chapter fully, it is important that you know what each of them means.

polygyny   the practice or the condition of having more than one wife at one time; marriage of one man to several women

monotheistic   pertaining to belief in only one god (as opposed to *polytheistic*, having to do with belief in and worship of many gods)

hierarchy   a system of placing persons or things in a graded order, from lower to higher, in wealth, power, status, and so on

sumptuary laws   laws regulating personal habits that offend the moral or religious conscience of the community

yeomen   free, landowning small farmers, below the gentry in status

capitalism   a system under which the means of production, distribution, and exchange are in large measure privately owned and directed, and in which prices and wages are determined by supply-and-demand market forces

indoctrination   teaching or inculcating a doctrine or set of beliefs

Eucharist   the Christian sacrament of the Lord's Supper; communion; the sacrifice of the Mass; also the consecrated elements of the Lord's Supper, such as the bread

gentry landowners with substantial amounts of property and without aristocratic titles; considered "gentlemen" and therefore not to do manual labor; played an important role in English government

caravel a type of small, maneuverable ship developed by the Spanish and Portuguese in the 1400s

astrolabe an astronomical instrument for taking the altitude of the sun or stars, useful in solving problems in astronomy and navigation

Huguenots French Protestants

patent an official document conferring a right (such as the exclusive right to make use of or sell an invention) or a grant of land (such as the charter given to the Virginia Company of London)

IDENTIFICATIONS

After reading Chapter 2, you should be able to identify and explain the historical significance of each of the following:

English "Poor Laws"

enclose (enclosure movement)

joint-stock company

indulgences, Martin Luther, and the Protestant Reformation

John Calvin and the doctrine of predestination

Counter-Reformation

Puritans versus Anglicans

conversion experience, "saints," and the "elect"

Prince Henry the Navigator

Vasco da Gama

Vasco Núñez de Balboa

Ferdinand Magellan

Northwest Passage

conquistadores and *encomiendas*

Hernán Cortés

Juan Ponce de León, Cabeza de Vaca, Hernán de Soto, Francis Drake, Humphrey Gilbert, and Walter Raleigh

Elizabeth I, James I, and Charles I

Samuel de Champlain

Virginia Company of London

Captain John Smith

John Rolfe

headrights

Peter Minuit

Separatists

Thomas Weston, Pilgrims, and Plymouth Plantation

Mayflower Compact

SKILL BUILDING: MAPS

1. On the map of Africa on the following page, locate each of the following and explain its historical significance.

   Sahara Desert

   Ghana

   Mali

   Songhai

   Timbuktu

   Benin

   Guinea

   Senegambia

   Arguin

   the Equator

   Cape of Good Hope

   Congo

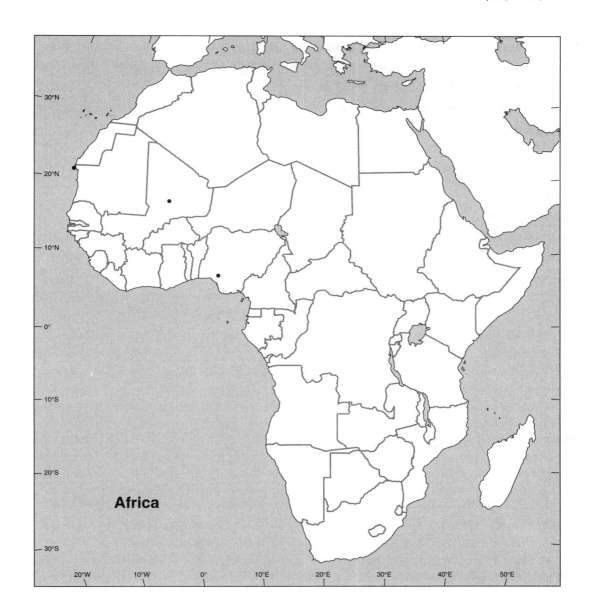

2. On the map of Central and South America and the Caribbean on the following page, locate each of the following places and explain which European explorer and conqueror is associated with it:

San Salvador and the Bahama islands

Hispaniola (Haiti and the Dominican Republic)

Isthmus of Panama

Caribbean Sea

Pacific Ocean

Atlantic Ocean

Strait of Magellan

Tenochtitlán (Mexico City)

Puerto Rico

Central and South America

3. On the map of North America on the following page, locate each of the following and indicate which European country had claimed and/or settled it by 1625:

Great Lakes

Chesapeake Bay

Mississippi River

Great Plains

Newfoundland

Acadia (Nova Scotia)

Santa Fe

St. Lawrence River

St. Augustine, Florida

Jamestown, Virginia, and James River

Bermuda

Quebec

Fort Nassau (later Albany, New York)

New Amsterdam (later New York City)

Roanoke Island (off the coast of North Carolina)

Plymouth Plantation

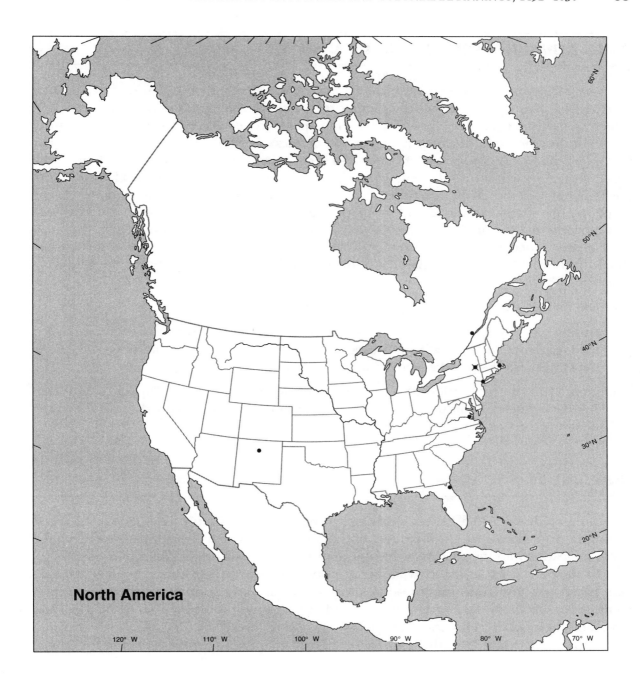

North America

SKILL BUILDING: GRAPH AND CHARTS

On page 27 in your textbook there is a line graph titled "Decline in Real Wages in England, 1500–1700." This graph shows the index of real wages, using 1500 as the base year. Real wages are not the amount of money a person earns but an estimate of what that amount of money at that time would allow the person to purchase. Economists derive these indexes by looking at the prices of a variety of goods and services offered in a given year and the actual wages earned by workers in the same period. Thus the index of real wages is a better indicator of people's standard of living than just looking at the amount of their earnings. In the graph the real wages, or standard of living, of English workers in 1500 is represented as 100. By following the line on the graph to 1700, one can see at a glance by how much that standard of living declined over the period. The importance of this graph is the light it can throw on historical causation. Based on this graph, how would you answer the following questions?

1. Did English people have strong economic motives for emigrating?

2. During which years would English people have had the greatest economic reasons for leaving home? Do these years correspond to periods of rapid population growth in the New England, Chesapeake, and Caribbean colonies?

3. After 1700 the proportion of non-English immigrants arriving in England's mainland colonies increased and the proportion of English immigrants declined. Does the graph offer any clues as to why this occurred?

HISTORICAL SOURCES

Too often students read a history textbook uncritically. They simply assume that the information in print is correct. Such readers do not ask the important questions: How does the historian learn about the past? How reliable are the sources historians commonly use?

In Chapter 2, for instance, what are the descriptions of West African society and religion based on? How does the historian know about the early years of the Plymouth settlement, the relations of the Pilgrims and the Indians, and the problems that the Pilgrims had paying off their debt to Thomas Weston?

Turn to pages 24–25 of the text. There the author quotes Olaudah Equiano on African religious beliefs and practices. Equiano, born in the area around Benin, was sold as a young man in 1756 to a British slaver who brought him to the New World. In 1766 he bought his freedom and settled in England, where he became active in the antislavery movement. The quotation in the text comes from *The Interesting Narrative of the Life of Olaudah Equiano or Gustavus Vasa, the African*, which Equiano published in 1791. This narrative is one of a number that were written by former slaves. Like Equiano's, most of them were published many years after their authors last lived in Africa. Why are the autobiographies of former slaves a useful historical source? Can you see any reasons to question their accuracy?

One of the earliest and best sources that historians have for learning about the Pilgrims and the Plymouth settlement is William Bradford's *Of Plymouth Plantation*. Bradford wrote this detailed history of the colony and its people between 1630 and 1650. A Separatist, he arrived on the *Mayflower* and was elected governor by the settlers over and over again from 1621 to 1656, the year before his death. Can you explain why *Of Plymouth Plantation* is an excellent source for historians but must also be used with caution?

Carefully read "A Place in Time: Roanoke, 1584–1590." Whose writings about the Indians of Roanoke does the author use? How does the author use Arthur Barlowe's account? Who was Arthur Barlowe? Are his observations a useful historical source? Why or why not?

MULTIPLE-CHOICE QUESTIONS

Circle the letter of the item that best completes each statement or answers the question.

1. By the 1500s the nuclear family unit was becoming increasingly important among
   a. Western Europeans.
   b. South American Indians.
   c. North American Indians.
   d. West Africans.

2. The beginnings of representative government in the European settlements in North America can be found in
   a. the Spanish colony at St. Augustine, Florida.
   b. the Dutch New Netherland, where the inhabitants were granted the right to elect their own legislature in the colony's charter.
   c. Virginia, when, in 1619, the company provided for election of an assembly by the inhabitants.
   d. the small Swedish fur-trading colony in the lower Delaware Valley.

3. Which of the following statements about West African society at the time of first contact with Europeans is correct?
   a. Slavery was unknown in West Africa.
   b. The majority of West Africans were either Muslims or Christians.
   c. Agriculture had not yet developed. The majority of West Africans were hunters and gatherers.
   d. Polygyny was permitted, and kinship groups were important.

4. The financing of the Virginia settlement came from
   a. the English government.
   b. a joint-stock company.
   c. the Church of England.
   d. all of the above.

5. In which European settlement was fur trading with the Hurons and other tribes the primary economic activity?
   a. New Mexico
   b. Florida
   c. New France
   d. Virginia

6. The first Europeans to develop the intercontinental African slave trade were
   a. English.
   b. French.
   c. Italian.
   d. Portuguese.

7. The primary aim of the explorations of Balboa, Magellan, Verrazano, and Cartier was to find
   a. a water passage through the Americas and reach Asia.
   b. the fabled fountain of youth.
   c. the Seven Cities of Gold.
   d. favorable places for their respective nations to plant new colonies.

8. All of the following statements about England's Queen Elizabeth I are correct *except*
   a. she eagerly embraced Puritanism and denounced the vestiges of Catholicism in the Church of England.
   b. she helped finance the raids of the English "sea dogs" on Spanish ports and shipping and shared in the plunder.
   c. she secretly aided Protestant revolts in Europe against Spanish domination.
   d. after the pope declared her a heretic, she viewed English Catholics as potential traitors.

9. All of the following statements about English Puritans are correct *except*
   a. they were Calvinists.
   b. they rejected the doctrine of predestination.
   c. the majority of them did not want to separate from the Church of England but to reform it from within.
   d. they rejected magnificent cathedrals and ornate rituals in favor of plain sermons in ordinary churches.

10. Which of the following is *incorrectly* matched with his deeds?
    a. Hernán Cortés—conquered the Aztecs, built Mexico City
    b. Francisco Coronado—found the Grand Canyon, plundered the New Mexico pueblos
    c. Giovanni da Verrazano—founded Quebec, sent *coureurs de bois* to live with the Indians
    d. Jacques Cartier—explored the St. Lawrence, made an early French attempt to colonize in North America

---

SHORT-ANSWER QUESTIONS

---

1. Explain what the Reformation and Counter-Reformation were. How did they lead to religious and political conflict in Europe?

2. Compare and contrast the attitudes of Native Americans, West Africans, and Europeans about land ownership and cultivation.

3. How and why did Elizabethan England challenge Spanish dominance in Europe and the Western Hemisphere?

4. Explain the beliefs of English Puritans. Why did James I and Charles I wish to suppress Puritanism?

5. Explain the various motives of the English for coming to America as settlers.

ESSAY QUESTIONS

1. Compare and contrast the founding and early development of Virginia and Plymouth. Since both were English colonies, how do you account for the differences?

2. "During the first third of the seventeenth century, the general outlines of European land claims in North America emerged, as did the basic elements of the various colonies' economic life." Discuss this statement with reference to the Spanish, French, Dutch, and English colonies in North America.

3. Discuss the religious and political conflicts and the economic conditions in sixteenth- and early seventeenth-century England that made the English interested in exploration and colonization in the Western Hemisphere.

4. "The displacement of Indians and the enslavement of Africans underlined the early history of European settlement in America." Illustrate this statement by discussing the African slave trade and relations between the Spanish, French, Dutch, and English settlers and the various Indian peoples.

5. Discuss the concept of social reciprocity. How did it operate in Native American, West African, and traditional European societies? In what ways was it breaking down in Western Europe by the sixteenth and seventeenth centuries?

3

Expansion and Diversity: The Rise of Colonial America

OUTLINE AND SUMMARY

I. Introduction

By 1700 more than 250,000 people of European ancestry, mostly English, lived in what would one day be the United States. Also, during the seventeenth century about 300,000 West African slaves were brought to North America and the Caribbean, the majority to the West Indian sugar colonies and the remainder to the mainland. These great migrations from Europe and Africa resulted in the depopulation and uprooting of the native inhabitants.

II. The New England Way

A. *A City upon a Hill*

In 1628 a group of Puritan merchants formed the Massachusetts Bay Company and obtained a charter from the king permitting them to establish a colony in North America. They decided that the company's officers and stockholders would emigrate along with the settlers. Thus, Massachusetts Bay would not be under the control of stockholders or proprietors back in England. In 1630 the company sent over eleven ships carrying seven hundred settlers under Governor John Winthrop. As the ships sailed westward, Winthrop delivered his lay sermon, "A Model of Christian Charity," in which he articulated the Puritans' mission. They would create a godly community, "a city upon a hill" that would serve as an example for sinful England to emulate. Unlike Virginia and the West Indies, Massachusetts was founded primarily for religious, rather than acquisitive, reasons. The Puritans did not object to material gain, but they believed that moral and/or government restraint must limit ruthless exploitation and profiteering.

During the first severe winter in Massachusetts, 30 percent of Winthrop's party died. Nonetheless, within a year the colony was economically self-sufficient, and the population grew because heavy English immigration persisted through the 1630s.

B. *Settlers and Natives*

At first Native Americans offered little opposition to Puritan colonization. But as the English pushed into the Connecticut Valley, the Pequots resisted. In 1637 the Puritans waged a bloody war of extermination against them. This cleared the way for Puritan settlement of Connecticut.

C. The Development of a Puritan Orthodoxy

Although claiming still to be part of the Church of England, the Puritans followed congregational practices that were quite different from Anglicanism. They had no church hierarchy. Each congregation was run by its male members and guided by its minister. Only those who could prove that they were saved through their public testimony about their conversion experiences were accepted by the congregations as church members. However, all residents of the colony had to attend services and pay taxes for support of the church. In other words, Massachusetts had a state (or established) church. Because the Puritans felt that everyone must be able to read the Bible to avoid Satan's snares, they passed the Old Deluder Act in 1647, requiring each town of fifty or more households to appoint a teacher for all children. To produce a continuing supply of learned Congregational ministers, they founded Harvard College in 1636. This early establishment of Harvard provided New England with a college-educated elite during the seventeenth century, which no other part of the English colonies possessed.

D. Dissenting Puritans

Despite the efforts of the Puritans to enforce conformity to their religious mission and doctrines, there were dissenters. The first challenge came from Roger Williams, a devout Puritan minister who preached that church and state should be separate and that government must not interfere with private religious beliefs or compel church attendance. Because the Massachusetts civil authorities held that the purpose of government was to protect the true religion and prevent heresy, they banished Williams in 1635 for his subversive opinions. He fled southward, bought land from the Indians, and eventually established the colony of Rhode Island, which was the first to practice religious tolerance and separate church and state. Massachusetts also expelled Anne Hutchinson, who was regarded as a troublemaker for meddling in theology and questioning the clergy's moral authority. She and many of her followers also migrated to Rhode Island, and Massachusetts imposed greater restrictions on women. In the long run the challenge that most undermined the Puritan mission came from merchants who resented community restrictions on their business practices.

E. Power to the Saints

Unlike the board of directors and stockholders of the Virginia Company of London, who stayed back in England, the Massachusetts Bay Company directors settled themselves and their charter in the colony. Male church members were eligible to vote for governor and members of the legislative body, at first called the General Court and after the bicameral Governor's Council and House of Representatives. In 1641 about 55 percent of adult males could vote under that church membership requirement, which was a higher percentage of the male population than was enfranchised in England or Virginia, where the vote was based on land ownership. The basic unit of local government, the town meeting, was generally open to participation by all male taxpayers (including non–church members).

F. Community Life

New Englanders generally lived in tightly clustered villages with everyone within walking distance of the meetinghouse. Each family's land was in fields or strips surrounding the town; people went out daily to farm but returned to town each night. This compact system of settlement promoted community interaction and allowed Puritans to watch each other to enforce godly conduct.

G. Puritan Families

"In a proper Puritan family, the wife, children, and servants dutifully obeyed the husband." Unlike Anglicans and Catholics, the Puritans allowed divorce, but it happened rarely. Because the Puritans believed healthy families were vital for the welfare of the community, the courts could and did discipline disobedient children, wives, and servants and irresponsible husbands. Puritans followed English common law in giving the wife no property rights independent of her husband's. Better living conditions resulted in a longer life expectancy in New England than in England. New Englanders also had larger families and therefore a faster rate of population growth. Most depended on the labor of their large families to support themselves modestly by farming. Rocky soil and a short growing season made it unlikely that anyone would become rich from agriculture. New Englanders seeking better opportunities turned to part- or full-time lumbering, fishing, rum distilling, and commerce. As they prospered, they became more worldly and materialistic and less preoccupied with religion.

H. The Demise of the Puritan Errand

The restoration of the Stuart kings in 1660, after the brief Cromwellian era, doomed the Puritan hopes that the Church of England would follow their Congregational example. Their mission in New England also was faltering as the founding fathers failed to pass on their intense religious fervor to the second and third generations. Declining church membership necessitated compromises like the Half-Way Covenant adopted in 1662.

I. Expansion and Native Americans

As European settlers increased and prospered, the Indian population declined. Many Native Americans died from diseases brought by the newcomers, such as diphtheria, measles, and tuberculosis. As Europeans cut down forests and cleared land to farm, they destroyed Indian hunting and gathering areas, reducing their food supply. New England's Indian population fell from 125,000 in 1600 to 10,000 by 1675. Demoralized, some Native Americans turned to alcohol; others agreed to convert to Christianity and live in the "praying towns" that the Puritans established for them. The last-ditch attempt of the Wampanoag chief Metacom (King Philip) to unite the remaining Indians and oust the English, in 1675–1676, ended in disaster. Metacom was killed, and many other Indians were captured and sold into slavery. King Philip's War reduced southern New England's Indian population by nearly 40 percent and ended all overt resistance to white expansion.

J. Economics, Gender, and Satan in Salem

Economic resentments, the breakdown of the religious mission and sense of community, and resentment of economically independent and assertive women all may have contributed to the witchcraft hysteria that began in Salem in 1691 and engulfed Massachusetts until the end of 1692. It started with accusations by a group of young girls in Salem against a few residents of low standing. It escalated as more and more people made charges against others, including the wife of the governor. Twenty persons were convicted of witchcraft and executed, and hundreds more were in jail by the time the governor halted the trials and released the imprisoned.

By 1700 the Puritan phase of New England's development was waning. Its mark remained, however, on the emerging Yankees of New England, who would build a thriving international trade and later pioneer the American Industrial Revolution.

III. Chesapeake Society

A. State and Church in Virginia

In 1619 the Virginia Company of London granted the settlers the right to elect a representative assembly. After Virginia became a royal colony, the settlers repeatedly petitioned the king to continue that right. In 1628 Charles I grudgingly agreed. The assembly eventually became a bicameral legislature composed of a House of Burgesses elected by landowners and an appointed Royal Governor's Council. Local government in Virginia, with most officials appointed rather than elected, was less democratic than in New England. The Anglican church was the established church, and all Virginians were required to pay fixed rates for its support. Religion was less important to Virginians than to New Englanders, but it touched them more than it did British West Indians.

B. Virginia's First Families

From the mid-1600s on, Virginia developed an elite upper class. Most members of that class were from English merchant families and had arrived with capital. They used their money to acquire and develop huge tobacco plantations in Virginia. By 1670 they controlled the Royal Council and, through their public offices, further enriched themselves with additional land grants. These first families, including the Byrds, Lees, and Randolphs, would dominate Virginia politics for two centuries.

C. Maryland

Maryland, the first proprietary colony, was founded by Cecilius Calvert, Lord Baltimore, on a tract of land given to him by Charles I. Lord Baltimore wanted to create a haven for fellow Catholics who could not worship in public, had to pay tithes to the Anglican church, and were barred from holding political office in England. However, Calvert remained in England, trying to govern as an absentee proprietor, and more Protestants than Catholics settled in Maryland. To protect the Catholic minority, Lord Baltimore drafted the Act of Religious Toleration and convinced the Maryland assembly to pass it in 1649. But in 1654 the Protestant majority disfranchised Catholics and repealed the act. Thereafter, the Protestant-controlled legislature battled continuously with the proprietary Calverts and resisted any political role for the Catholic minority.

D. Tobacco Shapes a Way of Life

Life in Virginia and Maryland was shaped by tobacco growing, the main occupation. The population spread out on farms and plantations near rivers. Few commercial centers or towns developed because ships from England came directly to riverfront docks built by the planters. There they sold their goods from Europe and bought the outgoing tobacco, with the planters serving as the middlemen for the surrounding small farmers.

Ninety percent of the English who arrived in Virginia and Maryland between 1630 and 1700 came as indentured servants.

E. Mortality, Gender, and Kinship

In the early decades in Virginia and Maryland, the life expectancy was twenty years shorter than that in New England and deaths exceeded births. Disease and overwork killed off perhaps 40 percent of indentured servants within six years of their arrival, and the shortage of women settlers prevented many men from marrying and starting families. By the late 1600s, however, death from epidemics had fallen off, there were almost as many women as men, and the population was growing through natural increase.

F. Tobacco's Troubles

The best chance for upward social mobility in the Chesapeake colonies was before 1660. After that, depressed tobacco prices afflicted Maryland and Virginia. Profits and wages fell. Former indentured servants were unable to earn enough money to buy land and become independent farmers. They formed a frustrated underclass that seemed destined to remain landless.

G. Bacon's Rebellion

Depressed tobacco prices and the resentments of the small farmers and landless toward the wealthy planters probably helped cause Bacon's Rebellion. Economically hard-pressed farmers on the Virginia frontier, under the leadership of Nathaniel Bacon, fought an unauthorized war against the Indians in 1676. When the royal governor tried to restrain them, they marched on Jamestown, burned it, and looted their enemies' plantations. The rebels dispersed, however, after Bacon's death later that year.

H. Slavery

The first Africans arrived in Virginia in 1619 and may have been treated initially as indentured servants. During the period 1640–1660, the status of Africans deteriorated into that of lifelong slavery. After 1660 the Chesapeake colonies recognized the institution of African slavery with laws that defined the condition and rigidly controlled blacks. Still, as late as 1660 fewer than one thousand slaves lived in Virginia and Maryland. Heavy importation of African slaves did not begin until late in the 1600s, and only after 1700 did slaves increasingly replace white indentured servants as plantation laborers. Even so, the population of the Chesapeake, unlike that of the West Indies, always remained predominantly white. As slaves became the predominant work force, whites of all classes closed ranks to cooperate in controlling the growing population of African origin.

IV. The Spread of Slavery: The Caribbean and Carolina

A. The Chaotic Caribbean

Despite Spain's claim to all of the Caribbean, the English were able to seize several islands from her after 1620, including Barbados, Antigua, and Jamaica. However, the British West Indies experienced repeated violent episodes between 1640 and 1713: Carib Indian, Spanish, French, and Dutch invasions; pirate raids; and slave revolts.

B. Sugar and Slaves

Tobacco was the first export of the British West Indies, but because sugar cane was a more profitable crop, those colonists who had enough capital to invest in the necessary land, equipment, and African slave laborers to produce it soon grew sugar cane instead. These sugar planters became fabulously wealthy. Many other whites, unable to make a decent living cultivating tobacco on the poorer land they could afford, left the islands, reemigrating to the mainland colonies, especially Carolina. The sugar planters imported so many African slaves that by 1713 blacks outnumbered whites by a margin of four to one. The masters bought fish and other foodstuffs from New Englanders to feed their slaves.

C. West Indian Society

The West Indies developed a starkly unequal society of masters and slaves. As sugar planters acquired most of the land, poorer whites deserted the islands for the mainland. The African slaves were ruthlessly controlled and exploited under slave codes enacted by the planters. These codes were later copied by several of the mainland colonies. Slaves were often worked to death within ten years of their arrival, but because blacks were in the majority, they retained more of their African heritage than slaves brought to the North American mainland. Whites in the West Indies had very high mortality rates, little religious life, weak family ties, and almost no sense of community. The richest planters often returned to England to live off their profits, while hired white overseers ran their estates.

D. Carolina: The First Restoration Colony

In 1663 King Charles II gave a group of his English supporters a grant of land in America, which they named Carolina in his honor. The proprietors organized their territory into two districts and created separate bicameral legislatures for each. To attract colonists the proprietors adopted the headright system, used earlier in Virginia and Maryland. Most of the settlers came from other English mainland colonies and Barbados. There were also some French Huguenots (Protestants). The northern Carolinians cultivated tobacco and exported it, along with lumber and pitch. The southern Carolinians raised livestock. They carried on these economic activities primarily with their own family labor, using few black slaves.

By the 1690s southern Carolinians had found a staple crop that would make them rich—rice. Those few who possessed sufficient capital to invest in the costly dams, dikes, and slaves necessary for large-scale rice production became fabulously wealthy, forming the only mainland elite that was as rich as the West Indian sugar planters. As the rice growers imported ever more African slaves, the black population burgeoned to 67 percent of South Carolina's residents, making South Carolina the only British mainland colony with an African majority. Outnumbered and frightened, the white minority adopted a brutal slave code similar to that of Barbados.

The Carolinians met resistance from the Indian tribes on whose lands they were encroaching, culminating in the Tuscarora and Yamasee wars that drove the natives from the area. In the 1700s the crown revoked the proprietary charter and turned South Carolina in 1720 and North Carolina in 1729 into royal colonies.

V. The Middle Colonies

A. Precursors: New Netherland and New Sweden

The Dutch-founded fur-trading colony of New Netherland became America's first multiethnic society. Its population included Dutch, Germans, Swedes, Africans (free and slave), Protestants, Catholics, Jews, and Muslims. Eighteen different languages were spoken there. In 1638, New Netherland's governor Peter Stuyvesant took over and annexed the Swedish fur-trading settlement in the lower Delaware Valley. By 1664 New Netherland had 9,000 people and a thriving port city of New Amsterdam.

B. English Conquests: New York and the Jerseys

In 1664 Charles II presented the seized Dutch colony, New Netherland, to his brother, James, Duke of York, who called it New York. Most of the Dutch settlers were allowed to keep their land and remained in the colony. When James became king in 1685, New York became a royal colony. The British royal governors rewarded their loyal followers with immense land grants, mostly along the Hudson River from New York City to Albany. These patroons, or manor lords, grew almost as wealthy as the South Carolina rice planters on the rents they collected from their tenant farmers.

James gave part of former New Netherland, which came to be known as the Jerseys, to two court favorites, Lord Berkeley and Sir Philip Carteret. The settlers, who were a mixture of New England Puritans, Quakers, Anglicans, Scottish Presbyterians, and Swedish Lutherans, quarreled continually with the absentee proprietors and with each other. In 1702 the king took over, and New Jersey became a royal colony.

C. Quaker Pennsylvania

Charles II, to repay a debt he owed the Penn family, gave a huge grant of territory in America to William Penn, a wealthy Englishman who had joined the much-persecuted Quakers. Penn hoped to found a colony based on Quaker principles that would offer a haven to his fellow worshipers, and, like other proprietors, he wanted to make a profit. In 1681 Penn laid out the city of Philadelphia and started the settlement. True to Quaker teachings against forced worship, he imposed no established church and allowed peoples of all faiths to settle. He also drafted a constitution known as the Frame of Government, which created a legislative assembly to give residents a voice in running the colony. Relations with the Indians were favorable, for the most part, because Penn bought land from them on fair terms. The settlers prospered by growing grains on the fertile land and selling them to the West Indies. Indeed the trade made Philadelphia a major port by 1700. Since most of the colonists had come as families, the population quickly expanded through natural increase as well as immigration. Despite all their good fortune, some of the colonists resented the proprietor and his request for rents. The counties on the lower Delaware, inhabited by many Swedes and Dutch, gave Penn the most trouble. In 1704 they gained the right to elect their own legislature and separate from the rest of Pennsylvania, eventually forming the colony of Delaware.

VI. Rivals for North America

A. France Claims a Continent

As the English colonies developed along the Atlantic coast, the French empire spread inland. In the 1660s and 1670s Louis XIV sent some six hundred settlers yearly, and French fur traders and missionaries fanned out over the Ohio Valley and explored the Mississippi from Wisconsin to the Gulf of Mexico. By the early 1700s the French claimed the entire Mississippi basin, called it Louisiana, and had erected forts and started fur-trading centers at Mobile, Alabama and Biloxi, Mississippi. Few Frenchmen lived in this vast empire but many of those who did mingled with the Indians, carrying on the all-important fur trade.

B. The Spanish Borderlands

To protect its hold on Mexico and the region north of it from the French, Spain established the province of Texas (Tejas) in 1691, but permanent settlement there did not begin until 1716. Rather, Spain was preoccupied with New Mexico, where long-standing Spanish attempts to suppress the Pueblo people's way of life resulted in a 1680 uprising led by Popé, an Indian religious figure. The Spanish did not fully regain control of New Mexico until 1700. As late as 1750, only about 3,800 Spaniards lived in the territory, most of them as sheep and cattle ranchers. In Florida, too, Spain faced recurring Indian resistance. In the 1690s, when a new round of European wars commenced, Spain's northern borderlands were in a weakened condition.

VII. Conclusion

By 1715, European nations had staked claims to most of the territory in the present-day United States east of the Mississippi River. Though the Spanish and French North American empires were larger in territory, the more compact English colonies along the Atlantic coast contained by far the most European settlers, about 250,000 in 1700. At the start of the eighteenth century, English America included three distinct regions: the southern colonies, with their plantation-slave systems; New England, where Puritan religious zeal was giving way to Yankee enterprise; and the ethnically and religiously diverse middle colonies, which had emphasized commerce from their beginning.

VOCABULARY

The following terms are used in Chapter 3. To understand the chapter fully, it is important that you know what each of them means.

tithes   taxes due for the support of the clergy and church, usually a tenth of one's income

established church   a church that is officially recognized and given legal and financial support by the government

dissent   to object or disagree

theocracy   government by priests or clergy

heresy   an opinion or doctrine at variance with established religious beliefs

subversive   tending to undermine existing or established institutions or doctrines; tending to cause the overthrow of existing governments or other established institutions

bicameral   composed of two houses, chambers, or branches, as in a two-house legislative body

sacrament   any of seven rites that the historical Christian church considered to have been instituted by Jesus to convey divine grace. In Catholicism that includes matrimony, but not in Puritan doctrine.

jeremiad   in New England, a long sermon or tale lamenting the decline of morals

social stratification   the different levels of caste, class, privilege, or status in a society

proprietor   a person who has legal title to something; the owner or owner-manager of a business or other institution

proprietary colony   a settlement organized in territory granted by the crown to a proprietor or proprietors, like Maryland, the Carolinas, and later Pennsylvania and New York

blasphemy   any contemptuous or profane utterance, act, or writing concerning God; any word or deed meant to dishonor God or his works

IDENTIFICATIONS

After reading Chapter 3, you should be able to identify and explain the historical significance of each of the following:

conversion relation

John Cotton and Congregationalism

John Winthrop and "A Model of Christian Charity"

Old Deluder (Satan) Act

Roger Williams

Anne Hutchinson and Antinomians

Massachusetts General Court

New England town meeting

indentured servants

Charles I and the English civil war

Oliver Cromwell

Stuart Restoration

Half-Way Covenant

"praying towns," "praying Indians"

King Philip's War

Puritans and Yankees

Virginia House of Burgesses and Royal Governor's Council

First Families of Virginia

Cecilius Calvert (Lord Baltimore)

Maryland Act for Religious Toleration

Anthony Ashley Cooper and John Locke

Peter Stuyvesant

William Penn and the Quakers

coureurs de bois

Popé and the Pueblo Revolt (1680)

SKILL BUILDING: MAPS

1. On the map of eastern North America and the Caribbean on the following page, locate each of the following and explain how its climate, soil, and other physical characteristics helped shape the economy and society there.

   Massachusetts

   Rhode Island

   Connecticut

   North Carolina

   South Carolina

   New York

   New Jersey

   Pennsylvania

   Jamaica

   the Bahamas

   Barbados

   Virginia

   Maryland

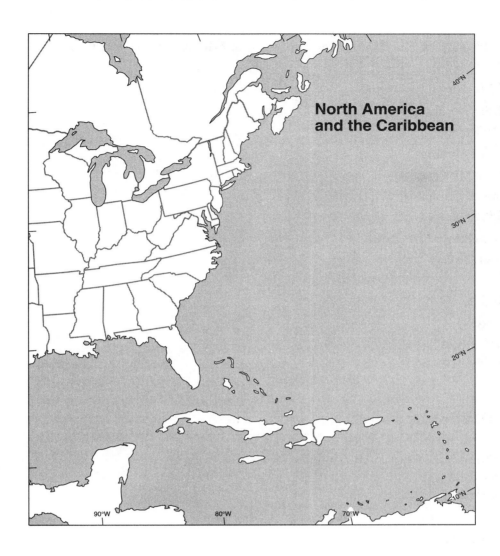

**North America
and the Caribbean**

2. On the map of North America, locate each of the following and explain its significance in seventeenth-century American history:

lands claimed by France

Mississippi River

Ohio River

Gulf of Mexico

Biloxi, Mississippi

Mobile, Alabama

lands claimed by England

lands claimed by Spain

Texas (Tejas)

Taos

Santa Fe

Florida

Great Lakes

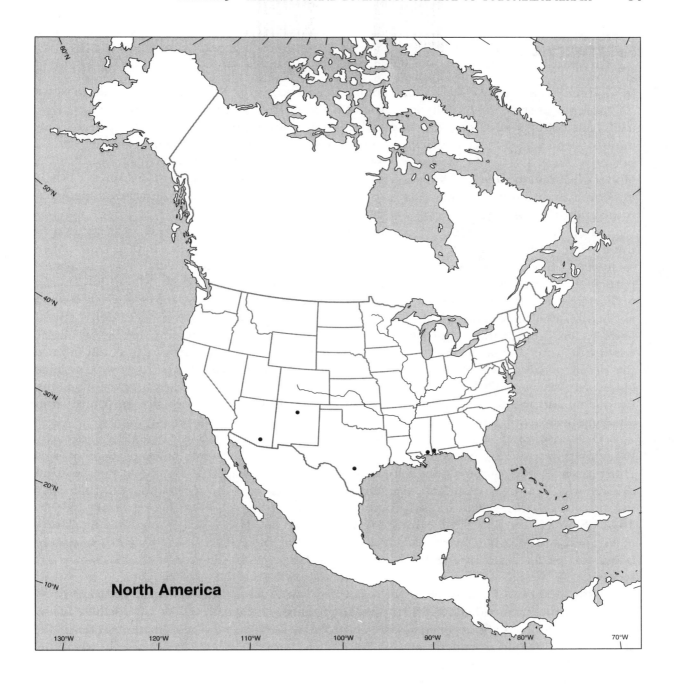

North America

HISTORICAL SOURCES

In Chapter 3 the author tells us much about Puritan hopes, beliefs, religious practices, views on church and state, and family life. How did the historian discover this information? One useful historical source on New England Puritan thinking is the numerous sermons that ministers and lay leaders gave, many of which were carefully written down and preserved for posterity. Look at page 54, where you will see a reference to John Winthrop's lay sermon "A Model of Christian Charity." What does the historian learn about the Puritans' sense of their mission from it? Find other places in Chapter 3 where references are made to sermons. How is the author using the sermon or sermons mentioned in each case?

Another valuable source for gaining insight into past societies is their legal codes. For example, if the historian reads the code known as the Body of Liberties adopted by the Massachusetts General Court in 1641, he or she finds there the guarantee that every man may participate in the town meeting. There are several sections of the Body of Liberties dealing with rights and duties of husbands, wives, children, and servants. Particularly revealing about the lack of separation of church and state is the part of the code titled "Capitall Laws." Here we see that religious or moral offenses, such as blasphemy, heresy, adultery, witchcraft, and "Carnall Copulation," were crimes for which civil authorities could impose the death penalty. As you review Chapter 3, look for other references to laws and legal codes. Notice particularly the discussions of the slave codes of the British West Indies, the Carolinas, and the Chesapeake colonies. In each case what has the historian found from studying these statutes?

Of course, laws are not always fully enforced and at times do not reflect what is really happening in a society. Therefore, the historian often does research among old records of court cases as well as consulting statutes. For instance, on page 61 of the text we read that divorce was legal in Puritan Massachusetts, but we learn how rarely it happened from looking at court records: "Massachusetts courts allowed just twenty-seven divorces from 1639 to 1692." Similarly, on page 75 the author states that the first laws officially recognizing slavery in Virginia and Maryland were passed after 1660, but there is evidence that Africans were being treated as slaves by the 1640s and 1650s. Some of that evidence comes from court records.

Now look at "A Place in Time: Taos Pueblo, New Mexico, in 1680." Here we learn of an uprising of the Taos and other Indians against Spanish civil and religious authorities. In the account we are told about Spanish officials arresting, executing, whipping, and selling into slavery Indian religious leaders, such as Popé. The historian also quotes Popé's words to his temporarily victorious people. How does the historian know these things? See if you can figure out possible historical sources.

MULTIPLE-CHOICE QUESTIONS

Circle the letter of the item that best completes each statement or answers the question.

1. The area that had the longest life expectancy and the fastest population growth through natural increase was
   a. England.
   b. New England.
   c. the Chesapeake colonies.
   d. the British West Indies.

2. The first colony in English America that had separation of church and state and practiced religious tolerance was
   a. Maryland.
   b. Massachusetts.
   c. Rhode Island.
   d. Virginia.

3. Harvard College was chartered in 1636 primarily to
   a. train learned Congregational ministers.
   b. produce an educated governing class.
   c. educate lawyers who could defend the rights of the colonists.
   d. teach Puritans how to farm the rocky New England soil.

4. A man's right to vote for governor and members of the General Court in seventeenth-century Massachusetts was based on
   a. land ownership.
   b. wealth.
   c. length of residence in America.
   d. church membership.

5. The greatest extremes of inequality in land ownership in the seventeenth century were found in
   a. New England.
   b. Maryland.
   c. the West Indies.
   d. Virginia.

6. The Half-Way Covenant was adopted because
   a. too few second- and third-generation Puritans were willing to testify publicly about their conversion experiences.
   b. Puritans believed that Indians were not capable of becoming fully Christian.
   c. Puritans wanted to justify enslavement of converted Indians and Africans.
   d. Puritans wanted to show Anglicans that they were willing to meet them halfway on resolving differences over religious doctrine.

7. African culture tended to survive most strongly among black slaves brought to
   a. New England.
   b. Maryland.
   c. Virginia.
   d. the West Indies.

8. Which of the following statements about Maryland is correct?
   a. It was founded by a joint-stock company.
   b. Although it was intended as a haven for Catholics, they were often more perse-cuted there than were Catholics back in England.
   c. The dominant crop that shaped its economy and society was sugar cane.
   d. Unlike neighboring Virginia, Maryland never adopted the institution of African slavery.

9. The great majority of those arriving in Virginia between 1630 and 1700 were
   a. Africans.
   b. British gentry.
   c. non-English middle- and working-class people.
   d. British indentured servants.

10. Which of the following statements about Virginia is correct?
    a. Unlike Massachusetts, it had no established church.
    b. It was governed by an appointed royal governor and governor's council and a House of Burgesses elected by landowners.
    c. By 1640 the great majority of its plantation laborers were African slaves.
    d. The indentured servants' chances of upward social mobility improved in the sec-ond half of the 1600s.

SHORT-ANSWER QUESTIONS

1. In what ways was New England Congregationalism different from Anglicanism? How did these differences affect life in Massachusetts?

2. Why did Massachusetts expel Roger Williams and Anne Hutchinson?

3. Discuss what happened to New England's Indian population between 1600 and 1700. Why did it happen?

4. Explain the impact of sugar growing on British West Indian society and rice growing on South Carolina's evolution.

5. How did New Netherland turn into New York and New Jersey?

6. Who was William Penn, and what were his motives for founding Pennsylvania?

7. Describe the extent of the British, French, and Spanish North American empires in 1700 and how they differed from each other in settlement and economic patterns.

ESSAY QUESTIONS

1. "In the course of the seventeenth century, New England evolved from a highly religious, community-oriented society to a region characterized by rising worldliness, individualism, and competitiveness." Discuss how and why this evolution took place.

2. Compare and contrast the economies, social structures, and racial and ethnic composition of New England, the Chesapeake colonies, the British West Indies and Carolinas, and the Middle colonies in the seventeenth century.

3. Discuss the evolution and spread of slavery in the Chesapeake colonies in the seventeenth century. Why did African slavery develop there? How did the gradual shift from a plantation labor force of indentured servants to one of African slaves affect life in Virginia and Maryland?

4. Discuss Bacon's Rebellion, telling first the known facts about what happened and then reviewing and evaluating the interpretation of the causes of the rebellion offered in Chapter 3.

5. Discuss the Salem witchcraft trials, telling first the known facts about what happened and then reviewing and evaluating the interpretation of the causes of the witchcraft accusations and hysteria offered in Chapter 3.

4

Colonial Society Comes of Age, 1660–1750

OUTLINE AND SUMMARY

I. Restoration and Rebellion

A. Introduction

Until the restoration of the Stuart kings in 1660, England made little effort to rule its overseas territories. However, with the accession of Charles II (ruled 1660–1685), the mother country sought to expand its empire and trade, impose royal authority on the colonies, and regulate their economic activities so as to benefit English commercial interests.

B. Stuart Policies

In furtherance of these objectives, Parliament passed the Navigation Acts of 1660 and 1663. These forbade colonists from exporting sugar, tobacco, and other products to any place outside the British empire and required all exports to be shipped on English vessels. Charles II also granted charters to some of his powerful political backers, permitting them to found new proprietary colonies (as discussed in Chapter 3).

C. Royal Centralization

The Restoration Stuart kings dreamed of becoming absolute monarchs like France's Louis XIV. They rarely called Parliament into session and ignored the colonial legislatures. In 1684 Charles II revoked Massachusetts's charter. Between 1686 and 1688 his successor, James II, consolidated all the New England colonies, New York, and New Jersey into a Dominion of New England, abolished their assemblies, and placed full power in the hands of his arbitrary and dictatorial royal governor, Sir Edmond Andros. The colonists bitterly resented this denial of their rights. Tensions ran particularly high in Massachusetts and New York.

D. The Glorious Revolution in England and America

In 1688–1689 James II's high-handed, pro-Catholic actions led to the Glorious Revolution in England. He was forced into exile. The throne went to William and Mary, who agreed to a limited monarchy and promised to summon Parliament annually and respect the civil liberties of English people. When news of the Glorious Revolution reached America in 1689, New Englanders also rebelled. The Boston militia arrested Andros and his councilors, and Massachusetts and other colonies appealed to William and Mary for return of their charters. The new monarchs dissolved the Dominion of New England and issued charters granting each colony the right to have a representative assembly. However, Massachusetts's new charter did not give it as much independence as it had formerly enjoyed. Its governors would be appointed by the crown, not elected, and it would have to tolerate and share power in the colony with Anglicans. Leisler's Rebellion in New York and John Coode's uprising in Maryland also were inspired by the Glorious Revolution.

E. A Generation of War

Between 1689 and 1713, the British and French fought against each other in two wars. The conflicts spread to North America, where the British colonists called them King William's and Queen Anne's wars. When peace returned in 1713, France still controlled the North American interior, and the English colonists felt a heightened sense of British identity and dependence on their mother country's protection from their powerful neighbor.

II. A Maturing Colonial Economy and Society

A. British Economic Policy Toward America

British economic policy toward America was guided by the economic doctrine of mercantilism, which held that, to increase the nation's wealth in gold and silver, the country should produce within its own empire as much of what it needed as possible: its exports to foreign competitors should exceed its imports. To achieve these goals, Parliament passed a series of laws known as the Navigation Acts between 1651 and 1733. The laws required all trade to be conducted on British-owned ships; barred Americans from selling certain products, such as tobacco, rice, furs, indigo, and naval stores, to foreign countries unless they first passed through England; placed high taxes on products that Americans bought from outside the empire, like molasses from the French Caribbean; and forbade colonials from competing with British cloth and iron manufacturers. Although Parliament intended these laws to benefit only England, the acts in practice did not unduly hamper the colonists. Although the laws cut into the profits of rice and tobacco planters and raised the price of foreign imports in America, the Navigation Acts also were beneficial. Colonials were considered English subjects, so the requirement that shipping be done on British vessels stimulated the growth of America's merchant marine, shipbuilding, and ports. The bounties paid to producers of hemp, lumber, and other items under the Navigation Acts encouraged the development of those industries in the colonies. The restrictions on large-scale manufacturing did little harm, since only home production and small workshops were economically feasible in America.

B. A Burgeoning, Diversifying Population

After 1700 British North America grew rapidly from both natural increase and the arrival of newcomers. The eighteenth-century immigrants came less from England and more from other places: 140,000 West Africans brought on slave ships under horrible conditions; 100,000 Irish and Scots-Irish; and 65,000 Germans. Consequently, the English colonies became more racially and ethnically diverse, a change sometimes resented by those of English extraction. Since most of the eighteenth-century white immigrants were too poor to buy land in the already developed coastal areas, they tended to push into the piedmont region, which stretched along the eastern slope of the Appalachians. By 1750 one-third of the colonial population resided there.

C. Eighteenth-Century Living Standards

Earnings from mounting exports of tobacco, grains, livestock, fish, lumber, and other products brought about a dramatic rise in American living standards between 1700 and 1770. The population of the middle colonies, New York to Delaware, enjoyed the greatest prosperity, but the overall standard of living in mid-eighteenth-century America exceeded that of Scotland and Ireland and equaled that of England.

D. Rural Men and Women

Most rural families worked small farms and depended on the labor of their sons and the supplemental production of clothing, vegetables, and poultry of their wives and daughters. Few inherited much land from their parents since holdings were modest and families were large. Therefore, most young couples starting out had to work for others for a time and borrow money to buy their own farms.

E. Colonial Farmers and the Environment

Colonial farmers rapidly cut down the forests to bring more land under cultivation. They used the timber for fences, fuel, and buildings. Farmers and planters also sold wood to townspeople. The resulting deforestation drove away large game and caused greater extremes in temperature and less dependable water levels in streams, which drastically reduced the amount of fish. As the farmers grew tobacco and other soil-depleting plants without fertilizer and without beneficial methods, such as crop rotation or letting fields lie fallow some years, the land lost its fertility and yields seriously diminished.

F. The Urban Paradox

By 1740 about 4 percent of the colonists lived in cities. The four largest were Philadelphia, New York, Boston, and Charles Town (now Charleston). All were thriving ports that shipped the livestock, grain, and lumber that enriched the countryside, but each also had escalating problems of urban poverty, crowding, poor sanitation, and periodic epidemics of contagious diseases.

G. Slavery's Wages

From 1713 to 1754, the importation of slaves to the mainland was greatly increased, with the result that the black colonial population rose from 11 percent to 20 percent. Most slaves lived in the South, but 15 percent were in colonies north of Maryland. The African-American population also multiplied through natural increase, despite the fact that slaves worked harder and longer and had lower standards of living than whites. As the number of slaves residing in cities mounted—they were 20 percent of New York's inhabitants and the majority in Charles Town and Savannah—urban racial tensions ran high, leading to incidents such as the 1739 Stono Rebellion in South Carolina and the 1712 and 1741 slave conspiracies in New York. All were brutally suppressed by frightened whites.

H. The Rise of the Colonial Elites

In the eighteenth century class differences were becoming more apparent in America. Wealthy rural gentry and urban commercial elites attempted to imitate the fashions and lifestyles of the European upper crust.

I. Elites and Colonial Politics

The elites also dominated politics. They were elected to the colonial assemblies and appointed to the governors' councils. Women, blacks, and Indians could not vote, and property qualifications probably excluded about 40 percent of white males from doing so. Still, the proportion of men who did have the vote was much higher than in England and Ireland of the same period.

The most significant political development after 1700 was the shift in power away from royal governors and appointed officials to the colonial assemblies. The legislatures exercised influence over the governors by controlling their salaries. The assemblies authorized spending and imposed taxes. The British Board of Trade, which could disallow laws passed by these legislatures, rarely interfered because of its own inefficiency. Thus America, or at least its upper classes, became more and more self-governing, except for trade regulations, restrictions on printing money, and declaring war.

Overall, most Americans prospered and some grew rich in the eighteenth century, but class distinctions were never as extreme as in Europe. The colonies had no hereditary nobility or privileged church or military hierarchy.

III. Competing for a Continent

A. France and Native Americans

After making peace in 1713 with its rivals, Britain and Spain, France resumed building its empire in North America. In 1718, the French founded New Orleans and made it the capital of their province of Louisiana. The government sent French paupers and criminals, German refugees, and African slaves to populate and develop Louisiana. These settlers survived by a combination of farming, hunting, fishing, and above all trading with the Indians. The French managed to forge an alliance with the Choctaws in Louisiana and tried to win over Native American trading partners in the Ohio Valley and on the Great Plains. While generally more successful in getting along with Indians than the British, the French also crushed tribes that stood in their way, such as the Natchez.

B. Native Americans and British Expansion

British colonies, too, were expanding at the expense of Native Americans. Pennsylvania coerced the Delaware Indians into ceding their lands and moving into territory adjacent to that of the Iroquois. Other eastern tribes also were pushed westward, where they were used by the Iroquois as a buffer between themselves and the aggressive English.

C. British Settlement in the South: Georgia

Georgia was the last of the original thirteen colonies to be established on the North American mainland and the only one to receive some financial support from the British government. James Oglethorpe, its founder and early guiding spirit, wanted it to be both a haven for English debtors who could rehabilitate themselves there and an outpost protecting the Carolinas from the Spanish empire to the south. Oglethorpe laid out the port city of Savannah in 1733, and by 1740 about 2,800 settlers had arrived. Most, however, were not English debtors. Nearly half were not even English, but German, Swiss, Scottish, and Jewish. To promote a society of industrious small farmers able to defend their homes from attack, Georgia banned African slavery and limited the size of landholdings. But once the settlers realized that their best chance of making their fortunes lay in rice cultivation, they chafed at these restrictions, which were dropped by 1750. In 1770 Georgia had 23,000 inhabitants, 45 percent of whom were black slaves.

D. Spain's Struggles

While trying to fend off the Indians, French, and British, Spain spread its empire throughout the Southwest and part of the Southeast. European population in New Mexico grew very slowly, but at least Navajo and Apache raids ceased. Instead, these tribes made an alliance with the Spanish against the Utes and Comanches, whom they all feared. In Texas the Spanish established four missions, including the one later known as the Alamo. However, the Indians in Texas seemed more interested in trading with the French than in farming for the Spanish. Periodic raids on the province by the French and Comanches discouraged Hispanic settlement in Texas: as late as 1760, only 1,200 Spaniards lived there. The Spanish attempted to weaken the British Carolinas and Georgia by offering freedom to English-owned slaves who fled to their colony of Florida.

IV. Enlightenment and Awakening

A. Introduction

New England had the highest literacy rates in America because its Puritan religion encouraged primary education to ensure that all could read the Bible. Among white males elsewhere in the colonies, literacy ranged from 35 to 50 percent, but this was still considerably higher than in England.

B. The Enlightenment in America

American intellectuals, like Benjamin Franklin, were much influenced by the ideals of the eighteenth-century Enlightenment. Enlightenment thinkers emphasized reason, progress, science, and the capacity for human improvement. Franklin and other enlightened Americans established libraries, organized the American Philosophical Society, and founded institutions of higher learning (the University of Pennsylvania grew out of Franklin's College of Philadelphia). Some enlightenment figures were Deists—that is, they believed in a god who created the universe and set it in motion according to natural laws discoverable by human intellect but did not intervene thereafter with miracles. Deists such as Franklin and Thomas

Jefferson, while formally considering themselves Christians and attending church, disliked zealots who persecuted others in the name of religion.

C. The Great Awakening

Enlightened intellectuals took a dim view of the emotional excesses of the 1740s Great Awakening, "an outpouring of passionate Christian revivalism" that swept through the thirteen colonies. Overcome by the fiery preaching of Jonathan Edwards, William Tennent, Theodore Frelinghuysen, and above all George Whitefield, thousands of colonists repented and flocked to churches and prayer meetings seeking salvation. This reawakened interest in religion caused unprecedented splintering of American Protestantism into ever more denominations. The many denominations began another round of college founding to educate ministers for their faiths: the New Light Presbyterians' Princeton, the Anglicans' King's College (Columbia), the Baptists' Brown, and the Congregationalists' Dartmouth. The Great Awakening may also have had unintended political effects through its insistence on the equality of all born-again Christians in God's eyes and the corruption of "unsaved" upper-class leaders.

V. Conclusion

By the 1750s British colonial society had matured. The colonies' population and wealth had swelled mightily. Their standard of living equaled that of England. Their literacy rate and number of institutions of higher learning exceeded those of the mother country. Further, Anglo-America was much more firmly planted in what would one day be the United States than were either the French or Spanish settlements. In the 1750s and 1760s, the British would expel the French entirely from North America and seriously weaken the Spanish, but in doing so England would open irreconcilable conflicts with its own colonies.

VOCABULARY

The following terms are used in Chapter 4. To understand the chapter fully, it is important that you know what each of them means.

provincialism   displaying a narrow or localized outlook or life-style; displaying a countrified or rustic outlook or life-style

dissemination   spreading abroad; diffusion; promulgation

manumission   releasing an individual from slavery or servitude

antithesis   opposition; contrast; the direct opposite

urbanization   the growth of cities

autonomous   self-governing; independent; subject to one's own will, choice, or law

dowry   the money, goods, or estate that a woman brings to her husband at marriage

artisans   persons skilled in industrial arts or crafts—for example, silversmiths, blacksmiths, cobblers, and printers

journeyman   person who has learned a skilled trade and works at it for another person

oral culture   a way of life in which people normally obtain most of their information and communicate by word of mouth

print culture   a way of life in which people rely on books, newspapers, and other printed sources for much of their information

IDENTIFICATIONS

After reading Chapter 4, you should be able to identify and explain the historical significance of each of the following:

Sir Edmond Andros and the Dominion of New England

the Glorious Revolution

Leisler's Rebellion

John Coode

King William's War and Queen Anne's War

redemptioners

James Oglethorpe

Francisco Menéndez

mercantilism and the Navigation Acts

Adam Smith, *The Wealth of Nations*

Stono Rebellion

Board of Trade

Enlightenment

Benjamin Franklin

American Philosophical Society

Royal Society

Deists

Great Awakening

Jonathan Edwards

George Whitefield

New Lights versus Old Lights

SKILL BUILDING: GRAPHS

Look at the pie graph titled "Distribution of Non-Indian Nationalities Within the British Mainland Colonies, 1700–1755" on page 102 of the text. It visually presents important demographic data about the British mainland colonies. Was the population of the British mainland colonies more ethnically and racially diverse in the seventeenth or the eighteenth century? How might these demographic shifts affect Britain's relationship with its mainland colonies? By 1755 which group made up roughly one-fifth of the population? How do you account for the growth of that group between 1700 and 1755? For comparison, find out what portion of today's total U.S. population that group makes up.

HISTORICAL SOURCES

In Chapter 4 the author has gathered information from many sources, including travelers' accounts of life in America. In the eighteenth century a number of Europeans took extended trips through the colonies and then published books about their experiences. A fairly typical one was Andrew Burnaby's *Travels Through the Middle Settlements in North America in the Years 1759 and 1760* (London, 1798). Burnaby, an Anglican clergyman, filled his book with detailed observations about the dress; housing; religion; money; and ethnic, racial, and class composition of the colonies. Although Burnaby and other travelers give us wonderful eyewitness accounts, the historian has to be wary of the "facts" found in their books. Why?

Benjamin Franklin's autobiography, *Poor Richard's Almanack,* and other writings have long been a gold mine for historians of colonial America. In Chapter 4 look for the many references to Franklin, his observations, and his opinions. For what purposes has the author used these writings? Although Franklin was an astute observer of his world, he had his biases, as we all do. Can you tell what some of them were from the quotations from his writings that appear in Chapter 4?

In "A Place in Time: Mose, Florida, in 1740" the historian has used a number of sources to discover the story of the black community of former slaves who lived there. These include written documents: letters, treaties, and government papers. In addition, the historian has drawn on findings from archaeological excavations. What did these "digs" show?

MULTIPLE-CHOICE QUESTIONS

Circle the letter of the item that best completes each statement or answers the question.

1. Which of the following statements about the Anglo-American colonies in 1750 is correct?
    a. Colonists living in the port cities were much more prosperous than those in the countryside.
    b. Black slaves made up a greater proportion of the population than they had in 1700.
    c. More immigrants to the colonies were from England and fewer came from other parts of Europe than in the 1600s.
    d. The overall standard of living had risen little since 1700.

2. James Oglethorpe
   a. led the Stono Rebellion.
   b. encouraged the importation of African slaves to Georgia in order to promote profitable rice cultivation there.
   c. hoped Georgia would be a place for the rehabilitation of English debtors and a barrier to Spanish expansion northward.
   d. did all of the above.

3. Which of the following statements concerning colonial government between 1700 and 1763 is correct?
   a. The royal governors and the Board of Trade frequently vetoed or disallowed laws passed by the colonial legislatures.
   b. All white men had the right to vote and hold office.
   c. The lower house of a colonial legislature was generally dominated by representatives of the lower and middle classes, whereas the upper house was dominated by the wealthy.
   d. The colonial legislatures became a powerful force in American government, controlling taxes, the budget, and executive salaries.

4. Which of the thirteen colonies was the last to be settled and the only one to receive some financial assistance from the British government?
   a. Georgia
   b. the Carolinas
   c. Pennsylvania
   d. Delaware

5. Which of the following statements about women in eighteenth-century America is correct?
   a. Women could not inherit their parents' land. Only sons could legally inherit family estates.
   b. Women could not choose their own husbands. The choice was made by their parents.
   c. Women in rural and urban families played an important part in helping to support their households.
   d. Women had legal control over their dowries and other property that they brought with them to marriage.

6. The Glorious Revolution in England touched off rebellions in all of the following colonies *except*
   a. Massachusetts.
   b. New York.
   c. Maryland.
   d. South Carolina.

7. Which of the following resulted from King William's and Queen Anne's wars?
   a. The French were driven from the North American continent.
   b. The Stuart kings were driven from power.
   c. The wars heightened Anglo-Americans' sense of their British identity and made them feel dependent on the mother country for protection.
   d. The British captured New Orleans and started to settle Louisiana.

8. The Dominion of New England was
   a. created by James II to consolidate his hold on the northern colonies and eliminate their colonial assemblies.
   b. welcomed by most New Englanders because it broke the dictatorial rule of the Massachusetts Puritans over the region.
   c. continued by William and Mary because the administrative consolidation made it easier to enforce the Navigation Acts.
   d. created as part of the reforms instituted after the Glorious Revolution.

9. The highest literacy rate in the eighteenth century was found in
   a. England.
   b. New England.
   c. the middle colonies, from New York to Delaware.
   d. Virginia and the Carolinas.

10. All of the following institutions of higher learning were originally founded by religious denominations *except*
    a. the University of Pennsylvania.
    b. Princeton.
    c. Rutgers.
    d. Columbia.

SHORT-ANSWER QUESTIONS

1. What actions of the Restoration Stuart kings led to the Glorious Revolution in England and America?

2. What was the Dominion of New England? What happened to it in 1689?

3. What was Leisler's Rebellion? How did the British royal governor deal with it?

4. What impact did the practices of colonial farmers in the eighteenth century have on the environment of the Atlantic seaboard settlements?

5. Explain why the Spanish and French had more trouble attracting European settlers to their North American colonies than did the British.

6. What were the ideals of the eighteenth-century Enlightenment?

7. What was Deism? Name some American Deists.

ESSAY QUESTIONS

1. How much equality, liberty, and self-government existed in the American colonies in the period 1700–1750? Back up your assessment with as many specific facts as possible.

2. What was the Great Awakening? Who was attracted to it? Who was repelled by it? What impact did it have on religious, social, educational, and political developments in eighteenth-century America?

3. Discuss the racial and ethnic makeup and the social class structure of mid-eighteenth-century America.

4. Historians have long debated the impact of Britain's mercantilist economic policy on the colonies. Explain the mercantilist economic theory and show how Parliament incorporated it into the navigation system. According to Chapter 4, in what ways did that system hurt and benefit America? Does the author believe the harm outweighed the benefits?

5. "In the second quarter of the eighteenth century, no American more fully embodied the Enlightenment spirit than [Benjamin] Franklin." Discuss Franklin's life, beliefs, career, and achievements, and explain how they embodied the Enlightenment spirit.

5

The Road to Revolution, 1744 – 1776

OUTLINE AND SUMMARY

I. Imperial Warfare

A. *King George's War*

King George's War, the third Anglo-French imperial conflict, proved indecisive. Although Americans seized the French stronghold at Louisbourg, in the peace treaty the British returned it in exchange for an outpost the French had taken in India.

B. *A Fragile Peace*

Since neither power gained dominance in North America, the skirmishing in the Ohio Valley continued. In 1753 the French Canadians began building a series of forts between the Ohio River and Louisiana. An expedition led by George Washington to block them misfired, leaving the Anglo-American frontier in danger. The attempt of seven colonies north of Virginia to forge an effective defensive union with the Albany Plan failed because the colonial legislatures refused to relinquish any of their authority over taxation.

C. *The Seven Years' War in America*

After the Anglo-French clash at Fort Necessity in 1754, war broke out in America. Then in 1756, full-scale hostilities between Britain and France resumed in the Seven Years', or French and Indian, War. At first British colonists fared poorly as France's Indian allies raided western settlements and the French seized key forts and threatened central New York and western New England. Unable to spare large British armies from the other military theaters where they were fighting the French, Prime Minister William Pitt offered British financial support to the colonials if they would do most of the fighting in America. Encouraged by the promise, colonials flocked to the struggle and drove the French from New York and much of the western frontier. Their success was aided by the decision of the Iroquois and other Ohio tribes to stop helping the French. After the fall of Quebec and Montreal, French resistance crumbled, and in the treaty of 1763 France ceded to Great Britain all of its territories in North America.

II. Imperial Reorganization

A. Introduction

After the Seven Years' War, Britain tried to tighten control over its now much-expanded colonial empire and to finance its administration by imposing new taxes on Englishmen at home and overseas. These efforts aroused opposition on both economic and constitutional grounds. At about the same time (1760), George III became king. He was determined to govern more actively than his predecessors, but his shifting policies and frequent ministerial changes further upset British-American relations.

B. Friction Among Allies

British supremacy in eastern North America opened the door to conflict between the mother country and the colonists. The war left the British people staggering under a huge debt and heavy taxes. The British resented repaying the Americans for defending themselves in the French and Indian hostilities and were equally upset that they now had to expend more money and military effort to put down Indian uprisings caused by the western surge of colonists beyond the Appalachians. Hoping to pacify Chief Pontiac and his followers, the British issued the Proclamation of 1763, forbidding whites to settle beyond the crest of the mountains until the crown had negotiated treaties with the Indians under which they agreed to cede their lands. The colonists were angered by this interference with their western land claims. Since continuing to protect the frontier and consolidate control over the newly acquired territories would cost around 6 percent of the peacetime budget, British government officials saw no reason that the colonials should not be taxed to help defray the expense.

C. The Writs of Assistance

To crack down on smuggling, British customs officers began to employ writs of assistance, or blanket search warrants that permitted officials to enter any ship or building to search for smuggled goods and seize them. Colonists protested that the writs violated traditional English guarantees against unreasonable search and seizure and that Parliament could not abridge their rights as Englishmen.

D. The Sugar Act

In 1764 Parliament adopted the Sugar Act, imposing import duties on sugar and other items to raise money for the British treasury. These taxes and a host of new regulations and restrictions burdened Massachusetts, New York, and Pennsylvania merchants particularly, but they also violated the long-standing guarantee of a fair trial. Accused smugglers were to be tried in vice-admiralty courts, without juries, by judges who had a financial stake in finding the defendants guilty. Nine colonial legislatures remonstrated against the Sugar Act.

E. The Stamp Act

Prime Minister George Grenville saw only that the Sugar Act brought in too little revenue to ease Britain's financial woes. He therefore proposed the Stamp Act and in 1765 convinced Parliament to pass it. It required colonists to purchase from government revenue agents special stamped paper for periodicals, customs documents, licenses, diplomas, deeds, and other legal forms. It also provided that violators would be tried in vice-admiralty courts. Since it was an internal tax, it touched many more colonials than the Sugar Act, which affected mainly merchants engaged in importing and exporting.

F. The Colonial Perspective

Colonists objected to Parliament's ability to impose upon them internal or external taxes designed to raise revenue because they elected no representatives to that body. Their own colonial legislatures had sole authority to tax them. Colonists conceded that Parliament might regulate trade within the empire, but there could be "no taxation without representation."

G. Resisting the Stamp Act

The Virginia House of Burgesses passed resolutions, proposed by Patrick Henry, denying Parliament's right to tax the colonies. Eight other provincial assemblies followed suit. In Boston a group of artisans, shopkeepers, and businessmen founded the Loyal Nine to fight the act. Similar organizations, usually called the Sons of Liberty, cropped up in other cities. The Loyal Nine and the Sons of Liberty directed outraged mobs in attacks on the homes and property of stamp distributors, causing all of them to resign their posts. In October 1765 representatives from nine colonies convened in the Stamp Act Congress in New York, where they reiterated the principle of no taxation without representation and no parliamentary denial of trial by jury and other English liberties. Most persuasive to the British, however, was the boycott of all English imports undertaken by American merchants. The decrease in their sales led British businessmen to plead for repeal of the Stamp Act. In March 1766 Parliament did revoke the law, but at the same time it adopted the Declaratory Act, restating its right to tax and legislate for the colonies "in all cases whatsoever." The colonists ignored the latter, rejoiced at the repeal, disbanded the Sons of Liberty, and concluded that the mother country would return to its earlier "salutary neglect."

H. Ideology, Religion, and Resistance

Resistance to the Stamp Act had revealed a deep split in thinking between England and its colonists. Influenced by John Locke; the oppositionists; the eighteenth-century English radicals; and the classical philosophers, such as Plato and Cicero, educated colonists saw in Parliament's actions a conspiracy of a corrupt government to deny them their natural rights and liberties. It was their duty as a free people to resist. Protestant clergymen, with the exception of the Anglicans and many pacifist Quakers, preached sermons to all classes of colonists backing these views. They declared that "solidarity against British tyranny and 'corruption' meant rejecting sin and obeying God."

III. Era of Anglo-American Crisis

A. The Quartering Act

In 1767 George III's new chancellor of the exchequer, Charles Townshend, like Grenville before him, looked to the colonies for much-needed revenue. That same year, Parliament's angry reaction to New York's refusal to comply with the Quartering Act indicated that it was ready to crack down on colonial self-government.

B. The Townshend Duties

Townshend pushed through Parliament the Revenue Act of 1767 (the Townshend duties), which imposed taxes on glass, paint, lead, paper, and tea imported into the colonies. Townshend intended to set aside part of the tax money to pay the salaries of royal governors so that they would no longer be subject to pressure from the colonial assemblies that had been compensating them.

C. The Colonists' Reaction

John Dickinson's *Letters from a Farmer* expressed the American majority view that Parliament could use duties to keep trade within the empire but not to raise revenue, as the Townshend duties did. The Massachusetts legislature sent Samuel Adams's "circular letter" making the same point to the other colonial assemblies. In August 1768 Boston merchants adopted a nonimportation agreement that spread to other cities.

D. "Wilkes and Liberty"

Although the boycott probably reduced imports only about 40 percent, this hurt many British merchants and artisans enough to make them again implore Parliament to rescind its taxes. Their appeal became part of a larger British protest movement against the domestic and foreign policies of George III and a Parliament dominated by a tiny elite of wealthy landowners. London journalist John Wilkes led the unrest. For this the government arrested him and denied him the seat in the House of Commons to which he had been elected. The government's actions prompted dissident Englishmen and American colonists to further question the authority of an unrepresentative Parliament.

E. Women and Colonial Resistance

Women bolstered the boycott by refusing to serve taxed tea and by organizing spinning bees to produce homespun apparel rather than buying British-made clothing.

F. Customs Racketeering

Meanwhile the high-handedness and corruption of customs officials, who seized ships and cargoes for technical violations of the Navigation and Sugar acts and broke open sailors' chests to search for small amounts of undeclared merchandise, contributed to Americans' growing alienation from the mother country. Violent attacks by seamen and others on customs inspectors, like the *Liberty* incident in Boston, happened more frequently. The way in which British officials enforced Parliament's trade regulations made more and more colonials broaden their cry from "no taxation without representation" to "no legislation at all without representation."

G. Repeal of the Townshend Duties

In 1770 Parliament again bowed to pressure and repealed all of the Townshend duties except the one on tea—to underscore its position that it had the right to tax the colonists. Americans responded by continuing to boycott tea, thus limiting its sale and the customs revenue from it so severely that there was not enough money to pay the salaries of the royal governors as Townshend had intended.

H. The Boston Massacre

To protect its officials, the British government stationed more troops in Boston. Tension between the seventeen hundred redcoats and the civilian population smoldered, ready to flare up. Then, on March 5, 1770, a group of British soldiers at a guardpost in front of the customs office fired into a disorderly crowd that was hurling dares, insults, and flying objects at them. Five civilians were killed and six more wounded in this so-called Boston Massacre. To defuse the situation, Massachusetts governor Thomas Hutchinson promised to try the soldiers, and the British removed their troops to a fortified island in Boston harbor. With John Adams as their lawyer, all but two of the redcoats were acquitted. After that, things quieted down.

I. The Committees of Correspondence

In 1772 Lord North revived trouble when he prepared to implement Townshend's plan to pay royal governors' salaries out of customs revenue. Sam Adams and others responded by organizing committees of correspondence in each New England town to exchange information and coordinate activities in defense of colonial rights. After a Rhode Island mob burned the British customs schooner *Gaspee*, the English announced they intended to ship the perpetrators, if they could be found, to England to stand trial. This threat to the right to a fair trial induced Virginians also to set up a committee of correspondence. Within a year every colony but Pennsylvania had such committees that linked Americans together in a communications web.

J. Frontier Tensions

Meanwhile, tensions in America among Indians, frontier settlers, and colonial authorities increased because of the relentless push of land-hungry whites westward. Colonial speculators and settlers ignored the Proclamation of 1763 and trespassed on Native Americans' lands. New Hampshire's Green Mountain Boys settled in Vermont, rejected New York's ownership of the area, and created a separate government and later new state. In North Carolina the frontier Regulator movement rebelled against the eastern-dominated colonial legislature and was suppressed. These and other incidents demonstrated the readiness of the westerners to defy all established authority violently.

IV. Toward Independence

A. The Tea Act

The British East India Tea Company was on the verge of bankruptcy in 1773 because Americans were buying so little taxed tea. Parliament tried to save it with the Tea Act, which allowed the company to sell its tea directly to American consumers, cutting out all middlemen's profits. As a result, the company would be able to sell its product, even with the import duty still on it, at a lower price than Americans paid for smuggled tea. The committees of correspondence denounced the act because they saw it as an attempt to seduce colonists into paying a parliamentary-imposed tax and they knew Lord North planned to compensate the royal governors with the customs receipts. That would surely endanger colonial representative government. At most ports, when the company's ships arrived, no one accepted the cargo and the captains turned around and left. But the governor of Massachusetts insisted on Bostonians' receiving and paying the duties on the shipment that arrived there. On the night of December 16, 1773, Sam Adams convened a protest meeting, at the end of which a band of colonials disguised as Indians boarded the East India Company's vessel and dumped its tea into the harbor.

B. The Coercive Acts

Infuriated by the Boston Tea Party, the British retaliated with a series of punitive laws, the Coercive Acts, which Americans dubbed the Intolerable Acts. These closed the Boston harbor, causing serious economic distress in Massachusetts; revoked the colony's charter and restructured its government to make it less democratic; banned the holding of more than one town meeting a year; provided for the housing of British troops in privately owned buildings; and permitted soldiers and other officials charged with killing colonials to be tried in England. General Thomas Gage, military commander in North America, took over as governor of Massachusetts. These measures and the unrelated Quebec Act, which provided no elected legislature for that province, convinced people in all the colonies that the British were out to destroy representative government and civil liberties in America. In Virginia the leading planters so successfully stirred up opposition to this parliamentary despotism that the southerners became ready to stand with Massachusetts in the coming struggle.

C. The First Continental Congress

To resist the Intolerable Acts, all the colonies except Georgia sent representatives to a Continental Congress that convened in Philadelphia in September 1774. The Congress approved the Suffolk Resolves, which, among other things, advised colonials to begin arming themselves against attacks by royal troops. The Congress also created the Continental Association to enforce a total cutoff of trade with England and the British West Indies and sent a Declaration of Rights to George III, begging him to dismiss the ministers responsible for the Coercive Acts.

D. The Fighting Begins

Committees of the Continental Association coerced wavering colonists into cooperating with the trade ban. Loyalists, or Tories, were intimidated. Volunteer militias, often calling themselves minutemen, drilled, and extralegal congresses met and tried to supplant the existing colonial assemblies headed by royal governors. On April 19, 1775, General Gage dispatched seven hundred soldiers to Lexington and Concord to seize the minutemen's weapons stockpiles and arrest key patriotic leaders. Forewarned by William Dawes and Paul Revere, the residents of Lexington and Concord challenged the redcoats arriving from

Boston, and the first fighting of the Revolution broke out. As news of the battles at Lexington and Concord spread, twenty thousand New Englanders rushed to besiege Boston and oust the English. The British defeated the colonials at Breed's and Bunker hills but suffered heavy casualties in doing so.

Soon after Lexington and Concord the Second Continental Congress convened in Philadelphia. The majority of the delegates still hoped for reconciliation with England and sent the Olive Branch Petition to George III, pleading for a cease-fire at Boston, repeal of the Coercive Acts, and negotiations to establish American rights. The British ignored the plea and, in December 1775, declared the colonists in rebellion.

E. The Failure of Reconciliation

Immediately after it met, the Second Continental Congress established an American continental army and appointed George Washington to command it, although it was not yet ready to declare independence. Loyalty to the king and hopes that he would restrain irritated ministers and members of Parliament lingered on through the summer and fall of 1775. Publication of Thomas Paine's pamphlet *Common Sense* in January 1776 did much to kill any remaining affection for monarchs.

F. Independence at Last

On June 7, 1776, Virginia delegate Richard Henry Lee proposed that Congress declare independence. The members first appointed a committee to draft a statement justifying the colonies' separation from England. Most of the writing was done by committee member Thomas Jefferson. Much influenced by the Enlightenment natural rights philosophy, Jefferson's Declaration of Independence emphasized equality of all men and their universal right to justice, liberty, and self-fulfillment. On July 2 the Congress formally adopted Lee's independence resolution and created the United States of America. On the third it reviewed and revised Jefferson's Declaration, approving and signing it on July 4.

V. Conclusion

In the years between 1763 and 1776, the colonists strove to reestablish the empire as it had existed earlier when British supervision was minimal and colonial assemblies controlled taxes and internal legislation. Failing in that goal, the Americans finally severed their ties with England and then had to fight for their independence on the battlefield. America also had to decide to what degree it would implement the idealistic statements in the Declaration of Independence.

VOCABULARY

The following terms are used in Chapter 5. To understand the chapter fully, it is important that you know what each of them means.

ceded   yielded or formally surrendered to another; given over, as by treaty

federation   a government body formed by a number of states, societies, or other units, each retaining control of its own internal affairs

boycott   an organized refusal to buy or use products or trade for the purpose of persuading, intimidating, or coercing

chancellor of the exchequer   the minister of finance in the British government, similar to the U.S. secretary of the treasury

rhetorical   pertaining to the art of influencing the thought and conduct of one's hearers

allusions   passing references to something either directly or by implication

lobby   to try to influence legislators

despotism   government exercising absolute power or control; tyranny

allegiance   faithfulness or loyalty to any person or thing; obligation or duty of a citizen to the government

beleaguered   surrounded by an army, troubles, or other adverse conditions

requisition   act of requiring or demanding; authorities taking or demanding something for military or public needs

Tories   the name given during the Revolution to Americans who remained loyal to England

vigilantes   members of groups using extralegal means to control or intimidate

---

IDENTIFICATIONS

After reading Chapter 5, you should be able to identify and explain the historical significance of each of the following:

King George's War

Albany Plan of Union

Acadians, Cajuns

Seven Years' War (French and Indian War)

Neolin, Pontiac's uprising, and the Proclamation of 1763

King George III

writs of assistance and James Otis

Sugar Act and vice-admiralty courts

George Grenville

Stamp Act and Stamp Act Congress

virtual representation

Patrick Henry

Loyal Nine and Sons of Liberty

Declaratory Act

Charles Townshend and the Townshend duties (Revenue Act of 1767)

John Wilkes

American Board of Customs Commissioners, customs racketeering

Samuel Adams

John Adams

spinning bees

Lord North

John Hancock

Crispus Attucks and the Boston Massacre

committees of correspondence

Tea Act and the Boston Tea Party

Coercive or Intolerable Acts and Quebec Act

Suffolk Resolves and Continental Association

minutemen, Paul Revere, and Lexington and Concord

Olive Branch Petition

Thomas Paine, *Common Sense*

Second Continental Congress and Declaration of Independence

SKILL BUILDING: MAPS

On the map of eastern North America on the next page, locate each of the following and explain its importance in the imperial wars between Britain and France or at the beginning of the American Revolution:

Nova Scotia

Louisbourg

Ohio River and Ohio Valley

Lake Champlain

Albany, New York

Fort Duquesne

Fort Necessity

Pittsburgh

Acadia

Quebec

Montreal

British North America under the terms of the Treaty of Paris, 1763

Detroit

Halifax, Nova Scotia

Fort Ticonderoga

Boston

Lexington, Massachusetts

Concord, Massachusetts

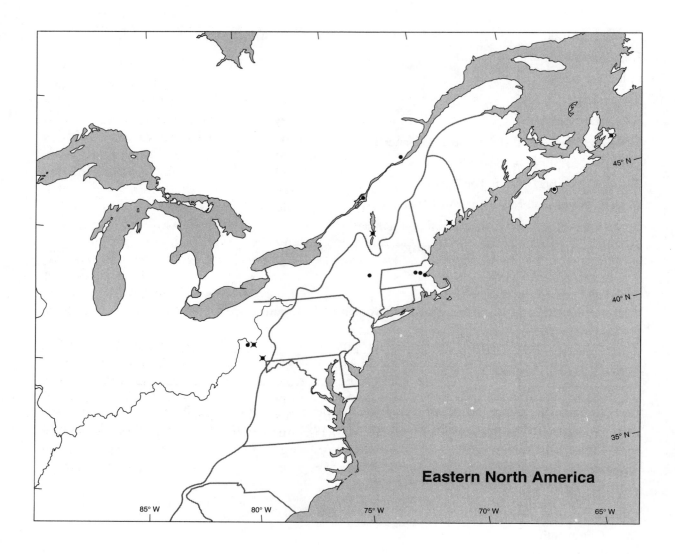

HISTORICAL SOURCES

The author of Chapter 5 has made considerable use of letters written by famous and ordinary people as historical sources. Letters dating from the 1760s and 1770s often contain colonial arguments against Parliament's actions and eyewitness accounts of riots, protest meetings, and other events, as well as expressions of the writers' fears, hopes, and opinions about the revolutionary situation that was brewing. Historians find letters in several places. The records of political leaders such as Benjamin Franklin, John and Sam Adams, Thomas Jefferson, and others frequently include letters that they wrote and received, some of which were intended for publication. Many were not for public consumption and therefore tend to be more candid. One also can read letters that were published in newspapers and periodicals. There are even private letters that were stolen or fell into the hands of others who disclosed them to the public, such as the letters of Massachusetts governor Thomas Hutchinson that Benjamin Franklin obtained and turned over to Sam Adams. These are referred to on page 151 of the text. There are abundant references to letters or information contained in letters in the chapter. In each case how has the author of Chapter 5 used these historical sources?

In addition to letters, the author of Chapter 5 has used newspapers and pamphlets printed during the revolutionary period and the records of proceedings kept by the various congresses, conventions, committees of safety, and committees of correspondence. Find places in Chapter 5 where material from newspapers, periodicals, and pamphlets is quoted. For what purposes does the author quote from these historical sources?

Now look at "A Place in Time: Concord, Massachusetts, in 1775." Try to figure out the sources of the information about what was happening in that town in the 1770s. Can you pinpoint what might have come from letters? From records of committees of correspondence? From local newspapers?

MULTIPLE-CHOICE QUESTIONS

Circle the letter of the item that best completes each statement or answers the question.

1. Both the Proclamation of 1763 and the Quebec Act of 1774
   a. interfered with colonial claims to western lands.
   b. extended religious freedom to Catholics.
   c. were repealed after colonial protests.
   d. imposed new taxes on goods imported from Europe.

2. The Albany Plan of Union
   a. was vetoed by the British because it challenged royal authority.
   b. united Anglo-Americans in a loose confederation during the Seven Years' War that fell apart after the French defeat.
   c. was not implemented because of opposition by colonial legislatures, but it set a precedent for future plans to unite the British mainland colonies.
   d. represented the earliest British attempt to suppress the colonial assemblies and exercise more imperial control.

3. Which of the following helped convince the delegates to the Second Continental Congress to vote for independence?
    a. the unexpected success of the colonists in clearing British troops out of New England
    b. Tom Paine's *Common Sense*
    c. the Boston Massacre
    d. John Dickinson's *Letters from a Farmer*

4. In the Declaratory Act, Parliament stated that
    a. it had the right to legislate for the colonies in all matters, including taxes.
    b. the colonists were in rebellion and therefore subject to martial law.
    c. it would repeal all the Townshend duties except the one on tea.
    d. it would take over payment of the salaries of the royal governors and other colonial officials.

5. Which of these events occurred last?
    a. the Battle of Bunker Hill
    b. fighting at Lexington and Concord
    c. adoption of the Declaration of Independence
    d. the Boston Massacre

6. How did the French and Indian War differ from King William's, Queen Anne's, and King George's wars?
    a. In the French and Indian War, France rather than Spain was England's chief enemy.
    b. Americans participated only in the French and Indian War.
    c. The French and Indian War was the only one in which the Indians sided with the French rather than the British.
    d. As a result of the French and Indian War, France lost her empire in North America.

7. The chief reason for the repeal of the Stamp Act and the Townshend duties by Parliament was the
    a. conviction that the colonists were on the verge of revolution.
    b. pleas of Burke and Pitt to conciliate the colonists by recognizing their right to tax themselves.
    c. harmful effects of colonial boycotts and nonimportation agreements on British business.
    d. expectation that the colonial assemblies would voluntarily vote for higher taxes.

8. Americans objected to the Tea Act because
    a. it would raise the price they had to pay for tea.
    b. there was still a tax on tea and the customs duties collected on it would be used to pay the salaries of royal governors.
    c. it forced them to drink tea when they preferred coffee.
    d. it forced them to buy from the British East India Tea Company, which sold low-quality, overpriced tea.

9. The Declaration of Independence was primarily written by
    a. John Adams.
    b. Patrick Henry.
    c. John Hancock.
    d. Thomas Jefferson.

10. John Adams, a key figure in the Revolution,
    a. drafted a "circular letter" to colonial legislatures condemning the Townshend duties.
    b. started committees of correspondence.
    c. served as the lawyer for the soldiers tried for shooting civilians in the Boston Massacre.
    d. convened the protest meeting at Old South Church that preceded the Boston Tea Party.

SHORT-ANSWER QUESTIONS

1. Explain why the colonists objected to writs of assistance and vice-admiralty courts.

2. Explain what the British meant by virtual representation and why the American colonists rejected the concept.

3. Why did the British pass the Coercive (Intolerable) Acts? What did the colonists think the laws showed about British intentions?

4. Where and when did the First Continental Congress meet? What actions did it take?

5. Why did General Gage send British troops to Lexington and Concord in 1775, and what happened as a result?

6. Why did the Second Continental Congress reverse itself on the question of independence between 1775 and 1776?

ESSAY QUESTIONS

1. Between 1689 and 1763 Britain and France and their respective allies fought four wars for supremacy in Europe and control of India and North America. Discuss the impact of those wars on America and relations between Britain and her thirteen colonies.

2. In 1763 a French statesman predicted that England would rue the day she expelled France from North America. Did events prove the Frenchman right? How are the French and Indian War and its outcome related to the American Revolution? Discuss.

3. One historian has written, "The British ruled the colonies for one hundred and fifty years and lost them in twelve." Do you agree with this statement? Why or why not? Use as many specific facts in your answer as possible.

4. Another historian claims, "A salient feature of our Revolution was that its animating purpose was deeply conservative. The colonials revolted against British rule in order to keep things the way they were, not to initiate a new era." Do you agree? Use as many facts in your answer as possible.

5. Discuss the role of each of the following groups in the events that led to America's break with England: colonial merchants, Virginia planters, workers, sailors, artisans, and women.

6

The Forge of Nationhood,
1776–1788

OUTLINE AND SUMMARY

I. America's First Civil War

A. *Introduction*

The Revolution was both a war of the American people against the British and a civil war between American patriots, or Whigs (supporters of independence), and American loyalists, or Tories (who were opposed to breaking with the mother country).

B. *Loyalists and Other British Sympathizers*

About 20 percent of all whites became loyalists. The proportion of loyalists was greatest in New York and New Jersey, where the leading families had split between the two sides. Recent British immigrants and French Canadians tended to be loyalists. Twenty thousand slaves escaped to the royal army, and most Indian tribes sided with the British against the westward-moving, land-hungry Americans.

C. *The Opposing Sides*

The British entered the war with major advantages: they outnumbered the Americans 11 million to 2.5 million, and they possessed the world's largest navy and one of the best professional armies. But they also had disadvantages. Because of their difficulty in recruiting soldiers, they had to employ twenty-one thousand loyalists and thirty thousand Hessian mercenaries. Supplying armies across three thousand miles of ocean was a formidable task. They managed to reach and hold coastal cities, but penetrating the interior with its poor roads proved especially trying. Further, as the financial strain of the conflict mounted, English domestic support for it waned. The Americans mobilized their smaller population behind the war more effectively, but they also were beset with problems: one-fifth of the free population was opposed to the Revolution, the state militias did well in guerrilla raids but lacked training for pitched battles, and there were few experienced officers to command the raw recruits of the Continental Army. Fortunately, the Americans did not have to conquer the redcoats; the rebels just had to keep resisting until the British public tired of the struggle.

D. George Washington

Washington, a Virginia tobacco planter who had sat in the House of Burgesses and the Continental Congress, was chosen commander of the army because of his military experience in the imperial wars with France. For much of the Revolution, America's fate depended on his ability to inspire his men to continue fighting despite numerous defeats.

E. War in Earnest

The British evacuated Boston in March 1776 and moved into New York, where they almost overwhelmed Washington's army on Long Island. In subsequent battles in and around the city, the British killed or captured a quarter of Washington's soldiers and forced him to make a hasty retreat across New Jersey. During the winter of 1776–1777, Washington struck back at Trenton and Princeton. The redcoats pulled back to New York, and New Jersey became a battleground between loyalists and Whigs. When the Whigs gained the upper hand and brutalized the loyalists, many of them dashed behind the royal army lines. The same pattern of bitter civil war was later repeated in New York, Georgia, and the Carolinas. During and at the end of the war, about one-sixth of the loyalists fled to Canada, England, or the British West Indies.

F. The Turning Point

The Americans realized that their best hope for victory lay in French diplomatic recognition and military alliance. Congress dispatched Benjamin Franklin to Paris to achieve this, but Louis XVI held back until he became convinced that the Americans had a chance of winning. When forces under General Horatio Gates foiled a major British offensive, surrounded General John Burgoyne's outnumbered army, and compelled the surrender of 5,800 British troops in October 1777 near Saratoga, New York, the French were impressed. By February 1778 France recognized the United States, and four months later she declared war on England. Subsequently the Spanish and the Dutch Republic also declared war on Britain. French and Spanish blows to British naval power and the diversion of English troops from America to fight in other theaters greatly aided the United States.

G. The Continentals Mature

In the fall of 1777, the British inflicted defeats on Washington's army at Brandywine Creek and Germantown, Pennsylvania, and occupied Philadelphia, compelling the Continental Congress to flee. While the royal army enjoyed the comforts of Philadelphia for the winter of 1778, Washington's men froze and drilled in nearby Valley Forge. In June the Continentals caught up with the British marching back to New York at the battle of Monmouth Court House, New Jersey. Badly mauled, the redcoats escaped to New York, where they sat under the protection of the British Navy, and Washington hovered across the Hudson keeping an eye on them.

H. Frontier Campaigns

Although the number of people involved in the frontier battles was small, the skirmishes were deadly, as the British, the new country, and the Indians realized what was at stake—

namely, who would control the area west of the Appalachians. The battles commenced in the South, where the Cherokees attacked from Virginia to Georgia. By 1777 the frontiersmen had crushed the Cherokees and forced them to cede much of their land in the Carolinas and Tennessee. Expeditions led by George Rogers Clark, John Bowman, and Daniel Brodhead inflicted heavy losses on hostile Ohio Indian tribes, who nonetheless kept up the struggle into the 1780s. Joseph Brant led the Iroquois on deadly raids against the western New York and Pennsylvania settlers until he was stopped at a battle near Elmira, New York. By the war's end the Iroquois population had dropped by a third.

I. Victory in the South

After 1778 the British shifted their attention to the South. They took Charles Town, South Carolina, in 1780, and General Charles Cornwallis led English forces into the Carolina backcountry. There he fought three major battles against American militiamen commanded by Nathaniel Greene. The British won all three encounters but suffered such heavy casualties that Cornwallis decided to leave the Carolina backcountry and head into Virginia. Cornwallis established a new base on Virginia's Yorktown Peninsula, where he was later cut off and surrounded by American and French armies and a French fleet under Admiral De Grasse. On October 19, 1781, Cornwallis surrendered, and the fighting in the Revolutionary War ended.

J. The Peace of Paris

John Adams, John Jay, and Benjamin Franklin represented the United States at the Paris peace negotiations that began in June 1782. Under the terms of the treaties signed in 1783, the British recognized American independence and promised to remove all troops from American soil. The Mississippi River became the western boundary of the United States, but New Orleans and the outlet of the river to the Gulf of Mexico, as well as East and West Florida, went to Spain. Although the United States agreed to compensate loyalists for their property losses and repay British creditors, several states later refused to comply. American victory had been costly: at least 5 percent of free white males between sixteen and forty-five years of age died in the war.

II. Revolutionary Society

A. Egalitarianism

Although there was no significant redistribution of wealth in America during the Revolution, the Declaration of Independence's bold assertion that all men are created equal did promote more egalitarian attitudes. The upper classes found it prudent to simplify their standard of living and treat common people with respect. Ordinary folks were less likely to defer to their "betters" or automatically leave governing to them. Americans began to feel that political leaders should come from the "natural aristocracy"—that is, men who demonstrated virtue, accomplishments, and dedication to the public good.

B. A Revolution for Black Americans

In 1776 blacks accounted for 20 percent of the U.S. population, and almost all of them were enslaved. Five thousand blacks served in the Continental Army. The Declaration of Independence's words about equality made Whigs uneasy about slavery. The Quakers had taken the lead in attacking slavery. Then, between 1777 and 1810, all the northern states instituted gradual emancipation. No southern states, however, where the majority of blacks lived, outlawed bondage. Several did make the voluntary freeing of slaves easier, and by 1790 about 5 percent of Virginia and Maryland blacks had been freed. Most free blacks remained poor laborers or tenant farmers. They relied on each other for help and began to build their own institutions, such as the African Methodist Episcopal church. Although most states granted freedmen certain civil rights, blacks continued in other respects to be treated as second-class citizens.

C. Women in the New Republic

The Revolution brought little change in the status of women. In the 1780s, as earlier, the great majority of people believed a woman's duty was to take care of her household and raise her children. The revolutionary emphasis on liberty and equality did, however, bring some improvements in female schooling. These were justified by the argument that women had to be educated so that they could inculcate republican virtues in their sons and daughters. But, the organized fight for women's rights did not begin until the nineteenth century.

D. Native Americans and the Revolution

The newly independent nation posed a serious threat to the Indians' future. For many whites the republic's promise of equal opportunity meant moving west to obtain their own land, thus impinging on Indian territory. The tribes of the Ohio Valley were especially vulnerable because between 1754 and 1783 war and uprooting had reduced the Native American population east of the Mississippi by nearly 50 percent. Those Indians still living east of the river adapted some features of white culture, combined it with their old ways, and carried on trade with whites, but they insisted on their right to control their own communities and lives.

E. The Revolution and Social Change

The overall distribution of wealth in the nation did not change as a result of the Revolution. Property taken from rich loyalists tended to end up in the hands of equally well-to-do Whigs. Slavery persisted in the South. Racial injustice and the subordination of women continued. But the Revolution did start the extinction of slavery in the North and increase the numbers of free blacks and the rights they had. The Revolution also gave rise to the earliest questioning of relations between the sexes.

III. Forging New Governments

A. Tradition and Change

Certain beliefs inherited from the colonial era stood in the way of a thorough democratization of politics. Most Whigs believed that voting and office holding must be tied to property ownership. They frowned on political parties as strife-causing factions and did not see the need for apportioning seats in a legislature on the basis of population. Their revolutionary experience did, however, make them wary of unchecked executive authority, inclined to augment the role of elected legislatures, and interested in framing governmental institutions that would balance the interests of different classes to prevent any one group from gaining absolute power.

B. Reconstituting the States

The first state constitutions reflected both the radical and traditional features of Whig thought. Except for Pennsylvania's, they did not provide for election districts that were equal in population. Nine of the thirteen states reduced property qualifications for voting, but none abolished them entirely. By 1784 all state constitutions included bills of rights. They provided for frequent elections and stripped the governors of most of their powers. In the 1780s, however, many states revised their constitutions to strengthen the executive branch and increase the political power of wealthy elites. Most of the states also enacted social reforms. In Virginia, for example, Thomas Jefferson framed legislation abolishing primogeniture, entails, and the established church, as well as guaranteeing religious freedom.

C. The Articles of Confederation

In 1777 the Continental Congress drafted a constitution called the Articles of Confederation and sent it to the states for ratification, which was finally achieved by 1781. The Articles created a weak central government. There was a unicameral congress in which each state had one vote, but there was no national court system or executive. Financial, diplomatic, and military affairs were managed by congressional committees. The congress could request funds from the states but could not tax the people directly. The Articles reserved to each state full sovereignty, freedom, and independence, leaving the national government "severely limited in important respects."

D. Finance and Trade Under the Confederation

The confederation proved too weak to meet its greatest challenge, putting the country's finances on a sound basis. Unable to tax the people or force the states to contribute funds, the congress could not pay off its Revolutionary War debt or meet its operating expenses. Its paper currency, the Continental, depreciated by 98 percent. Nor could the government under the Articles win diplomatic concessions from the British, who badly hurt northern shippers and merchants by shutting them out of the West Indian trade and imposing steep customs fees on goods entering England.

E. The Confederation and the West

The confederation also had to decide on the future of the trans-Appalachian west. The confederation was caught between speculators and settlers resolved to acquire these lands immediately and Native Americans determined to keep their homes. It responded by forcing Indian leaders to sign treaties ceding western lands, which the tribes then repudiated. In addition, the congress passed the Ordinance of 1785 and the Northwest Ordinance of 1787. These laws set a successful pattern for surveying, selling, and administering western lands, as well as providing the way for territories to become states with the same powers and privileges as the original thirteen states. Equally important, the Northwest Ordinance for the first time banned slavery from a territory.

Meanwhile the British and Spanish governments made life difficult for western settlers. The British refused to evacuate seven forts in the Ohio Valley and supplied Indians in the region with arms and ammunition. The Spanish, too, sided with the Indians against American frontier families and closed off New Orleans to western farmers who wanted to ship their produce down the Mississippi and out to eastern cities and Europe through that port. The ineffectual confederation failed to persuade Britain and Spain to stop these practices.

F. Shays's Rebellion

Shays's Rebellion, in 1786 in Massachusetts, led some Americans to fear that the government was unable to protect even domestic law and order. Further, producers wanted a stronger government to regulate interstate and foreign commerce. Merchants and shippers desired a government that could secure foreign trade opportunities for them. Westerners hoped for better protection from the Indians. A 1786 Annapolis, Maryland meeting to promote interstate commerce instead called for a general convention of all the states to amend the Articles and thereby create a more effective national government.

G. The Philadelphia Convention

Fifty-five delegates from every state but Rhode Island gathered during the spring and summer of 1787 in Philadelphia. The majority of them were wealthy, had legal training, and shared a nationalist rather than a local perspective. In sessions closed to the press and the public, they decided to abandon the Articles and write a new constitution. The convention worked from a draft written by delegate James Madison. His Virginia Plan proposed a national government with broad powers to tax, legislate, and use military force against states. There would be a two-house congress, with representation in both chambers based on population. The small states, worried that they would always be outvoted, objected and countered with William Patterson's New Jersey Plan. It called for a unicameral congress in which each state, regardless of population, had an equal voice. The convention finally agreed to the Connecticut Compromise, with a two-chamber legislature: representation in the House based on population and representation in the Senate based on the principle of equality for each state.

The Constitution, finished in September 1787, vested in the federal government the power to levy and collect taxes, conduct diplomacy, and protect domestic order. It also granted to the national government (and denied to the states) authority to coin money and regulate interstate and foreign commerce. The Constitution carefully balanced state and federal power, the interests of one social group against another, and the authority of one branch of the national government versus another with its systems of federalism, separation of powers, and checks and balances. Many features of the Constitution were not democratic. It recognized and in some ways protected slavery and allowed direct election only of members of the House of Representatives. On the other hand, it acknowledged the people as the "ultimate source of political legitimacy" and, through the amendment process, opened the door for democratization of the government in the years ahead. Finally, the delegates provided for ratification of the Constitution by special state conventions composed of delegates elected by the people. As soon as nine conventions had approved the document, the new government would commence.

H. Ratification

During 1787 and 1788 the country divided into pro-ratification Federalists and opposing Antifederalists. Antifederalists feared that the Constitution concentrated too much centralized power in the hands of a national elite and that individuals' freedoms would be trampled because the document contained no bill of rights. Leading Antifederalists included Virginia's Patrick Henry, George Mason, and James Monroe and New York governor George Clinton. The Federalists ultimately prevailed, because of their vigorous leadership and promise that they would amend the Constitution to provide a bill of rights once the new government was under way. In an effort to win New Yorkers over to the Constitution, John Jay, Alexander Hamilton, and James Madison published a series of articles, later collected in a book called *The Federalist* papers. These articles still afford us a valuable commentary on the Constitution and insight into the political philosophy of the Founding Fathers.

IV. Conclusion

The final triumph of the nationalism born of the War for Independence came in late 1789 and early 1790, when the last two reluctant states, North Carolina and Rhode Island, ratified the Constitution and joined the new union.

VOCABULARY

The following terms are used in Chapter 6. To understand the chapter fully, it is important that you know what each of them means.

mercenaries   hired soldiers serving in an army

egalitarian   asserting the equality of all people

confiscate   to seize for public use; to take away property as a penalty

emancipation   freedom from slavery

peers   persons of the same civil rank or standing; equals before the law

sovereignty   supreme or independent power or authority in government

republic   a government in which the supreme power rests in the body of citizens entitled to vote and is exercised by representatives chosen directly or indirectly by them. Also, the head of government is nominated and/or elected rather than inheriting the position as a king.

ideology   the body of doctrine, myth, and symbols of a social movement, institution, social class, or large group

agrarian   relating to farming, agricultural economy, or a rural way of life

connotations   secondary, implied, or associated meanings of a word or term rather than its dictionary definition

compact   an agreement between parties; a contract; a treaty

prorogue   to dismiss a legislature or discontinue its session

entails   legal requirements that prevent an heir and all his descendants from selling or dividing an estate

primogeniture   legal requirement that, in the absence of a will, only the eldest son inherits all a family's property

confederation   a league or alliance; a body of sovereign states more or less united for common purposes

interstate commerce   business carried on in more than one state; transactions across state lines (as opposed to business done entirely within one state, or *intrastate* commerce)

anarchy   a state of society without government or law; political and social disorder due to absence of government control

ratification   the act of confirming by expressing formal consent or approval

---

IDENTIFICATIONS

After reading Chapter 6, you should be able to identify and explain the historical significance of each of the following:

Henry Knox

loyalists (Tories) versus patriots (Whigs)

Hessians

Marquis de Lafayette

General John Burgoyne, General Horatio Gates, and Saratoga

Frederick von Steuben

George Rogers Clark

Joseph Brant

Yorktown

John Adams, John Jay, Benjamin Franklin, and the Peace of Paris

"natural aristocracy"

Benjamin Banneker

African Methodist Episcopal church

Abigail Adams

"republican motherhood"

Virginia Statute for Religious Freedom

John Dickinson and the Articles of Confederation

Ordinance of 1785 and Northwest Ordinance of 1787

Continentals

Shays's Rebellion

Virginia Plan, New Jersey Plan, and Connecticut Compromise

checks and balances, functional separation of powers, and federalism

Federalists versus Antifederalists

John Jay, Alexander Hamilton, James Madison, and *The Federalist* papers

SKILL BUILDING: MAPS

1. On the map of eastern North America on the following page, locate each of the following and explain its importance in the Revolutionary War.

   Fort Ticonderoga

   Boston

   New York City

   Long Island

   Delaware River

   Trenton, New Jersey

   Princeton, New Jersey

   Albany

   Philadelphia

   Saratoga, New York

   Brandywine Creek and Germantown, Pennsylvania

   Valley Forge, Pennsylvania

   Monmouth, New Jersey

   Appalachians

   Jenuchshadago, Pennsylvania (on the Allegheny River)

   Tennessee

   Illinois

   Vincennes, Indiana

   Detroit, Michigan

   Ohio River

   Elmira, New York

   Savannah, Georgia

   Charles Town, South Carolina

   Yorktown, Virginia

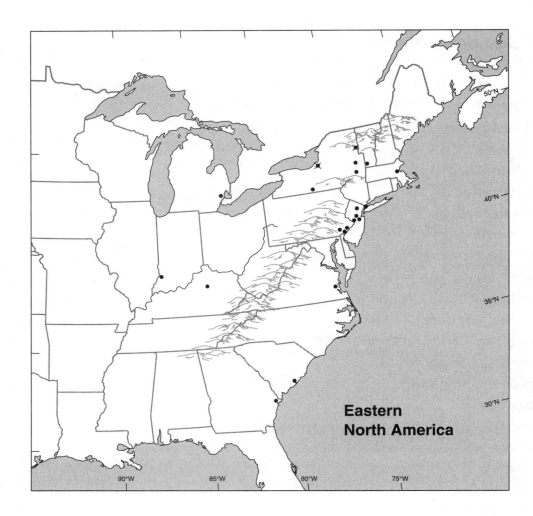

2. Draw on the map the boundaries of the United States as set by the Peace of Paris in 1783. Also draw the boundaries of the Northwest Territory created by the Ordinances of 1785 and 1787.

HISTORICAL SOURCES

On page 191 the author tells us that the sessions of the Constitutional Convention were closed to the press and the public and that the delegates kept no official journal of their proceedings. How, then, do historians know what went on at the convention? How does the author of Chapter 6 know who said this or that about the Virginia Plan or the New Jersey Plan? How does he know about the "grand committee," or that Madison and the Virginians continued to fight against the Connecticut Compromise until they were overruled by the July 17, 1787, vote? Much of our information comes from detailed notes that James Madison took on the debates as he attended and participated in the sessions. He did not make these notes public during his lifetime, but after his death in 1836, Congress purchased Madison's papers that contained the notes. They were first published in 1840. While Madison's notes have proved a most valuable source of information, can you see why it is wise for historians also to look at any memoirs, letters, and comments they can find by other convention participants?

A way that historians have learned much about the thinking of Federalists and Antifederalists is by reading the articles and letters that they published in the press during the fight over ratification. John Jay, Alexander Hamilton, and James Madison wrote many essays, which appeared in such New York newspapers as the *Daily Advertiser* in 1787, arguing in support of the Constitution. New York governor Clinton, a leading Antifederalist, countered with letters attacking the proposed Constitution in the *New York Journal*. In addition to these newspaper pieces, historians can turn to the records of the speeches given for both sides at the state ratifying conventions.

As well as finding their sources, historians also have to decide which past events they will focus on. Understandably, most accounts of the 1780s have concentrated on the post–Revolutionary War problems of whites under the Articles of Confederation and the writing of the present U.S. Constitution. The author of Chapter 6 seeks to give a broader, more balanced view of the period by including consideration of what Native Americans faced and how they responded to their situation. Look at "A Place in Time: Jenuchshadago, Pennsylvania, in the 1780s." What does this brief description of a Seneca community demonstrate about Indian problems and responses?

MULTIPLE-CHOICE QUESTIONS

Circle the letter of the item that best completes each statement or answers the question.

1. The long delay in approval of the Articles of Confederation was caused primarily by
    a. Maryland's demand that Virginia and New York give up their western land claims.
    b. fear that it created too strong a central government.
    c. bitterness between northern and southern states.
    d. feuding between loyalists and Whigs.

2. Which statement about the men who wrote the U.S. Constitution is correct?
    a. Most of them doubted that a republic could effectively govern so large a nation as the United States.
    b. Most were wealthy men who were convinced that unless the national government was strengthened, the country would fall victim to foreign aggression or simply disintegrate.
    c. Most were men in their fifties and sixties who distrusted the younger revolutionaries.
    d. They wanted to get on with creating a democratic government that would enforce their belief that all men are created equal.

3. The Northwest Ordinance did all of the following *except*
   a. forbid slavery in the Northwest Territory.
   b. permit the citizens of a territory to elect a legislature and make their own laws.
   c. permit the citizens of a territory to write a state constitution and apply to Congress for admission as a new state.
   d. remove Native Americans and guarantee white settlers the right to buy land in the territory.

4. The British justified their refusal to evacuate their military forts in the Ohio Valley after the Revolution by pointing to America's failure to
   a. stop Indian attacks against Canada.
   b. pay for damage done to British shipping during the war.
   c. return or pay for loyalists' property and pay British creditors.
   d. allow British goods to enter the United States duty free.

5. Which of the following represented the most serious difficulty facing American commercial interests at the end of the Revolution?
   a. loss of the protection of the British Navy
   b. British restrictions on trade with the West Indies
   c. decreased demand for American goods in Europe
   d. France's refusal to sign a commercial treaty

6. Shays's Rebellion was provoked by
   a. retention of the northwest posts by Britain.
   b. the failure of the government to protect frontier settlements from Indian attacks.
   c. an excise tax imposed by Congress on whiskey.
   d. the heavy burden of taxes on the farmers of western Massachusetts.

7. Which of the following men was both an author of the U.S. Constitution and an outspoken supporter of its ratification?
   a. Thomas Jefferson
   b. Patrick Henry
   c. James Madison
   d. George Clinton

8. The greatest achievement of the Antifederalists was to
   a. force the Federalists to agree to add a bill of rights to the Constitution.
   b. convince New York and Virginia to turn over their western lands to the new national government.
   c. delay ratification of the Constitution until a section guaranteeing all white men the right to vote and hold office was added.
   d. force the Federalists to bestow citizenship under the new government to free blacks.

9. Who was the author of Virginia's Statute for Religious Freedom and bills abolishing entails and primogeniture?
   a. George Washington
   b. Richard Henry Lee
   c. Thomas Jefferson
   d. Patrick Henry

10. All of the following were true of the state constitutions adopted during the Revolution *except*
   a. they concentrated power in the popularly elected legislatures.
   b. they all contained bills of rights.
   c. they provided for weak executives and frequent elections.
   d. they abolished property and tax-paying qualifications for voting.

SHORT-ANSWER QUESTIONS

1. Which groups of people tended to be loyalists, or British sympathizers, during the American Revolution?

2. Why is the Battle of Saratoga considered a turning point in the American Revolution?

3. In the Peace of Paris ending the revolutionary war, what were the terms affecting America?

4. What was the relationship between Shays's Rebellion and the calling of the Constitutional convention?

5. Explain the differences between the Virginia plan and the New Jersey plan for the Constitution. In what ways was the Connecticut proposal a compromise between them?

6. What was the three-fifths controversy at the Constitutional convention? In what other ways did the Constitution recognize and deal with slavery?

7. Briefly describe the checks and balances and separation of powers in the U.S. Constitution. Give examples to illustrate.

8. Who were the Antifederalists, and what were their objections to the U.S. Constitution?

ESSAY QUESTIONS

1. Besides being a war for independence from Britain, the American Revolution was also a civil war of American against American and a war of Native Americans to defend their homelands. Discuss and illustrate this statement with as many facts as possible.

2. Discuss the advantages and disadvantages the British and the Americans each had in fighting the Revolutionary War. What do you think accounts for the Americans' ultimate victory?

3. Discuss the social, economic, and political changes within the thirteen states produced by the American Revolution. Be sure to consider things such as slavery, status of women, property distribution, voting rights, and religion.

4. Discuss the domestic and foreign difficulties the United States experienced under the Articles of Confederation. What were the accomplishments of the government under the Articles?

5. Discuss the backgrounds and political beliefs of the men who wrote the U.S. Constitution. What did they hope to accomplish by establishing this Constitution?

7

Launching the New Republic, 1789–1800

OUTLINE AND SUMMARY

I. The Fragile New Nation

A. *The West and the South*

After America won its independence, Britain and Spain both connived to deny the United States its western lands between the Appalachians and the Mississippi. The British held on to forts in the Northwest Territory and armed the Indians who were resisting white settlers. The Spanish aided Indians in the lower Mississippi Valley and closed the port of New Orleans to American frontier farmers. Spanish officials indicated that westerners could gain access to the Gulf of Mexico and end Indian attacks by seceding from the United States and joining the Spanish Empire. Some American settlers and land speculators were tempted. If the new federal government could not subdue the Indians and win concessions from Britain and Spain, it might lose the West. Virginia and North Carolina had rewarded Revolutionary War soldiers with western land, and many members of the southern gentry hoped to profit by speculating on frontier real estate. Therefore, southerners resented the British and Spanish actions in the West and advocated strong measures against them.

B. *Regional Economies*

The post–Revolutionary War slump in tobacco and rice exports heightened southern resentment of foreign interference with westward movement. Pennsylvania and New York farmers, conversely, were doing well selling their foodstuffs to Europe. The New England economy languished as British economic restrictions strangled the Northeast's formerly lucrative trade with the West Indies and its shipping and fishing industries. The depressed economy made the Revolutionary War debt particularly burdensome.

C. *Entrepreneurs, Artisans, and Wage Earners*

In the North, entrepreneurs were trying to make the American economy more diversified and self-sufficient. The earliest factories were opening, as well as banks and commercial associations like the New York Stock Exchange. But most items were still being handmade by mechanics (artisans) and journeymen in small workshops. Unable to compete with industrially advanced British factories, American mechanics wanted the new national government to impose protective tariffs on imported items.

II. Constitutional Government Takes Shape

A. Introduction

The men elected to Congress under the new Constitution began assembling in New York City, the first national capital, in March 1789. George Washington arrived on April 23 and was sworn in as president on April 30. The lawmakers immediately devoted their attention to filling in the details in areas left vague in the Constitution: the president's cabinet, the national court system, and rights of the individual.

B. Defining the Presidency

The Constitution mentions executive departments only in passing. Through legislation Congress established the first cabinet. It consisted of four departments headed by secretaries of state, treasury, and war and an attorney general.

C. National Justice and the Bill of Rights

The Constitution authorized Congress simply to provide for federal courts below the level of the Supreme Court. This the lawmakers did by passing the Judiciary Act of 1789. It created a three-tier system of federal district courts, circuit courts of appeals, and the Supreme Court.

James Madison, who had been elected to the House of Representatives, led the way in drafting the first ten amendments, which became known as the Bill of Rights when they were ratified by the states in December 1791. The first eight protected individual rights, including freedom of speech, press, assembly, and religion, and procedures for a fair trial and punishment. The Ninth and Tenth amendments reserved to the people and the states powers not specifically granted to the federal government by the Constitution.

III. National Economic Policy and Its Consequences

A. Hamilton and His Objectives

Washington's secretary of the treasury, Alexander Hamilton, soon emerged as the leading figure in the administration. He wanted to promote national economic self-sufficiency through industrialization and a strong merchant marine. He also believed that the federal government's success depended on gaining the support of the politically influential commercial classes by benefiting them economically.

B. Report on the Public Credit

Hamilton's Report on the Public Credit, sent to Congress in January 1790, outlined a plan to establish the country's credit while at the same time wedding the upper classes to the government. He proposed that the federal government quickly pay off the outstanding foreign debt. Domestic holders of Revolutionary War bonds issued by the Continental Congress and the states could exchange them at full face value for new U.S. government bonds carrying 4 percent interest. Further, Hamilton urged Congress to maintain a perpetual debt, issuing new interest-bearing bonds as the old ones were retired. Hamilton hoped with these arrangements to provide former state creditors and other bond holders with a safe, attractive investment opportunity that would in turn give them a stake in the continued survival and economic health of the U.S. government.

Repayment of foreign creditors aroused no opposition, but Hamilton's other proposals provoked bitter controversy. Most of the domestic Revolutionary War bond holders had long since sold their certificates to speculators for a fraction of their value. Now these speculators, mostly well-to-do northeasterners, stood to reap a fortune. The states that had already paid back their creditors also objected to the federal government's assuming the burden for states that had lagged in discharging their financial obligations, most of which were northern states, except South Carolina. James Madison led the southern congressional opposition to both proposals but was unable to defeat them. Hamilton garnered just enough southern votes to put through his assumption of state debt scheme by making a deal to round up northern votes for placing the nation's permanent capital on the Potomac, where the Virginians wanted it. Hamilton's measures dramatically improved America's credit rating but alienated many southerners.

C. Reports on the Bank and Manufactures

Next Hamilton asked Congress to charter a national bank. The government would own one-fifth of its stock, and private individuals would own the other four-fifths. This bank would serve as a depository for federal tax receipts, make low-interest loans to the government, issue notes that would circulate as a national currency, regulate practices of state-chartered banks, and provide credit to expand the country's economy. The bank would, of course, further Hamilton's objective of tying rich businessmen to the federal government by affording them still another profitable investment. The secretary of the treasury also proposed to encourage manufacturing and other industries by enactment of protective tariffs and subsidies.

D. Hamilton's Challenge to Limited Government

Some government leaders began to see in Hamilton's bank and other proposals a disturbing pattern of favoring the interests of, and giving undue influence to, an elite group of investors. Led by Secretary of State Thomas Jefferson and Representative James Madison, opponents of the bank charter argued that it endangered the republic and was unconstitutional. When Congress passed the bill by a slim margin, a troubled President Washington asked Hamilton and Jefferson to advise him on the measure's constitutionality. The opinion each wrote presented the first clear-cut statements of the strict versus loose interpretations of the Constitution. Washington, more impressed with Hamilton's loose interpretation than Jefferson's strict reading of the Constitution, signed the bank bill into law. But Hamilton was not able to convince Congress to enact a high protective tariff, although it did aid shipping and fishing in other ways.

E. Hamilton's Legacy

Beneficiaries of Hamilton's policies, including speculators, merchants, and other monied men of the port cities, rallied behind the administration in a budding political party calling itself Federalist. The Federalists had their strongest support in New England, New Jersey, and South Carolina. They also had many adherents in Pennsylvania and New York. But the agricultural interests of the South, West, and Middle Atlantic states saw no gains for themselves in Hamilton's programs. They began to coalesce in opposition to the administration and in favor of the "true principles" of republicanism.

F. The Whiskey Rebellion

To fund the assumption of state debts, Congress in March 1791 imposed a federal excise tax on domestically produced whiskey. Western Pennsylvania farmers who earned a little cash income by turning their surplus grain (which was too bulky to ship) into compact corn liquor for sale viewed the excise tax as an unfair levy. In July 1794 a mob of frontier farmers attacked U.S. marshals who had come west to serve summonses on sixty persons for nonpayment of the tax. Washington and Hamilton decided to crush this Whiskey Rebellion forcefully to demonstrate that citizens must obey federal law. Almost thirteen thousand militiamen marched west and rounded up rebellious farmers. Twenty were sent to Philadelphia for trial, and two received death sentences, but Washington later pardoned them.

IV. The United States in a Hostile World

A. Introduction

After 1793 the political polarization created by Hamilton's financial policies became even more pronounced as Americans argued over foreign policy.

B. Foreign Powers and Native Americans in the West

The greatest danger in the West lay in British and Spanish assistance to Native Americans resisting settlers moving in and in the attempts of those foreign powers to detach the region from the United States. To counter this peril, the federal government, between 1791 and 1796, admitted Vermont, Kentucky, and Tennessee as new states. Both whites and Native Americans rejected Washington's efforts to "civilize" and integrate the eastern tribes into white society. The government instead continued to pressure the Indians to cede their lands and move farther west.

C. France and Factional Politics

In 1789 the French Revolution began. Almost all Americans were initially sympathetic, but when the revolution became more radical and France went to war with Britain, Spain, and other European monarchies, opinion in this country divided. Most southerners and westerners remained pro-French. Western settlers and southern land speculators hoped a French victory would leave Britain and Spain too weak to keep stirring up Indians on America's frontier. However, northeastern merchants, shippers, and seamen were dependent on trade with England and feared a pro-French foreign policy would lead to British retaliation against U.S. commerce. Meanwhile, the French ambassador, Edmond Genet, was actively recruiting

Americans to fight for France. Instead of abiding by the 1778 treaty of alliance, however, Washington, in 1793, proclaimed U.S. neutrality.

D. The British Crisis

To discourage the pro-French activities of some Americans, the British began seizing U.S. merchant ships and impressing seamen, as well as stepping up their incitement of the Indians in the Ohio Valley. The Spanish also increased their incursion on American western lands. To halt the drift into war, Washington dispatched John Jay to England and Thomas Pinckney to Spain. Jay's Treaty with England won few concessions except a British promise to evacuate their western forts, which owed much to Anthony Wayne's victory at the Battle of Fallen Timbers. Most southerners and westerners denounced Jay's Treaty, but a Federalist-dominated Senate ratified it to avoid war. Pinckney's Treaty with Spain was more satisfactory, especially because it opened full use of the port of New Orleans to western farmers. Disagreements about foreign policy, especially ratification of Jay's Treaty, furthered the partisan split.

V. Battling for the Nation's Soul

A. Ideological Confrontation

Horrified by the intensifying radicalism of the French Revolution, the Federalists grew more suspicious of the common people and of unchecked democracy. But the Jeffersonian Republicans retained their sympathy for revolutionary France and did not fear popular participation in politics. Jefferson and Madison sought the support of ordinary citizens against Federalist policies by encouraging the publication of anti-administration newspapers like the *National Gazette*. They also approved of the Democratic societies that were springing up in various locations.

B. The Republican Party

By 1793 President Washington was clearly identified with the Federalists and Jefferson had resigned from his cabinet to lead the opposition. Federalist and Republican newspapers were engaged in a press war of exaggerated charges and countercharges. Stung by partisan criticism, Washington decided to retire after 1796. In his farewell address, he warned Americans to avoid political parties and entangling alliances with European countries. His decision not to run, however, opened the presidential election of 1796 to the first partisan contest.

C. The Election of 1796

The Republicans ran Thomas Jefferson; the Federalists, John Adams. The Federalists won control of Congress and the presidency by a narrow margin. Jefferson, who lost, became vice president, however, because the Constitution (written without providing for an organized opposition and political parties) had provided that the runner-up should have the number-two spot.

D. The French Crisis

The French, angered by America's signing of Jay's Treaty with the British, began to seize U.S. merchant ships. Hoping to avoid war with France, President Adams sent a peace commission to Paris to negotiate. There, in what became known as the XYZ Affair, agents of the French government demanded a bribe as the price for negotiations. The affair outraged Americans and provoked an anti-French and anti-Republican backlash. Republican candidates were defeated in the 1798 congressional elections, and an undeclared naval war broke out with France.

E. The Alien and Sedition Acts

The Federalist-dominated Congress took advantage of the anti-French hysteria to push through a series of repressive measures known as the Alien and Sedition Acts, which aimed at silencing the opposition press and in other ways weakening the Republican party. One measure attempted to rob the Republicans of the votes of their Irish- and French-immigrant supporters by imposing a fourteen-year wait for citizenship. Under the Sedition Act, which made it a crime to speak, write, or print anything unfavorable about the government or the president that would bring him "into contempt or disrepute," the Federalists prosecuted and jailed a number of Republican journalists and political candidates. Madison and Jefferson fought back with the Virginia and Kentucky resolutions. Passed by the legislatures of those two states, the resolutions claimed that state governments could interpose themselves between their residents and the enforcement of unconstitutional federal laws such as the Alien and Sedition Acts. The resolutions set a precedent for the later states' rights position that states were the proper judges of federal actions and could nullify unconstitutional statutes.

F. The Election of 1800

The election took place in an atmosphere of tense and bitter partisanship. The Republicans nominated Jefferson and Aaron Burr for president and vice president. President Adams, running for a second term, greatly disappointed the "High Federalists" and hurt his own election prospects by reopening negotiations with France and thus quieting the war scare on which Federalist fortunes had thrived. The negotiations eventually patched things up with France and spared this nation an unnecessary war. The Republicans won the election, but Jefferson and Burr ended up tied for president because, under the Constitution as originally written, electors did not vote separately for president and vice president. The tie threw the election into the House of Representatives, which took thirty-six votes to name Jefferson president. The nation soon added the Twelfth Amendment to the Constitution to prevent such muddled elections in the future.

VI. Deferring Equality

A. Indians in the New Republic

By 1800 eastern Indians had suffered devastating losses of land and population, and Indian culture was buckling under the strain of continual frontier warfare. As the broken survivors sank into alcoholism and clung to their traditional ways, whites increasingly perceived

Native Americans as an inferior people who would never be assimilated successfully into the dominant white society.

B. Redefining the Color Line

As the revolutionary idealism that had eased out slavery in the North and won some rights for free blacks ebbed in the 1790s, the position of African-Americans deteriorated. In the late 1790s and early 1800s, states such as Delaware, Maryland, Kentucky, and New Jersey, which had earlier given freedmen the vote, rescinded it. Congress protected southern masters with the 1793 Fugitive Slave Law. White fears generated by the slave uprising in Saint Domingue and the 1800 Gabriel's Rebellion in Virginia further eroded any sentiment for abolition and racial equality. The demand of the British textile industry for cotton and Eli Whitney's invention of the cotton gin in 1793 also revived southern plantation slavery, making the institution too profitable to question.

VII. Conclusion

By 1801 the dangers of civil war and national disintegration had declined, if not disappeared. Two rival political parties had developed, but with the election of 1800 the nation managed a peaceful transfer of power from Federalists to Republicans. Slavery and racism, after some abatement, were again on the rise.

VOCABULARY

The following terms are used in Chapter 7. To understand the chapter fully, it is important that you know what each of them means.

speculator   a person trading in land, commodities, or stocks and bonds in the hope of profiting from changes in the market price; one who engages in business transactions involving considerable risk but offering large gains

default   to fail to meet financial obligations; to fail to perform a legally required act or obligation

secession   formal withdrawal from an association, as in states withdrawing from the union

entrepreneurs   persons who develop and carry out new economic enterprises

mechanic   an artisan who practices a trade using his home as a workshop and employing family members, apprentices, journeymen, and servants

journeyman   a person who has served an apprenticeship in a trade and who works at it for another

tariff   a tax imposed on products imported from abroad

excise tax   a tax levied on goods and services manufactured, sold, or offered within the country

ex post facto law   a law criminalizing previously legal actions and punishing those who have been engaging in such actions

bill of attainder   a legislative act proclaiming a person's guilt and stipulating punishment without a judicial trial

bounties or subsidies   rewards or payments given (usually by governments) to encourage certain actions or economic activities

privateer   a privately owned and manned armed vessel commissioned by a government in time of war to fight the enemy, especially its commercial shipping

impress   to force into service, as with a seaman; to seize or take for public use or service

constituents   the voters and residents of a district, state, or country whom an elected official represents

abomination   an object greatly disliked or hated; a horror

demagoguery   using the methods or practices of a demagogue—that is, a leader who uses the passions or prejudices of the people for his or her own interests; using the methods or practices of an unprincipled popular orator or agitator

partisan   a supporter of a political party or cause; actions motivated by support of a political party or cause

cabal   a small group of secret plotters

libelous   writing that contains damaging or malicious misrepresentation

emoluments   profits or rewards arising from office, such as government service

apostate   one who forsakes his church, cause, or party

electorate   the body of persons entitled to vote in an election

sedition   incitement of discontent or rebellion against the government; action or language promoting such discontent or rebellion

---

IDENTIFICATIONS

After reading Chapter 7, you should be able to identify and explain the historical significance of each of the following:

Samuel Slater

Stephen Girard

Judiciary Act of 1789

Bill of Rights

Hamilton's Report on the Public Credit, 1790

James Madison

Hamilton's Report on a National Bank

Hamilton's Report on Manufactures

strict versus loose interpretation and the "necessary and proper" clause of the Constitution

Federalists versus Republicans

Whiskey Rebellion

citizen Edmond Genet

Jay's Treaty

Treaty of San Lorenzo (Pinckney's Treaty)

Washington's farewell address

XYZ Affair

Quasi-War with France

Alien and Sedition Acts, 1798

Virginia and Kentucky resolutions, 1798

interposition and nullification

election of 1800

Jefferson-Burr tie and the Twelfth Amendment

Handsome Lake

Fugitive Slave Law, 1793

Saint Domingue (Haiti) slave uprising

Gabriel Prosser and Gabriel's Rebellion, 1800

Eli Whitney and the cotton gin

SKILL BUILDING: MAPS

On the map of the eastern half of the United States, locate and explain the historical importance of each place in the period 1789–1800.

Fort Miami (Toledo, Ohio)

Fort San Fernando (Memphis, Tennessee)

Ohio River

Northwest Territory

Appalachians

Marietta, Ohio

Cincinnati, Ohio

New Orleans

Vermont

Kentucky

Tennessee

thirty-first parallel

SKILL BUILDING: CHARTS AND GRAPHS

Look at the chart titled "Number and Percentage of Free Blacks, by State, 1800" on page 230 of the textbook. By studying that bar graph, you should be able to answer the following questions:

1. Had the revolutionary ideology of the Declaration of Independence resulted in the freeing of most African-Americans?

2. Had slavery been totally eliminated in any state by 1800?

3. Which northern states had made the least progress in eliminating slavery by 1800?

4. Which southern or border states had made the most progress in eliminating slavery by 1800? Which had made the least?

5. In which four states did the bulk of free blacks live in 1800?

HISTORICAL SOURCES

In Chapter 7 the author discusses the birth and development of opposing political parties. One source for historians writing on this topic is the newspapers that aligned themselves with either the Federalist or Republican party, like the *Gazette of the United States* and the *National Gazette*. Early in the Washington administration, Alexander Hamilton helped set up John Fenno's *Gazette of the United States* to build public opinion behind the treasury secretary's financial program. James Madison countered in the 1790s by encouraging his friend Philip Freneau to establish the *National Gazette* to arouse the people against Federalist policies. On page 222 there is a reference to the contents of these newspapers. How is the author of Chapter 7 using these historical sources? Can the historian rely on these newspapers for accurate, unbiased reporting of events in the 1790s? If not, why is the press of the 1790s still a valuable historical source?

On page 231 Gabriel's Rebellion of 1800 is discussed and a statement of one of the rebels is quoted. Where do historians gain this information? Gabriel Prosser and thirty-five of his followers were tried. James Monroe, then governor of Virginia, questioned Prosser about the uprising. Prosser would say little, but some of his codefendants did testify about their plans, motives, and intentions. These records are preserved in Documents Relating to the Trial and Execution of Gabriel in the Virginia State Historical Library. Such state historical archives afford historians much of the material they use to learn about the past.

Now look at "A Place in Time: Philadelphia in the 1790s." What illustrations of economic, social, and political developments of the 1790s can one find in this short urban history? Note the brief references to the position of black Philadelphians and to the yellow-fever epidemic in 1793. A pertinent historical source on these two subjects is a pamphlet written by two black Philadelphia clergymen, Absalom Jones and Richard Allen, *A Narrative of the Proceedings of the Black People, During the Late Awful Calamity in Philadelphia . . . 1793 . . .*, published in 1794. Today historians can look at a copy of the pamphlet in the Library of Congress, which houses a treasure trove of publications and documents pertaining to American history.

MULTIPLE-CHOICE QUESTIONS

Circle the letter of the item that best completes each statement or answers the question.

1. The main purpose of the Alien and Sedition Acts was to
   a. publicize the activities of French revolutionaries in the United States.
   b. strengthen the policy of neutrality.
   c. strengthen the Republican party.
   d. suppress the Republican opposition to Federalist policies.

2. Hamilton wanted the federal government to take over in full the Revolutionary War debt of the Continental Congress and the states because he believed that
   a. this would cause a heavy loss to speculators in certificates.
   b. the payment of all such obligations was guaranteed in the Constitution.
   c. this would cause well-to-do creditors to favor the new federal government and the extension of its powers.
   d. the states unanimously favored such a policy.

3. Hamilton's financial program was designed to do all of the following *except*
   a. gain the support of the commercial classes for the new national government.
   b. encourage the rapid industrialization of the United States.
   c. pay off the national debt as quickly as possible.
   d. establish the credit of the United States at home and abroad.

4. Hamilton's national bank
   a. provoked the first clear-cut argument over the strict versus loose interpretation of the Constitution.
   b. was a fully government-owned-and-operated institution.
   c. helped the United States retire its old revolutionary debt as quickly as possible.
   d. did or was all of the above.

5. The XYZ Affair
   a. arose out of the French government's demand for a bribe as the price of negotiating.
   b. increased the popularity of the Republican party and hurt the fortunes of the Federalists.
   c. was provoked by Hamilton to increase the popularity of the Washington administration.
   d. arose out of the Whiskey Rebellion.

6. The Virginia and Kentucky resolutions
   a. attacked the Alien and Sedition Acts.
   b. were written by Madison and Jefferson.
   c. claimed the right of a state to protect its people from unconstitutional federal laws.
   d. all of the above.

7. Speculators were able to take advantage of which of these Federalist measures?
   a. the excise tax
   b. the refunding of the national debt by paying full face value of Revolutionary War bonds
   c. the tariff
   d. placing the federal capital on land donated by Virginia and Maryland

8. Which action of President John Adams angered the "High Federalists"?
   a. his handling of the XYZ Affair
   b. his signing of the Alien and Sedition Acts
   c. his decision to improve relations with France in 1799–1800
   d. his request for a larger army

9. Which of these people would probably *not* be a supporter of Jefferson's Republican party?
    a. a Virginia planter
    b. a Boston merchant
    c. a western Pennsylvania farmer
    d. a recent Irish immigrant

10. Which of the following people scored a victory over the Indians that opened Ohio to white settlement and won a promise by the British to evacuate forts in the Northwest Territory?
    a. Gabriel Prosser
    b. Anthony Wayne
    c. Stephen Girard
    d. Matthew Lyon

SHORT-ANSWER QUESTIONS

1. What problems in the West faced the new federal government in 1789?

2. Briefly describe the drafting, content, and ratification of the Bill of Rights.

3. Explain Hamilton's reasoning in support of a loose interpretation of the U.S. Constitution and Jefferson's in defense of a strict interpretation.

4. Why did farmers in western Pennsylvania object to the excise tax on whiskey? How did the Washington administration deal with their rebellion? Why?

5. Why did President Washington make his Farewell Address? What advice did it offer his fellow citizens?

6. What happened to eastern Indians in the 1790s and early 1800s, and why?

7. Explain the reasons for heightened racism and declining abolitionist sentiment in the 1790s and early 1800s.

ESSAY QUESTIONS

1. Discuss the rise of political parties in the United States. Did the Constitution provide for political parties? If not, when and why did the first two parties develop? Who led and supported each party?

2. Discuss the economic and financial programs of Secretary of the Treasury Alexander Hamilton. What did they include? What was Hamilton trying to accomplish? How and why did his programs politically divide Americans?

3. Discuss the deteriorating positions of African-Americans and Native Americans in the post–Revolutionary War period. How do you account for the deterioration? What were the major changes or events that marked the declining status of each group?

4. Explain how differences over foreign policy in the period 1789–1800 encouraged the development of political parties and partisanship.

5. "By 1801 the dangers of civil war and national disintegration had abated though they had not vanished." Discuss the dangers the nation faced during the Federalist era (1789–1800) and how it overcame or survived them. In your answer be sure to include conflict among social, economic, and sectional interest groups; challenges from foreign nations; and threats to individual liberties and the Bill of Rights.

8

Jeffersonianism and the Era of Good Feelings

OUTLINE AND SUMMARY

I. Introduction

When Thomas Jefferson entered the presidency, he was dedicated to restoring "republican simplicity" to the United States government.

In 1800 the United States had no major cities. Poor roads made travel and communication difficult, and these conditions promoted localism. National issues dividing Federalists and Republicans were often of minor interest to voters scattered in rural areas. Besides, large segments of the population—women, slaves, and the propertyless—were excluded from voting.

Despite this localism, the United States between 1800 and 1823 would experience major national events: (1) adding new territory that more than doubled its size, (2) surviving alleged conspiracies of a former vice president, (3) becoming embroiled in a European war, (4) fighting a battle over Missouri statehood and the spread of slavery, and (5) making important foreign-policy agreements and statements. Also during this period, Jefferson and Madison faced the challenge of applying republican political theory to day-to-day government operations.

II. The Age of Jefferson

A. Introduction

Thomas Jefferson, a complex, contradictory, and gifted individual, championed equality but owned over two hundred slaves. He distrusted power concentrated in the federal government as a danger to republican liberty, preferring the state governments, which he saw as closer and more responsive to the people. Republican liberty could best be retained by a virtuous and vigilant citizenry that put the public good ahead of selfish private interests. To Jefferson, the group that best displayed those qualities were small farmers. Cities and their landless inhabitants, on the other hand, were a potential menace to the republic. Jefferson as president, whatever his philosophy, showed himself to be flexible and practical.

B. Jefferson's "Revolution"

Jefferson attempted to repeal Federalist measures that he felt were a danger to the simple republic, such as parts of Alexander Hamilton's economic program and the Alien and Sedition Acts. He reduced taxes and the national debt, primarily by slashing expenditures for the army and for the diplomatic establishment. In these ways he felt he was lifting an economic burden from hardworking farmers.

C. Jefferson and the Judiciary

Although Jefferson was willing to cooperate with the moderate Federalists in many ways, he attacked the underhanded Federalist move to retain control of the judiciary. Jefferson demanded that Congress repeal the Federalist-sponsored Judiciary Act of 1801 and remove the partisan Federalist judges that outgoing President Adams had just appointed. Jefferson had little success with impeachment of Federalist judges, however, gaining only one conviction and removal from the bench. The reason was that the majority in Congress apparently viewed the impeachment process as an inappropriate way to solve the problem of partisan judges. Jefferson's drive to keep additional Federalists out of the judiciary led to the landmark Supreme Court case of *Marbury* v. *Madison*. Chief Justice John Marshall used the case to claim that federal courts had the right to review laws passed by Congress—the right of judicial review. For the first time, the Supreme Court declared a portion of a law passed by Congress unconstitutional. Jefferson did not oppose the concept of judicial review, but he believed that other branches of government, including state legislatures, should share that right with the federal courts.

D. The Louisiana Purchase

Napoleon Bonaparte forced Spain to cede the Louisiana Territory to France. The French action alarmed Jefferson because it placed a major European power on the U.S. border and blocked the gradual expansion of the United States. The problem became especially pressing in 1802, when Spanish authorities, just before the territory's transfer to France, denied western farmers use of the port of New Orleans. Jefferson sent James Monroe and Robert R. Livingston to France with a request to buy the city. Napoleon countered with an offer to sell the entire Louisiana Territory for $15 million. Since the Constitution did not explicitly give the federal government the power to acquire new territories, and since Jefferson was wedded to strict interpretation, he briefly thought of first seeking an enabling amendment to the Constitution. His practicality won out, however, and he submitted the purchase treaty to the Senate, where it was quickly ratified.

E. The Lewis and Clark Expedition

Jefferson requested funding from Congress for an expedition across the continent to explore the new Louisiana Purchase. The party, led by Meriwether Lewis and William Clark, left St. Louis in 1804; followed the Missouri, Snake, and Columbia rivers; crossed the Rockies; and reached the Pacific. It returned with a wealth of scientific information (and some misinformation), descriptions, and maps that stimulated interest in the West.

F. The Election of 1804

Republicans in Congress renominated Jefferson for president and dropped Aaron Burr in favor of George Clinton for vice president. The Federalists chose Charles C. Pinckney and Rufus King. The successes of Jefferson's first term—doubling the size of the United States, maintaining peace, and reducing taxes and the national debt—won over many former Federalist voters, resulting in an overwhelming Republican victory.

III. The Gathering Storm

A. Introduction

Jefferson's second term as president was beset by problems caused by the breakdown of Republican party unity and the renewal of the Napoleonic Wars.

B. Jefferson's Coalition Fragments

Aaron Burr, Jefferson's first-term vice president, stirred up factionalism within the Republican party. Jefferson believed that Burr was the chief plotter in a conspiracy to separate the western states from the Union. The president had Burr arrested and tried for treason. At the trial, over which John Marshall presided, the jury found the charges "not proved."

C. Jefferson and the Quids

Jefferson also was attacked by another faction of Republicans known as the Quids, led by John Randolph. They criticized the president's handling of the Yazoo land scandal and other actions that they saw as compromising Republican simplicity.

D. The Suppression of American Trade

The British and French, at war with each other, forbade American ships from entering each other's ports and trading with the other side. Both powers seized U.S. ships, but the actions of the British caused greater harm because they had the larger navy and their warships often hovered just off the U.S. coast.

E. Impressment

Also, the British removed sailors on American ships and forced (pressed) them into service in the Royal Navy.

F. The Embargo Act

Jefferson persuaded Congress to pass an embargo as a means of "peaceable coercion." He hoped that U.S. refusal to export any goods or to buy any products from abroad would put sufficient economic pressure on Britain and France to make them respect U.S. neutral rights. Unfortunately, the cutoff of trade did not hurt them enough to change their actions, but it proved disastrous to the U.S. economy. Seamen were unemployed; merchants and farmers who depended on foreign sales were ruined. The impact was hardest on New England. An unintended consequence of the embargo was to encourage transfer of capital into domestic manufacturing, a development Jefferson had initially opposed.

G. The Election of 1808

The unpopularity of the embargo, especially in New England, revived the Federalist party. In 1808 it nominated Charles C. Pinckney to run against Republican James Madison. Although the Federalists carried much of New England, Madison won because of continued Republican strength in other sections.

H. The Failure of Peaceable Coercion

Just before Jefferson left office, Congress repealed the embargo and replaced it with the weaker Non-Intercourse Act. This law worked no better than the previous one. For the next year and a half, President Madison tried variations on the theme of peaceable coercion, such as Macon's Bill No. 2, but all failed to change British and French behavior.

I. The Push into War

By 1810 Madison faced increasing pressure from Republican congressmen from the South and West who demanded a more aggressive policy toward Britain and France. These "war hawks" resented the insults to American honor and blamed the interference in trade for the economic recession hitting their home states.

J. Tecumseh and the Prophet

The war hawks wanted the British to get out of Canada, partly because they believed the British were arming and inciting the Indians on the American frontier. Tecumseh and his brother the Prophet were two Shawnees attempting to unite the tribes of Ohio and Indiana against white settlers. They initially had no connection with the British, but after William Henry Harrison attacked the Prophet's town and won the battle at Tippecanoe, Tecumseh did join forces with England.

K. Congress Votes for War

Madison, on June 1, 1812, asked Congress to declare war on England. The vote reflected party and sectional splits. Most of the no votes came from New England Federalists, while the majority of Republicans passed the declaration.

L. The Causes of the War

The United States declared war in 1812 because of Britain's incitement of the Indians, the belief that continuing British restrictions on U.S. shipping were causing the recession in the South and West, and Madison's view that England intended to ruin America as a commercial rival.

IV. The War of 1812

A. *On to Canada*

In 1812 American attempts to conquer Canada failed. The British took Detroit and were routed only by Oliver H. Perry's victory on Lake Erie and William Henry Harrison's success in 1813 at the Battle of the Thames.

B. *The Naval War*

Although Americans won some encounters at sea, the British continued to dominate the Atlantic. They clamped a blockade on the American coast and repulsed U.S. efforts to invade Canada and control Lake Ontario.

C. *The British Offensive*

In 1814 the British landed on the shores of Chesapeake Bay and marched to Washington, which they captured and burned. After they failed to take Baltimore, they broke off the campaign.

D. *The Treaty of Ghent*

U.S. and British commissioners met at Ghent, in Belgium, to make peace. At first the British, based on their superior military position, demanded territory from the United States. When the Americans refused, the British, anxious for peace now that they had defeated Napoleon, backed down. In December 1814 they signed a treaty with the United States that restored the prewar status quo. The United States' victory at the Battle of New Orleans, fought two weeks after the treaty was concluded, had no bearing on its terms.

E. *The Hartford Convention*

The unpopularity of the war in the Northeast contributed to the revival of the Federalists. In the election of 1812, antiwar Republicans and Federalists supported De Witt Clinton for president against Madison. Although Madison won reelection, Clinton carried most of the Northeast. American military losses intensified Federalist discontent to the point that, in the fall of 1814, a group of party members from New England convened at Hartford, Connecticut, and passed resolutions aimed at strengthening their region's power within the Union. The return of peace and public disapproval of the Hartford Convention led to the rapid demise of the Federalist party. In the election of 1816, the Republican presidential nominee, James Monroe, scored an easy victory over his Federalist opponent. In 1820 Monroe won reelection with every electoral vote but one.

V. The Awakening of American Nationalism

A. *Madison's Nationalism and the Era of Good Feelings*

The postwar period, characterized by a heightened spirit of nationalism and a new political consensus, has been called the Era of Good Feelings. As the Federalist party disappeared, the Republicans, to make the nation more economically self-sufficient, enacted many of the measures that the Federalists had earlier supported. Among these were the chartering of a new national bank and help for domestic manufacturing with a protective tariff. The sectional harmony started to break down almost immediately, however, because of the issue of slavery and its spread westward.

B. John Marshall and the Supreme Court

During the Era of Good Feelings, Chief Justice John Marshall wrote opinions that strengthened the power of the federal government at the expense of state sovereignty. Among these were *Dartmouth College* v. *Woodward*, which forbade state interference with contracts, and *McCulloch* v. *Maryland*, which favored the Hamiltonian broad interpretation of the Constitution and prohibited states from interfering with the exercise of federal powers.

C. The Missouri Compromise

National harmony began to crumble in the 1819 controversy over Missouri's application for statehood. For the first time, bitter sectional debate took place over the issue of the spread of slavery because the institution had become embroiled in political and economic issues dividing North and South, Republicans and Federalists. Admitting Missouri as a slave state would upset the balance of eleven free and eleven slave states that existed in 1819 and would give the South a political advantage. The issue was settled for the time being when Congress in 1820 approved the Missouri Compromise: (1) Missouri entered the Union as a slave state; (2) Maine entered as a free state; (3) in the remainder of the Louisiana Territory slavery would be permitted only south of 36 degrees, 30 minutes latitude, the southern boundary of Missouri.

D. Foreign Policy Under Monroe

Under the leadership of president James Monroe and his able secretary of state, John Quincy Adams, the United States achieved several foreign-policy successes. Good relations with the British were cemented by the Rush-Bagot Treaty and the British-American Convention. In the 1819 Adams-Onís Treaty, Spain ceded East Florida to the United States and renounced its claims to West Florida.

E. The Monroe Doctrine

In December 1823 President Monroe proclaimed a policy later known as the Monroe Doctrine. Its purpose was to discourage European powers from helping Spain regain her lost colonies in the Americas while, at the same time, reserving the right of the United States to expand further in the Western Hemisphere. The Monroe Doctrine stated that (1) the United States would not become involved in strictly European affairs, (2) the American continents were not available for further European colonization, and (3) the United States would look upon any attempt by European countries to regain lost colonies or to interfere in the Americas as an "unfriendly act."

VI. Conclusion

The key accomplishment of the political leaders in the period 1800–1820s was the creation of a "workable body of political institutions and customs to govern the young nation." The disappearance of the Federalists and the takeover of many of their economic policies by the Republicans softened earlier political divisions. Short-lived national harmony peaked in the years following the War of 1812, only to crumble with the dispute over Missouri. Thereafter, new signs of sectional and political conflict emerged.

VOCABULARY

The following terms are used in Chapter 8. To understand the chapter fully, it is important that you know what each of them means.

infidel   an unbeliever; one who does not accept a particular religion, such as Christianity

judicial review   right of the federal courts to declare legislative acts unconstitutional

impeach   to charge a public official, such as a judge or president, with misconduct in office; an impeachment is equivalent to an indictment, not to a conviction

caucus   a meeting of political party members to nominate candidates and/or decide on other party actions

coalition   a combination or alliance among different groups, parties, or states in support of a particular cause, individual, or purpose

internal improvements   roads, canals, and other projects to improve transportation and communication

consensus   general agreement

Brahmins   in American history, an elite group of New England families whose influence was based on family heritage, wealth, and culture

IDENTIFICATIONS

After reading Chapter 8, you should be able to identify and explain the historical significance of each of the following:

Tripolitan (Barbary) pirates

Judiciary Act of 1801

midnight judges

Marbury v. *Madison*

John Marshall

Lewis and Clark Expedition

Sacajawea

Aaron Burr conspiracy

British Orders in Council and Napoleon's Continental System

impressment

Chesapeake-Leopard Affair

Embargo and Non-Intercourse acts

war hawks

John C. Calhoun

Henry Clay and the American System

Tecumseh and the Prophet

William Henry Harrison and the battles of Tippecanoe and the Thames

Oliver H. Perry and the Battle of Lake Erie

Treaty of Ghent and the *status quo ante*

Battle of New Orleans

Hartford Convention

Era of Good Feelings

Dartmouth College v. *Woodward*

McCulloch v. *Maryland*

Missouri Compromise

John Quincy Adams

Rush-Bagot Treaty and British-American Convention, 1818

Adams-Onís, or Transcontinental, Treaty

Monroe Doctrine

SKILL BUILDING: MAPS

On the map of the United States on the following page, locate each of the places listed below. How is each connected with one or more of the following historical events: U.S. treaties with Spain and France, Lewis and Clark expedition, War of 1812, sectional conflict and compromise?

East and West Florida

New Orleans

Louisiana Territory

Appalachian Mountains

Mississippi River

Missouri River

Snake River

Columbia River

St. Louis

Ohio River

Indiana Territory

Lake Erie and Lake Champlain

Chesapeake Bay

36° 30 latitude

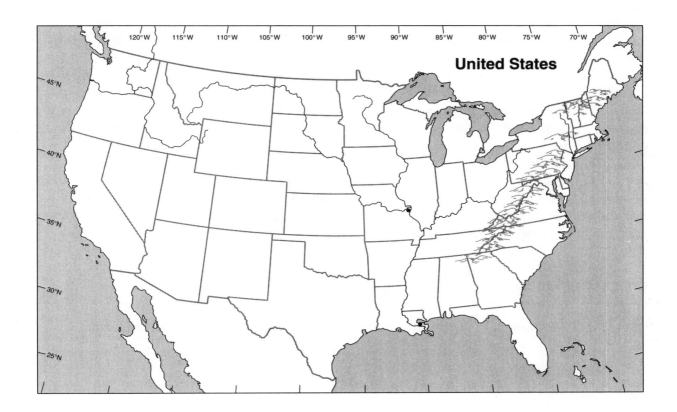

HISTORICAL SOURCES

Pages 243–244 of Chapter 8 give an account of the Lewis and Clark expedition. How did the author find out about the adventures of the party, the role of Sacajawea, and the mass of scientific information and some tall tales that Lewis and Clark brought back with them? Much of what we know about the expedition and its findings comes from the journals kept by Meriwether Lewis and William Clark, first published in 1814. Probably the definitive edition of the record of Lewis's and Clark's trip is the eight-volume *Original Journals of the Lewis and Clark Expedition, 1804–1806,* edited by Reuben Gold Thwaites and published in

1904–1905. A single-volume, abridged version, *The Journals of Lewis and Clark*, edited by Bernard De Voto, is available for the general reader who would like to taste the flavor of this valuable historical source.

The author of Chapter 8 also discusses the reasons for America's declaration of war on England and the sectional controversies over that war. How does the historian know which congressmen from which states voted for war? How does the author know that John C. Calhoun and other southern and western congressmen believed that British policy was damaging America's economy, or that President Madison attributed British actions to their desire to monopolize trade? The historian can read the speeches of senators and representatives and find the record of their votes in the *Debates and Proceedings in the Congress of the United States*, often cited as *Annals of Congress*, printed by the U.S. government. Madison's statement about British motives was part of his war message to Congress. Like all public communications of American presidents, it is published in the multivolume *A Compilation of the Messages and Papers of the Presidents*.

Some of the bitterest criticism of the Republicans and their war came from Federalist Boston. In "A Place in Time: Bulfinch's Boston," we see a close-up picture of that city's political and social-class structure. How does this urban portrait help explain why the Federalist party survived in Boston longer than elsewhere in the United States?

MULTIPLE-CHOICE QUESTIONS

Circle the letter of the item that best completes each statement or answers the question.

1. Between 1800 and 1823, the United States did all the following *except*
   a. fight a war it almost lost.
   b. extend the right to vote to women and blacks.
   c. double in territorial size.
   d. warn European powers not to claim new colonies in the Americas.

2. Thomas Jefferson believed that
   a. educated farmers were the most virtuous citizens and best upholders of republican liberty.
   b. state governments had too much power, and the federal government had not enough.
   c. the United States should develop prosperous cities, filled with new industries.
   d. the rich should pay heavier taxes so that government could provide more social services for the poor.

3. Chief Justice John Marshall's opinions backed
   a. a broad definition of treason that made it easier to convict the accused.
   b. a narrow interpretation of the Constitution, denying that the federal government had any powers beyond those enumerated in the document.
   c. the right of federal courts to declare acts of Congress unconstitutional.
   d. the doctrine that states could nullify illegal actions of the federal government.

4. The Embargo Act
   a. badly damaged the British economy.
   b. stimulated the growth of manufacturing in the United States.
   c. convinced the French to drop their trade restrictions against the United States.
   d. was favored by New England but resisted in the South.

5. By the terms of the Treaty of Ghent, ending the War of 1812,
   a. the United States gained Florida and some territory from Canada.
   b. the British agreed to stop impressment and other violations of U.S. neutral rights.
   c. neither the United States nor Britain gained territory or made concessions.
   d. the British agreed to evacuate New Orleans and compensate the United States for burning Washington.

6. The war hawks were
   a. mostly from New England.
   b. eager for war against Napoleon to gain the Louisiana Territory.
   c. supporters of Jefferson's and Madison's policy of economic coercion.
   d. Republicans from the West and South who wanted to take Canada from Britain and Florida from Spain.

7. Which of the following occurred during Madison's presidency?
   a. The United States sent a naval squadron against the Barbary pirates of North Africa.
   b. Congress chartered a second national bank.
   c. The United States bought Florida from Spain.
   d. Congress passed the embargo.

8. Secretary of State John Quincy Adams is associated with which of the following foreign-policy initiatives?
   a. purchasing Texas from Mexico
   b. purchasing Louisiana
   c. formulating the Monroe Doctrine and purchasing Florida
   d. British sale of the Oregon Territory to the United States for $15 million.

9. During the Era of Good Feelings
   a. the Federalist party disappeared but the Republican party adopted some of its policies.
   b. the United States won a war against England.
   c. sectional and partisan conflicts became more acute.
   d. President Monroe signed new treaties of alliance and friendship with Britain and France.

10. During the War of 1812
   a. the United States successfully occupied Canada.
   b. the British captured Baltimore, Maryland.
   c. Tecumseh, the Prophet, and their Indian followers proved valuable allies to the Americans against the British.
   d. the northeastern states became increasingly unhappy about the war.

SHORT-ANSWER QUESTIONS

1. Explain what the Federalists were trying to accomplish with passage of the Judiciary Act of 1801 and appointment of the midnight judges.

2. Explain why Napoleon first forced Spain to cede Louisiana to France, and then turned around and offered to sell the territory to the United States.

3. Why did President Jefferson want to buy Louisiana from France? Why did the purchase pose a dilemma for him? How did he justify the purchase?

4. What happened at the Hartford Convention in 1814? What impact did it have on the Federalist party? Why?

5. Why did Missouri's request for statehood touch off a sectional crisis? How was the crisis resolved, at least, in the short run?

ESSAY QUESTIONS

1. Compare and contrast the political and economic views of the Hamiltonian Federalists and the Jeffersonian Republicans. When, why, and how did the differences between the two parties blur?

2. Thomas Jefferson's first term as president was so successful that he overwhelmingly won reelection in 1804. His second term, in contrast, was marked by frustration and failure. Discuss the achievements of Jefferson's first term and the problems that beset his second.

3. Discuss the foreign-policy achievements of President James Monroe and his secretary of state, John Quincy Adams. How do those achievements still affect the United States and its foreign policy today?

4. Why did the United States engage in a nearly disastrous war against the British from 1812 to 1814? What, if anything, did the United States gain from that war?

5. "[T]he greatest accomplishment of the political leaders of the early Republic was to fashion a workable body of political institutions and customs to govern the young nation." Discuss the ways in which political leaders such as Thomas Jefferson, John Marshall, and James Madison fashioned political institutions and customs. Use as many specific examples as possible to illustrate your points.

9

The Transformation of American Society, 1815–1840

OUTLINE AND SUMMARY

I. Westward Expansion and the Growth of the Market Economy

A. *The Sweep West*

The sweep of population westward had by 1821 added the states of Vermont, Kentucky, Tennessee, Ohio, Louisiana, Indiana, Mississippi, Illinois, Alabama, Maine, and Missouri to the Union. Although New York merchant John Jacob Astor established a fur-trading post in the Oregon territory and hardy "mountain men" like Jedidiah Smith roamed and trapped on the Great Plains and beyond, most westerners prior to 1840 settled in the region between the Appalachians and the Mississippi River.

B. *Western Society and Customs*

Pioneers usually migrated west with families rather than alone. Between 1790 and 1820, they clustered near the navigable rivers; only after the coming of canals and railroads in the 1820s and 1830s could they afford to fan out a bit. Westerners also tended to settle near others who had come from the same region back east. Before 1830 life in the West was crude and difficult. Easterners often looked down on westerners' lack of refinement, and westerners in turn resented eastern pretentions to gentility.

C. *The Federal Government and the West*

Midwestern settlement was encouraged by the Ordinance of 1785; the Northwest Ordinance; the Louisiana Purchase; the Transcontinental Treaty of 1819; the land warrants given to War of 1812 veterans; the extension of the National Road into Illinois by 1838; and the declining strength of the Indians, who by 1820 no longer received Spanish and British aid.

D. *The Removal of the Indians*

By the 1820s the Cherokees, Creeks, Choctaws, Chickasaws, and Seminoles of the South were under heavy pressure to cede their lands to whites. In 1830 Andrew Jackson pushed through Congress the Indian Removal Act, which granted the president the power to move all Native Americans, by force if necessary, west of the Mississippi River. The Creeks in Georgia and Alabama had already started to migrate by that point, and in 1836 the remainder were forced out. The Choctaws and Chickasaws suffered a similar fate. The Cherokees, the most assimilated of the Indians, appealed to the U.S. Supreme Court for protection. Although Chief Justice John Marshall ruled in their favor, President Jackson ignored the court and compelled the tribe to cede its land and travel the "Trail of Tears" westward, a trip on which between two thousand and four thousand of the sixteen thousand migrating Cherokees died. After putting up some futile resistance in the Black Hawk War, the Sac, Fox, and other Northwest Indians also had to move west of the Mississippi.

E. The Agricultural Boom

The removal of the Indians and the high prices and escalating demand for wheat and corn drew more whites than ever into the old Northwest. Eli Whitney's invention of the cotton gin in 1793 and the boundless need of the British textile industry for raw cotton had similar results in the old Southwest. After the War of 1812, southeasterners poured into Alabama and Mississippi, driving land prices skyward and tripling the nation's cotton production. By 1836 cotton accounted for two-thirds of America's foreign exports.

F. The Rise of the Market Economy

High crop prices after the War of 1812 tempted many western farmers to switch from subsistence to commercial agriculture and to borrow money to buy additional land and tools. This left them vulnerable, however, to the fluctuations of distant markets over which they had no control.

G. Federal Land Policy

Jeffersonian Republicans introduced land policies aimed at a speedy transfer of the public domain to small farmers. Between 1800 and 1820, the government cut the minimum price per acre and the minimum number of acres that could be purchased. However, most government land was sold at auction, and speculators, believing it would soon shoot up in value, often bid the price up far above the minimum. The easy availability of credit encouraged this speculation.

H. The Speculator and the Squatter

Many poor settlers who did not have the money to buy at auction simply squatted on government land. They exerted mounting pressure on Congress to grant them preemption rights over speculators and finally won their demand in 1841. Squatters, wanting to accumulate the cash to buy their farms, quickly turned to commercial agriculture. Many western farmers, after exhausting the soil's fertility growing cash crops, simply moved on to new land.

I. The Panic of 1819

Crop and western land prices plummeted and many speculators were ruined in the panic and depression of 1819. The National Bank tightened credit and called in the notes of the overextended western banks, many of which failed. The hard times experienced by agriculture and industry had long-term political effects. Many westerners hated the National Bank, blaming it for the crisis. Manufacturers redoubled their cries for high protective tariffs, and western farmers intensified their search for internal improvements that would cut transportation expenses for shipping their produce to market.

J. The Transportation Revolution: Steamboats, Canals, and Railroads

Before 1820 available transportation facilities were unsatisfactory. The National Road and privately constructed turnpikes were adequate for transporting people, but moving bulky loads over them by horse-drawn wagons was slow and costly. Midwestern farmers who floated their produce downriver on flatboats to New Orleans had to travel home by foot or horseback, which took months. Robert Fulton's invention of the steamboat and the institution of regular ferry service on all of the major rivers greatly improved the transportation picture. However, rivers did not always exist where they were most needed for trade. Therefore, Americans in the 1820s began to build canals. Between 1817 and 1825, the State of New York constructed the 363-mile Erie Canal connecting Albany on the Hudson River with Buffalo on Lake Erie. The canal lowered freight rates to a fraction of what they had been and made New York City a leading outlet for midwestern produce. The Erie Canal's success encouraged dozens of other projects, including the Blackstone, the Main Line, and the Ohio canals. The canal-building boom deflated with the depression of the late 1830s, but by 1840 some three thousand miles of railroad track had been laid and trains were beginning to supplement and compete with canal shipping.

K. The Growth of the Cities

This transportation revolution stimulated the rapid development of towns and cities. First the coming of the steamboat to western waterways caused the growth of such river port cities as Pittsburgh, Cincinnati, Louisville, St. Louis, and New Orleans. Then the Erie Canal made the fortunes of lake port cities like Buffalo, Cleveland, Detroit, Chicago, and Milwaukee.

II. The Rise of Manufacturing

A. Causes of Industrialization

Industrialization was brought about by the Embargo Act of 1807, which induced merchants barred from foreign trade to divert their capital to founding factories. After the War of 1812 fledgling industries received protection from high tariffs, especially in the 1820s. Transportation improvements opened to manufacturers distant markets where customers quickly showed their preference for factory over homemade items. The 5 million immigrants arriving between 1790 and 1860 also stimulated industrialization by bringing technological know-how with them, such as Samuel Slater, and by providing factories with labor and customers. Relatively high wages paid to American workers also made employers eager to adopt labor-saving techniques like Eli Whitney's interchangeable parts.

B. New England Industrializes

New England was the first region to industrialize because its merchants were particularly hard hit by foreign trade disruptions and it had swift-flowing rivers for waterpower and excess female farm population for labor. Textile manufacturing became its leading industry. In 1790 Samuel Slater opened the first American cotton spinning mill in Rhode Island, but the weaving was still given to women working in their homes. The Waltham and Lowell, Massachusetts mills, started by the Boston Associates, were the first to concentrate total cloth production within the factory. Originally 80 percent of the mill operatives were unmarried young women, who lived in company housing under the strict supervision of management. During the 1830s these Lowell women staged two of the largest strikes in American history to that date.

C. Manufacturing in New York City and Philadelphia

In New York City and Philadelphia manufacturing of products such as shoes, saddles, tools, rope, hats, and ready-made clothing was done in small shops as well as factories. Much of the work was still done by hand rather than machine, but increasingly production was subdivided into small, specialized tasks performed by low-paid, semiskilled or unskilled laborers, including widows and immigrants. This resulted in a declining importance for skilled artisans, who, in protest in the late 1820s, formed trade unions and "workingmen's" political parties.

III. Equality and Inequality

A. Growing Inequality: The Rich and the Poor

The gap between the rich and the poor grew during the first half of the nineteenth century. The extremes were especially obvious in the cities, where the mansions of the wealthy lined the fashionable avenues while the poor crowded into noxious slums like New York's Five Points district. Contrary to the self-made man, rags-to-riches myth, 90 percent of the very wealthy had started out with considerable means. At the other end of the scale, cities were developing a pauperized class consisting of the aged and infirm; widows; and, in the 1840s and 1850s, destitute Irish immigrants fleeing starvation in their homeland.

B. Free Blacks in the North

Overwhelming discrimination kept most free blacks in poverty. They were generally denied the vote; educated in inferior segregated schools, if at all; forced to use separate and unequal facilities; and kept out of all but the lowest paying, least skilled occupations.

C. The "Middling Classes"

The majority of white Americans were neither rich nor poor but belonged to what was then called the middling classes. For most people in that group the standard of living rose between 1800 and 1860, although members of the middle class experienced a lot of insecurity. And like other Americans, they also exhibited a high degree of transiency, moving from neighborhood to neighborhood, city to city, and region to region.

IV. The Revolution in Social Relationships

A. *The Attack on the Professions*

One sign that economic changes were disrupting traditional relationships and forms of authority could be seen in the intense criticism of professionals such as lawyers, doctors, and ministers between 1820 and 1850. The denial that professionals had any special expertise was particularly prevalent on the frontier.

B. *The Challenge to Family Authority*

Children became more inclined to question parental authority. Young men left home at an earlier age and struck out on their own. Young women increasingly made their own choice of whom to marry or even whether to marry.

C. *Wives, Husbands*

Relations between spouses also were evolving. Wives continued to be legally subordinate to their husbands, but under the doctrine of separate spheres, middle-class women were demanding and winning greater voice in those areas where they were deemed to be particularly competent: exerting moral influence on the family and creating within the home a calm refuge from the harsh, competitive world outside. As middle-class women gained more control over the frequency of their pregnancies, the size of white middle-class families declined markedly. However, the birthrate remained high among black and immigrant women.

D. *Horizontal Allegiances and the Rise of Voluntary Associations*

While the authority of fathers, husbands, professionals, and other social "superiors" waned, new relationships among persons in similar positions were forged through the proliferation of voluntary associations. Temperance and moral-reform societies of white middle-class women, union and workingmen's parties, and black fraternal and other clubs encouraged sociability among members and were attempts to enhance their influence on outside groups.

V. Conclusion

The economic transformations of the period 1815–1840 were modest compared to those that would occur later in the nineteenth century. Nevertheless, they were widespread enough to erode traditional family and social relationships and to promote both individualism and horizontal allegiances among like-minded Americans.

VOCABULARY

The following terms are used in Chapter 9. To understand the chapter fully, it is important that you know what each of them means.

mulatto   the offspring of one white and one black parent; a person of mixed black and white ancestry

public domain   the land owned by the government

injunction   a court order to a person or persons to do or not to do a particular thing

annuities   specified payments made at intervals for a period of time, often for life

subsistence agriculture   growing crops to feed and satisfy the needs of the farmer and his family, not cash crops for sale on the market

commercial agriculture   growing crops for sale on the market; farming as a business, big or small

squatter   one who settles on land, especially public or new land, without title or right

preemption   the act or right of purchasing before others or in preference to others

specie   gold, silver, or other coined money (as opposed to paper)

capital   wealth (money) used or capable of being used in the production of more wealth

technology   the industrial arts; technical advances in production methods

antebellum   before the war; pre–Civil War

myth   a collective belief that is built up in response to the wishes of the group rather than having a base in fact

pauperism   the condition of being without means of support and living on public or private charity

transiency   moving frequently from place to place (as opposed to establishing permanent residency over long periods)

IDENTIFICATIONS

After reading Chapter 9, you should be able to identify and explain the historical significance of each of the following:

transportation revolution

John Jacob Astor

"mountain men": Kit Carson, Jedidiah Smith, and Jim Beckwourth

Five Civilized Tribes

Indian Removal Act, 1830

Cherokee Nation v. *Georgia* and *Worchester* v. *Georgia*

Trail of Tears

Black Hawk War

Eli Whitney, the cotton gin, and interchangeable parts

Panic of 1819

Robert Fulton, the *Clermont*, and the Livingston-Fulton monopoly

Gibbons v. *Ogden*

Erie Canal

Samuel Slater

the putting out system and cottage industry

Boston Associates, Waltham and Lowell mills

Alexis de Tocqueville, *Democracy in America*

New York's Five Points district

middling classes

individualism

doctrine of separate spheres

Andrew Jackson Downing

SKILL BUILDING: MAPS

On the map of the United States on the following page:

1. Indicate the states that entered the Union between 1790 and 1821.

2. Indicate the main area of western settlement between 1815 and 1840.

3. Locate each of the following rivers or lakes and explain its economic importance to white Americans between 1815 and 1840:

   Columbia

   Missouri

   Mississippi

   Hudson

   Ohio

   Great Lakes

4. Locate each of the following internal improvements and explain its economic and political impact on American life between 1815 and 1840:

   National Road

   Erie Canal

   Blackstone Canal

   Main Line (or Pennsylvania) Canal

   Ohio Canal

   Baltimore and Ohio Railroad

   Boston and Worcester Railroad

   Massachusetts Western Railroad

5. Indicate the areas from which the Five Civilized Tribes were removed and the areas in which they were resettled between 1820 and 1840.

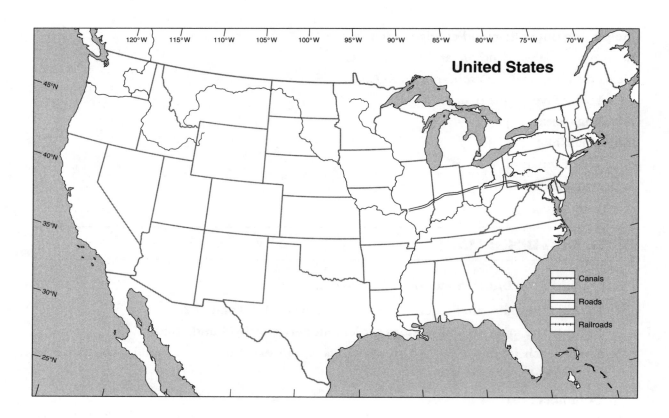

HISTORICAL SOURCES

The workers and working conditions in the Waltham and Lowell textile mills are described on pages 283–285 of Chapter 9. Where did the author find this information? There are numerous historical sources on Lowell and other New England mills, but they do not all paint the same picture. Lowell employees produced their own periodicals: *Operatives' Magazine* (1841–1842), *Lowell Offerings* (1840–1845), and *New England Offerings* (1848–1850). The articles appearing in these publications give quite a favorable view of conditions in Lowell. This makes it difficult to account for the walkout of eight hundred women in 1834 and fifteen hundred in 1836. A group of dissident workers denounced the *Lowell Offerings* as "a mouthpiece of the corporations," which had to approve all items that appeared in it. These unhappy laborers started rival publications, *Factory Tracts* and the *Voice of Industry*, that stressed the oppressiveness of life in the mills. In 1845 a Massachusetts legislative committee held public hearings on labor conditions in the textile mills.

Female workers testified that the overly long workdays and insufficient pay had damaged their health. Management officials, on the other hand, spoke of the contented farm girls who worked a few years in the mills, saved hundreds of dollars from their pay, and then returned home to marry with this nest egg. In addition, European visitors and a Lowell Unitarian minister published accounts of life in the town and mills, which were mostly laudatory. But two thousand textile workers signed petitions sent to the Massachusetts House of Representatives pleading for a ten-hour-day law and other factory reforms. Obviously, such conflicting sources do not make the historian's task easy. In writing about the past, the historian, inevitably influenced by his or her own beliefs and predilections, weighs and evaluates evidence and chooses among available sources.

Just as there are conflicting sources concerning Lowell, Massachusetts, so there are about the conditions of the southeastern tribes after their removal to the Indian Territory. Look at "A Place in Time: Tahlequah, Indian Territory." What impressions does one receive from the report of the white agent? Why have some historians concluded that Native Americans established the best school system west of the Mississippi River? How did the Cherokee chief John Ross see the situation of his people?

MULTIPLE-CHOICE QUESTIONS

Circle the letter of the item that best completes each statement or answers the question.

1. Andrew Jackson's remark, "John Marshall has made his decision; now let him enforce it," refers to the president's intention to
   a. destroy the National Bank despite the Supreme Court ruling upholding its constitutionality.
   b. use force, if necessary, to make South Carolina obey federal laws that it thought unconstitutional.
   c. move the Cherokees west of the Mississippi River, regardless of Supreme Court rulings.
   d. disregard Chief Justice Marshall's ruling in *Gibbons* v. *Ogden*.

2. By 1840 about what portion of Americans lived between the Appalachian Mountains and the Mississippi River?
   a. one-quarter
   b. one-third
   c. one-half
   d. two-thirds

3. Which of the following was most responsible for the spread of cotton growing into the old Southwest?
   a. the discovery of methods for getting sea-island cotton to flourish in the interior uplands
   b. the removal of the Five Civilized Tribes
   c. the adoption of a homestead law making the available land free to qualified settlers
   d. Eli Whitney's invention of the cotton gin

4. Which of the following statements about the Erie Canal is correct?
   a. It linked New York City through inland waterways to Ohio and made the city a major outlet for midwestern produce.
   b. It and the National Road were the only major internal improvements financed by the federal government before the Civil War.
   c. It contributed to the growing importance of Mississippi River cities such as New Orleans.
   d. It had little impact on shipping costs.

5. As a result of the Panic of 1819,
   a. western farmers returned to subsistence farming.
   b. many westerners hated the national bank.
   c. westerners became reluctant to see federal tax monies spent on expensive internal improvements.
   d. industrialists denounced high U.S. tariffs for ruining their sales abroad.

6. In the 1820s and 1830s the majority of the workers in the Lowell and Waltham textile mills were
   a. children from poor immigrant families.
   b. Irish and French-Canadian immigrants.
   c. displaced artisans and skilled workers.
   d. young women from New England farms.

7. Which of the following statements about the professions in the late 1840s is correct?
   a. Lawyers, doctors, and clergymen were highly paid and respected.
   b. Women were entering the professions in significant numbers.
   c. No state required a person to have medical education or a license to be a doctor.
   d. Increasing numbers of doctors, lawyers, and ministers moved to the West because they were most needed and valued there.

8. By the mid-1830s which of the following accounted for two-thirds of America's foreign exports?
   a. wheat and corn
   b. textiles
   c. cotton
   d. farm machinery

9. The transportation revolution in the years after the War of 1812 contributed to the growth of all of the following *except*
   a. industry in the Deep South.
   b. towns and cities in the North and West.
   c. new markets for northeastern manufacturers.
   d. commercial agriculture in the West.

10. The majority of the immigrants who arrived in the United States in the 1840s and 1850s were from
    a. England and Scotland.
    b. Italy and Eastern Europe.
    c. Ireland and Germany.
    d. Asia and Latin America.

SHORT-ANSWER QUESTIONS

1. Explain the developments between 1815 and 1840 that encouraged white settlement in the Midwest.

2. What stimulated northeastern manufacturing in the years after the War of 1812?

3. Explain why New England led the way in industrialization.

4. Compare and contrast manufacturing in New England with that in New York and Philadelphia.

5. In the period 1815–1840, how much truth was there to the rags-to-riches idea?

6. What changes occurred in the economic and social status of artisans and skilled workers in the period 1815–1840?

ESSAY QUESTIONS

1. Discuss the transportation revolution of the period 1815–1840. What changes took place? What was the impact of those changes on the country economically, politically, and socially?

2. Discuss the doctrine of separate spheres for women. What changes, if any, did the doctrine produce in the lives of white middle-class, white working-class, and black and immigrant women?

3. Alexis de Tocqueville in his *Democracy in America* was impressed by the "general equality of condition among the people." Writing about the same period, New York merchant Philip Hone stated "the two extremes of costly luxury in living, expensive establishments, and improvident waste are presented in daily and hourly contrast with squalid misery and hopeless destitution." How do you account for these very different assessments? Which man came closer to the truth? Why?

4. Discuss federal government policy toward Native Americans during the period 1815–1840.

5. Chapter 9 states that "the pre–Civil War period witnessed the widespread substitution of horizontal allegiances for vertical allegiances." What does this mean, and what evidence is offered in the chapter to support the claim?

10

Politics, Religion, and Reform in the Age of Jackson

OUTLINE AND SUMMARY

I. The Transformation of American Politics, 1824–1832

A. Introduction

In 1824 only one political party existed, the Republican, but it was fragmenting because of pressures produced by the industrialization of the Northeast, the spread of cotton growing in the South, and westward expansion. Out of this fragmentation grew two new political parties. On the whole, those who retained Jefferson's distrust of strong federal government and preferred states' rights became Democrats, while those who favored an active federal government that encouraged economic development became Whigs. Both Democratic and Whig politicians had to adapt to the democratic idea of politics as the expression of the will of the common man rather than "an activity that gentlemen conducted for the people."

B. Democratic Ferment

Politics became more democratic as property qualifications for voting were eliminated, written ballots replaced voting aloud, appointive offices became elective, and presidential electors were chosen by the people. This broadening of suffrage was often brought about by competition between Republicans and Federalists in the 1790s and early 1800s. "Wherever one party was in the minority, it sought to increase the number of eligible voters in order to turn itself into the majority party."

C. The Election of 1824

The fragmenting Republican party could not agree on a single nominee for president. Instead, four Republicans ran. Andrew Jackson received the most popular and electoral votes, but not a majority. Therefore, as the Constitution requires, the House of Representatives had to choose among the three top contenders—Jackson, John Quincy Adams, and William Crawford. Henry Clay, who came in fourth, used his considerable influence with Congress to gain the selection of John Quincy Adams. President Adams in turn appointed Clay his secretary of state. Jackson supporters charged that a "corrupt bargain" had been made, and that charge hung like a cloud over the Adams administration.

D. John Quincy Adams as President

President Adams tried to encourage economic growth, but he was a poor politician with little interest in playing the role of party leader in a democratic age.

E. The Rise of Andrew Jackson

Andrew Jackson's victory over the British in the Battle of New Orleans in 1815 had made him a popular hero. The fact that he was a slave owner and advocated removing all Indians from the East endeared him to southerners. Jackson supporters like Martin Van Buren began to build a strong political organization that increasingly called itself the Democratic party. The Democrats in 1828 nominated Jackson for president. Those who remained loyal to Adams called themselves National Republicans and renominated him in 1828.

F. The Election of 1828

Although Jackson was a wealthy planter when he ran for president, the Democrats portrayed him as a man of the people opposing Adams the aristocrat. Jackson won the election with this common-man appeal. His victory also showed a clear sectional split, with the South and Southwest going heavily for Jackson and New England going mostly for Adams.

G. Jackson in Office

Jackson did not initiate the spoils system, but he defended and practiced it on the grounds that frequent rotation in office gave more people a chance to serve and prevented the development of an elite bureaucracy. He also opposed federal support for internal improvements, as demonstrated in his Maysville Road veto. While southerners liked that stand, they resented his lack of action against the 1828 "Tariff of Abominations," which protected northern manufacturers and western farmers from foreign competition but raised the price that southerners had to pay for finished products.

H. Nullification

The tariff issue prepared the way for a break between Jackson and his vice president, John C. Calhoun, who was becoming the chief spokesman for the southern planter class. Calhoun wrote and circulated the *South Carolina Exposition and Protest* in opposition to the Tariff of 1828. In it he argued that protective tariffs were unconstitutional and that states had the right to nullify federal laws that violated the U.S. Constitution.

I. Jackson Versus Calhoun

In November 1832 South Carolina, acting on Calhoun's doctrine, nullified the Tariff of 1828 and the slightly less protectionist Tariff of 1832 and forbade collection of customs duties at its ports. Jackson denounced the state's defiance and threatened to use the army and navy to enforce federal laws. A clash of arms was avoided only by the Compromise of 1833, proposed by Henry Clay. South Carolina rescinded its nullification, and Congress passed a new tariff law that gradually lowered duties over the next nine years.

J. The Bank Veto

Jackson disliked all banks and the issuance of paper money, and he particularly hated the Second Bank of the United States. He regarded it as a privileged monopoly that made the "rich, richer and the potent, more powerful." This national bank, which controlled the nation's credit and was the depository for federal government monies, was run by its private stockholders, "Monied Capitalists," with little control from the federal government. In 1832 Nicholas Biddle, president of the Second Bank, applied for its recharter. The recharter bill passed Congress, but Jackson vetoed it.

K. The Election of 1832

In 1832, for the first time, the candidates were chosen by national party nominating conventions. The Democratic convention named Jackson and Martin Van Buren for president and vice president, respectively, while the National Republicans ran Henry Clay. Clay opposed Jackson's record and advocated instead his American System of protective tariffs, rechartering of the national bank, and federally supported internal improvements. Jackson won easily and was ready to complete his destruction of the Second Bank.

II. The Bank Controversy and the Second Party System

A. The War on the Bank

Jackson quickly tried to bankrupt the Second Bank by removing federal government deposits and distributing them to accounts in state-chartered banks. The "pet banks" that received the deposits, now having no restraint on them from the defunct national bank, extended much more credit and issued many more bank notes (paper money). This loosening of credit touched off a period of headlong economic expansion, reckless speculation, and rapid inflation. These results dismayed Jackson and other Democrats who opposed use of paper money and bank credit.

B. The Rise of Whig Opposition

During Jackson's second term, the National Republicans changed their name to Whigs. They began to attract broader support, including southerners angry over Jackson's denunciation of nullification; temperance and public-school reformers; anti-immigrant and anti-Catholic Protestants; followers of the Anti-Masonry movement; and the commercial community of merchants, manufacturers, and bankers.

C. The Election of 1836

The Democrats ran Martin Van Buren for president in 1836; the Whigs, unable to agree on a single nominee, ran four candidates. They hoped that no man would receive a majority of the electoral votes, putting the choice into the House of Representatives, where one of their nominees might win. Their strategy failed, however, because Van Buren won a clear majority.

D. The Panic of 1837

Just as Van Buren was inaugurated, the country's economy went into a severe depression. Its causes were both international and national. Jackson's bank policies had produced a wave of speculation and inflation that so alarmed him that in July 1836 he issued the Specie Circular, a proclamation that barred the purchase of government-owned land with anything but gold. This move burst the speculative bubble and contributed to the panic and depression that followed.

E. The Search for Solutions

President Van Buren, with little understanding of economics, dealt with the depression by divorcing the federal government from banking. In 1840 he signed the Independent Treasury bill, which provided that federal government money would be kept in its own treasury instead of being deposited in banks.

F. The Election of 1840

The Democrats renominated Van Buren in 1840. The Whigs chose the hero of Tippecanoe, William Henry Harrison, for president and John Tyler of Virginia for vice president. The Whigs adopted the popular appeal-to-the-common-man campaign techniques pioneered by the Democrats in the previous decade. These campaign tactics, along with Van Buren's unpopularity caused by the depression, gave the election to Harrison.

G. The Second Party System Matures

Between 1836 and 1840, the number of people who voted increased by 60 percent. This rapid increase in voter interest was caused by popular campaign techniques, strong contrast and competition between rival parties, and controversial issues like tariffs and banking, all of which characterized the mature second party system.

III. The Rise of Popular Religion

A. Introduction

In the 1820s and 1830s, Americans turned to preachers who rejected the Calvinist belief in predestination. Just as politics was becoming more democratic, so was religious doctrine. The primary message was that any individual could be saved through his or her own efforts and faith. This democratic transformation was produced in part by a series of religious revivals known as the Second Great Awakening.

B. The Second Great Awakening

From New England the Second Great Awakening moved rapidly to frontier areas where thousands gathered at religious camp meetings. These frontier revivals helped to promote law and order and diminish the violence prevalent in new western areas.

C. Eastern Revivals

By the 1820s the center of religious revivals had moved east again and was particularly strong in an area of western New York known as the Burned-Over District. The revivalist leader Charles G. Finney preached that, rather than being naturally depraved, humans were capable of living without sin once they experienced an emotional religious conversion.

D. Critics of Revivals: The Unitarians

In New England the educated and wealthy were often repelled by the emotional excesses of revivalism and turned instead to Unitarianism. This denomination preached that goodness should be cultivated by a gradual process of character building and by emulating the life and teachings of Jesus. Although the Unitarians were critical of the revivalists, both shared the belief that humans could shape their own destiny and improve their behavior.

E. The Rise of Mormonism

Joseph Smith started Mormonism in the 1820s in the Burned-Over District. He and his followers founded a model city at Nauvoo, Illinois, but when they began the practice of polygyny, they were prosecuted by authorities and attacked by a mob that murdered Smith. The Mormons continued to make converts, however, many of whom followed their new leader, Brigham Young, to the Great Salt Lake area of Utah. There they created an independent, cooperative republic, the State of Deseret.

F. The Shakers

Started by Mother Ann Lee, the Shakers also founded cooperative religious communities. The Shakers and Mormons were unusual in that they rejected economic individualism and tried to withdraw from American society. Most of the religious revivalists encouraged their followers to get ahead economically, stay in society, and improve it and themselves. This message inspired many of the reformers of the period.

IV. The Age of Reform

A. Introduction

The reform movements were strongest in New England and in areas of the Midwest settled by New Englanders.

B. The War on Liquor

The temperance movement began by preaching moderation in the use of liquor. With the formation of the American Temperance Society, however, the movement began to demand total abstinence and prohibition laws. Most members of temperance societies were middle class, though in the 1840s the Washington Temperance Societies attracted workers. The movement was successful in cutting per capita consumption of alcohol in half between the 1820s and 1840s.

C. Public-School Reform

Secretary of the Massachusetts Board of Education Horace Mann advocated many educational innovations. These included state tax support of schools, grouping pupils into classes by age and level of competence, longer school terms, use of standardized textbooks, and compulsory attendance laws. Despite opposition from various groups, many northern states adopted these reforms because they were backed by three powerful constituencies: businesses that needed disciplined, literate workers; workingmen's groups that saw education as a road to social mobility; and native-born Americans who viewed public schools as an instrument for assimilating immigrant children.

D. Abolition

Opposition to slavery in the 1820s came mostly from black Americans. Not until 1831, when William Lloyd Garrison started publishing *The Liberator*, was there a militant white abolitionist movement. Most northern whites in the 1830s and 1840s, however, were hostile to the abolitionists. Moreover, the American Anti-Slavery Society, founded in 1833, suffered from internal quarrels between its Garrisonian wing and its New York and western wings. The main points of dispute were whether to support rights for women as well as blacks and whether to take abolitionism into politics. Despite hostility and internal division, the abolitionist movement kept the issue of slavery alive, put the South on the defensive, and gained supporters for the side issue of the constitutional rights of free expression and petition.

E. Women's Rights

Many of the women's rights leaders began their reform careers in the abolitionist movement. When women were denied full participation in that movement, Elizabeth Cady Stanton and Lucretia Mott in 1848 called a women's rights convention in Seneca Falls, New York. The convention adopted a Declaration of Sentiments, which launched the feminist movement. Thereafter, women gained a few rights, but they did not get the vote until 1920.

F. Penitentiaries and Asylums

In the 1820s and 1830s, religious revivalists and reformers came to believe that crime, poverty, and deviancy were caused by defects of character that could be mended by institutions providing the proper discipline and environment. Following that belief, reformers created penitentiaries and workhouses for criminals and the indigent. Dorothea Dix fought for the establishment of insane asylums to treat the mentally ill.

G. Utopian Communities

A few reformers founded "ideal" or "utopian" communities to demonstrate ways of life that they thought were superior to those prevailing in antebellum America. Among these model communities were New Harmony, Hopedale, and Brook Farm. Most of these settlements were short-lived.

V. Conclusion

During the 1820s and 1830s Americans responded to economic and social changes by finding new political leaders, creating the second party system, and launching reform movements. By the 1840s some of the reformers were entering the political arena to try to further their particular aims.

VOCABULARY

The following terms are used in Chapter 10. To understand the chapter fully, it is important that you know what each of them means.

suffrage   the vote; the right to vote

bureaucracy   the body of nonelected government officials

nullify   to render or declare legally void or inoperative

itinerant   one who travels from place to place

utopian   founded upon or involving perfection in law, politics, and human relations

deviancy   behavior differing from the normal, accepted behavior and/or morality of society

indigence   neediness, poverty

IDENTIFICATIONS

After reading Chapter 10, you should be able to identify and explain the historical significance of each of the following:

Henry Clay and the American System

second American party system

spoils system

"Tariff of Abominations," 1828

John C. Calhoun and the *South Carolina Exposition and Protest*

Compromise of 1833

Nicholas Biddle and the Bank of the United States

"pet banks"

Specie Circular

Log Cabin campaign, "Tippecanoe and Tyler too," and the election of 1840

Second Great Awakening

Burned-Over District

Charles G. Finney and "perfectionism"

William Ellery Channing and Unitarianism

Joseph Smith, Brigham Young, and Mormonism

Lyman Beecher and the American Temperance Society

Horace Mann

William Lloyd Garrison, *The Liberator*, and the American Anti-Slavery Society

Frederick Douglass

Sojourner Truth

James G. Birney and the Liberty party

Angelina and Sarah Grimké

John Quincy Adams and the "gag rule"

Elizabeth Cady Stanton, Lucretia Mott, the Seneca Falls convention, and the Declaration of
    Sentiments

penitentiaries and the "Auburn and Pennsylvania systems"

Dorothea Dix

Robert Owen and New Harmony

Transcendentalists, Brook Farm, and *The Dial*

John Humphrey Noyes and Oneida

SKILL BUILDING: MAPS

On the map of New York and New England, on the following page, locate each of the places
listed below. How is each connected with the religious and reform movements of the Age of
Jackson?

Burned-Over District

Albany

Buffalo

Erie Canal

Hudson River

Lake Erie

Seneca Falls

Oneida

Boston

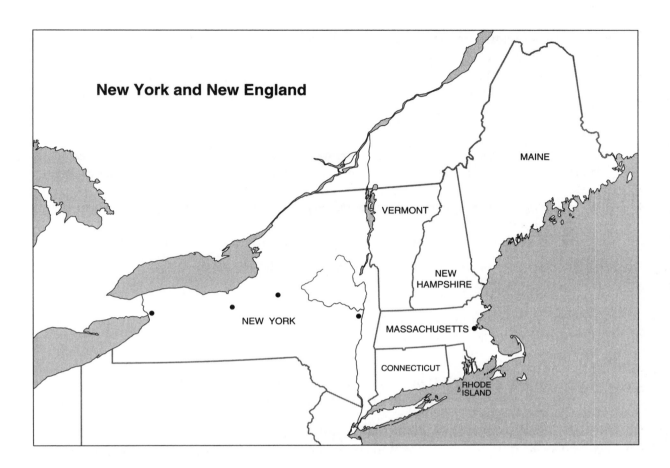

New York and New England

MAINE

VERMONT

NEW HAMPSHIRE

NEW YORK

MASSACHUSETTS

CONNECTICUT

RHODE ISLAND

MULTIPLE-CHOICE QUESTIONS

Circle the letter of the item that best completes each statement or answers the question.

1. The immediate result of Jackson's distribution of federal funds to state banks was to
    a. bring about rapid economic expansion, speculation, and inflation.
    b. increase the power of the Second Bank of the United States.
    c. make the purchase of land more difficult.
    d. increase the effectiveness of the Specie Circular.

2. The *South Carolina Exposition and Protest* was drawn up in opposition to the
    a. Missouri Compromise.
    b. spoils system.
    c. "Tariff of Abominations."
    d. Compromise of 1833.

3. All of the following were founded as utopian communities *except*
   a. New Harmony, Indiana.
   b. Oneida, New York.
   c. Brook Farm, Massachusetts.
   d. Rochester, New York.

4. Which of the following statements about William Lloyd Garrison is *incorrect*?
   a. He favored removal of freed blacks from the United States to colonies in Africa.
   b. He opposed abolitionists who wanted to start a political party and run candidates for office.
   c. He favored giving women equal positions and influence with men in the anti-slavery movement.
   d. He insisted that slavery was sinful and its continued existence unacceptable.

5. The "gag rule" was repealed in 1845 largely due to the efforts of
   a. Theodore Weld.
   b. Horace Mann.
   c. John Quincy Adams.
   d. Andrew Jackson.

6. Martin Van Buren did *not*
   a. create one of the first Democratic state party machines, the Albany Regency.
   b. sign the Independent Treasury Bill, which provided for deposit of federal funds in government vaults.
   c. serve as president during a severe economic depression.
   d. defect to the newly formed Whig party in protest over Andrew Jackson's handling of the nullification crisis.

7. Reformers of the antebellum period
   a. were usually Democrats rather than Whigs.
   b. were often inspired by the writings of Karl Marx.
   c. received their best response in New England and areas to which New Englanders had migrated.
   d. rarely advocated legal coercion to force people to live morally.

8. Revivalists and Unitarians were similar in
   a. the social classes that they appealed to.
   b. their emotionalism.
   c. their belief that human behavior could be changed for the better.
   d. the cities and towns where most of their followers lived.

9. Which of the following quotations is *not* correctly paired with its source?
   a. "Our Union: It must be preserved." John C. Calhoun's *South Carolina Exposition and Protest*
   b. It makes "the rich richer and the potent more powerful." Andrew Jackson's veto message of the recharter of the Bank of the United States
   c. "I will not equivocate—I will not excuse—I will not retreat a single inch—AND I WILL BE HEARD." William Lloyd Garrison's *The Liberator*
   d. "All men and women are created equal." The Declaration of Sentiments of the Seneca Falls convention

10. The Seneca Falls Declaration of Sentiments called for
    a. state tax support for public schools.
    b. equal rights for women.
    c. immediate abolition of slavery.
    d. humane treatment of the mentally ill and establishment of insane asylums for their care.

SHORT-ANSWER QUESTIONS

1. Explain the ways in which politics became more democratic in the 1820s and 1830s. What were the effects of greater popular participation in politics on parties and politicians?

2. Why were John Quincy Adams and Henry Clay accused of entering into a "corrupt bargain" in the election of 1824? How did that charge affect Adams's presidency?

3. Explain why the South disliked high tariffs and what John C. Calhoun proposed to do about such protective import duties.

4. Discuss the role Henry Clay played in the Compromise of 1833. Did the compromise settle the nullification question?

5. Why did Andrew Jackson hate the Second Bank of the United States? What actions did he take to destroy it?

ESSAY QUESTIONS

1. Andrew Jackson deserves to be ranked among America's greatest presidents. Accept or refute this statement and back up your position with a discussion of Jackson's policies and actions as president.

2. Discuss the origins and development of the second party system. Which parties were involved? Who supported each of them? What, if anything, did they stand for? What impact did their actions have on voter interest and participation in politics?

3. Discuss the reform movements of the antebellum period. Who participated? What inspired the reformers? What assumptions did they make? What were their aims and accomplishments?

4. Discuss the rise of "popular religion" in antebellum America. In what ways did religious doctrine become democratized? What assumptions did the new theologies make? How did these assumptions affect religious, social, and political life?

5. Compare and contrast the positions of Jacksonian Democrats and Whig supporters of Henry Clay's American System on the issues of the proper role of the federal government, protective tariffs, internal improvements, and banking. How do you account for their similarities and differences?

11

Life, Leisure, and Culture,
1840 – 1860

OUTLINE AND SUMMARY

I. Introduction

Americans in the 1840s and 1850s believed in progress, which they defined largely in terms of material betterment. The period was filled with material advances. New agricultural machinery, for example, produced a surplus of food despite a rapidly growing population. Railroad building, use of steam power, and adoption of the principle of interchangeable parts in manufacturing helped to make more products available at lower prices and thus contributed to a rise in real income. Also, the 1840s and 1850s were so rich in literary and artistic achievements that historians speak of the decades as an American Renaissance. These advances, however, did not prevent a severe economic depression or much improve the life of the poor. In fact, some of the writers and thinkers of the time were led to question the widely held belief that material progress automatically meant a better life for everyone in all respects.

II. Technology and Economic Growth

A. Agricultural Advancement

Between 1830 and 1860 settlers moved onto the grasslands of Indiana, Michigan, and Illinois, where John Deere's steel-tipped plow, developed in 1837, aided them in breaking the tough prairie sod. When Cyrus McCormick started to mass-produce mechanical reapers in 1847, farmers could harvest grain seven times faster than before, with half the labor. This made wheat the dominant crop of the Midwest. Although Americans quickly adopted these laborsaving inventions, they generally farmed wastefully, rapidly depleting soil and then moving to virgin land. Only in the East did some farmers introduce fertilizers to increase their yields to the point where they could compete with those of the new western fields.

B. Technology and Industrial Progress

Americans of the antebellum period readily invested in new technology. A most important advance was Eli Whitney's principle of using interchangeable parts. Manufacturing such parts was greatly facilitated by improved machine tools. Readiness to invest in innovations, interchangeable parts, and better machine tools resulted in rapid acceptance, mass production, and use of new inventions such as Samuel Colt's revolving pistol, Elias Howe's sewing machine, and Samuel F. B. Morse's telegraph.

C. The Railroad Boom

The desire to conquer time and space with technology encouraged Americans to invest heavily in railroad development. By 1860 the United States had thirty thousand miles of track, more than the rest of the world combined. Most of the new rail lines linked the East and Midwest. As a result, much of the produce of the Midwest, which had formerly been shipped downriver and out of the port of New Orleans, was now shipped via railroads radiating from Chicago eastward. These railroads stimulated settlement of the Midwest; growth of wheat farming there; and the development of cities, towns, and industry. As America's first big business, the railroads pioneered new forms of financing in the 1850s, particularly the sale of stock and other securities. Many of the transactions were handled through Wall Street, making New York the nation's leading capital market.

D. Rising Prosperity

Technological improvements reduced the price of commodities to consumers, which in turn contributed to an average 25 percent rise in the real income of American workers between 1840 and 1860. The increased annual income of working families also was attributable to the use of steam power, which allowed factories to operate in all seasons and therefore offer more work to laborers. Furthermore, the growth of towns and cities that accompanied industrialization opened new employment opportunities for women and children, who often had to work to supplement the inadequate wages of the husband and father. These economic opportunities, plus the comforts and conveniences of urban life, attracted a steady stream of Americans to cities.

III. The Quality of Life

A. Introduction

Technological advances improved the quality of life for those in the middle class. They now enjoyed luxuries formerly reserved to the rich, but these changes were slower to reach the poor. Medical knowledge lagged behind the strides made in industry and agriculture, leaving Americans to look to popular health fads for the prevention and cure of illness.

B. Housing

In the cities the typical dwellings of the period were row houses. The row houses that the middle class lived in became increasingly elaborate, while the poor were forced into crowded row houses that were further subdivided by several families and boarders. The worst of these were called tenements. On the frontier, one-room log cabins were common. These were replaced by the much more comfortable balloon-frame houses as the community matured and prospered.

C. Home Furniture

The upper and middle classes, between 1840 and 1860, favored ornate home furnishings in the rococo style. The wealthy imported such furniture from Europe, but the middle class bought mass-produced imitations from new furniture manufacturing centers like Cincinnati and Grand Rapids. The poor, on the other hand, made do with simple, functional furniture.

D. Heating, Cooking, and Diet

Industrialization and improved transportation affected home heating, cooking, and diet. By the 1840s coal-burning stoves were replacing fireplaces for heating and cooking. Although these stoves were more convenient and made it possible to cook several dishes simultaneously, coal burning contributed to fouling the urban environment. Railroads brought fresh produce, meat, and fish to city dwellers, but only the rich could afford fruits and vegetables out of season. Because home iceboxes were rare before 1860, most Americans still ate meat preserved by salting rather than fresh meat.

E. Water and Sanitation

In rural areas people obtained their water from wells, springs, and cisterns. By the 1840s and 1850s, cities such as New York, Philadelphia, Cleveland, and Detroit began to construct aqueducts, reservoirs, and water works. These brought pure water to street hydrants, but the majority of houses were not yet hooked up to the water mains. Even those homes with indoor faucets rarely had hot water. As a result, Americans of the period bathed infrequently. Because few cities had sanitation departments and most people used outdoor privies, American cities often stank.

F. Disease and Health

American cities also were racked by recurring epidemics of cholera, yellow fever, and other diseases. By the 1850s most big cities had established municipal boards of health to try to prevent these outbreaks, but the boards had almost no power. Furthermore, the medical profession, which was divided and uncertain about the causes and cures of epidemic diseases, was held in low esteem. In the 1840s the development of anesthetics by Crawford Long and William T. G. Morton advanced the field of surgery, but the achievements of surgeons were still blighted by their failure to recognize the importance of disinfection.

G. Popular Health Movements

Since neither public-health boards nor doctors seemed able to prevent disease, many Americans put their faith in various popular therapies, such as hydropathy and the Grahamite regimen.

H. Phrenology

Phrenology was the most popular of the scientific fads of the antebellum period. Its claim that a skilled phrenologist could make an accurate analysis of an individual's character by examining the contours of his skull appealed to Americans for the same reason that they turned to popular cures. All promised to teach the principles of life and give the individual control over his or her own fate.

IV. Democratic Pastimes

A. *Introduction*

New technology transformed leisure as well as work in the years 1830–1860. Imaginative entrepreneurs used new inventions and advances in manufacturing to sell the kinds of entertainment they believed the public wanted.

B. *Newspapers*

James Gordon Bennett, publisher of the *New York Herald,* was one of the first journalists to take advantage of new techniques in paper making and printing and the invention of the telegraph. He realized that a newspaper could make money by building mass circulation. He and other publishers slashed the price of their papers to a penny and used newspaper boys to sell hundreds of thousands of copies daily. The penny papers filled their columns with human-interest stories of crime and sex. Bennett's *New York Herald* and Horace Greeley's *New York Tribune* also pioneered in modern financial and political reporting.

C. *The Popular Novel*

Printing and transportation improvements made it possible to sell paperback books for as little as seven cents, which contributed to the popularity of the sentimental novel. Most of its authors and readers were women. Although neither the writers nor most of the readers were active feminists, many of the novels did illustrate the moral that "women could overcome trials and make the world a better place."

D. *The Theater*

Antebellum theaters were filled with large, rowdy audiences from all social classes. People liked best melodramas with plots similar to those of the sentimental novels, although William Shakespeare's plays were performed more often than those of any other single dramatist.

E. *Minstrel Shows*

Starting in the 1840s, minstrel shows—performances of songs, dances, and skits by white men in blackface—became popular with white working-class audiences. These shows catered to and reinforced the prejudices of whites by depicting blacks as stupid, comical, musical, and irresponsible.

F. *P. T. Barnum*

P. T. Barnum, with his display of curiosities, flair for publicity, and development of the American Museum in New York, was the ultimate "entrepreneur of popular entertainment" in the antebellum period.

V. The Quest for Nationality in Literature and Art

A. Introduction

Whereas entrepreneurs promoted popular culture, intellectuals like Ralph Waldo Emerson called on American writers and artists to develop creative, original, indigenous literature and art. Emerson and other intellectuals of the 1830s to 1860s were influenced by the international literary and artistic movement known as romanticism, which preached that people had to discover their own unique character as a nation. Moreover, a nation's literature and art should explore this national character as well as the deep emotions of the writer or artist. Emerson and his admirers developed an American form of romanticism called transcendentalism.

B. Literary Geography

Emerson's call for a new American creativity coincided with a "flowering of distinctively American literature and art, often called the American Renaissance." In producing new writers of merit, New England led the way with figures such as Emerson, Nathaniel Hawthorne, Henry David Thoreau, John Greenleaf Whittier, and Henry Wadsworth Longfellow. New York was not far behind as the home of Washington Irving, James Fenimore Cooper, Walt Whitman, and Herman Melville. All regions, however, participated in the literary renaissance.

C. James Fenimore Cooper and the Stirrings of Literary Independence

The success of Cooper's novels—*The Last of the Mohicans, The Pathfinder,* and others— "marked the first step in a process that saw Americans develop an imaginative literature of their own." Cooper's innovations included the creation of the American frontiersman character and the American theme of the conflict between the wilderness and the advance of civilization.

D. Emerson, Thoreau, and Whitman

All three tried to write prose or poetry that was a spontaneous and vivid expression of their emotions. Emerson, in his essays and lectures, used striking language to call for independence of thought. He also encouraged younger writers like Thoreau and Whitman. Emerson and Thoreau were often critical of the materialism and aggressiveness of Americans, whereas Whitman celebrated everything in his country but slavery. Thoreau excelled in his descriptions of nature and in arguing the lessons to be learned from contemplating it. Whitman, in *Leaves of Grass,* abandoned the poetic conventions of his time to write free verse that was "lusty" and "blunt."

E. Hawthorne, Melville, and Poe

These three authors did not answer Emerson's call to write about the American scene or distinctly American characters. Rather, they were more interested in analyzing moral dilemmas and probing psychological states. Unlike Emerson and Whitman, who were essentially optimistic, Hawthorne, Melville, and Poe shared an "underlying pessimism about the human condition."

F. American Landscape Painting

American artists between 1820 and 1860 sought to depict their native land, especially in its primitive grandeur before pioneers deforested and plowed it. George Catlin, for example, in hundreds of pictures portrayed Indians as "noble savages" doomed by the "march of progress." Others, like Thomas Cole, painted allegorical scenes on themes of importance to a young republic.

Many of the artists belonged to the Hudson River school, which included Thomas Cole, Asher Durand, and Frederic Church. Their works, which subordinated realism to emotional effect, reflected the romanticism of the period. The designers of New York's Central Park, Frederick Law Olmsted and Calvert Vaux, also shared a romantic view of nature. In their plan they aimed to refresh the souls of harried urbanites by creating for them an idealized pastoral landscape in the midst of the city.

G. The "Diffusion" of Knowledge

Many intellectuals believed that in a democratic society the educated had a duty to diffuse knowledge and culture to the masses. They attempted to enlighten the common people not only through the public schools but also through lyceums—local organizations that sponsored public lectures. Lyceums spread from New England to other sections of the country; by 1840, thirty-five hundred towns had lyceums. These efforts to popularize high culture "bridged the . . . gap between classes but never closed it." In trying to have wide popular appeal, creative artists, writers, and lecturers had to simplify their ideas.

VI. Conclusion

New technology changed the lives of millions of Americans between 1840 and 1860. Advances in transportation and manufacturing improved the American diet, made a greater variety of necessities and luxuries available at lower prices, transformed leisure pursuits, and encouraged efforts to diffuse and popularize culture. "The bright possibilities rather than the dark potential of technology impressed most antebellum Americans." But all these advances did not significantly reduce inequality between the poor and the affluent, or wipe out ethnic and sectional differences and tensions.

VOCABULARY

The following terms are used in Chapter 11. To understand the chapter fully, it is important that you know what each of them means.

despoliation   stripping of riches or resources; ruining

machine tools   machines that shape metal products

real income (real wages)   how much one's income or wages will purchase, given the prices at the time

tenements   subdivided houses or apartments in the poorer, crowded parts of large cities

celerity   speed

rococo   a style of architecture and decoration, originating in France about 1720, that was distinguished by abundant and elegant ornamentation

precepts   rules of action or conduct

stereotype   characteristics, usually negative, attributed to all members of a group

poll tax   a tax that must be paid to exercise the right to vote

allegory   a figurative or symbolic treatment of an abstract idea or spiritual concept

IDENTIFICATIONS

After reading Chapter 11, you should be able to identify and explain the historical significance of each of the following:

James Fenimore Cooper

Edgar Allan Poe

American Renaissance

Henry David Thoreau

John Deere's steel-tipped plow and Cyrus McCormick's mechanical reaper

American system of manufacturing, or interchangeable parts

Samuel F. B. Morse

Catharine Beecher, *A Treatise on Domestic Economy*

contagion theory versus miasm theory

Crawford Long and William T. G. Morton

hydropathy

Sylvester Graham

phrenology

James Gordon Bennett, the *New York Herald,* and the penny press

P. T. Barnum and the American Museum

Horace Greeley and the *New York Tribune*

Astor Place riot

minstrel shows

Ralph Waldo Emerson and "The American Scholar"

transcendentalism

Nathaniel Hawthorne

Bronson Alcott and Fruitlands

Walt Whitman

Herman Melville

Thomas Cole, Asher Durand, Frederic Church, and the Hudson River school

lyceums

Frederick Law Olmsted and Calvert Vaux

SKILL BUILDING: MAPS

1. Locate on the map on the following page each of the important railroad hubs and/or terminal cities listed below:

   Chattanooga, Tennessee

   Atlanta, Georgia

   Chicago, Illinois

   Buffalo, New York

   Pittsburgh, Pennsylvania

   Baltimore, Maryland

   Wheeling, Virginia (later West Virginia)

2. Trace on the map the routes of each of these main antebellum railroad lines:

   New York Central

   Erie

   Pennsylvania

   Baltimore and Ohio

   Illinois Central

3. What economic, social, and political effects did the building of these railroads have on the United States?

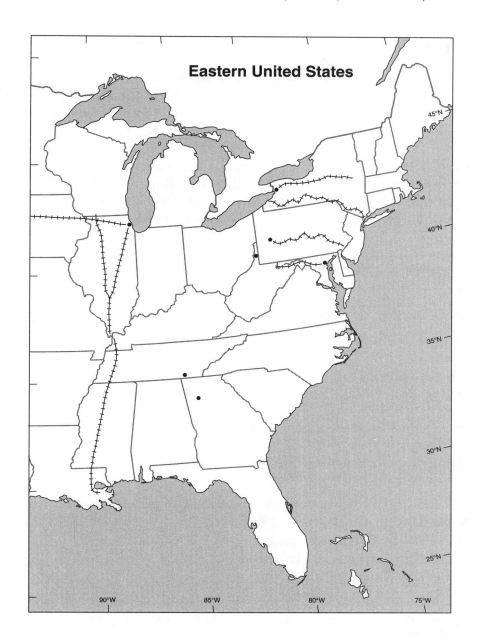

Eastern United States

HISTORICAL SOURCES

Pages 344–345 in Chapter 11 describe the deplorable sanitation and periodic epidemics that plagued America's antebellum cities. How do historians know about these conditions? Our most valuable sources on this are the investigative reports made to early municipal health boards by city inspectors. One of the most thorough of these, *The Sanitary Conditions of the Laboring Classes* (1845), was written by New York's crusading city inspector Dr. John H. Griscom.

Historians also try to learn about the attitudes, values, and interests of people in the past by reading what they read. Although many Americans today still read the works of Whitman, Hawthorne, Melville, and Poe, few but historians wade through the popular novels of the antebellum period, like Susan Warner's *The Wide, Wide World* and E. D. E. N. Southworth's *The Hidden Hand*. What did the author of Chapter 11 learn about American life and values from these and other popular novels, as well as the penny press and advertisements of that time?

Now look at "A Place in Time: Frances Trollope Invents Popular Culture in Cincinnati." What does the historian's description of the exhibits Trollope helped plan for the Western Museum (or for that matter the exhibits in Barnum's American Museum) indicate about antebellum American values, interests, and levels of sophistication?

MULTIPLE-CHOICE QUESTIONS

Circle the letter of the item that best completes each statement or answers the question.

1. The 1840s and 1850s in the United States were characterized by all of the following *except*
   a. heightened literary and artistic output and inventiveness.
   b. advances in medical knowledge that lessened the danger and frequency of epidemics.
   c. improvements in transportation and increases in productivity that raised the standard of living for the middle class.
   d. building of municipal water works in many of the big cities to supply the needs of urban dwellers.

2. All of the following were inventions of the antebellum period that were mass-produced and/or widely used in the 1840s and 1850s *except*
   a. Alexander Graham Bell's telephone.
   b. Cyrus McCormick's mechanical reaper.
   c. Samuel F. B. Morse's telegraph.
   d. Elias Howe's sewing machine.

3. Which of the following cities declined in importance as a commercial center because of the railroad building that took place in the 1840s and 1850s?
   a. Atlanta
   b. Chicago
   c. Pittsburgh
   d. New Orleans

4. An urban middle-class home in the 1850s would probably *not* have
   a. several stories.
   b. indoor faucets supplying hot and cold running water.
   c. conspicuously ornamented furniture.
   d. a coal-burning stove for cooking and heating.

5. James Gordon Bennett was the
    a. founder of the American Museum.
    b. inventor of the cylindrical steam-driven press.
    c. founder of the penny press.
    d. founder of the lyceums.

6. Which of the following statements about transcendentalism is *incorrect?*
    a. It was an American form of romanticism.
    b. It claimed that knowledge of God and truth were born in each individual.
    c. It claimed that great literature must conform to universal standards of form and beauty.
    d. It claimed that a new democratic republic could produce art and literature as great as the old traditional societies of Europe.

7. The region of the nation that produced the greatest number of and most influential writers during the American Renaissance was
    a. the South.
    b. New England.
    c. New York and the Middle Atlantic states.
    d. the Midwest.

8. Which of the following writers introduced into fiction the character of the American frontiersman and the theme of conflict between primitive life in the wilderness and the advance of civilization?
    a. Herman Melville
    b. Edgar Allan Poe
    c. James Fenimore Cooper
    d. Nathaniel Hawthorne

9. Which of the following writers defended the right to disobey unjust laws, criticized the materialism of American society, and doubted the beneficial effects of technological advances?
    a. Walt Whitman
    b. Henry David Thoreau
    c. John Greenleaf Whittier
    d. James Fenimore Cooper

10. Which of the following statements about the Hudson River school of painters is *incorrect?*
    a. Its members painted only landscapes of the Hudson River and its vicinity.
    b. Its members subordinated realism to heighten emotional effect through the use of color and composition.
    c. It included Thomas Cole, Asher Durand, Frederic Church, and about fifty other painters.
    d. Its members sought to capture on canvas the natural grandeur of the American landscape.

SHORT-ANSWER QUESTIONS

1. Why were interchangeable parts and improved machine tools extremely important in the growth of American manufacturing?

2. How was most American railroad building in the 1850s financed? What role did New York City play in this financing?

3. Why did Americans' real and annual income increase between 1840 and 1860?

4. Why did antebellum American cities make little headway against recurring epidemics of cholera, yellow fever, and other diseases?

5. Explain the beliefs of American transcendentalists, such as Emerson and Thoreau.

ESSAY QUESTIONS

1. In the 1830s Ralph Waldo Emerson called for a probing exploration of American nationality in literature and art. To what extent did the writers and painters of the American Renaissance answer that call?

2. What technological advances were made in agriculture, industry, and transportation between 1830 and 1860? How did these affect the daily lives of antebellum Americans? What impact did these have on the environment?

3. "The bright possibilities rather than the dark potential of technology impressed most antebellum Americans." To what extent did Americans' lives and experiences between 1830 and 1860 justify that attitude?

4. Discuss the rise of popular culture in the period 1830–1860, including the penny press, the sentimental novel, theater and minstrel shows, and popular health and science movements. How did technological advances of the period affect popular culture?

5. Discuss the attempts of intellectuals to bridge the gap between the high culture of the educated elite and the popular culture of the masses. What techniques and organizations did they use? How successful were they?

12

The Old South and Slavery, 1800–1860

OUTLINE AND SUMMARY

I. Introduction

The Old South developed gradually between the 1790s and 1860. Its most distinctive feature was its defense of slavery at a time when the institution was being condemned and ended almost everywhere else in the civilized world. In all the southern states, the majority of the white population never owned any slaves. The Upper South relied less on slavery and cotton growing than the Lower South. It also seceded from the Union more hesitantly and reluctantly. However, defense of slavery gradually united almost all white southerners. Antislavery sentiment in the South peaked at the time of the Virginia debate on emancipation, 1831–1832, and thereafter it all but disappeared.

II. King Cotton

A. Introduction

The main cash crop of the colonial South, tobacco, declined in the late eighteenth century. Cotton culture revived southern agriculture and encouraged its rapid expansion southward and westward. Cotton growing was stimulated by growth of the British textile industry, development of the cotton gin, and removal of Indians from southern and western lands.

B. The Lure of Cotton

The climate of the Lower South was ideal for growing cotton. Cotton could be grown profitably on any scale, with or without slave labor. However, cotton cultivation and the institution of slavery did increase side by side. Cotton and corn were often grown together so that the South did not have to spend money on imported food.

C. Ties Between the Lower and Upper South

The Upper South identified with the Lower South rather than with the free states because many Lower South residents had migrated from the Upper South; all southern whites benefited from the three-fifths clause in the Constitution; almost all southerners resented the criticism from northern abolitionists; and the residents of the Upper South enjoyed a large, profitable business in the sale of slaves to the Lower South.

D. The North and South Diverge: Economic Patterns

While the North was rapidly industrializing and urbanizing, the South remained primarily rural and agricultural. Slaves could be and were employed in southern factories, but much of the South's capital was tied up in slave ownership and, therefore, not available for investment in industrial development. Southerners believed that raising cash crops through slave labor would continue to be profitable, and hence they lacked the incentive to switch their capital from land and slaves to financing of industry.

E. The North and South Diverge: Education in a Cotton Economy

The Old South made less provision for public schools than the North. School attendance was not compulsory for southern whites, and the law forbade teaching slaves to read and write. The South's agricultural, slave economy did not require a high rate of literacy.

F. Cotton and Southern Progress

"Rather than viewing the Old South as economically backward, it is probably better to see it merely as different."

III. Social Relations in the White South

A. Introduction

Southern white society showed a mixture of aristocratic and democratic elements. There were great differences in wealth between classes, but most whites did own land. Planters were overrepresented in state legislatures but did not always pass the laws they wanted.

B. The Social Groups of the White South

In 1860 only one-quarter of southern whites owned slaves; 1 percent of southern whites owned one hundred or more slaves. The whites of the Old South fit into four classes (although there was considerable variation within each category): (1) planters—owners of twenty or more slaves; (2) small slaveholders; (3) yeomen—nonslaveholding small family farmers; (4) people of the pine barrens.

C. Planters and Plantation Mistresses

Characterized by a high degree of division of labor, the plantation was almost a factory in the field. The planters' income depended on profits from the sale of a cash crop. The pursuit of profit led planters to look constantly for additional and more fertile land, organize their slave crews as efficiently as possible, and seek favorable merchant-banker connections to market their crops and extend needed credit. Psychological strains that plantation agriculture placed on planters and their wives included physical isolation from other whites of their class; frequent moves; crude living conditions, especially for the many who lived on the new frontier; and responsibilities of running a major economic enterprise. An additional stress on planters' wives was the sexual double standard that accepted illicit sexual relations between masters and their bondswomen, while demanding absolute sexual purity from white females.

D. The Small Slaveholders

There were many more small slaveholders than planters. "In 1860, 88 percent of all slaveholders owned fewer than twenty slaves." In the upland regions, the small slaveholders tended to identify with the more numerous yeomen, while in the low country and delta, they identified with the planters and aspired to rise into that class, which they sometimes did.

E. The Yeomen

These nonslaveholding family farmers were by far the largest group among southern whites. Those with the least fertile land tended to be subsistence farmers, but most yeomen grew at least some crops for sale. Their farms ranged in size from fifty to two hundred acres. The yeomen farmers were congregated in the upland, hilly, and less fertile regions. They were, on the whole, a proud and self-sufficient group.

F. The People of the Pine Barrens

They made up about 10 percent of the white population and owned neither slaves nor land. They typically squatted on unfenced land, on which they grazed hogs and cattle and grew corn for their subsistence. The men supplemented the family diet with hunting. Able to survive in this manner, they refused to work as hired help for others and were viewed by more affluent whites as lazy and shiftless.

G. Conflict and Consensus in the White South

Planters and yeomen inclined toward opposing political parties, the elite being Whigs; the small farmers, Democrats. Other characteristics of the Old South, however, minimized conflict: the four main social groups clustered in different regions and often had little contact, both yeomen and planters were independent landowners, and whites rarely worked for other whites. Although planters dominated state legislatures, all white men had the right to vote by the 1820s; therefore, the planters could not ignore the desires of the yeomen majority.

H. Conflict over Slavery

There was a potential for conflict between slaveholders and nonslaveholders. The majority of nonslaveholding southerners, however, supported slavery. Why? (1) Some hoped to become slaveholders; (2) they feared freedmen would demand social and political equality with whites; (3) southern whites shared racist beliefs about blacks and feared that emancipation would be followed by a race war, which would endanger the lives of all whites.

I. *The Proslavery Argument*

The proslavery argument also was used as a tool to unite southern whites behind the institution. The argument, which was constructed by southern intellectuals between 1830 and 1860, claimed that slavery was a positive good rather than a necessary evil. It claimed that slavery was sanctioned by history and religion and that southern slaves were better treated than northern factory "wage slaves." By the 1830s most southern churches had adopted this proslavery position.

In addition to persuading themselves of the righteousness of their "peculiar institution," southerners increasingly suppressed all public criticism of slavery. They seized and destroyed abolitionist literature mailed to the South, smashed the presses of southern anti-slavery newspapers, and mobbed anyone who dared to question.

IV. Honor and Violence in the Old South

A. *Violence in the White South*

During the colonial and pre–Civil War periods, violence was more prevalent among southern whites than it was among the white population of the North.

B. *The Code of Honor and Dueling*

Behind much southern violence was an exaggerated notion of personal pride. White men must "react violently to even trivial insults in order to demonstrate that they had nothing in common with slaves." Among gentlemen this pride took the form of a code of honor. Any intentional insult to one's reputation had to be redressed by a challenge to a duel.

C. *The Southern Evangelicals and White Values*

The code of honor was potentially in conflict with the values preached by southern evangelical churches, such as humility and self-restraint. From the 1830s on, evangelical religion grew in influence to the point that some southern gentlemen, while clinging to the value of reputation in the eyes of others, did denounce drinking, gambling, and dueling as un-Christian practices.

V. Life Under Slavery

A. *Introduction*

Slavery was an exploitative institution that took by force the life and labor of one race for the profit of another.

B. *The Maturing of the Plantation System*

The institution of slavery changed between 1700 and 1830. In the earlier period, the majority of the black population were recent African or Caribbean arrivals, disproportionately young males who spoke little English and were isolated on small farms. By 1830 there was a more even balance between males and females. Most were American-born and English-speaking and worked on large plantations. These changes facilitated a more rapid natural increase in the black population.

C. Work and Discipline of Plantation Slaves

No other nineteenth-century Americans worked as many hours under as harsh discipline as slave field hands. Slave craftsmen and domestics on the plantations had higher status and easier work but also were subjected at times to physical brutality.

D. The Slave Family

The slave family was not recognized or protected by southern law. Slave families were disrupted by sale; physical separation of husbands and wives and of parents and children; and sexual demands made on black females by masters and other white men. Despite these hazards, the black family did not dissolve but evolved in ways that were different from those of middle-class whites.

E. The Longevity, Diet, and Health of Slaves

Slaves in the Old South lived longer and reproduced faster than those in Brazil or the Caribbean because of a more even sex ratio among U.S. blacks and a more adequate diet. On the other hand, southern slaves had a higher mortality rate than their white countrymen.

F. Slaves off Plantations

Although the majority of slaves worked on plantations, the Old South also used slaves in mining, lumbering, manufacturing, and performing a variety of skilled artisan jobs in cities and villages.

G. Life on the Margin: Free Blacks in the Old South

Not all blacks in the Old South were slaves; there were more than a quarter million free blacks in 1860. The position of the free blacks in the South deteriorated from the 1830s on. Southern law forbade teaching blacks, free or slave, to read. Obstacles were put in the way of manumission, and free blacks were barred from entering or remaining in many states. Nonetheless, many of the post–Civil War black leaders came from this group.

H. Slave Resistance

There were only three organized slave rebellions in the Old South: Gabriel Prosser's rebellion (1800), Denmark Vesey's conspiracy (1822), and Nat Turner's rebellion (1831). More uprisings did not occur because slaves did not form a large majority anywhere in the South, whites had all the weapons and soldiers, blacks were reluctant to endanger their families, and they rarely had allies in southern Indians and never in nonslaveholding whites. An alternative way to freedom was to try to escape to the North. Black abolitionists such as Frederick Douglass, Harriet Tubman, and Josiah Henson were escaped former slaves, some of whom returned repeatedly to the South to help others escape, giving rise to the legend of the Underground Railroad. Relatively few slaves, however, made it to the North successfully.

More than by either running away or violent revolt, blacks resisted slavery by furtive means: theft, negligence, arson, and work stoppages and slowdowns.

VI. The Emergence of African-American Culture

A. Introduction

American blacks under slavery developed a distinctive culture that drew on African and American cultures but was "more than a mixture of the two."

B. The Language of Slaves

Blacks in the antebellum South developed an English pidgin.

C. African-American Religion

The first Africans brought to the South were Muslims or followers of a variety of indigenous African religions. By 1800 many had been converted to Christianity, especially as Methodists or Baptists. Masters hoped that by preaching Christian humility and acceptance to their slaves, they could make blacks docile and obedient. This did not necessarily work, since the rebels Gabriel Prosser, Denmark Vesey, Nat Turner, and many of their followers were devout Christians who were inspired by their interpretation of the Bible. While Christianity did not turn most slaves into revolutionaries, it did serve as a unifying force among blacks, as well as a source of hope and comfort. Few blacks accepted the white preachers' message that slavery was right in God's eyes.

D. Black Music and Dance

Compared to the cultural patterns of upper-class whites in the Old South, the culture of blacks was "extremely expressive." Blacks expressed their feelings in shouts, music, and dance. They composed work songs and religious songs, later known as spirituals.

VII. Conclusion

The Old South, with its African-American culture, lack of industry, and dispersed farmers and planters, became increasingly a world apart. Northerners saw it as backward and different because of its institution of slavery. Southern whites reacted to outside criticism by defending their "peculiar institution" as a benevolent way to handle the innate inferiority of the black race. Few slaves agreed. While most of them did not revolt or escape successfully, they did engage in covert resistance. They also looked to Christianity for solace and the message that slavery was a gross injustice.

VOCABULARY

The following terms are used in Chapter 12. To understand the chapter fully, it is important that you know what each of them means.

yeomen   nonslaveholding family farmers, the Old South's most numerous white class

malapportioned   unfairly divided and assigned, as when seats in a legislature are divided to give one group or geographical area more than its fair share of representation

portico   a structure consisting of a roof supported by columns, usually attached to a building as a porch

social structure   the classes or groups that make up a society and their relations with each other

planters   large landholders, especially those who owned twenty or more slaves, who were a small elite class of the Old South

alluvial soil   soil built up by the mud deposits of flowing rivers, usually very fertile, the best cotton-growing land

evangelical   referring to certain movements and/or denominations within the Protestant churches that stress the importance of personal experience of guilt for sin and of reconciliation to God through Christ

pidgin   a simplified language, with no original, native speakers, in which people of different native languages can communicate

IDENTIFICATIONS

After reading Chapter 12, you should be able to identify and explain the historical significance of each of the following:

Nat Turner's rebellion

debate in the Virginia legislature over slavery, 1831–1832

three-fifths clause of the Constitution

J. D. B. De Bow

Tredegar Iron Works

Whig party

Democratic party

Hinton R. Helper, *The Impending Crisis of the South*

proslavery argument

George Fitzhugh

southern code of honor

northern "character"

Gabriel Prosser

Denmark Vesey

Henry "Box" Brown

Frederick Douglass

Harriet Tubman

Josiah Henson

Underground Railroad

SKILL BUILDING: MAPS

On the map of the South, locate each of the areas listed below. In what states do you find these geographical areas? What was the historical significance of each?

Upper South

Lower (Deep) South

tidewater

pine barrens

piedmont

Mississippi Delta

uplands

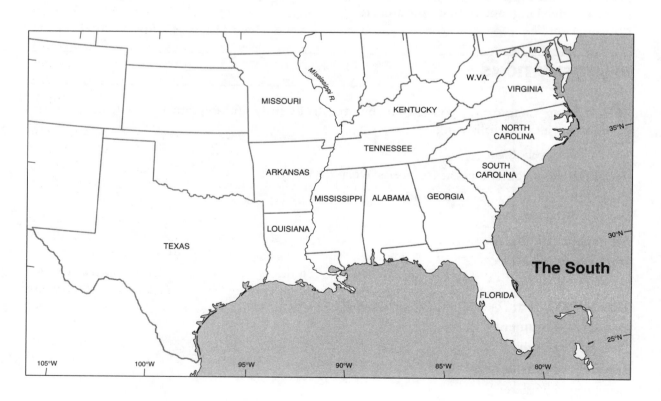

HISTORICAL SOURCES

The author of Chapter 12 has relied on many and varied historical sources to try to achieve a balanced and accurate account of life in the Old South. To see slavery as the bondsmen and bondswomen experienced it, the author has turned to accounts of former slaves, written or oral. Probably the most famous of the published narratives are those of black abolitionist, writer, and political leader Frederick Douglass, including his *Narrative of the Life of Frederick Douglass: An American Slave, Written by Himself* (1845); *My Bondage and My Freedom* (1855); and *Life and Times of Frederick Douglass* (1881). On pages 384, 385, and 393 the works of Frederick Douglass are referred to and/or quoted. How has the author used these historical sources in each instance? Another of the well-known written narratives, Solomon Northup's *Twelve Years a Slave* (1854), also is quoted. What does the author illustrate with this quotation? Northup was a free black living in New York who was kidnapped in 1841 and sold into slavery on a Louisiana cotton plantation. Find other places in the chapter where the memories of former slaves are cited. Many of these stories come from interviews that were conducted by unemployed writers and researchers who, during the depression in the 1930s, worked for the WPA Federal Writers Project. The government hired these persons to seek out elderly black people who had been slaves as children, ask them about their experiences, and record their answers. A sampling of these interviews, edited by Benjamin A. Botkin, was published in 1945 in a book titled *Lay My Burden Down*.

Historians have learned much about the life and attitudes of the planter class from letters and diaries. One of the most informative of these is the diary kept by Mary Boykin Chesnut, wife of a South Carolina planter. On page 375, of Chapter 12, she is cited on the "sorrows of plantation mistresses," many of whom were reminded daily of their husbands' infidelities by the features of the mulatto children in the slave quarters. The historian can find confirmation of this charge against planters and see how one bondswoman felt about the unwanted advances of her master by looking at the narrative of escaped slave Harriet A. Jacobs, *Incidents in the Life of a Slave Girl, Written by Herself* (1861).

Chapter 12 also lets us see the Old South as it appeared to visitors from the outside. On pages 383, 384, 390, and 393 the author refers to and/or quotes from Frederick Law Olmsted's books *A Journey in the Seaboard Slave States* (1856), *A Journey Through Texas* (1857), and *A Journey in the Back Country* (1860). Olmsted, who later became one of America's foremost landscape architects and designer of New York's Central Park, took a fourteen-month tour of the slave states in the 1850s on a journalistic assignment from the *New York Times*. Olmsted's mostly critical observations about the Old South and its "peculiar institution" were different from the glowing defense of black slavery that historians encounter in the writings of its southern defenders. Chapter 12 cites the works of two such defenders, James Henry Hammond's "Letters on Slavery" in *The Pro-Slavery Argument* (1853) and George Fitzhugh's *Sociology for the South* (1854). What arguments did these books present in favor of black slavery?

Historians also conduct intensive studies of local records to gain insights into both regional and national history. Look at the account of the Edgefield District, South Carolina. What generalizations about the Old South does it seem to bear out?

MULTIPLE-CHOICE QUESTIONS

Circle the letter of the item that best completes each statement or answers the question.

1. The majority of white men in the antebellum South were
   a. planters.
   b. small slaveholders.
   c. nonslaveholding family farmers.
   d. merchants or shopkeepers.

2. All of the following were true of planters *except*
   a. they searched constantly for more and better land.
   b. they were often in debt to Northern bankers and brokers.
   c. they usually managed their own estates.
   d. they almost always built mansions on their plantations for their families.

3. The yeomen farmers of the Old South
   a. were congregated in the upland and hilly regions.
   b. did not grow cash crops for market.
   c. did not have the right to vote.
   d. were generally tenants rather than landowners.

4. In 1857 a book calling on nonslaveholding southern whites to abolish slavery in their own interest was published by
   a. James Henry Hammond.
   b. Hinton R. Helper.
   c. George Fitzhugh.
   d. Gabriel Prosser.

5. As compared to the North, the Old South had a higher
   a. literacy rate.
   b. proportion of its people living in cities.
   c. murder rate.
   d. proportion of its white population working for other whites.

6. Southern evangelical churches generally preached against all of the following *except*
   a. slavery.
   b. gambling.
   c. dueling.
   d. intemperance.

7. The black family under slavery
   a. received no legal recognition or protection.
   b. disintegrated.
   c. copied the customs and patterns of white families.
   d. was protected against separation of young children and mothers.

8. Why weren't there more slave revolts in the Old South?
    a. Blacks were outnumbered by whites almost everywhere in the South and lacked allies and guns.
    b. Blacks had no strong desire for freedom, which they did not understand.
    c. Blacks had no inspired leaders.
    d. Blacks were restrained by strong bonds of loyalty to masters who treated them fairly.

9. Most blacks in the antebellum South
    a. rejected Christianity as the religion of the slave masters.
    b. accepted the preaching of white clergy that slavery was divinely sanctioned.
    c. drew from Christianity the view that slavery was an affliction to test their faith and for which masters would be punished.
    d. became obedient and docile because of the Christian promise of reward in heaven for faithful servants.

10. Which of the following statements about white people of the pine barrens is *incorrect*?
    a. They generally "squatted" on their land rather than owning it.
    b. They usually favored the institution of slavery, though they owned no slaves.
    c. They usually worked for the planters as tenant farmers, sharecroppers, or overseers.
    d. They carried on subsistence farming, supplemented by hunting.

SHORT-ANSWER QUESTIONS

1. Explain the differences between the Upper and Lower South. What tied them together?

2. Explain why the Old South failed to industrialize.

3. Summarize the proslavery argument developed by southern intellectuals to defend the "peculiar institution."

4. Discuss the free black population of the Old South. How many were there by the eve of the Civil War? Where did most of them live? Under what economic and legal constraints did they exist?

5. Describe the "furtive resistance" of slaves in the Old South.

ESSAY QUESTIONS

1. Compare and contrast economic, social, and political developments in the North and South between 1800 and 1860. How do you account for the divergence between the two sections?

2. Discuss the white social structure of the Old South. How egalitarian was it? What social classes or groups existed? What was their relationship to each other and to the institution of slavery?

3. The great majority of white southerners never owned a single slave, yet the majority supported the institution of slavery. Write an essay explaining why.

4. Was slavery in the South essentially a paternalistic institution in which most slaves were treated reasonably well, or was it primarily an exploitative institution? Back up your conclusions by citing as much evidence as possible.

5. Discuss the emergence of African-American culture in the Old South. In what ways did it draw on African experiences? In what ways did it incorporate the American slave experience? How did it differ from white southern culture and values?

13

Immigration, Expansion, and Sectional Conflict, 1840–1848

OUTLINE AND SUMMARY

I. Introduction

Between 1840 and 1848 the United States expanded its territory by 50 percent through occupation, conquest, and negotiation. The 1840s and 1850s also saw a marked increase in population, much of it produced by a great rise in European immigration. American aggressive expansionism and rising population and immigration were linked in several ways: (1) the penny press inflamed a passion for expansion among the urban, often immigrant masses; (2) the overwhelmingly Democratic immigrant vote helped elect James K. Polk, an ardent expansionist, as president; (3) some influential Democratic politicians saw acquisition of more land and a return to a republic of self-sufficient farmers as a way of relieving the growing class and ethnic conflicts in the nation's industrializing cities. The United States paid a heavy price for its expansion, however; sharpened sectional strife and a split in the Democratic party drove the country toward civil war.

II. Newcomers and Natives

A. *Introduction*

Between 1840 and 1860, 4.2 million immigrants entered the United States. The two biggest groups came from Ireland and the German states.

B. *Expectations and Realities*

Immigrants came in hope of improving their economic condition. Few of the Irish immigrants possessed enough capital to acquire farms. Instead they settled heavily in northeastern cities, where they took jobs in construction and railroad building. Germans and Scandinavians, on the other hand, tended to concentrate in Illinois, Ohio, Wisconsin, and Missouri. Although more of them entered farming than did the Irish, they too were drawn to cities. By 1860 the Irish and Germans accounted for approximately 50 percent of the population of cities such as St. Louis, New York, Chicago, Cincinnati, Milwaukee, Detroit, and San Francisco.

C. The Germans

The German immigrants were quite diverse, including people of different social classes and religions, but they were bound together by their common language and often settled in German neighborhoods. They prospered and built many ethnic institutions: German-language newspapers, voluntary associations, and schools. Native-born Americans criticized them for being clannish.

D. The Irish

Between 1815 and 1844 almost 1 million Irish entered the United States, most of them Catholic, poor, and seeking greater economic opportunity. From 1845 to 1855, another 2 million arrived, now overwhelmingly Catholic and fleeing the potato famine that was ravaging their homeland. They usually entered the urban work force at the bottom, competing for jobs with equally poor blacks. The competition led to animosity between the two groups and made most Irish hostile to abolition and abolitionists. Those Irish who rose to the level of skilled and semiskilled workers competed against native-born, white, Protestant mechanics, again producing ethnic and religious hostilities.

E. Anti-Catholicism, Nativism, and Labor Protest

The antagonism of white, Protestant, native-born workers took the form of anti-Catholic and anti-immigrant outbursts and organizations. Such sentiments and organizations were behind the founding of the Know-Nothing (or American) party, which played a significant political role in the 1850s. Labor also responded to low wages and job competition by advocating land reform (including free 160-acre homesteads in the West for all who wanted them) and by forming unions and waging strikes. Unions won a few gains, but their growth was limited by government and employer opposition and by the deep splits along ethnic and religious lines in the antebellum working class.

F. Labor Protest and Immigrant Politics

Almost all Irish and German immigrants became supporters of the Democratic party. They saw it as an antiprivilege party, more sympathetic to the common man than the Whigs were. The Irish and Germans also resented Whig connections with the temperance movement and nativism. The Irish suspected the northern Whigs of antislavery views, and since the Irish feared economic competition from emancipated slaves, they wanted no part of abolitionism.

III. The West and Beyond

A. The Far West

In the 1820s, 1830s, and 1840s Texas and the present-day southwestern regions of the United States belonged to Mexico. The Oregon Territory (including what are now the states of Oregon, Washington, and Idaho and parts of Wyoming, Montana, and Canada) was under joint occupation by Britain and the United States.

B. Far Western Trade

The earliest Americans to enter the Far West were fur trappers and traders. They blazed trails, such as the Santa Fe; introduced eastern manufactured goods in exchange for beaver pelts or Mexican silver; and set up encampments and trading posts. They also spurred the interest of pioneer farmers with their tales of favorable climate and fertile soil in the Far West.

C. Mexican Government in the Far West

Much of northern Mexico (including Texas, California, New Mexico, Colorado, Nevada, Arizona, and Utah) was sparsely occupied by Hispanic ranchers and native Indian tribes. These Indians were forced into slave labor on the ranches, or they roamed and repeatedly attacked the intruding Hispanics. Poor protection from the Mexican army against Indian attacks discouraged more Mexicans from settling in those territories. This small Mexican population, increasingly dependent on American traders for needed supplies, presented little obstacle to the penetration of U.S. pioneers into the Far West.

D. The American Settlement of Texas

In the 1820s the Mexican government gave generous land grants to Americans and encouraged their settlement in Texas as a way to hasten the economic development of the province. So many came, primarily from the southern states, that by 1830 twice as many Americans as Mexicans were living in Texas. Alarmed, the Mexican government in the 1830s attempted to end American immigration and prohibit slavery in Texas. Its efforts antagonized the Americans but failed to stop the flood of immigrants that by 1836 had raised the American population in Texas to thirty thousand whites and five thousand slaves. Meanwhile, in 1834 the new president-dictator of Mexico, Santa Anna, started to tighten his hold on Texas. The Americans in the province rebelled.

E. The Texas Revolution

In 1836 Santa Anna led an army into Texas to suppress the uprising. The Mexicans defeated the Americans at the Alamo and at Goliad. Under the leadership of Sam Houston, however, the Americans in April at San Jacinto routed the Mexicans, took Santa Anna prisoner, and forced him to sign a treaty granting Texas independence. The Mexican government later refused to ratify the treaty, but Texas remained independent.

F. American Settlements in California, New Mexico, and Oregon

The Mexicans also initially welcomed American colonists to California. By the 1840s a growing number were settling in the Sacramento Valley, where they lived apart from the Mexicans. In the 1830s American missionaries entered Oregon's Willamette Valley to convert the Indians there. The missionaries' glowing reports of the territory's climate and resources aroused keen interest back in the United States.

G. The Overland Trail

In the 1840s, despite faulty maps and guidebooks, fears of Indian attacks, and other real and imagined dangers, more than fourteen thousand Americans joined wagon trains on the Overland Trail headed for Oregon or California.

IV. The Politics of Expansion

A. Introduction

At the start of the 1840s western expansion was not an important political issue. Only after politicians failed to deal effectively with troubling economic issues did some of these leaders seize on expansion as a primary goal.

B. The Whig Ascendancy

The Whig party won the election of 1840 with William Henry Harrison. The party planned to enact Clay's American System of a new national bank, protective tariffs, and federal aid for internal improvements. These plans were thwarted, however, by Harrison's death after only one month in the White House. This brought Vice President John Tyler into office. Tyler, a states' rights Virginian, vetoed all the economic measures the congressional Whigs passed.

C. Tyler and the Annexation of Texas

At odds with his party on economic issues, Tyler attempted to gain popularity by achieving success in foreign policy. He supported U.S. annexation of Texas and appointed John C. Calhoun as his secretary of state to draw up a treaty. Calhoun wrote undiplomatically that one reason for annexation was to provide more territory for the expansion and protection of slavery. This added fuel to already existing northern suspicions that acquiring Texas was part of a southern conspiracy to expand slavery, and the Senate therefore rejected Tyler's and Calhoun's annexation treaty.

D. The Election of 1844

The annexation of Texas became an important issue in the 1844 election. The Whig nominee, Henry Clay, wavered on annexation, first opposing it as sectionally divisive, then softening his opposition, and finally opposing it again. His shifts lost southern votes to the Democrats and northern antislavery votes to the Liberty party. The Democrats nominated the ardently expansionist James K. Polk, who called for admitting Texas immediately. Many Irish and other recent immigrants voted for Polk because they disliked the Whigs' association with nativism, temperance, and anti-Catholicism. Polk won in a close election.

E. Manifest Destiny

The election demonstrated, among other things, that expansionism had become a popular cause by the 1840s. Many expansionists repeated journalist John L. O'Sullivan's claim that it was the "manifest destiny" of the United States to spread its experiment in liberty and self-government from coast to coast. Others eyed the excellent harbors of California and Oregon as the natural outlets for American trade with Asia. Expansionists argued that acquiring additional fertile soil would safeguard the U.S. future as a democratic republic of self-sufficient farmers and combat the social stratification and class strife that accompanied industrialization and urbanization. These ideas, carried in the penny press, strongly appealed to struggling immigrants in the cities.

F. Polk and Oregon

In his 1844 presidential campaign, Polk had called for American ownership of all the Oregon Territory as well as the annexation of Texas. After he entered the White House, neither the British nor the United States wanted a war, and so they settled for a compromise treaty that split Oregon at the forty-ninth parallel. The Senate ratified the treaty in 1846.

G. The Origins of the Mexican War

In February 1845 Congress passed a joint resolution to annex Texas, although Mexico had never recognized the independence of the province. After Polk was inaugurated, he backed the Texan claim that its southern boundary was the Rio Grande as opposed to Mexico's contention that it was the Nueces River, one hundred miles to the northeast. This support encouraged Texas to accept annexation on July 4, 1845.

Polk also wanted to gain California and New Mexico, and he sent John Slidell to Mexico with an offer to buy them for $25 million. After Mexico refused, Polk ordered American troops under General Zachary Taylor into the disputed region south of the Nueces, hoping to provoke a war that would give the United States a chance to seize California and New Mexico. When Mexican troops clashed with Taylor's, Polk told Congress that Mexico had forced war with the United States. A minority in Congress accused Polk of aggressive, proslavery actions, but the majority supported the war.

H. The Mexican War

In February 1847 Zachary Taylor defeated an army commanded by Santa Anna at the Battle of Buena Vista. Colonel Stephen Kearny took New Mexico, and California fell to combined naval and land assaults under commodores John D. Sloat and David Stockton and army officers Kearny and John C. Frémont. Mexico surrendered in September 1847 when an American force led by General Winfield Scott conquered Mexico City. Under the terms of the Treaty of Guadalupe Hidalgo, Mexico accepted the Rio Grande boundary and ceded to the United States almost all of the present-day U.S. Southwest in return for $15 million and a promise by the U.S. government to pay claims of U.S. citizens against Mexico.

I. The Mexican War in the Popular Mind

The Mexican War was widely reported in the penny press (it was the first time that war correspondents were used) and became the background for numerous popular novels. This coverage romanticized the war, softened opposition to it, whipped up nationalism, and made Zachary Taylor a popular hero.

J. Intensifying Sectional Divisions

Despite the patriotism generated by the war, sectional conflict grew between 1846 and 1848. The Polk administration, dominated by southerners, angered the North and West by lowering tariffs and vetoing federal aid for internal improvements. More important, arguments began over expansion of slavery into the Mexican cession.

K. The Wilmot Proviso

A northern Democratic congressman, David Wilmot, in 1846 tacked on to an appropriations bill an amendment that would bar slavery from the new territory acquired from Mexico. With much northern support, the so-called Wilmot Proviso passed the House but not the Senate. Extremist southerners led by Calhoun claimed it was unconstitutional for Congress to forbid slavery in any territory.

L. The Election of 1848

The Whigs nominated Zachary Taylor for president. The Democrats chose Lewis Cass, who tried to solve the sectional controversy by proposing squatter or popular sovereignty, giving the settlers who lived in a territory the right to decide whether to permit slavery. Not satisfied with this position, a faction of Democrats called Barnburners joined antislavery "conscience" Whigs and Liberty party abolitionists to create the Free-Soil party. It nominated Martin Van Buren, who ran on a platform opposing any further spread of slavery. Taylor, a military hero whose position on slavery was unknown, won the election. The good showing of the Free-Soilers in the North, however, demonstrated the popular appeal of keeping slavery out of the West and using it as a place of opportunity for poor white men.

M. The California Gold Rush

Just before the signing of the Treaty of Guadalupe Hidalgo, an American carpenter living in California discovered gold near Sacramento. The news, which soon reached the East, produced a rush of prospectors. California's population surged, and the weak military government proved unequal to containing the violence and disorder of the gold fields and mining boom towns. Californians demanded a civilian state government. This brought to a head the issue of slavery in California and the rest of the Mexican cession.

V. Conclusion

Americans considered expansion their manifest destiny. More land in the West, they believed, would enable most people to avoid city life and factory work and provide instead continuing opportunities for small, independent farmers. In fact, in the 1840s social tensions intensified between the native-born and the recent immigrants and between the North and the South. The issue of whether slavery should be allowed in the territory acquired from Mexico split the Democratic party, widened the schism between northern and southern Whigs, and gave birth to the Free-Soil party.

VOCABULARY

The following terms are used in Chapter 13. To understand the chapter fully, it is important that you know what each of them means.

steerage   the section of a ship, originally near the rudder, providing the cheapest accommodations for passengers

freethinker   one who has rejected authority and ritual, especially in religion, in favor of rational inquiry and speculation

nativism   dislike and suspicion of immigrants; the policy of protecting the interests of native inhabitants versus those of immigrants

secularize   to transfer control or ownership of something from the church or religious authorities to civil authorities, such as the government

allegiance   a feeling of duty, obligation, or faithfulness to a person, idea, country, or government

dark horse   a little-known or unlikely political figure who unexpectedly wins nomination and/or election

proviso   a clause in a statute, contract, or the like by which a condition is introduced; a stipulation or condition

IDENTIFICATIONS

After reading Chapter 13, you should be able to identify and explain the historical significance of each of the following:

Maria Monk, *Awful Disclosures of the Hotel Dieu Nunnery in Montreal*

Know-Nothing, or American, party

George Henry Evans

Commonwealth v. *Hunt* (1842)

Spanish missions and presidios

Stephen F. Austin and American *empresarios* in Texas

Antonio López de Santa Anna

the Alamo

Sam Houston

Overland Trail and the Donner party

John Tyler

John C. Calhoun

Henry Clay

James K. Polk ("Young Hickory")

John L. O'Sullivan and manifest destiny

Zachary Taylor ("Old Rough and Ready")

Winfield Scott

John C. Frémont and the Bear Flag Republic

Treaty of Guadalupe Hidalgo

Wilmot Proviso

squatter or popular sovereignty

Martin Van Buren and the Free-Soil party

SKILL BUILDING: MAPS

On the map of the West on the following page, locate each of the following and explain its historical significance:

forty-ninth parallel

Great Plains

Rocky Mountains

Oregon Territory

54°40 latitude

St. Louis

Santa Fe

Santa Fe Trail

Texas and the Mexican cession

Sacramento Valley

Columbia River

Vancouver Island

Rio Grande

Nueces River

San Francisco

36°30 latitude

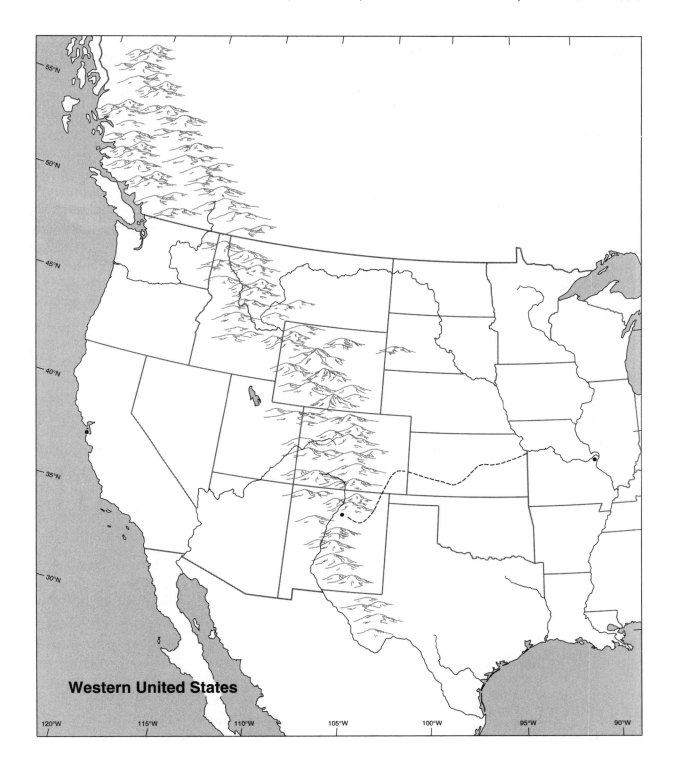

Western United States

MULTIPLE-CHOICE QUESTIONS

Circle the letter of the item that best completes the statement or answers the question.

1. The two biggest sources of immigration to the United States between 1840 and 1860 were
   a. Italy and Eastern Europe.
   b. China and Japan.
   c. Ireland and the German states.
   d. Britain and Scotland.

2. In the case of *Commonwealth* v. *Hunt* (1842), the Massachusetts Supreme Court ruled that
   a. slavery was unconstitutional in Massachusetts.
   b. labor unions were not necessarily illegal combinations or monopolies.
   c. Massachusetts tax money could not be used to support an unjust war against Mexico.
   d. segregated schools for blacks in Massachusetts did not violate the U.S. Constitution.

3. Squatter or popular sovereignty meant
   a. allowing residents of a territory to decide whether to permit slavery there.
   b. extending the right to vote to all male settlers in the Far West.
   c. deciding the ownership of a territory by vote of its residents.
   d. the right of the native Indian peoples to keep the lands they were already cultivating.

4. Which of the following statements about President Polk's actions is *incorrect?*
   a. He sent John Slidell to Mexico with an offer to buy California and New Mexico.
   b. He ordered Zachary Taylor to keep his troops north of the Nueces River to avoid a confrontation with Mexico.
   c. He agreed to split the Oregon Territory with the British at the forty-ninth parallel, although he had demanded all of it during his presidential campaign.
   d. He signed a bill lowering the tariff and vetoed one giving federal aid for internal improvements.

5. The expansionist phrase *manifest destiny* was first coined by
   a. George Henry Evans.
   b. Horace Greeley.
   c. John C. Frémont.
   d. John L. O'Sullivan.

6. All of the following people or groups were nativist and anti-Catholic *except*
   a. the Know-Nothings.
   b. Martin Van Buren.
   c. Samuel F. B. Morse.
   d. Lyman Beecher.

7. The fate of the Donner party best illustrates
    a. the hazards faced by pioneers traveling west on the Overland Trail.
    b. the lack of appeal of abolitionism to the majority of immigrants.
    c. the widespread lack of interest among Americans in Henry Clay's American system by the 1840s.
    d. the vicious attacks on Catholics and immigrants that took place in the 1830s and 1840s.

8. The Senate rejected the treaty annexing Texas that was drawn up by Secretary of State John Calhoun because
    a. he defended annexation as a way to protect and defend slavery.
    b. the Texans made it clear that they were not yet ready to give up their independence and join the United States.
    c. the British threatened to break off diplomatic relations if the United States took the territory without compensating them.
    d. Mexico threatened to declare war on the United States if it stole her province.

9. The Wilmot Proviso called for
    a. annexation of Texas.
    b. prohibiting slavery in any territory acquired from Mexico.
    c. drawing the Missouri Compromise line of 36°30 to the West Coast.
    d. legislation to limit immigration into the United States.

10. Presidios were
    a. agents who contracted with the Mexican government to bring American settlers into Texas.
    b. Mexicans who owned huge ranches worked by enslaved Indians.
    c. Franciscan priests who endeavored to convert the Indians to Christianity.
    d. forts constructed by the Spanish to protect their missions in the Southwest.

SHORT-ANSWER QUESTIONS

1. In the antebellum period, why did Irish and German immigrants generally favor the Democratic party over the Whig party?

2. Why did Polk first demand all of the Oregon Territory from Britain and then agree to a compromise? What were the terms of that compromise?

3. Why did many northern Democrats who were not abolitionists favor the Wilmot Proviso?

4. What was the platform of the Free-Soil party in the election of 1848? How well did the party do in the election? Why was its showing significant?

5. Describe the impact of the gold rush on the sleepy Mexican village of San Francisco.

6. How did the California gold rush bring to a head the issue of slavery in the Far West?

ESSAY QUESTIONS

1. Discuss immigration to the United States in the 1840s and 1850s. Who came? Why did immigrants come? Where did they settle? What economic and political roles did they play?

2. Discuss the rise of anti-Catholic and nativist sentiment and movements in the United States in the 1840s. What caused them? Who supported such groups? What impact did these groups have on American politics?

3. What did expansionists mean by the term *manifest destiny?* What arguments did they use to justify expansion? To whom did these arguments appeal? Why?

4. Discuss the causes of the Mexican War. To what extent did the United States provoke the confrontation? Why did some members of Congress and the public oppose the war?

5. Explain the following statement with as much illustrative evidence as possible: "[E]xpansion brought sectional antagonism to the boiling point, split the Democratic party in the late 1840s, and set the nation on the path to the Civil War."

14

From Compromise to Secession,
1850 – 1861

OUTLINE AND SUMMARY

I. Introduction

In the 1850s northerners increasingly adopted the free-soil doctrine. Unlike abolitionists, free-soilers did not call for the end of slavery everywhere in the United States. Rather, they held that slavery must be kept from spreading to the western territories. Free-soilers wanted the West to be kept as a land of opportunity for poor white men, where they would not be degraded by having to compete against slave labor. Some free-soilers, such as William H. Seward and Abraham Lincoln, also saw the containment of slavery as necessary to the future of the nation. If slavery was restricted to the South, it might gradually die out; if it was not confined, it would spread over the entire country. Most southerners, on the other hand, defended slavery as a positive good that elevated the position of all whites while treating blacks humanely. Southerners regarded attempts to exclude slavery from the West as an insult to them and a denial of their constitutional right to take their property wherever they chose. They also came to believe that free-soilers, like abolitionists, intended ultimately to destroy slavery even in the South.

II. The Compromise of 1850

A. Introduction

When the treaty ending the Mexican War was signed in 1848, a delicate balance existed between free and slave states: there were fifteen of each. All the proposed solutions for handling slavery in the Mexican cession—whether to prohibit it, open the whole area to slave-holders, extend the Missouri Compromise line to the Pacific, or apply popular sovereignty—were controversial. Other issues also divided the North and South. Then, in 1849, California drew up a constitution banning slavery and petitioned Congress for statehood.

B. Zachary Taylor at the Helm

President Taylor had encouraged California to make this request for statehood. Believing that the majority of its residents opposed slavery, he urged Congress to welcome it into the Union as a free state. Southerners were horrified, however, at the prospect of losing the balance of power in the Senate by admitting California and perhaps next New Mexico as free states. In protest nine southern states sent delegates to a convention at Nashville.

C. Henry Clay Proposes a Compromise

Senator Clay proposed a compromise to settle the territorial problem and other sectional controversies:

1. Admit California as a free state.
2. Divide the rest of the Mexican cession into the New Mexico and Utah territories, with the future of slavery in each left up to its residents.
3. Settle the border dispute between Texas and New Mexico in New Mexico's favor.
4. Compensate Texas by having the federal government pay off the state's past public debt.
5. Allow slavery to continue in Washington, D.C., but ban slave trading there.
6. Pass and enforce a tough new fugitive-slave law.

After heated debate and much maneuvering, the compromise passed.

D. Assessing the Compromise

The compromise did not settle the underlying differences between the sections. The one clear advantage that the South gained, the passage of the stringent Fugitive Slave Act, backfired.

E. Enforcement of the Fugitive Slave Act

The law, which was blatantly stacked against black people and sent federal marshals all over the country looking for runaways, aroused widespread opposition in the North. Northern mobs attacked marshals to rescue arrested fugitives, vigilance committees helped runaways escape to Canada, and nine states passed personal liberty laws designed to interfere with enforcement of the act. Whereas the act embittered northerners against the South, southerners resented the North's refusal to live up to the terms of the compromise.

F. Uncle Tom's Cabin

The publication of Harriet Beecher Stowe's *Uncle Tom's Cabin* and the many dramatizations of it further aroused anti-southern feelings and sympathy for slaves in the North.

G. The Election of 1852

The Whigs nominated war hero General Winfield Scott to run against Democrat Franklin Pierce for president. The Democrats rallied behind the compromise and popular sovereignty in the territories. Pierce and the Democrats trounced the Whigs, whose northern and southern wings were being torn apart by the sectional controversy.

III. The Collapse of the Second Party System

A. Introduction

During Pierce's administration the second party system—Whig against Democrat—collapsed. In the 1850s the issues that had been the main focus of partisan politics (banking, internal improvements, tariffs, temperance) were pushed from center stage by the debate over slavery's extension. The Whig party, more internally divided on the question than the Democrats, disintegrated when Stephen A. Douglas's Kansas-Nebraska bill threw the future of slavery in the territories wide open.

B. The Kansas-Nebraska Act

Passage of this act in 1854 dealt a shattering blow to the second party system and renewed the sectional strife that the compromise aimed to quiet. Stephen A. Douglas was eager to advance settlement of Kansas and Nebraska and promote the building of a transcontinental railroad through the area. To accomplish these goals he needed to organize a territorial government for the region, but he was running into southern opposition because the area was north of the Missouri Compromise line and would therefore be free. To gain southern support, Douglas introduced the Kansas-Nebraska bill, which repealed the Missouri Compromise, organized two territories, and left the question of slavery in both Kansas and Nebraska up to popular sovereignty. That gave the South a chance to gain at least Kansas (adjacent to the slave state of Missouri) for the "peculiar institution."

C. The Surge of Free Soil

Douglas was surprised at the angry reaction in the North, where many regarded the law as part of an atrocious southern plot to spread slavery into Kansas, the rest of the Louisiana Territory, and even into the North. Free-soil sentiment had grown tremendously in the North, not primarily because of sympathy for black slaves—many free-soilers were racists—but because northerners wanted the territories to be the place where upwardly mobile, enterprising, poor Americans could become independent, self-employed farmers and businessmen. If slavery invaded the territories, it would discourage and drive out free labor.

D. The Ebbing of Manifest Destiny

Enthusiasm for expansion, which had unified the Democratic party, waned in the free states as northerners saw in each southern move to acquire territory a plot to gain additional slave states. This northern attitude became so pronounced that President Pierce had to repudiate southern-backed plans to buy or seize Cuba.

E. The Whigs Disintegrate

Southern Whigs had joined Democrats in voting for the Kansas-Nebraska Act. Northern "conscience" Whigs, led by Senator William Seward, and free-soil Democrats reacted angrily against both of the major parties. In the elections of 1854 and 1855 many of the disaffected voters turned first to the American, or Know-Nothing, party and later increasingly to the new Republican party. As a result of these moves the Whig party fell apart.

F. The Rise and Fall of the Know-Nothings

The American party (Know-Nothings) evolved out of a secret nativist society called the Order of the Star-Spangled Banner. In the North the party combined hatred of Catholics, immigrants, and slavery-extension. It took a conspiratorial view of the world in which the Pope and the Slave Power were both plotting to extinguish the American democratic republic. In 1854 and 1855 the Know-Nothings scored major victories in northern states such as Massachusetts. However, the party declined rapidly thereafter because, like the major parties, it was pulled apart by the slavery-expansion issue. Its southern adherents supported the Kansas-Nebraska Act, a position unacceptable to northern nativists, who deserted to the emerging Republicans.

G. The Origins of the Republican Party

The Republican party first appeared in several northern states in protest against the Kansas-Nebraska Act. As the Know-Nothings waned by 1856, the Republicans became the main opposition party to the Democrats. The Republicans were basically a coalition of former northern Whigs and Democrats who wanted to restore the Missouri Compromise, Liberty party abolitionists, and free-soilers. Little united them at first except their opposition to the Kansas-Nebraska Act. However, the subsequent fighting in Kansas between proslavery and antislavery forces greatly strengthened the party and its freesoil stand.

H. Bleeding Kansas

Both proslavery and antislavery settlers rushed to Kansas. In 1855, when the first election for a territorial legislature took place, thousands of proslavery Missourians invaded Kansas for the day and voted illegally. This fraud produced a rabidly proslavery legislature, which from its capital in Lecompton, Kansas, passed repressive laws aimed at squelching the free-soilers. The free-soilers, considering the Lecompton legislature a sham, organized a rival government in Topeka. After the sack of Lawrence and John Brown's Pottawatomie massacre, civil war broke out in Kansas between the two governments and their followers. Popular sovereignty had not worked. Instead it caused angry debate between Pierce, who recognized the fraudulent Lecompton government, and dismayed northern Democrats and Republicans. It also spread violence to Congress with Preston Brooks's attack on Senator Charles Sumner.

I. The Election of 1856

The Republicans nominated John C. Frémont, whose platform called on Congress to exclude slavery from all remaining territories. The Democrats nominated James Buchanan and backed popular sovereignty. Millard Fillmore ran as a Know-Nothing. Buchanan won, but the Republicans did remarkably well in the North. Had Frémont carried Pennsylvania and either Illinois or Indiana, he would have been elected despite receiving almost no southern votes.

IV. The Crisis of the Union

A. *The Dred Scott Case*

Two days after Buchanan's inauguration, the Supreme Court entered the controversy over slavery in the territories with its *Dred Scott* decision. A court composed mostly of southerners ruled that blacks, slave or free, were not citizens of the United States and that the Missouri Compromise had always been unconstitutional because Congress had no right to exclude slavery from any territory. To do so violated the Fifth Amendment protection of property and property holders. The Republicans denounced the decision and prepared to ignore it.

B. *The Lecompton Constitution*

In Kansas the proslavery Lecompton legislature proposed a state constitution that protected slaveholders and gave the settlers the right to vote only on whether to allow more slaves into Kansas. President Buchanan backed the Lecompton constitution and called on Congress to grant Kansas statehood under it. Stephen Douglas, author of the Kansas-Nebraska Act, broke with Buchanan and denounced the actions of the Lecompton legislature. Northern Democrats and Republicans applauded Douglas; southern Democrats applauded Buchanan.

C. *The Lincoln-Douglas Debates*

In 1858 Douglas ran for reelection to the Senate. His lesser-known Republican opponent, Abraham Lincoln, challenged Douglas to a series of debates. In the debates Lincoln attacked slavery as morally evil but denied that Congress had the right to abolish it in the South or that he favored equality for blacks. Rather, he stuck to his position of barring slavery from the territories. Lincoln also forced Douglas into making his Freeport Doctrine statement, which pleased northern Democrats but made Douglas and his views unacceptable to the South. Although Douglas won the Illinois Senate seat, the election further split the Democratic party. It also made Lincoln "famous in the North and infamous in the South."

D. *John Brown's Raid*

In the hope of arming blacks and leading them in a slave uprising, John Brown and twenty-one followers in October 1859 seized the federal arsenal at Harpers Ferry. Brown and his men were quickly defeated, and Brown was convicted of treason and hanged. The raid touched off a wave of fear and hysteria in the South. Southerners believed Brown had the backing of abolitionists and Republicans who were plotting to incite more slave rebellions. These fears played into the hands of southern extremists.

E. *The South Contemplates Secession*

Southerners began to speak of secession as the only way to protect themselves. They regarded northern opposition to the Fugitive Slave Act and to slavery in Kansas as unconstitutional and an offense to the South, which wounded southern pride. Some argued that separation from the Union also would permit the South to seize more territory in the Caribbean and the West for slavery.

F. The Election of 1860

The Republicans broadened their appeal in the free states in 1860 by supporting a protective tariff, federal aid for internal improvements, and a homestead act. For president they nominated the Illinois moderate, Lincoln. The northern and southern Democrats, unable to agree on a platform, split. Northern Democrats nominated Douglas, who still advocated popular sovereignty. Southern Democrats selected John C. Breckenridge, who insisted that Congress must pass laws protecting slavery in all territories. The Constitutional Union party, with appeal mostly in the border states and Upper South, ran John Bell. Lincoln won a majority in the electoral college, but only 39 percent of the popular vote.

G. The Movement for Secession

Believing that a Republican president would unleash more John Browns upon them, the states of the Deep South began to secede even before Lincoln took office. South Carolina led the way in December 1860, followed by Alabama, Mississippi, Florida, Georgia, Louisiana, and Texas. On February 4, 1861, delegates from these seven states met in Montgomery, Alabama, to form the Confederate States of America. The states of the border and Upper South hesitated to secede and join the Confederacy for a number of reasons.

H. The Search for Compromise

Kentucky senator John Crittenden proposed a compromise to bring the Deep South back into the Union. It included constitutional amendments that guaranteed the federal government would never interfere with slavery in the South and that drew the Missouri Compromise line across the remaining territories, with slavery permitted south of the line in all present and future U.S. territory. Lincoln rejected the Crittenden plan because he would not abandon the free-soil promise on which he had been elected. He regarded the plan as an invitation to the South to seize territory in the Caribbean for slavery. He also felt that he had won an honest election and that giving in to a losing minority would damage the American tradition of majority rule.

I. The Coming of War

The Confederacy began to take over federal forts within its region. Soon after Lincoln's inauguration, it bombarded Fort Sumter in Charleston's harbor, thus firing the first shot. Lincoln responded by proclaiming that a rebellion existed in the Lower South and calling for seventy-five thousand militia volunteers from the loyal states to subdue it. Rather than send their troops to fight against sister southern states, Virginia, North Carolina, Arkansas, and Tennessee seceded and joined the Confederacy. The North was now aroused and ready to fight to save the Union, though not yet ready to abolish slavery.

V. Conclusion

During the 1850s the gulf between the North and South over the issues of slavery and its spread into the territories widened. Civil war in Kansas proved that the fate of slavery in the territories could not be decided peacefully by the settlers themselves. By the late 1850s southerners, encouraged by the *Dred Scott* decision, were demanding that Congress protect slavery throughout the territories. On the other hand, increasing numbers of northerners had concluded that stopping the spread of slavery was essential to the liberties and opportunities of white men. Southerners finally took the drastic step of seceding because they were convinced that the North, led by Lincoln and the Republicans, intended not only to bar slavery from the territories but also to undermine the "peculiar institution" in the South itself, thus corroding "the moral and political foundations of southern society."

VOCABULARY

The following terms are used in Chapter 14. To understand the chapter fully, it is important that you know what each of them means.

omnibus bill   a bill including numerous items or subjects

defector   one who withdraws allegiance from a political party, group, or country

stalwart   a steadfast or uncompromising political party supporter

conspiracy   a secret agreement to perform an evil or unlawful act; a secret plot

naturalization   the legal process that confers the rights and privileges of citizenship upon an immigrant

capital crime or offense   a crime or offense punishable by death

doughface   in the 1850s, a northern politician whose views were acceptable or even sympathetic to the South

plaintiff   one who brings suit in a court

due process of law   the enforcement of laws through established judicial proceedings

referendum   the procedure of submitting legislative measures directly to the voters for approval or rejection

insurrection   an armed uprising or other open resistance against a government or other established authority; a revolt

lynch   to put a person to death for some alleged offense by the actions of a mob or group having no legal authority

vigilantes   members of extralegal citizen groups organized to maintain order and punish offenses

IDENTIFICATIONS

After reading Chapter 14, you should be able to identify and explain the historical significance of each of the following:

doctrines of free soil and free labor

William H. Seward and irrepressible conflict

popular (squatter) sovereignty

Daniel Webster

Henry Clay's omnibus bill and the Compromise of 1850

Millard Fillmore

Fugitive Slave Act of 1850 and personal-liberty laws

Harriet Beecher Stowe, *Uncle Tom's Cabin*

American (or Know-Nothing) party

Stephen A. Douglas and the Kansas-Nebraska Act

Gadsden Purchase

John A. Quitman, William Walker, and filibustering

Ostend Manifesto

"Bleeding Kansas"

Lecompton versus Topeka legislature and the Lecompton constitution

sack of Lawrence and Pottawatomie massacre

Charles Sumner and Preston Brooks

John C. Frémont

James Buchanan

Roger B. Taney and *Dred Scott* v. *Sandford*

Lincoln-Douglas debates and Douglas's Freeport Doctrine

John Brown's raid on Harpers Ferry

Panic of 1857

John C. Breckenridge

John Bell and the Constitutional Union party

Jefferson Davis and the Confederate States of America

Crittenden compromise

Fort Sumter

SKILL BUILDING: MAPS

On the map of the United States, locate and draw in each of the following. How is each related to sectional conflict and the coming of the Civil War?

Missouri

Kansas and Nebraska territories

36°30 latitude

New Mexico Territory

Utah Territory

California

Gadsden Purchase

states that seceded by February 1861 (Lower South)

states that seceded after fighting at Fort Sumter (Upper South)

border slave states that did not secede

Charleston, South Carolina

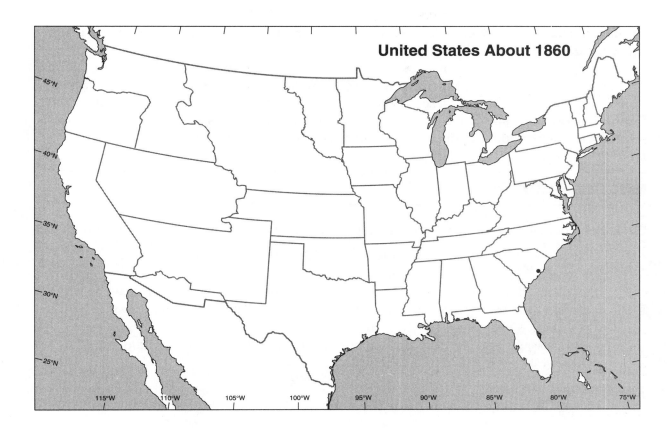

United States About 1860

HISTORICAL SOURCES

Chapter 14 concentrates on the widening gulf between North and South on the questions of slavery and its extension into western territories. How do historians attempt to understand what northerners and southerners felt and believed in the 1850s? One historical source that the author of Chapter 14 uses is literary works published during the period, as well as the letters and comments of well-known poets and novelists. The most famous and influential piece of fiction in the 1850s was Harriet Beecher Stowe's *Uncle Tom's Cabin.* Look at the discussion of the novel on pages 436–437. By analyzing that novel, what does the historian learn about its emotional appeal to antebellum northerners? How did it touch their family values? Despite its abolitionist position, how did the book reflect the negative stereotypes about blacks that were prevalent among white northerners?

The historian can see the differing reactions to the novel in the North and South by reading reviews of it that appeared in northern and southern periodicals. For example, in December 1852 in a magazine called the *Southern Literary Messenger,* the historian can read a scathing denunciation of *Uncle Tom's Cabin,* which, according to the reviewer, criminally prostitutes the "high functions of the imagination to the pernicious intrigues of sectional animosity, and to the petty calumnies of willful slander."

The author of Chapter 14 also quotes Ralph Waldo Emerson on page 451 and a poem by John Greenleaf Whittier on page 436. Why does the author cite each of these 1850s writers? The historian can read an equally impassioned defense of the southern way of life and its planter elite in the poems, letters, and novels of the South Carolinian writer William Gilmore Simms.

Another way to gauge feelings in the Deep South on the eve of the Civil War is by taking a close look at a single city of the region. Turn to "A Place in Time: Charleston in the Secession Crisis." How does this description of Charleston add to our understanding of the southern mood in 1860 and the reasons why the Lower South seceded? What does this selection illustrate about the interplay of social class and race in the antebellum South?

MULTIPLE-CHOICE QUESTIONS

Circle the letter of the item that best completes each statement or answers the question.

1. Which of the following statements about the Compromise of 1850 is correct?
    a. It ended slavery in Washington, D.C.
    b. It allowed the California voters to decide by popular vote whether to have slavery.
    c. It had the backing of John C. Calhoun and almost all southerners but was opposed by Daniel Webster and most northerners.
    d. Its passage was helped by Stephen Douglas's strategy of breaking up Clay's Omnibus bill into separate measures.

2. Personal-liberty laws were
    a. state laws aimed at hampering enforcement of the Fugitive Slave Act.
    b. federal laws guaranteeing the right of slaveholders to protection of their slave property.
    c. state laws prohibiting blacks, free or slave, from entering a state.
    d. federal laws guaranteeing that states would not deny any person life, liberty, or property without due process of law.

3. Stephen Douglas's Freeport Doctrine
    a. angered northern Democrats by repudiating popular sovereignty.
    b. pointed out how settlers could exclude slavery from a territory despite the *Dred Scott* decision.
    c. undermined Lincoln's free-soil position by showing it was unworkable.
    d. helped to unify the Democratic party for the election of 1860.

4. Which is the most valid statement describing the Republican party position in the election of 1860?
    a. There should be immediate, complete emancipation of slaves in the South.
    b. A program of gradual, compensated emancipation should be started.
    c. There should be no further extension of slavery into the territories.
    d. The principle of popular sovereignty should be applied honestly in the remaining territories.

5. What did the South gain from the Compromise of 1850?
    a. a stronger fugitive slave law
    b. a slave code for the territories
    c. the right to bring slaves into all territories taken from Mexico
    d. a lower tariff

6. The Lecompton Constitution would have provided
    a. a policy for the Supreme Court to follow in cases involving slavery.
    b. an independent country in Africa for freed slaves.
    c. a permanent compromise on slavery for future states.
    d. a proslavery government for Kansas.

7. The Ostend Manifesto pertained to
    a. Cuba.
    b. California.
    c. Mexico.
    d. Florida.

8. The *Dred Scott* decision declared that Congress could *not*
    a. admit new slave states.
    b. prohibit slaveholders from taking slaves into northern states.
    c. bar slavery in the territories.
    d. pass a fugitive-slave law.

9. The secession of southern states began immediately after
    a. announcement of the *Dred Scott* decision.
    b. civil war in Kansas.
    c. Lincoln's inauguration.
    d. Lincoln's election.

10. The Crittenden compromise was not acceptable to Lincoln for all of the following reasons *except*
    a. he would not abandon the promise of free soil on which he had been elected.
    b. he had decided soon after his election to issue the Emancipation Proclamation.
    c. he believed that loyal southerners would soon overturn secession.
    d. he thought the plan would encourage southerners to seize more territory for slavery in the Caribbean.

SHORT-ANSWER QUESTIONS

1. Discuss the provisions of the Fugitive Slave Act of 1850. How did northerners attempt to prevent its enforcement?

2. What were the provisions of the Kansas-Nebraska Act? Why did it anger and alarm many northerners?

3. What brought about civil war in Kansas in 1856?

4. Explain Lincoln's position on slavery when he ran for the Senate in 1858 and for President in 1860.

5. Explain the impact of John Brown's Harpers Ferry raid on the South's mood and thought.

6. Discuss the political impact of the Confederacy's seizure of Fort Sumter.

ESSAY QUESTIONS

1. Imagine that you are a Virginia cotton planter or planter's wife. Compose a letter to a friend in New York explaining why your state has just seceded from the Union.

2. Repeated sectional compromises in 1820, 1833, and 1850 held the Union together and averted civil war. Why did compromise fail in 1860–1861?

3. Although the Compromise of 1850 postponed secession and civil war for a decade, it also contributed to embittered feelings in each section toward the other. Discuss and illustrate this statement.

4. Discuss the birth of the Republican party. How and why did it come about? Who supported it and why? What did it stand for? How and why did it broaden its appeal in the late 1850s?

5. Discuss the demise of the second party system. How is its breakdown related to immigration, nativism, slavery, and the spread of slavery into the West?

Reforging the Union: Civil War, 1861–1865

OUTLINE AND SUMMARY

I. Mobilizing for War

A. Recruitment and Conscription

Initially, local governments and private citizens recruited volunteers for the armies, but their efforts proved insufficient. The Confederacy in April 1862 was the first to pass a conscription law. The act exempted from the draft people in several occupations, including those who owned or oversaw twenty or more slaves. The 20-Negro law led nonslaveholders to complain that this was "a rich man's war but a poor man's fight." The South managed to procure the arms it needed but was less successful in providing its troops with food and clothing. Therefore, in 1863 it imposed the Impressment Act, which allowed government agents to take food supplies from farmers at a set price and seize slaves to work for the army. This law was hated even more than the Conscription Act.

In 1863 the North passed the Enrollment Act, making all able-bodied white males aged twenty to forty-five eligible for the draft. The northern law also granted exemptions. Most resented were the provisions that permitted men to buy substitutes to serve in their places and excused those who paid the government a $300 commutation fee.

B. Financing the War

Both sides sold war bonds and printed unbacked paper money. The Union's greenbacks did not depreciate unduly in value because the federal government made greenbacks legal tender and imposed stiff new taxes to keep the government solvent. The South, which was reluctant to impose and collect new taxes and tried to pay its bills by printing more and more paper money, saw its currency depreciate drastically. The North also passed the National Bank Act, permitting federally chartered banks to issue national bank notes for up to 90 percent of the value of the war bonds they held.

C. Political Leadership in Wartime

Lincoln faced opposition from northern Democrats, who disliked the National Bank Act, the draft, and emancipation of slaves, as well as from the Radical Republicans. Led by Salmon

Chase, Charles Sumner, and Thaddeus Stevens, the Radicals pressed Lincoln to end slavery and, after 1863, criticized his lenient reconstruction plans. By his political skill, however, Lincoln held his party together. Jefferson Davis, president of the Confederacy, was less successful in containing factionalism. He was embroiled in destructive fights with his vice president, Alexander Stephens, and other states' rights southern leaders. The absence of an opposition party in the South further contributed to the factionalism of the southern Democrats.

D. Securing the Union's Borders

Because loss of the border states to the Confederacy would endanger Washington, D.C., and make fighting the war tougher, Lincoln took extraordinary measures. He occupied those states militarily and suspended the writ of habeas corpus there. The Supreme Court in *Ex parte* Merryman ruled Lincoln's actions unconstitutional, but he defied the Court and, with his emergency measures, kept Maryland, Delaware, Kentucky, and Missouri in the Union.

II. In Battle, 1861–1862

A. Armies, Weapons, and Strategies

Northern advantages over the South included a larger population, many more white men of fighting age, and control of 90 percent of the country's industry and two-thirds of its railroad track. The South's advantages were fighting a defensive war on its home territory and, with a slave labor force to carry on nonmilitary activities, being able to use a larger percentage of its white men for fighting.

The improved bullets and Springfield and Enfield rifles used during the Civil War increased the infantry's firepower, which in turn reduced the effectiveness of cavalry, encouraged the digging of trenches, and put a premium on the element of surprise in an attack.

At the start of hostilities the Union adopted the Anaconda plan, which called for sealing off the South with a blockade of its coastline and cutting it in two by gaining control of the Mississippi River. In 1861 the Union did not yet have enough ships and troops to carry out this plan. Instead, west of the Appalachians Union soldiers occupied Kentucky and moved southward into Tennessee, while in the eastern theater the North made repeated, futile attempts to capture Richmond.

B. Stalemate in the East

After the Confederates routed the Union at the first Battle of Bull Run (First Manassas), General George McClellan tried to take Richmond from the South, moving his army up the York Peninsula. Robert E. Lee's smaller Confederate army stopped McClellan, and Lincoln called off the Peninsula campaign. Then Lee and Stonewall Jackson headed north, defeated the Union at the Second Battle of Bull Run (Second Manassas), and continued into western Maryland. Lee hoped with this invasion to seize needed food; threaten Washington, D.C.; increase peace sentiment in the North; and convince Britain and France to recognize the Confederacy. At the bloody Battle of Antietam (Sharpsburg) in September 1862, Union forces under McClellan halted Lee's advance and forced him to retreat southward. After

Antietam Lincoln issued his preliminary Emancipation Proclamation. Another Union attempt to take Richmond, under General Burnside, failed miserably at the Battle of Fredricksburg.

C. The War in the West

The western theater saw important Union victories. In 1861–1862 Ulysses S. Grant secured control of Missouri and Kentucky and then moved into Tennessee, capturing two key forts. Next he headed south toward Mississippi. Confederate attempts failed to stop him at the bloody Battle of Shiloh in southern Tennessee. Meanwhile a naval force under Admiral David G. Farragut captured New Orleans and pushed northward on the Mississippi. A second Union flotilla moving southward captured Memphis. By 1863 the North controlled the entire river except for a two-hundred-mile stretch between Port Hudson, Louisiana and Vicksburg, Mississippi.

Fighting also broke out in the Trans-Mississippi West, where northern and southern forces were joined by Mexican-Americans and Indians. After defeating the Confederates, much of the Union army in the Southwest and on the Great Plains turned to the final conquest of Native Americans.

D. Ironclads and Cruisers: The Naval War

The Union gradually tightened its blockade. It further disrupted foreign trade vital to the Confederacy by capturing its ports and coastal areas. Confederate attempts to break the stranglehold with an ironclad ship led to the battle of the *Merrimac* and the *Monitor,* the first clash of ironclads, but did not disrupt the blockade. The South inflicted serious damage on northern shipping with commerce raiders, but this did not hinder the Union's winning the war.

E. The Diplomatic War

The Confederacy tried to convince Britain and France that it was in their interests to extend diplomatic recognition. It even expected active help from the British, who, desperate for the South's cotton, might be counted on to break the Union blockade. There was tension between the Union and the British over the *Trent* affair and over the commerce raiders and rams built for the Confederacy in England, but the South's "cotton diplomacy" failed. The British had stockpiles of cotton on hand at the start of the war and then found alternative sources of supply. Lincoln's Emancipation Proclamation, which turned the struggle into a war against slavery, won British sympathy for the Union.

III. Emancipation Transforms the War

A. From Confiscation to Emancipation

In his inaugural address Lincoln proclaimed that he had no intention of interfering with slavery in the South. Whenever Union armies approached, however, slaves fled to them. Some commanders, calling these people contraband of war, refused to return them to their masters. In August 1861 Congress backed this policy with the First Confiscation Act but stopped short of freeing the slaves. Lincoln at first resisted calls for emancipation because he did not want to push the border slave states into secession; further, he knew many northerners feared that freedmen might come north and compete for jobs. Radical Republicans, however, demanded immediate emancipation and pointed out that the South's use of slave labor was helping it militarily. After early Union defeats, many northerners agreed that it was necessary to strike a blow against slavery to beat the Confederacy. In July 1862 Congress passed the Second Confiscation Act, which authorized freeing slaves who came within Union lines and using blacks as soldiers. Lincoln hesitated a while longer to enforce this law, but when he failed to persuade the loyal slave states to accept voluntary, federally compensated abolition, he drafted his Emancipation Proclamation. The Proclamation stated that, as of January 1, 1863, all slaves in areas then in rebellion were "forever free." Since it applied only in areas not controlled by the Union, the Proclamation at first freed no slaves, but issuing it was a masterful move. It satisfied the Radicals, appealed to antislavery sentiment in Britain and France (forestalling their recognition of the Confederacy), and encouraged slaves to run away and join the Union army.

B. Crossing Union Lines

By 1865 about half a million former slaves were in Union territory. Some worked for the army. Others worked for loyal planters or on abandoned plantation lands. Many Union soldiers were bitterly prejudiced against blacks but began to change their attitudes as black spies and scouts helped them. Freedmen's aid societies in the North sent agents into the South to distribute relief and open schools. In March 1865 Congress created the Freedmen's Bureau to educate, dispense relief to, and find employment for the former slaves.

C. Black Soldiers in the Union Army

After Lincoln issued the Emancipation Proclamation, large numbers of blacks were accepted in the Union army. By 1865, 186,000 blacks had served, making up approximately one-tenth of all Union soldiers. The black troops suffered much discrimination. Placed in segregated regiments and commanded by white officers, they received less pay and suffered a higher mortality rate than whites. Despite unfair treatment, they served well.

D. Slavery in Wartime

Southerners attempted to maintain control over their slaves by stepping up patrols, telling slaves horror stories about the Yankees, and moving slaves far from Union lines. Nonetheless, blacks ran to Union camps. Others remained on the plantation doing little or no work.

E. The Turning Point of 1863

In the summer and fall of 1863 the Union scored important victories. Lee's invasion of the North was turned back at Gettysburg in July. Simultaneously, Grant took Vicksburg and Port Hudson fell to another Union force. The North then controlled the whole Mississippi River. In September the North also routed the Confederacy from Chattanooga, leaving the way clear for Union troops to invade Georgia.

IV. War and Society, North and South

A. *The War's Economic Impact: The North*

War-related industries and the railroads boomed. The Republican-dominated Congress enacted measures that encouraged further business development: raising tariffs, chartering and granting land and loans to the Union Pacific and Central Pacific railroad corporations to build a transcontinental line, and creating a new national banking system. Other legislation benefited the West particularly, such as the Homestead and the Morrill Land Grant acts (1862). Everyone did not benefit equally from the rising economy. While manufacturers and speculators made fat profits, workers' wages lagged behind inflation. Women, who increasingly replaced drafted men, received even less pay than males. Workers protested their economic lot by forming national unions.

B. *The War's Economic Impact: The South*

The war destroyed the South's economy, wrecking its railroads and cutting its cotton and food production. Food shortages worsened the South's already rampant inflation and caused such hardships for soldiers' families that many Confederates deserted to try to provide for their wives and children.

C. *Dealing with Dissent*

The Union and the Confederacy both faced internal dissent. In the South nonslaveholders with Unionist sentiments and states' rights politicians denounced Jefferson Davis's government. On the whole the Confederate government took little action against these dissidents. In the North peace Democrats (Copperheads) criticized the Emancipation Proclamation and demanded an immediate peace settlement with the South. Peace Democrats had their strongest following in the border states, in the Midwest, and among immigrant workers in northeastern cities. Attempts to begin drafting men in July 1863 sparked riots in New York City that had to be quelled by federal troops. Lincoln suspended the writ of habeas corpus and imposed martial law more frequently than Jefferson Davis did. Although Lincoln was hardly the despot his opponents charged, his actions did lead to the Supreme Court case *Ex parte* Milligan (1866), in which the justices ruled that civilians cannot be tried by military tribunals when the regular civil courts are open.

D. *The Medical War*

Northern citizens formed the U.S. Sanitary Commission, a civilian organization that raised money for medical supplies and distributed extra food and medicine to army camps. Some thirty-two hundred women volunteered their services as nurses to either the Union or Confederate army. Nevertheless, limited medical knowledge about sanitation and germs led to a frightful death toll from disease and infected wounds. Conditions in prisoner-of-war camps were particularly grim. The Confederate prison camp at Andersonville, Georgia was the most notorious.

E. The War and Women's Rights

Feminists hoped that the war would win equality for women as well as blacks. Elizabeth Cady Stanton and Susan B. Anthony organized the National Woman's Loyal League in 1863 to campaign for amendments ending slavery and granting blacks and women the vote. The Civil War, however, did not change women's inferior political status.

V. The Union Victorious, 1864–1865

A. The Eastern Theater in 1864

In 1864 Lincoln put Grant in command of all Union armies. Grant moved his headquarters to the eastern theater and proceeded to attack Lee in Virginia. At the same time, he ordered Sherman to invade Georgia. Despite heavy casualties at the Battles of the Wilderness, Spotsylvania, and Cold Harbor, Grant pressed forward, forcing Lee to pull back to trenches outside Petersburg and Richmond. Grant dispatched another Union force under Philip Sheridan, which devastated and conquered the Shenandoah Valley.

B. Sherman in Georgia

While Grant battled Lee in the Wilderness, Sherman advanced relentlessly into Georgia. Confederate forces had to evacuate Atlanta, which fell to Sherman in September 1864.

C. The Election of 1864

Lincoln faced a tough election fight first from the Radical Republicans, who would have preferred to nominate Salmon Chase, and then from the peace Democrats, who nominated George McClellan. To win the votes of prowar Democrats, Lincoln and the Republicans renamed their party the National Union Party and nominated a prowar Tennessee Unionist, Andrew Johnson, for vice president. Sherman's capture of Atlanta in September clinched Lincoln's victory in November.

D. Sherman's March Through Georgia

After burning much of Atlanta, Sherman marched across Georgia to Savannah. His army lived off the countryside and seized or destroyed everything of possible military value. In December 1864 Sherman took Savannah and turned north to South Carolina. The destruction visited on that state was even greater and was climaxed with the gutting of its capital, Columbia. Sherman then continued into North Carolina.

E. Toward Appomattox

While Sherman swung north, Grant closed in on Lee's army. By spring 1865 Confederate morale had broken and men were deserting in droves. On April 3 Grant entered Richmond. Lee made a last attempt to escape from the Union armies but soon after surrendered to Grant at Appomattox Courthouse. Within a month all remaining Confederate resistance ended. On April 14 John Wilkes Booth shot Lincoln, who died the next day, bringing Andrew Johnson to the presidency.

VI. Conclusion

The Civil War killed some 620,000 Americans, more than any other war the nation has fought. It ruined the southern economy but stimulated industrialization and capital investment in the North. While the Civil War did not wipe out the states' rights doctrine, it did greatly strengthen the federal government: there would be no more attempts at secession. The war ended slavery, but it left undecided the future of 3.5 million freedmen and the form that reconstruction of the South would take.

VOCABULARY

The following terms are used in Chapter 15. To understand the chapter fully, it is important that you know what each of them means.

conscription   compulsory enrollment of men for military or naval service; the draft

gross national product (GNP)   the sum, measured in dollars, of all goods and services produced in a given year

tithe   a tax amounting to one-tenth of income or agricultural produce due to the government or the church

writ of habeas corpus   a formal order requiring that an arrested person be brought before a judge or court and either charged with a specific crime or released (The right to such a writ is guaranteed in the U.S. Constitution.)

reconnaissance   a search in the field to uncover useful military information

flotilla   a group of small naval vessels; a subdivision of a fleet

emissaries   agents sent out on a mission, sometimes of a secret nature

belligerent   when used as a diplomatic term, as in this chapter, a state or nation at war

bigotry   intolerant attachment to a particular belief, prejudice, or opinion

dissent   to disagree with the opinions and policies of the government, church, or social majority

martial law   law imposed on an area by military forces when civil authority has broken down or been pushed aside

feminist   an advocate of equality for women in political, economic, and social life

IDENTIFICATIONS

After reading Chapter 15, you should be able to identify and explain the historical significance of each of the following:

20-Negro law

bounty jumpers

Legal Tender Act and greenbacks

National Bank Act, 1863, and national bank notes

Jefferson Davis

Charles Sumner, Thaddeus Stevens, and the Radical Republicans

Ex parte Merryman, 1861, and *Ex parte* Milligan, 1866

Winfield Scott and the Anaconda plan

first and second battles of Bull Run (First and Second Manassas)

George B. McClellan

Thomas "Stonewall" Jackson

Robert E. Lee

Battle of Antietam (Sharpsburg)

Ulysses S. Grant

William T. Sherman

ironclads and the battle of the *Merrimac* and the *Monitor*

Trent affair

Charles Francis Adams, the *Florida*, *Alabama*, and Laird rams

cotton diplomacy

First and Second Confiscation Acts and Emancipation Proclamation

Fort Pillow massacre

Gettysburg

Vicksburg

Homestead Act, 1862

Morrill Land Grant Act, 1862

Copperheads and Clement L. Vallandigham

New York City draft riot

Elizabeth Cady Stanton, Susan B. Anthony, and the National Woman's Loyal League

National Union party and Andrew Johnson

surrender at Appomattox Courthouse

SKILL BUILDING: MAPS

On the map of the South on the following page, locate each of the areas or places listed below. What is the political and/or military importance of each in the Civil War?

western theater

eastern theater

Appalachian Mountains

Mississippi River

Montgomery, Alabama

Richmond, Virginia

Washington, D.C.

Shenandoah Valley

Maryland

Missouri

Kentucky

Memphis, Tennessee

Vicksburg, Mississippi

Gettysburg, Pennsylvania

Atlanta, Georgia

route of Sherman's march to the sea

Port Royal, South Carolina

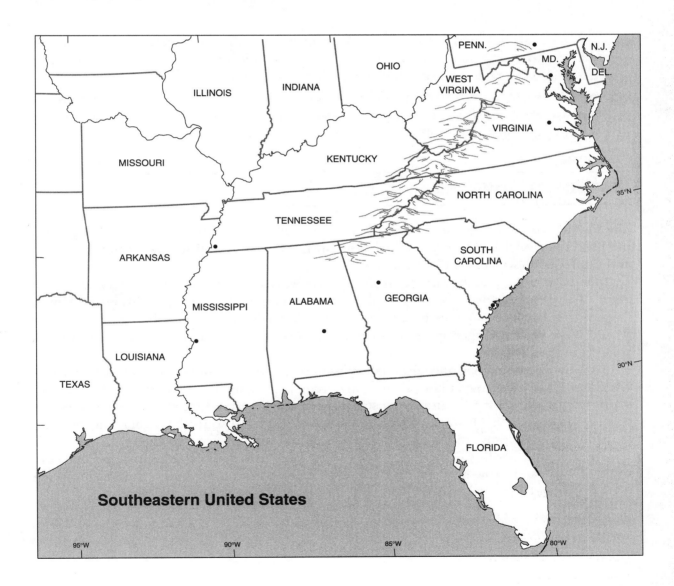

Southeastern United States

SKILL BUILDING: GRAPHS AND CHARTS

Look at the bar graphs under the title "Brothers in Combat: The Opposing Armies of the Civil War" on page 464. These graphs present in a kind of visual shorthand many historically important facts. By glancing at them, you should be able to answer the following questions, among others:

1. In which of America's wars, from the Revolution to Vietnam, did the United States suffer the greatest number of deaths? How do you account for this?

2. How significant an advantage did the Union have over the Confederacy in the size of the army it was able to put into the field?

3. Which side had the greater percentage of its army made up of volunteers? Which had more draftees and substitutes?

4. Given the size of their respective armies, which side suffered the greater percentage of deaths? Why do you think that might be? Which side had the greater percentage of desertions? How do you explain that?

5. New York City draft rioters in 1863 complained that the Civil War was a rich man's war and a poor man's fight. Looking at the graph on draftees and substitutes, do you see any merit to their complaint?

HISTORICAL SOURCES

Among the many historical sources used in Chapter 15 are two particularly interesting ones: published personal narratives of participants in the Civil War and letters written by Union and Confederate soldiers and their families.

On page 479 the author quotes from Thomas W. Higginson's *Army Life in a Black Regiment*. Who was Higginson? What does the author intend to show by using his book? Why is Higginson's book a valuable historical source? Was Higginson an "objective" observer? Would there be any danger in a historian's relying on this source alone to learn about black soldiers in the Civil War?

Another personal narrative used is Ray Billington, ed., *The Journal of Charlotte Forten*. Charlotte Forten was a member of a wealthy, free black family from Philadelphia who went south during the Civil War and Reconstruction to teach and aid freedmen. What does her account on page 479a illustrate? Why is it a valuable historical source? Are there any dangers in using it as one's only source on the experiences and reactions of freedmen?

In many places in Chapter 15, letters of soldiers and their families are quoted. Find some of these and show how the historian uses them. Would these letters tend to duplicate what the historian can learn from William T. Sherman's *Memoirs?* Why or why not?

MULTIPLE-CHOICE QUESTIONS

Circle the letter of the item that best completes each statement or answers the question.

1. Lincoln's Emancipation Proclamation
   a. freed the slaves in the slave states that remained in the Union.
   b. freed the slaves in the western territories.
   c. freed the slaves in areas in rebellion against the U.S. government.
   d. freed all slaves in the Union and Confederacy.

2. Which of the following Union military objectives proved the hardest and took the longest to accomplish?
   a. taking Richmond
   b. gaining control of the Mississippi River
   c. taking New Orleans
   d. seizing the sea islands off the South's Atlantic coast to strengthen the blockade

3. Andrew Johnson was nominated as Lincoln's running mate in 1864 to
   a. please the Radical Republicans.
   b. win the votes of prowar northern Democrats.
   c. influence the South to rejoin the Union, since he would be a southern vice president.
   d. reward Tennessee for remaining loyal to the Union.

4. Which of the following men, denouncing Lincoln's Emancipation Proclamation and suspension of the writ of habeas corpus, called for immediate peace with the Confederacy?
   a. Thaddeus Stevens
   b. Salmon Chase
   c. Clement L. Vallandigham
   d. Charles Sumner

5. Union capture of Vicksburg and Port Hudson was strategically important because
   a. it opened the way to Richmond.
   b. it completed Union control over the Atlantic coast.
   c. it gave Lincoln the victories he was waiting for to issue the Emancipation Proclamation.
   d. it gave the North control over the whole Mississippi River.

6. The Supreme Court ruled in *Ex parte* Milligan that
   a. civilians could not be tried by military tribunals when the civil courts were open.
   b. Lincoln had no constitutional right to free slaves in the Confederacy.
   c. the Union had no right to confiscate the property of rebel leaders.
   d. Congress rather than the president had the right to direct Reconstruction of the South.

7. Slaves during the Civil War
    a. mostly remained loyal to their masters and the South.
    b. often served as officers in the Union army over other blacks.
    c. ran to Union lines when they could and worked for or fought for the North.
    d. were never allowed to enlist as soldiers in either the Union or the Confederate army.

8. By 1865, African-Americans constituted about what portion of the Union army?
    a. 1/10
    b. 1/4
    c. 3/4
    d. 1/20

9. Which of the following statements about women in the Civil War is correct?
    a. Women were *not* allowed to enter army camps to nurse soldiers.
    b. Women replaced draftees in many of the industrial jobs in the North.
    c. Loyal Unionist women were allowed to vote and run for political office.
    d. Northern missionary and freedmen's aid societies refused to use women volunteers.

10. Which of the following statements is correct?
    a. Both the Union and the Confederacy printed unbacked paper money to help finance their war efforts.
    b. The Union had to resort to conscription to get enough soldiers, but the Confederacy recruited enough volunteers to avoid imposing the draft.
    c. Neither the Union nor the Confederacy exempted the wealthy from the draft.
    d. Both the Union and the Confederacy ruthlessly suppressed all internal dissent for the duration of the war.

SHORT-ANSWER QUESTIONS

---

1. Explain how President Lincoln kept the four border slave states in the Union.

2. Why didn't the British recognize the Confederacy as a nation? What help did the British give the South?

3. Who were the Radical Republicans? On what grounds did they criticize Lincoln during the Civil War?

4. How were African-Americans in the Union army discriminated against?

5. What caused the 1863 New York City draft riot?

ESSAY QUESTIONS

1. In his inaugural address in 1861 Lincoln said, "I have no purpose, directly or indirectly, to interfere with the institution of slavery in the states where it exists." In September 1862 he issued his preliminary Emancipation Proclamation. Explain why and how this marked change of policy took place.

2. Discuss the military advantages and disadvantages of each side at the start of the Civil War. Considering that the preponderance of advantages belonged to the Union, why did it take the North four years to defeat the South?

3. Compare and contrast the economic impact of the Civil War on the Union and the Confederacy.

4. The Civil War has been called a second American Revolution that significantly transformed the social, economic, and political fabric of the nation. Write an essay agreeing or disagreeing with that assessment and offer as much evidence as possible to back up your position.

5. Pretend that you are one of the following: a northern woman or young man working in a factory, the wife of a Confederate soldier, or a rank-and-file Confederate soldier. Write a journal or letter, based on the content of Chapter 15, explaining your attitudes, experiences, hardships, aspirations, and gripes.

16

The Crises of Reconstruction,
1865 – 1877

OUTLINE AND SUMMARY

I. Reconstruction Politics

A. Lincoln's Plan

Differences between President Lincoln and Congress on reconstruction of the Confederate states began as early as 1863. In December Lincoln issued a plan that would allow the formation of a new state government when as few as 10 percent of the state's voters took an oath of loyalty to the Union and recognized the end of slavery. This plan said nothing about votes for the freedmen. Lincoln hoped with this plan to win over southern Unionists and draw them into the Republican party. Republicans in Congress thought the plan inadequate and passed the Wade-Davis bill instead. This bill required that at least 50 percent of the voters take an oath of allegiance, and it excluded from participation in government all those who had cooperated with the Confederacy. Lincoln pocket-vetoed the bill, and at the time of his death he and Congress were at an impasse.

B. Presidential Reconstruction Under Johnson

President Andrew Johnson, who was unconcerned about the blacks but wished to promote the interests of the poorer whites in the South, announced his Reconstruction plan in May 1865. Johnson required whites to take an oath of allegiance to the Union, after which they could set up new state governments. These had to proclaim secession illegal, repudiate Confederate debts, and ratify the Thirteenth Amendment (abolishing slavery). Whites who had held high office under the Confederacy and all those with taxable property of $20,000 or more could not vote or hold office until they applied for and received a special pardon from the president. During the summer, Johnson undermined his own policy of excluding planters from leadership by handing out pardons to them wholesale. The new governments created under Johnson's plan were soon dominated by former Confederate leaders and large landowners. Some of the Johnson governments refused to ratify the Thirteenth Amendment, and all showed their intention of making black freedom only nominal by enacting "black codes." Horrified by such evidence of continued southern defiance, the Republican-dominated Congress, in December 1865, refused to recognize these governments or to seat the men they sent to the House and Senate.

C. Congress Versus Johnson

The Radical Republicans, who wished to give black men the vote and transform the South into a biracial democracy, were in a minority in 1866. The majority Moderate Republicans wanted only to get rid of the black codes and protect the basic civil rights of blacks. The Moderates attempted to accomplish these limited goals by continuing the Freedmen's Bureau and passing the Civil Rights Act of 1866. When Johnson vetoed both of these measures, he drove the Moderates into alliance with the Radicals, and together they overrode his vetoes. The now radicalized Republicans also moved to protect the provisions of the Civil Rights Act by embodying them in a constitutional amendment.

D. The Fourteenth Amendment

With the Fourteenth Amendment, the federal government for the first time defined citizenship and intervened to protect persons from state governments. The amendment stated that all persons born in the United States or naturalized were citizens. No state could deny any person's rights without due process of law or deny equal protection of the law. States that refused black men the vote could have their representation in Congress reduced. Former Confederate officials were excluded from voting and officeholding until pardoned by a two-thirds vote of Congress. The southern states, except for Tennessee, refused to ratify the amendment and Johnson denounced it, but in the congressional elections of 1866 the Republicans won huge majorities, giving them a mandate to force ratification of the Fourteenth Amendment and proceed with congressional Reconstruction of the South.

E. Congressional Reconstruction

In 1867 and 1868 Congress enacted its Reconstruction program over Johnson's vetoes. The earlier Johnson governments, black codes, and all other laws they had passed were invalidated. All the former Confederate states except Tennessee, which had been readmitted, were divided into districts under the temporary rule of the military. Each state was required to write a new constitution enfranchising black men and to ratify the Fourteenth Amendment. When these things had been done, Congress could readmit the state to the Union. Congressional Reconstruction was more radical than Lincoln's or Johnson's, since it enfranchised blacks and temporarily disfranchised many whites. It did not, however, go as far as the Radicals wanted, since it failed to confiscate southern land and redistribute it to blacks and poor whites. Johnson, as commander in chief of the army, dragged his feet in enforcing congressional Reconstruction, thus convincing Republicans that he had to be dealt with.

F. The Impeachment Crisis

In March 1867 Congress passed laws aimed at reducing the president's power. Johnson violated one of them by firing Secretary of War Stanton, at which point the Republicans in Congress began impeachment proceedings. Some Republicans wavered, however, fearing that removal of Johnson would upset the constitutional balance of power. As a result, the vote to convict and remove the president fell one short of the necessary two-thirds of the Senate.

G. *The Fifteenth Amendment*

Congress passed a final amendment to complete its Reconstruction program. The Fifteenth Amendment stated that the right to vote could not be denied because of race, color, or previous condition of servitude. The Republicans hoped with this amendment to protect southern blacks, extend suffrage to northern blacks, and gain many new voters for their party. When Congress refused to include women's suffrage, some feminists denounced the amendment and its Republican sponsors. By 1870 the three new amendments—ending slavery, guaranteeing the rights of citizens, and enfranchising black men—were a part of the Constitution and Congress had readmitted all the former Confederate states. Thereafter congressional efforts at Reconstruction weakened.

II. Reconstruction Governments

A. *A New Electorate*

The Reconstruction laws of 1867–1868 created a new electorate in the South by enfranchising blacks and temporarily disfranchising 10 percent to 15 percent of the whites. This new electorate put in power Republican governments that were made up of a coalition of carpetbaggers (northerners who had come south for a variety of reasons), scalawags (cooperating southern whites), and blacks.

B. *Republican Rule*

The Republican Reconstruction governments democratized southern politics by abolishing property and racial qualifications for voting and officeholding, redistricting state legislatures, and making formerly appointive offices elective. They undertook extensive public works, offered increased public services, and established the South's first public schools. All of this cost money, and therefore taxes rose. Southern landowners bitterly resented the increased taxes and accused the state governments of corruption and waste. Some of their charges were true, but many were exaggerated.

C. *Counterattacks*

White southern Democrats refused to accept black voting and officeholding and launched a counterattack to drive the Republican Reconstruction governments from power. White vigilante groups began a campaign of violence and intimidation against blacks, Freedmen's Bureau officials, and white Republicans. Congress investigated this reign of terror and attempted to suppress it with the Enforcement Acts, but only a "large military presence in the South could have protected black rights" and preserved the black electorate. By the 1870s Congress and President Grant were no longer willing to use military force to remake the South.

III. The Impact of Emancipation

A. *Confronting Freedom*

Freedmen, usually lacking property, tools, capital, and literacy, left the plantations where they had been enslaved and searched for family members from whom they had been separated. Once reunited many took the first opportunity to legalize their marriages so that they could raise their children and live an independent family life.

B. Black Institutions

The desire to be free of white control also led blacks to establish their own institutions. Most important were the black churches, which played major religious, social, and political roles. Many black schools were started with the help of the Freedmen's Bureau and northern philanthropists, including the earliest black universities: Howard, Atlanta, and Fisk. Segregation of all facilities in the South became a way of life despite Charles Sumner's Civil Rights Act of 1875, which was unenforced and later invalidated by the Supreme Court.

C. Land, Labor, and Sharecropping

Above all freedmen wanted to become landowning, independent farmers, but few did because the Republicans believed that property rights were too sacred to violate by confiscation and redistribution of white planters' land. Besides, blacks did not have the capital to buy land and agricultural tools. With the end of slavery, the planters continued to own the land but had no work force. Therefore, landless laborers and landholding planters developed the form of tenantry known as sharecropping. Many white small farmers also lost their land and became sharecropping tenants. By 1880, 80 percent of the land in the cotton states was worked by landless tenants.

D. Toward a Crop-Lien Economy

Rural merchants (often themselves landlords) sold supplies to sharecroppers on credit—with a lien on the tenants' share of the crop as collateral. Because interest rates were exorbitant, cotton prices low, and merchants often dishonest, sharecroppers fell deeper and deeper into debt. Southern law prohibited their leaving the land until they had fully repaid their debts. Thus sharecroppers were locked into poverty and "debt peonage."

IV. New Concerns in the North

A. Grantism

The popular Civil War hero Ulysses S. Grant won the presidency in 1868 on the Republican ticket. His administration was marred by rampant corruption, as were many state and local governments of the time. In 1872 Republicans disgusted by the scandals broke with Grant and formed the Liberal Republican party.

B. The Liberals' Revolt

The Liberal Republicans nominated Horace Greeley for president, and the Democrats endorsed him as well. The regular Republicans renominated Grant, who won the 1872 election, but the split in Republican ranks seriously weakened Republican efforts to remake the South.

C. The Panic of 1873

During Grant's second term the nation suffered a financial panic and a severe economic depression. These produced business failures, mass unemployment, heightened labor-management conflict, and disputes over the country's currency system, all of which further diverted Republican attention from Reconstruction.

D. Reconstruction and the Constitution

The Supreme Court in the last quarter of the nineteenth century also undermined Republican Reconstruction. In a series of decisions, the Court interpreted the Fourteenth and Fifteenth amendments in a way that made them all but useless for protecting black citizens. It declared the Civil Rights and Enforcement acts unconstitutional and upheld state segregation laws.

E. Republicans in Retreat

By the 1870s the Republicans were abandoning their Reconstruction policy. Most of them were more interested in economic growth than in protecting black rights. The Radicals who were committed to biracial democracy in the South were dead or had been defeated in elections. Many northerners wanted to normalize relations with the white South. They shared the racist belief that blacks were inferior to whites, and the federal government could not force equality.

V. Reconstruction Abandoned

A. Redeeming the South

After 1872 congressional pardons restored voting and officeholding rights to all ex-Confederates. These men and the South's rising class of businessmen led the Democratic party in a drive to redeem the South from Republican rule. Using economic pressure, intimidation, and violence, the Democrats had regained control of all the southern states but South Carolina, Florida, and Louisiana by 1876. Once in power the Democrats cut taxes and public works and services, and they passed laws favoring landlords over tenants. Some blacks responded to the deteriorating situation by migrating from the South, but most were trapped where they were by debt and poverty.

B. The Election of 1876

The Republicans nominated Rutherford Hayes; the Democrats, Samuel Tilden. Tilden won in the popular vote, but because of fraud and intimidation at the polls, the electoral votes in four states were disputed. A special electoral commission stacked in favor of the Republicans awarded all the disputed votes to Hayes. The Democrats refused to accept the finding until a compromise deal was worked out by southern Democrats and Republican supporters of Hayes. In exchange for southern acceptance of Hayes as president, the Republicans promised (1) to let Democrats take over the last Republican Reconstruction governments in Louisiana, South Carolina, and Florida; (2) to remove the remaining troops from the South; (3) to give more federal patronage to southern Democrats; and (4) to provide federal aid for building railroads and for other internal improvements in the South.

VI. Conclusion

By the end of the Reconstruction era the Republicans had firm support in the Northeast and Midwest; the Democrats were solidly entrenched in the South and would remain so for nearly a century. Many historians today look back on Reconstruction as a democratic experiment that failed partly because Congress did not redistribute land to the freedmen, and without any property they were too economically vulnerable to hold on to their political rights. The Republicans also were unwilling to continue using military force to protect blacks and remake southern society. Reconstruction did, however, leave as a lasting legacy the Fourteenth and Fifteenth amendments. During that brief era, southern blacks reconstituted their families, created their own institutions, and for the first time participated in government.

VOCABULARY

The following terms are used in Chapter 16. To understand the chapter fully, it is important that you know what each of them means.

suffrage   the vote; the right to vote

enfranchisement   the giving of the rights of citizenship and voting (the taking away of these rights is called disfranchisement)

allegiance   faithfulness and obligation to a person, idea, country, or government

amnesty   a general pardon for offenses against a government

partisan   a supporter of a political party or cause; having to do with actions motivated by support of a political party or cause

yeomen   nonslaveholding, small landowning farmers

status quo antebellum   the way things were before the war

referendum   the procedure of submitting legislative measures to the voters for approval or rejection

mandate   instruction about policy given or supposed to be given by the voters to a legislative body or government

confiscate   to seize private property by government authority

impeachment   the charging of a public official, such as a judge or president, with misconduct in office

vigilantes   members of extralegal citizens' groups organized to maintain order and punish offenses

electorate   the body of persons entitled to vote in an election

stereotype   a characteristic or set of characteristics, usually negative, attributed to all members of a group

coalition   a combination or alliance between different groups, parties, or states in support of a particular cause, individual, or purpose

mulatto   the offspring of one white and one black parent; a person of mixed black and white ancestry

mobilization   putting forces or resources into active service for a cause

writ of habeas corpus   a formal order requiring that an arrested person be brought before a judge or court and be charged with a specific crime or released; the right to such a writ is guaranteed in the U. S. Constitution

capital   wealth (especially money) that can be used to produce more wealth

segregation   the act of separating or setting apart from others, especially on the basis of race (the undoing of such separation is called desegregation or integration)

collateral   security or property pledged for the payment of a loan

debt peonage   the practice of holding someone in servitude or partial slavery until that person's debt is paid off

speculator   one who trades in commodities, securities, or land in the hope of making a profit from changes in their market value; a person who engages in business transactions that involve considerable risk but offer the chance of large gains

filibuster   to use delaying tactics, such as long speeches, to prevent a vote or action by a legislative body

---

IDENTIFICATIONS

After reading Chapter 16, you should be able to identify and explain the historical significance of each of the following:

Charles Sumner, Thaddeus Stevens, and the Radical Republicans

Lincoln's 10 percent plan versus Wade-Davis bill

Thirteenth Amendment

black codes

Freedmen's Bureau

Civil Rights Act of 1866

Fourteenth Amendment

Reconstruction Act of 1867

Tenure of Office Act

Fifteenth Amendment

Elizabeth Cady Stanton and Susan B. Anthony

carpetbaggers and scalawags

Ku Klux Klan, Enforcement Acts (Ku Klux Klan Act)

Civil Rights Act of 1875

Jay Gould and Jim Fisk

Crédit Mobilier

William M. Tweed

"Seward's Ice Box"

Liberal Republicans and Horace Greeley

greenbacks and the Greenback party

Slaughterhouse cases

Mississippi Plan and redemption

"Exodus" movement

Rutherford B. Hayes, Samuel J. Tilden, and the Compromise of 1877

SKILL BUILDING: CHARTS

1. Look at the table titled "The Duration of Republican Rule in the Ex-Confederate States" on page 527 in the textbook.
    a. For how many years on average did Republicans control the governments of the ex-Confederate states?
    b. Can you explain why Republican rule lasted less than a decade in every one of them?
    c. Which state was readmitted to the Union before the start of congressional Reconstruction? After reading the chapter, can you explain why?
    d. In what three states did Republicans hold power the longest? Can you explain what brought about the return of the Democrats to power in those three states?
2. Look at the table titled "Percentage of Persons Unable to Write by Age Group, 1870–1890, in South Carolina, Georgia, Alabama, Mississippi, and Louisiana" on page 518 of the textbook.
    a. What percentage of whites in each age group were unable to write in 1870? After reading the textbook, can you explain why these figures are so high?
    b. Did the educational levels of whites improve by 1890? Can you explain why it did or did not?
    c. Was the educational level of blacks higher or lower than that of whites in 1870? What about 1890? How might a critic of Republican Reconstruction of the South use these figures?
    d. After reading the text, can you explain the reasons for the differences between whites and blacks?

HISTORICAL SOURCES

Among the many historical sources used in Chapter 16 are three that are often useful to historians writing political history: (1) law codes, statutes, and constitutional amendments passed by the states and the federal government; (2) records of congressional speeches, remarks, and votes, as found in the *Congressional Globe,* later named the *Congressional Record;* (3) records of congressional hearings and investigations that are printed and made public by the federal government.

Page 503 of the text refers to laws known as black codes passed by the ex-Confederate states. By studying these laws, what does the historian learn about the intentions and attitudes toward blacks among the governing whites? What other conclusions does the textbook come to on the basis of this source?

Find at least three places in Chapter 16 where remarks of congressmen or important votes in the House or Senate are discussed. In each example, analyze what the author is illustrating or proving with this evidence.

Page 515 of the text cites testimony about vigilante violence in the South that was given before a joint congressional committee. Why are records of hearings and investigations by congressional committees a rich source for historians? Could a historian get a distorted or biased view of a past situation by relying solely on such a source? Why or why not?

Intensive studies of local or regional areas also provide useful historical insights. Look at "A Place in Time: A Georgia Plantation, 1865–1880." What light does this account of the Barrow plantation shed on the questions of why and how the sharecropping system developed? In what ways would the article written in 1881 by David Barrow for *Scribner's* magazine be a good historical source for learning about blacks and sharecropping? Why should the historian using it also be skeptical about its claims and observations?

MULTIPLE-CHOICE QUESTIONS

Circle the letter of the item that best completes each statement or answers the question.

1. Lincoln's plan of reconstruction
   a. required southern states to enfranchise blacks.
   b. required that 50 percent or more of white voters in an ex-Confederate state take an oath of allegiance to the Union before a new state government could be established.
   c. was intended to gain the support of southern Unionists and attract them to a southern Republican party.
   d. was eventually accepted by Congress.

2. Which of the following statements about Andrew Johnson is *incorrect*?
   a. He wanted to exclude the planters from political leadership in the South, but then he undermined his intention by granting many pardons to this group.
   b. He cared deeply about obtaining just treatment for the freedmen.
   c. He was a lifelong Democrat with no interest in building the strength of the Republican party.
   d. He vetoed all of the congressional Reconstruction acts, only to have Congress override his vetoes.

3. The black codes
   a. were imposed by Congress on the ex-Confederate states.
   b. guaranteed such basic liberties as freedom of movement and employment, the right to testify in court, and the use of all public facilities.
   c. were seen by Thaddeus Stevens and other Radical Republicans as a necessary legal step to help blacks make the transition from slavery to freedom.
   d. were laws passed by the Johnson governments in the South to keep blacks as a semifree, cheap labor force.

4. Which of their plans did Radical Republicans persuade Congress to embody in the Reconstruction acts and in the Fourteenth and Fifteenth amendments?
   a. black suffrage, a period of military occupation of the South, temporary exclusion of ex-Confederates from voting and officeholding
   b. confiscation and redistribution of land in the South, imprisonment of ex-Confederate leaders
   c. forty acres and a mule for each freedman, temporary disfranchisement of whites, enfranchisement of blacks
   d. exile of Jefferson Davis and other ex-Confederate leaders, upholding of all Civil War debts, extending the right to vote to all citizens over age twenty-one

5. Andrew Johnson was impeached but not convicted because
   a. he proved that he had not violated the Tenure of Office Act.
   b. he resigned before the Senate voted on his guilt.
   c. seven Republicans, fearing that removal of the president would upset the balance of power among the three branches of government, voted "not guilty" with the Democrats.
   d. the Supreme Court ruled that he had not engaged in misconduct in office.

6. The Fifteenth Amendment
   a. defines citizenship and requires states to extend to all persons equal protection of the laws.
   b. states that no one shall be denied the right to vote because of race, color, or previous condition of servitude.
   c. extends suffrage to all citizens over twenty-one years of age.
   d. gives Congress the power to deny seats in the House to states that do not allow black men to vote.

7. In the Republican Reconstruction governments of the South, the group that held the most political offices consisted of
   a. carpetbaggers.
   b. scalawags.
   c. blacks.
   d. the planter elite.

8. The Republican Reconstruction governments of the South
    a. gave the region the most honest, efficient governments it had ever had.
    b. excluded almost all whites from officeholding and were run almost exclusively by blacks.
    c. created public-school systems, built and repaired roads and bridges, and opened institutions to care for orphans and the disabled.
    d. cut taxes and passed laws favoring the interests of landlords over those of tenants and sharecroppers.

9. The sharecropping and crop-lien systems that developed in the post–Civil War South
    a. contributed to soil depletion, agricultural backwardness, and southern poverty.
    b. reduced the portion of southern land owned and controlled by the planter elite.
    c. forced most black people out of agriculture and into southern cities.
    d. tied white planters and black tenants together economically but had no effect on white small farmers.

10. Most historians today view Radical Reconstruction as a democratic experiment that failed because
    a. it left blacks without property and thus economically unable to defend their political rights.
    b. it relied on excessive military force instead of political persuasion.
    c. it was unrealistic in its expectation that illiterate blacks could be turned into responsible citizens overnight.
    d. it was overly vindictive and harsh toward all white southerners.

SHORT-ANSWER QUESTIONS

1. What actions of President Johnson drove Moderate Republicans in Congress into cooperation with Radical Republicans?

2. Why did Elizabeth Cady Stanton, Susan B. Anthony, and some other feminists oppose the Fifteenth Amendment?

3. Why did the Liberal Republicans break with President Grant? What impact did the split have on Republican Reconstruction?

4. Explain how Supreme Court decisions in the 1870s and 1880s undermined Republican Reconstruction.

5. What were the terms of the Compromise of 1877? Which of the terms were actually carried out after the inauguration of Rutherford B. Hayes?

ESSAY QUESTIONS

1. Compare and contrast Lincoln's, Johnson's, and Congress' plans of reconstruction (as represented by the Reconstruction Acts of 1867–1868 and the Fourteenth and Fifteenth amendments). What were the objectives of each plan? Why did each fail to achieve its goals?

2. Discuss the transformation of southern agriculture during the Reconstruction period. Why did the sharecropping and crop-lien systems evolve? What were the consequences of those systems for the economy of the South and for white and black farmers?

3. Discuss the achievements and failures of the Republican Reconstruction governments in the South. Who supported and who opposed them? Why? Why and how were they driven from power?

4. Imagine that you are a Freedmen's Bureau agent in the South during the Reconstruction period. Using the information in Chapter 16, write an account of what you have seen black people doing and experiencing. As such an agent, how have you been involved with the blacks in your district?

5. Write an essay discussing the Grant administration. What were its policies on Reconstruction and the freedmen? What was meant by "Grantism" and Grant's "Great Barbecue"? What successes and failures did the administration have in foreign policy? Why did the Liberal Republicans break with Grant?

17

The Trans-Mississippi West

OUTLINE AND SUMMARY

I. Native Americans and the Trans-Mississippi West

A. *The Plains Indians*

In the mid-nineteenth century, the Sioux, Blackfoot, Cheyenne, Arapaho, Crow, and other Indian tribes roamed the northern Great Plains. In the central and southern Plains lived the Five Civilized Tribes and the Comanches, Kiowas, Pawnees, and others. Such diverse peoples as the Hopis, Zunis, Navajos, Apaches, southern Arapahos, and southern Cheyennes inhabited the Southwest. Many of the Plains Indians, among them the Dakota Sioux, Blackfeet, Crows, and Cheyennes, hunted the migrating buffalo herds. They ate the meat and used the hides for tepees and clothing, the sinews and bones for tools and weapons, and skulls and other parts for religious rituals. In the 1870s the demand for buffalo hides in the eastern markets grew so great that white hunters, aided by the expanding railroads, became professional buffalo killers. By the 1880s hunting had reduced the once great herds to only a few thousand animals and doomed the nomadic, buffalo-centered way of life of the Plains tribes.

B. *The Transformation of Indian Life*

Not only did white hunters destroy most of the game on the Great Plains, but settlers began to invade the area as well. In the 1850s and 1860s the U.S. government forced the Dakota Sioux to cede 24 million acres of land in the Minnesota Territory in exchange for promises of payments, agricultural help, and two reservations. When the government failed to deliver promised supplies and farming help, the angry Sioux attacked white settlers in Minnesota, only to be defeated and pushed out of the territory almost entirely. By the time of the Civil War, the government was pressuring other Plains tribes to surrender their vast hunting grounds and settle as farmers on restricted reservations. Some tribes, such as the Pueblos and Crows, accepted the change peacefully, but in the 1860s and 1870s some 100,000 Indians of the Sioux, Cheyenne, Arapaho, Kiowa, Comanche, and other tribes engaged in almost constant warfare with the army over possession of the Great Plains and the Southwest. In this struggle both whites and Indians committed atrocities, such as the Chivington and Fetterman massacres. In 1868 the government signed peace treaties with many of these tribes that assigned most of them to two large reservations, one in present-day Oklahoma (then known as the Indian Territory) and the other the Great Sioux Reserve in present-day Montana and South Dakota. The government failed to keep its promises of supplies and help with learning to farm, and much of the land was unsuitable for cultivation. The Indians, therefore, left the reservations and harried white pioneers. The army retaliated by attacking any bands off their reservations, even if those groups did not happen to be the ones that had committed hostile acts.

C. Custer's Last Stand

When the Sioux refused to report to the government-run agencies on their reservation and to sell the Black Hills part of their reserve, on which gold had been discovered, the army made war against them. The most famous casualties in that campaign were Colonel George A. Custer and his Seventh Cavalry, whom the Sioux annihilated at the Battle of the Little Bighorn in 1876. Despite their brief triumph, the Sioux were subsequently forced to settle near the government agencies and to surrender the Black Hills. In the late 1870s the army crushed brief resistance by Chief Joseph's Nez Percés and Chief Dull Knife's northern Cheyennes.

D. "Saving" the Indians

Humanitarian reformers in the East began to cry out against government mistreatment of the Indians. In 1881 Helen Hunt Jackson's *A Century of Dishonor* called attention to the sorry record. These reformers thought the best way to end the injustice was to assimilate Indians quickly into mainstream white society. Therefore, well-intentioned reformers, as well as whites who were interested only in seizing more Indian land, supported the 1887 Dawes Severalty Act. The law ended collective tribal ownership of land and split the reservations into 160-acre farms that were assigned to the head of each Indian family. Any remaining reservation land was sold to whites. At the end of twenty-five years, the Indians were to receive full title to their farms and U.S. citizenship. The government also attempted to suppress tribal languages and culture. The new policies proved disastrous for most Indians. By 1934 the total acreage owned by Indians had fallen by 65 percent. What was left in Indian hands was often too dry or infertile to be farmed.

E. The Ghost Dance and the End of Indian Resistance on the Great Plains

Desperate because of their plight, the Sioux and other tribes turned to the Ghost Dance movement. The army's decision to stop the movement led to the last battles between whites and Indians and the 1890 Wounded Knee massacre of three hundred Sioux.

II. Settling the West

A. The First Transcontinental Railroad

With the meeting of the Union Pacific and Central Pacific tracks at Promontory Point, Utah, in 1869, the United States completed its first transcontinental railroad. Construction had been authorized by the Pacific Railroad Act of 1862, and much of the labor was performed by Chinese and Irish immigrants. Because the government granted land to the companies for every mile of track laid, the railroads emerged as the biggest landlords in the West. By the end of the 1800s, nine major railroads linked the country, making westward travel and shipping much faster and easier.

B. Settlers and the Railroad

The railroad attracted settlers to the Great Plains. To encourage railroad companies to lay track across the country, state and federal governments granted them millions of acres of land. Eager both to sell these lands and to create future customers for rail service, the companies made all-out efforts to attract settlers. They opened land bureaus, sent agents to the East Coast and Europe, offered easy credit and free transportation out west to potential purchasers, and promised land buyers that the railroads would transport their future crops to market inexpensively. The railroads wielded great economic and social influence over western development. Their pressure for quick payment from land buyers pushed western farmers into concentrating on producing a single cash crop, such as wheat or corn, which made them very vulnerable to price fluctuations on the world market.

C. Homesteaders on the Great Plains

Settlers also were attracted to the Great Plains by the Homestead Act, which provided a free 160-acre farm to anyone who would live on and improve it over a five-year period. This offer was especially attractive to immigrants from western and northern Europe, where land was extremely expensive. Some 400,000 families registered claims under the Homestead Act between 1862 and 1900, although there were flaws in the provisions and implementation of the law that allowed the most valuable western land to end up in the hands of the railroads, land speculators, lumber companies, and big ranchers.

D. New Farms, New Markets

Railroads, improved farm machinery, soaring eastern demand for food, and improved milling techniques all led to the development of 2.5 million new farms and the doubling of American agricultural production between 1870 and 1900. Starting a new farm on the Great Plains was a risky business. Most settlers had to go heavily into debt to acquire horses, machinery, and seed even if they obtained free land. To meet debt payments to railroads and banks, farmers specialized in growing cash crops, which made them vulnerable to world market conditions and dependent on the railroads to reach the markets. Uncertain rainfall and severe weather conditions added to the farmers' problems.

E. Building a Society and Achieving Statehood

The difficulties of living in crude frontier conditions—sod houses, backbreaking labor, isolated surroundings, storms, and extremes of heat and cold—drove out many early settlers. Within a decade, however, most of those who stuck it out had built decent wood houses. "Civilized" communities with churches, schools, lyceums, libraries, and social clubs began to emerge. Residents drew up state constitutions, and one after another Kansas, Nevada, Nebraska, and Colorado entered the Union in the 1860s and 1870s. Most of the northern portions of the Great Plains achieved statehood in the late 1880s and 1890s. With the entrance to the Union of Oklahoma, Arizona, and New Mexico early in the twentieth century, the trans-Mississippi West completed its transition from frontier territories to statehood. Although most western governments were conservative, they did lead the eastern states in granting women's suffrage. By 1910 Idaho, Wyoming, Utah, and Colorado women had full voting rights.

F. The Grange

When prices of wheat and other agricultural products dropped in the 1870s, debt-burdened farmers fell on hard times. They responded by forming the first nationwide agricultural organization, the Patrons of Husbandry, or Grange, led by Oliver H. Kelley. The Grange tried to help farmers economically by organizing cooperatives to market their crops and buy supplies. It also lobbied state legislatures to regulate the railroads, which were overcharging farmers, giving discounts to large shippers, and bribing state officials. A number of states did pass "Granger Laws," but they were bitterly attacked by the railroads as unconstitutional. At first federal courts upheld state regulation, but in the *Wabash* case (1886) the Supreme Court ruled that states could not regulate interstate railroads. Congress stepped into the void by passing the Interstate Commerce Act (ICA) (1887), which created the Interstate Commerce Commission (ICC) to investigate and oversee railroad practices. The ICA did little to curb railroad abuses, but the law and the ICC set a precedent for future federal regulation of interstate commerce. The failure of the Granger Laws and the Grange's other efforts to help farmers economically led to the organization's decline after 1878.

G. The Southwestern Frontier

After the Mexican War, American ranchers and settlers in the Southwest took over the territorial governments and forced most of the Spanish-speaking population off the land. The Mexican minority tended to become low-paid day laborers who faced discrimination and periodic violent attacks. The large numbers of Mexicans in the region nonetheless gave the Southwest a strongly Spanish cultural and linguistic coloration.

III. Exploiting the West

A. The Mining Frontier

Starting with the California gold rush in 1849, a series of mining booms swept the West. In the 1850s gold rushes took place in the Sierra Nevada and in British Columbia. New gold and silver strikes followed in Nevada, Colorado, Idaho, Montana, Wyoming, South Dakota, and the Alaskan Klondike. Each new discovery brought a rush of eager prospectors who believed in the get-rich-quick myth of the West. Infamous boomtowns such as Virginia City, Nevada, sprang up and then declined into ghost towns when the mines were depleted. Although a few individual prospectors with picks, shovels, and strainers did make their fortunes, most barely earned a living. The real profits from the mining frontier went to large mining companies backed by European and eastern capital. They had the expensive equipment necessary to mine the gold and silver deposits deep underground.

B. Cowboys and the Cattle Frontier

Confinement of the Plains Indians on reservations, extension of the railroad into Kansas, and the construction of new stockyards at railheads such as Abilene made possible the open-range cattle industry. Railroad promoters enticed thousands of people to enter the business by predicting great profits. For a time open-range ranchers did make fortunes, although this was not true for the ordinary cowboys who tended the cattle on the long drives to the railheads. Most cowboys were poorly paid young men, about one-fifth of them black or Mexican. The open-range cattle bonanza reached its peak in the years 1880–1885. Thereafter the industry declined rapidly because of overgrazing, fencing of the open range by farmers, and freezing winters in 1885 and 1886 that killed 90 percent of the steers in some regions. The open range and great cattle drives disappeared, to be replaced by smaller, fenced-in ranches that were close to one of the many rail lines serving the West by the 1890s.

C. Bonanza Farms on the Plains

Believing that enormous profits could be made in large-scale wheat growing, speculators in the late 1870s and 1880s established ten-thousand-acre farms and invested heavily in the latest equipment. For a while these bonanza farms did reap handsome profits, but overproduction, poor weather conditions, and falling wheat prices sent most of the enterprises into bankruptcy by 1890.

D. The Oklahoma Land Rush

The federal government initially set aside Oklahoma as a reservation for various Indian tribes, but as pressure from land-hungry farmers mounted, the government reconsidered. In 1889 Congress opened some 2 million acres in the heart of the Indian Territory to white settlers. Within weeks Oklahoma pioneers filed six thousand homestead claims, and in the following years, under the provisions of the Dawes Act, more and more Oklahoma land passed into the hands of whites.

IV. The West of Life and Legend

A. The American Adam and the Dime-Novel Hero

In the 1860s and 1870s eastern dime-novel writers created the western novel, with its frontiersman hero who fought Indians and "bad guys" and rescued maidens. One of the novelists, Ned Buntline, made Buffalo Bill so famous that his real-life model, William F. "Buffalo Bill" Cody, cashed in on the fame by founding a Wild West touring show that became extremely popular.

B. Revitalizing the Frontier Legend

The dime novels and Wild West shows caught the fancy of three young members of the eastern elite: Theodore Roosevelt, Frederic Remington, and Owen Wister. The three visited the West and made it the subject of their histories, art, and novels. In doing so they fostered the frontier legend of the West as a testing ground in which the fittest and best survived and as the home of the cowboy, who embodied the essence of manly virtue.

C. Beginning a Conservation Movement

The frontier legend aroused limited public interest in protecting some of the West's natural beauty and wonders. Also, in response to the work of John Wesley Powell, Henry D. Washburn, George Perkins Marsh, and John Muir, the nation created its first national parks (Yellowstone and Yosemite), and Muir founded the first organization dedicated to conservation, the Sierra Club.

V. Conclusion

In the 1890s, as the untamed West vanished, historian Frederick Jackson Turner advanced his thesis that American self-reliance, inventiveness, individualism, and freedom had been nurtured by the frontier experience. While most modern historians reject Turner's "frontier thesis," they do acknowledge the important role of the West and its resources in "influencing our thinking about society, government, and ourselves."

VOCABULARY

The following terms are used in Chapter 17. To understand the chapter fully, it is important that you know what each of them means.

entrepreneur   one who owns, launches, manages, and assumes the risks of a business venture

cede   to hand over land or valuable rights, usually by treaty

severalty   the legal situation in which property, such as land, is held or owned by separate or individual right, as opposed to collective ownership

polygamy   the practice of having several spouses at one time

lobby   to seek to influence legislators' votes for or against a bill; many groups hire persons called lobbyists to do this for them

indigenous   native to a region or to the original population of an area

bonanza   a rich mass of ore, as in mining; a sudden find of wealth

subsidize   to give governmental aid to a private business to encourage its development

cavalier   disdainful, dismissive, showing superiority toward others

IDENTIFICATIONS

After reading Chapter 17, you should be able to identify and explain the historical significance of each of the following:

John M. Chivington and the Sand Creek Massacre

Fetterman Massacre

Great Sioux Reserve

Sitting Bull

George Armstrong Custer

Chief Joseph

Chief Dull Knife

Carlisle Indian School

Helen Hunt Jackson, *A Century of Dishonor*

Dawes Severalty Act, 1887

Wovoka, the Ghost Dance, and Wounded Knee

Pacific Railroad Act, 1862

Homestead Act, 1862

Timber Culture, Desert Land, and Timber and Stone acts, 1870s

the Grange and the Granger Laws

Wabash v. *Illinois*, 1886

Interstate Commerce Act, 1887

Henry Comstock and the Comstock Lode

Joseph G. McCoy and the cattle frontier

Oklahoma "sooners"

Frederick Jackson Turner's "frontier thesis"

Ned Buntline and William F. "Buffalo Bill" Cody

John Wesley Powell, Henry D. Washburn, George Perkins Marsh, John Muir, and the birth of the conservation movement

SKILL BUILDING: MAPS

1. On the outline map of the Great Plains and the Far West, identify each state and indicate the decade in which it entered the Union.

2. Each of the following places was significant in the history of the frontier West. Locate each and explain its importance.

    100th meridian

    Sierra Nevada

    Rocky Mountains

    Virginia City, Nevada

    Denver, Colorado

    Missouri River and Great Sioux Reserve

    Indian Territory (Oklahoma)

    Black Hills, South Dakota

    Little Big Horn, Montana

    Wounded Knee, South Dakota

    Abilene, Kansas

    Chisholm Trail

    Promontory Point (near Ogden, Utah)

    Colorado River

    Yellowstone National Park

    Yosemite National Park

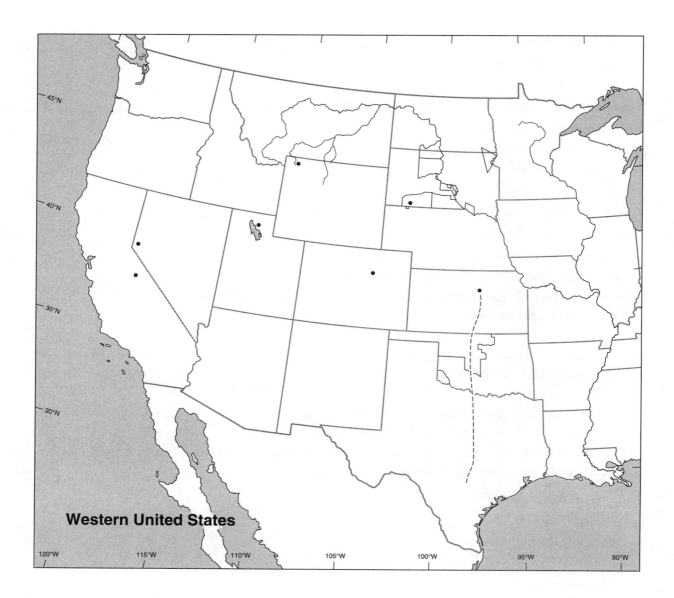

Western United States

HISTORICAL SOURCES

Historians try to discover not only what life was like for different groups of people living in the past but also what those people believed, valued, and perceived. Unless we know these things, it is difficult to understand motivation, to answer the question, Why did people do what they did?

In Chapter 17 the author uses popular novels published in the last forty years of the nineteenth century to shed some light on beliefs, values, and perceptions. Some examples are Edward L. Wheeler, *Deadwood Dick* (1877), cited on pages 559–560; and Ned Buntline, *Buffalo Bill, King of the Border Men* (1869), cited on pages 562–563. What do each of these popular novels try to convey to the reader? Why are popular novels good historical sources? How can we know whether their readers shared the values and perceptions of their authors?

While these novels may be historical sources, they have little lasting literary merit. In Chapter 17 the author also uses the works of more gifted writers and artists as historical sources. Hamlin Garland wrote vivid stories about farm life on the Great Plains. On page 554 the author refers to two of Garland's books. What do *Son of the Middle Border* and *Main-Travelled Roads* illustrate? Page 557 refers to a book by Mark Twain, one of the best nineteenth-century writers, and page 563 discusses the paintings and sculptures of Frederic Remington, the fine western artist. How does the author use the work of Twain and Remington? What is illustrated in each case? Look at some reproductions of Remington paintings and sculptures of cowboys and Indians. Do you see the same message in them as the author does in Chapter 17?

Look at "A Place in Time: Like-a-Fishhook." How does this capsule history of the Hidatsas illustrate the generalizations made in Chapter 17 about Plains Indian culture and the adjustments forced on Indians?

MULTIPLE-CHOICE QUESTIONS

Circle the letter of the item that best completes each statement or answers the question.

1. Most Great Plains Indians in the mid-nineteenth century
   a. lived in semipermanent villages and did some farming.
   b. lived in nuclear family units and seldom saw others beyond their immediate relatives.
   c. hunted the migratory buffalo herds and utilized the animals' meat, hides, and bones.
   d. adjusted quickly to reservation life because they were used to living in tribal communities.

2. Custer's Last Stand occurred during an army campaign aimed at
   a. suppressing the Ghost Dance.
   b. forcing the Sioux to settle at government agencies and give up the Black Hills.
   c. forcing Dull Knife and his northern Cheyennes to return to their reservation in Wyoming.
   d. capturing Chief Joseph and his fleeing band of Nez Percés.

3. The Dawes Severalty Act
   a. was opposed by Helen Hunt Jackson and other eastern friends of the Indians.
   b. gave each tribe legal title to its reservation land.
   c. attempted to preserve Indian culture once the Indians were no longer a military threat.
   d. benefited land-hungry whites much more than it did Indians.

4. Which of the following statements about the Homestead Act is *incorrect?*
   a. It attracted many immigrants from Northern and Western Europe to the Great Plains.
   b. Because of this law, the great majority of federal government land on the Great Plains went to pioneering family farmers.
   c. The law provided 160-acre farms to anyone who would live on the land for five years and improve it.
   d. Because of flaws in the law and its enforcement, much of the best land went to speculators and railroads.

5. In the latter half of the nineteenth century, the federal government attempted to confine all Plains Indian tribes on two big reservations located in
   a. Texas and Arizona.
   b. California and Oregon.
   c. Nebraska and Kansas.
   d. Oklahoma and South Dakota.

6. In the case of *Wabash* v. *Illinois*, the Supreme Court ruled that
   a. states could regulate railroads and other businesses serving the public so as to protect public safety.
   b. the federal government could not interfere in businesses operating wholly or partly in a particular state.
   c. states could not regulate interstate railroad rates.
   d. the Interstate Commerce Act was unconstitutional.

7. Although the new state governments in the West were generally conservative, the one area in which they were ahead of the eastern states was in
   a. granting women suffrage.
   b. ending all discrimination on the basis of race.
   c. enacting legislation against prostitution.
   d. desegregating public education.

8. Whose campaign to protect the wilderness led to establishing Yosemite National Park and the founding of the Sierra Club?
   a. Joseph G. McCoy
   b. Hamlin Garland
   c. Owen Wister
   d. John Muir

9. The days of the open range and great cattle drives came to an end after 1886 for all of the following reasons *except*
   a. overgrazing and crowding of the range.
   b. severe winters and dry summers in 1885 and 1886.
   c. a decline in the demand for beef.
   d. expansion of the railroads throughout the West.

10. He was the Indian leader who helped defeat Custer at the Little Big Horn, traveled with Buffalo Bill's Wild West show, and was killed in 1890 by reservation agents trying to suppress the Ghost Dance.
    a. Chief Joseph
    b. Chief Dull Knife
    c. Goodbird
    d. Sitting Bull

SHORT-ANSWER QUESTIONS

1. What was the Grange? What did it attempt to do for farmers? Did it succeed? Why or why not?

2. Discuss early state and federal efforts to regulate railroads. Why were they ineffective?

3. What happened to the Hispanic population of the Southwest after 1848?

4. What was Frederick Jackson Turner's "frontier thesis"? How do today's historians regard it?

5. Discuss the beginnings of the conservation movement. Who were some of its early advocates? What were their motives?

ESSAY QUESTIONS

1. One historian has written a book about the Plains Indians in the period 1840–1900 titled *The Long Death*. Drawing on the material in Chapter 17, explain why this is an appropriate title. Include in your discussion the impact of the slaughter of the buffalo, the reservation policy, the Dawes Act, and the attempts of government and reformers to "civilize" and assimilate the Indians.

2. The railroads, more than any other agency, stimulated settlement of the Great Plains and shaped the pattern of development there. Discuss this statement, explaining why and how railroads helped shape the West.

3. The myth of the frontier celebrated the economic opportunities that the West offered to everyone. Judging from the material in Chapter 17, how much truth was there in that myth? (Cite as much specific evidence as possible.)

4. Compare and contrast the picture of cowboys and their lives in the West as presented in Chapter 17, Owen Wister's novel *The Virginian*, and the dime novels of writers such as Ned Buntline.

5. "Unlike earlier westward expansion, almost every aspect of the settlement of the final frontier was influenced by the transformation occurring within American industry and the American economy." Explain and illustrate this statement with material about the development of farming, mining, and cattle raising found in Chapter 17.

18

The Rise of Industrial America

OUTLINE AND SUMMARY

I. The Character of Industrial Change

A. Railroad Innovations

By 1900 the United States had more rail miles tying the country together than did all of Europe. Building this extensive railroad system opened a vast internal market to American industry. The railroad companies also led the way in developing financial and managerial practices that made large-scale corporate enterprise possible, such as the sale of stock to raise needed capital. Railroad management innovations became the model for other businesses trying to sell products in a national market.

B. Creativity, Cooperation, and Competition

A group of innovative and unscrupulous railroad entrepreneurs, including Collis P. Huntington, Jay Gould, and James J. Hill, bought out their smaller competitors one by one. By the 1890s they had established great trunk lines that controlled most of the track. These integrated lines, with their standardized equipment and track gauge, carried goods all over the country much more efficiently than had been done formerly. The railroad companies also abused their powers. They cheated investors by watering their stock, bribed politicians with free passes and other favors, and gave rebates and kickbacks to big shippers while overcharging small businesses and farmers.

Suffering from these railroad abuses, small shippers demanded legislation to curb the unfair practices. In the 1870s many midwestern states outlawed rate discrimination, and in 1887 Congress passed the Interstate Commerce Act, which established the Interstate Commerce Commission (ICC) to investigate complaints and unreasonable rates. The legislation proved ineffective for several reasons, among them federal court decisions, which nearly always sided with the railroads.

In the early twentieth century, under the guidance of investment bankers, railroad consolidation proceeded still further. By 1906 seven giant corporations controlled two-thirds of all the track. These companies had become the largest business enterprises in the world, pioneering new accounting and organizational methods and stimulating iron, steel, and other industries with their need for rails and engines.

C. Applying the Lessons of the Railroads to Steel

Andrew Carnegie's career illustrates the close connection between railroad expansion and the growth of heavy industry. Carnegie's best customers were the railroad companies. From his early experiences working in the railroad industry, he learned the organizational, accounting, and managerial innovations that he later applied to his steel business. He also copied the railroad practice of consolidating smaller enterprises into fewer and fewer huge companies. Carnegie integrated his business both vertically and horizontally. When J. P. Morgan's Federal Steel and Carnegie Steel combined in 1901 to form U.S. Steel, it was the world's first corporation capitalized at over $1 billion.

D. Consolidating the Industrial Order

By 1900 the consolidation process that had placed the railroad and steel businesses in the hands of a few corporate giants had also taken place in the oil, sugar, meat-packing, and many other industries. In the oil-refining business, John D. Rockefeller led the way toward consolidation. His Standard Oil Company, like Carnegie Steel, was quick to adopt the latest technology. He advertised heavily, made deals with the railroads to get special shipping discounts, engaged in deception and aggression to ruin competitors, and created the first trust to extinguish all competition in oil refining.

The growth of trusts and monopolies in one industry after another led to public pressure for government intervention. In 1890 Congress passed the Sherman Anti-Trust Act, which outlawed all contracts and consolidations that were in restraint of trade in interstate commerce. The law proved ineffective in stopping the growth of trusts because it was vaguely worded, presidents rarely brought suits against companies under it, and the Supreme Court in the *E. C. Knight* case interpreted the meaning of interstate commerce so narrowly as to prevent the law's use against manufacturing corporations. In fact, between 1897 and 1903, large-scale consolidations in industry accelerated.

E. The Triumph of Technology

The invention and patenting of new machines in the period 1860–1900 also brought about the growth of huge corporations. For example, Alexander Graham Bell's invention of the telephone in 1876 gave rise to Bell Telephone, which by 1900 had installed some 800,000 phones in the United States. Thomas A. Edison, with the founding of his Menlo Park laboratory, perfected the light bulb and invented the phonograph, microphone, motion-picture camera, and over a thousand other items. These men proved that new inventions could be the foundation of profitable big business.

F. Mass Production, Mass Marketing

Aggressive marketing and advertising were effective in expanding sales and beating out competitors in the late nineteenth century. Procter and Gamble, American Tobacco, and Pillsbury Flour all built huge demand for their products this way.

G. Industrialization: Costs and Benefits

By 1900 the chaos of thousands of small companies competing for the national market had been replaced by an economy dominated by a small number of enormous corporations offering a dazzling array of new products. The price of these accomplishments was the crushing of thousands of small- and medium-sized businesses, the exploitation of millions of workers, and the fouling of the environment.

II. The New South

A. Obstacles to Southern Economic Development

The South industrialized more slowly than the North and until 1900 lagged far behind it. The reasons for this included the destruction of the South's credit system by the Civil War and its subsequent shortage of capital. Other factors were federal government policies that hurt the South economically, such as high protective tariffs, and the South's poor educational facilities and high rate of illiteracy.

B. The New South Creed and Southern Industrialization

In the 1870s southern newspaper editors, planters, and businessmen began to preach the "New South Creed"—the region must industrialize. Eager to attract northern capital, southern states offered tax exemptions for new businesses that would locate there. They also held industrial fairs, leased convicts from state prisons as cheap labor, and practically gave away land, forests, and mineral rights to northern corporations. Northern lumber syndicates cut down the forests of Alabama, Louisiana, and other southern states, making lumber production soar. Iron and steel production expanded dramatically around Birmingham, Alabama.

C. The Southern Mill Economy

Southern industry developed in its own distinctive pattern. Unlike the North, where factories were usually in or near urban areas, southern textile mills opened in the countryside, and towns and villages were created around them. Most of the textile mills were located in the Piedmont region of Virginia, the Carolinas, Georgia, and Alabama. The southern mills combined northern technical expertise with southern rural paternalism. They recruited workers from the poor white farm population of the Piedmont, hiring whole families, including many women and children. The owners, despite substantial profits, paid the laborers 30 percent to 50 percent less than New England mills did. The textile companies dominated life in the mill towns they started. They provided their employees with housing, stores, schools, and churches. Because the mills underpaid their workers and overcharged for rent and supplies, the employees often fell into debt to the companies, just as sharecroppers were indebted to their landlords and credit-merchants.

D. The Southern Industrial Lag

Despite impressive advances, southern industrialization occurred on a smaller scale and at a slower pace than in the North. Furthermore, the southern economy remained essentially in a colonial status, owned largely by northern firms. U.S. Steel, for example, controlled the foundries in Birmingham.

III. Industrial Work and the Work Force

A. From Workshop to Factory

As the number of industrial workers in the United States climbed from 885,000 to 3.2 million by 1900 and the trend toward large-scale, increasingly mechanized production speeded up, the nature of work changed markedly. There were fewer artisans, and the remaining skilled workers had less control over their work and derived less satisfaction from it. Factories hired more low-skilled, low-paid women and children to do jobs that had become simple, machine-paced, repetitive, and boring.

B. The Hardships of Industrial Labor

Already by the 1880s almost one-third of the labor force in the steel and railroad industries were unskilled workers. Common laborers drifted from city to city and from industry to industry, working for wages that were one-third of those paid to skilled artisans. In the expanding factories and on railroads, workers were exposed to a variety of industrially induced diseases, such as black and brown lung. They also had appallingly frequent accidents resulting in permanent disability or death. The excessive hours of work and the presence of many child laborers contributed to the high rate of industrial accidents. Employers rarely paid compensation to injured workers and opposed passage of state health and safety codes.

C. Immigrant Labor

More and more, immigrants filled the least skilled, lowest-paid, dirtiest, and most dangerous jobs in the expanding mines, factories, and railroads. Impoverished French Canadians crossed the border to work in the New England textile mills; the Chinese constructed railroads and mined ore in the West. If immigrant workers stayed healthy, they often lived better than they had in their homelands. They even saved small amounts of money. Although most of the immigrants worked very hard, they did not adjust easily to the fast pace and monotony of factory work. As much as possible, they resisted management's attempts to tighten factory discipline and increase production quotas. When worker resentment boiled over in response to wage cuts and speed-ups, they struck and often became violent.

D. Women and Work in Industrializing America

Since women could be paid even less than men and could do unskilled industrial jobs just as well, management hired more and more women. Married, working-class women and their children often spent hours finishing garments, rolling cigars, and performing other labor for manufacturers in their tenement apartments. Young, single women readily took jobs in factories because they preferred them to domestic service, almost the only alternative for uneducated females. Immigrant parents regularly sent their daughters into the mills and factories to supplement inadequate family incomes. By 1900 women made up 17 percent of the labor force. In the late nineteenth and early twentieth centuries, women also began to enter clerical positions. Office work paid better and offered more prestige than factory jobs, but women clerical workers had almost no chance of moving up to managerial positions.

Despite the increase in female wage earners, women's work outside the home was viewed as temporary. A woman's career was that of housewife and mother.

E. Hard Work and the Gospel of Success

Newspapers and magazines preached the gospel that, for male workers, America was the land of opportunity and hard work led to success. The papers were filled with rags-to-riches stories of poor immigrant boys such as Andrew Carnegie who rose to become heads of major corporations. In fact, Carnegie was the exception. Ninety-five percent of executives of big corporations came from middle- and upper-class families. There was some opportunity, however, for skilled workers to move into ownership and management of small businesses. For unskilled immigrant laborers, there was less mobility. At best they moved from unskilled to semiskilled or skilled industrial jobs, and they remained in the working class. A huge gulf existed between the rich and poor. By 1890 America's richest families, the top 10 percent, owned 73 percent of the country's wealth. At the other extreme, better than 50 percent of all industrial laborers earned incomes that placed them below the poverty line.

IV. Labor Unions and Industrial Conflict

A. Organizing the Workers

In response to the unfavorable changes that rapid industrialization was forcing upon them, workers turned to labor unions. In 1866 William H. Sylvis recruited workers from several trades into the National Labor Union. As it declined in membership in the 1870s, it was overshadowed by the Knights of Labor, led by Terence V. Powderly. The Knights called for advanced social and economic reforms, including equal pay for men and women; abolition of child labor; inclusion of black workers in unions; a graduated income tax; and cooperative ownership of factories, mines, and other businesses. Despite its egalitarian ideals, the Knights and other labor groups favored immigration restriction. Labor opposition to the Chinese, whom they accused of working so cheaply that they undercut native-born workers, was especially strong. The federal government responded to anti-Chinese sentiment by passing the Chinese Exclusion Act in 1882. When the Knights won a series of strikes in the 1880s, workers rushed to join, swelling its membership to 700,000. In the late 1880s, however, the Knights suffered setbacks: it lost several big strikes, its craft unions broke away to form a separate American Federation of Labor, and its membership declined to 100,000.

The AFL, led by Samuel Gompers, did not attempt to organize unskilled workers, and it dropped the far-reaching social-reform goals of the National Labor Union and the Knights. Instead, the AFL concentrated on winning short-term improvements in wages and hours for its skilled members. The AFL grew, but by 1900 less than 5 percent of America's workers belonged to it or any other union. The development of unions was seriously impeded by splits in the labor force between skilled artisans and common laborers, religious and ethnic divisions, and differences among labor leaders concerning goals and tactics.

B. Strikes and Labor Violence

Between 1881 and 1905 almost thirty-seven thousand strikes took place, involving nearly seven million workers. In many of these, violence erupted as strikers attacked employers' property and the scab laborers hired to replace them. Some of the biggest and most violent confrontations were the railroad strikes of 1877, the eight-hour strikes of 1886, the Haymarket Square bombing (for which four anarchists were unjustly convicted and executed), the Homestead steel strike, and the Pullman strike.

To combat labor unrest, employers forced workers to sign yellow-dog contracts and hired their own private police forces. Because of the violence, the public regarded strikers as dangerous radicals. The federal government intervened repeatedly on the side of management, using the army to quell disturbances and injunctions to order union members back to work. When injunctions were disobeyed, union officers like Eugene Debs, leader of the Pullman strike, were thrown in jail. As a result of employer, public, and government hostility, strikes almost always failed and unions languished.

C. Social Thinkers Probe for Alternatives

The growing extremes of poverty and wealth and the violent clashes between labor and management troubled middle-class Americans. A number of social commentators tried to explain these developments and put forward their own solutions. Conservative Social Darwinists, like Andrew Carnegie and William Graham Sumner, believed that labor's misery was an inevitable product of the constant struggle for survival that weeded out all but the fittest. They opposed any government interference with the workings of these natural laws. On the other hand, Lester F. Ward, Henry George, and Edward Bellamy attributed the social problems to a man-made economic system that placed private property and unrestrained profit seeking above all else. They called, respectively, for government regulation, tax reform, and a cooperative commonwealth. Tiny socialist and anarchist groups preached that only the overthrow of the capitalists and the government that protected them would make possible a just and humane society.

V. Conclusion

Industrialization had brought great benefits to America: international power status, lower-cost goods, more jobs, and a tremendous array of new consumer products. But the price had been high. Shoddy business practices and polluted factory sites abounded. Much of the industrial work force lived in urban slums and grinding poverty. Exploited laborers periodically vented their rage and frustrations in violent outbursts and strikes. Middle-class Americans were ambivalent about the new industrial order. They wanted to keep the benefits but somehow alleviate the accompanying social evils.

VOCABULARY

The following terms are used in Chapter 18. To understand the chapter fully, it is important that you know what each of them means.

"watering" stock   issuing stock certificates far in excess of the value of a corporation's assets; stock in a company that has overissued in this manner is called "watered stock"

rebate   a return of part of an original amount paid for some service or merchandise

pool   an agreement among formerly competing companies to set uniform prices and divide the business among themselves according to a predetermined formula; the purpose is to maximize profits by ending competition

vertical integration   organization of a single corporation to control all stages of manufacturing, from obtaining raw materials to marketing the finished product

horizontal integration   organization of a single corporation, through consolidation measures, to gain broad control over all manufacturing of a particular product

postbellum   after the war; usually meaning after the Civil War

"bread-and-butter" unionism   (also trade unionism "pure and simple") the union practice of concentrating on issues of immediate concern to its members, such as reducing hours and raising wages, rather than promoting broad social reforms

yellow-dog contract   an agreement that employers forced employees to sign swearing that they would not join unions or strike

anarchist   a person who advocates the overthrow of all established governments and of capitalist economic institutions

injunction   a court order requiring a person to do or not do a particular thing

laissez faire   the doctrine that government should intervene as little as possible in economic affairs, such as regulating business

---

IDENTIFICATIONS

After reading Chapter 18, you should be able to identify and explain the historical significance of each of the following:

Jay Gould

Interstate Commerce Act and Interstate Commerce Commission, 1887

J. Pierpont Morgan

Andrew Carnegie

John D. Rockefeller and Standard Oil

Sherman Anti-Trust Act, 1890

United States v. *E. C. Knight Co.*

Thomas A. Edison

Henry W. Grady and the "New South Creed"

William H. Sylvis and the National Labor Union

Terence V. Powderly and the Knights of Labor

Mother Jones

Chinese Exclusion Act, 1882

Samuel Gompers and the American Federation of Labor

railroad strikes of 1877

Haymarket Square bombing, 1886

Homestead strike, 1892

Pullman strike, 1894

Eugene Debs

William Graham Sumner and conservative Social Darwinism

Lester Frank Ward

Henry George, *Progress and Poverty*

Edward Bellamy, *Looking Backward*

Marxist socialists

SKILL BUILDING: MAPS

Locate each of the following sites and explain why each was important in the rise of industrial America from 1860 to 1900:

Pittsburgh, Pennsylvania

Homestead, Pennsylvania

Mesabi range, Minnesota

Titusville, Pennsylvania

Birmingham, Alabama

Piedmont region of Virginia, the Carolinas, Georgia, and Alabama

Cincinnati, Ohio

Chicago, Illinois

Pullman, Illinois

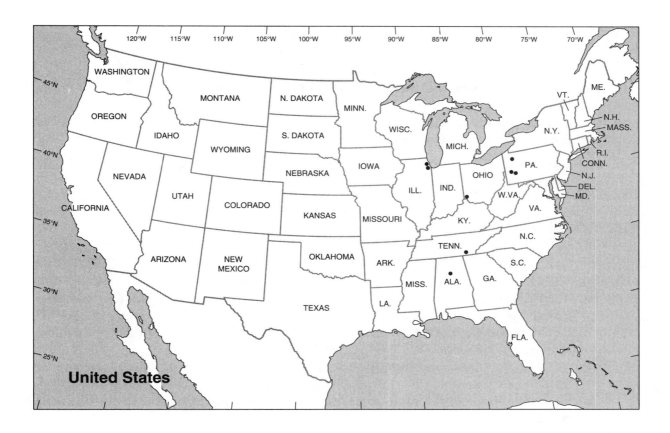

United States

MULTIPLE-CHOICE QUESTIONS

Circle the letter of the item that best completes each statement or answers the question.

1. Rapid industrial development in the United States between 1860 and 1900
   a. increased the demand for and importance of skilled artisans.
   b. produced by 1900 an economy dominated by enormous corporations.
   c. increased the opportunities by 1900 for small- and medium-sized companies to succeed.
   d. reduced by 1900 the use of women and child laborers in mines and mills.

2. Why did the South's industrialization lag behind the North's?
   a. The post-Civil War South lacked capital and technically trained personnel.
   b. Southern industry paid higher wages than northern factories and therefore could not compete effectively with northern plants.
   c. The South had almost no natural resources and not enough people to supply the necessary industrial labor force.
   d. The South clung to its agrarian tradition and rejected the building of factories and mills.

3. The Interstate Commerce Act
   a. outlawed trusts and monopolies in manufacturing in interstate commerce.
   b. was effective in stopping railroad abuses of small shippers.
   c. stopped the trend toward a few giant companies' controlling most of the economy.
   d. created the Interstate Commerce Commission but left enforcement of the law to the federal courts, which seldom upheld ICC rulings.

4. The first U.S. corporation capitalized at over $1 billion and created by merging more than two hundred companies was
   a. Standard Oil.
   b. Union Pacific.
   c. U.S. Steel.
   d. American Telephone and Telegraph.

5. The Supreme Court in *United States* v. *E. C. Knight Company*
   a. diminished the effectiveness of the Sherman Anti-Trust Act by ruling that manufacturing was not interstate commerce.
   b. declared the Granger Laws unconstitutional because states could not regulate interstate commerce.
   c. ruled that all trusts and monopolies in interstate commerce are illegal and can be broken up by the federal government.
   d. held that employers could force employees to sign and abide by yellow-dog contracts.

6. The New South Creed preached the need for the South to
   a. industrialize.
   b. combat racial prejudice.
   c. promote the interests of agriculture ahead of those of industry.
   d. bring its wage scale up to that prevailing in the North.

7. Studies of top managers in large corporations in the late nineteenth century show that
   a. the majority of them rose from the ranks of skilled workers.
   b. the majority of them started out as poor but ambitious immigrant boys like Andrew Carnegie.
   c. the great majority of them came from middle- and upper-class families.
   d. women were beginning to make their way into executive positions.

8. Which of the following explains why unions did not have much success in the nineteenth century?
   a. Workers had little interest in joining unions because their real wages were rising and their conditions improving.
   b. Most workers did not remain in the working class permanently but quickly went on to become self-employed farmers or small businessmen.
   c. Labor and management saw eye-to-eye on most issues, and as a result there was little need for unions.
   d. Public, employer, and government hostility toward unions as well as divisions within the labor force impeded union growth.

9. Which of the following people argued that poverty was *not* the result of unchangeable natural laws and could be eliminated by government intervention and social planning?
    a. William Graham Sumner
    b. Lester Frank Ward
    c. Andrew Carnegie
    d. John D. Rockefeller

10. In the Pullman strike
    a. the federal government used an injunction and troops against workers and threw the union leaders in jail.
    b. the state of Illinois tried eight anarchists for throwing a bomb, found them guilty, and executed four of them.
    c. workers walked out to protest conditions at Carnegie's steel mills but eventually returned to work without gaining any improvements.
    d. the Knights of Labor led railroad workers in demands for an eight-hour day and finally won this concession from the railroads.

SHORT-ANSWER QUESTIONS

1. Explain how the building of the nation's railroad network stimulated American industrialization and the growth of large corporations.

2. Discuss government attempts to stop the growth of trusts and monopolies in the late nineteenth century. Why were these efforts ineffective?

3. Explain the actions Andrew Carnegie and Henry Clay Frick took at Homestead to crush unionism in the steel industry.

4. How were the objectives of the American Federation of Labor different from those of the earlier National Labor Union and Knights of Labor?

5. What was the theme of Horatio Alger's novels? How realistic were these books in terms of late-nineteenth-century American experience?

6. Explain what a conservative Social Darwinist would believe that government should do about poverty and exploitation of labor. How would the Social Darwinist justify such recommendations?

ESSAY QUESTIONS

1. Discuss the reasons for rapid industrial expansion and the growth of huge corporations between 1860 and 1900. What were some of the benefits the American people reaped from these developments? What were some of the social and economic costs or problems produced by industrialization and the growth of big business?

2. Discuss the impact on labor of industrial development in the post–Civil War period. In your answer include the effects on skilled, unskilled, southern, immigrant, and women workers.

3. Discuss the contemporary intellectual response to late-nineteenth-century industrialism and the social problems that accompanied it. Be sure to include in your answer the ideas of the conservative Social Darwinists, such as William G. Sumner, and their opponents, including Lester F. Ward, Henry George, and Edward Bellamy.

4. Discuss the industrialization of the South in the post–Civil War period. Why did the South lag behind the North? How much had the South's industry grown by 1900? In what ways was southern industrial development different from that in the North? Why?

5. Between 1881 and 1905, there were almost thirty-seven thousand strikes, and workers made numerous attempts to unionize. Yet by 1900 less than 5 percent of the labor force belonged to any union, and workers lost most strikes. What obstacles stood in the way of unionization and successful strikes?

19

The Transformation of Urban America

OUTLINE AND SUMMARY

I. Introduction

In the post–Civil War years, the United States experienced rapid urbanization. By 1900 New York, Chicago, and Philadelphia each had more than 1 million inhabitants, and 40 percent of all Americans lived in cities. Because they offered work and other opportunities, cities attracted thousands from the surrounding rural districts and most of the 11 million immigrants who arrived in this nation between 1870 and 1900. The runaway population growth swamped municipal services and facilities, and terrible housing and sanitary conditions developed. The physical deterioration, ethnic diversity, and social instability alarmed native-born reformers who tried to clean up cities and quickly "Americanize" the often resistant immigrants.

II. Urban Expansion

A. *The New Urban World*

Urbanization changed people's way of life. Small-town residents knew each other and usually shared a common heritage and similar traditions and values. The city bristled with activity, anonymity, and heterogeneity. City industry or industries also polluted the urban environment and surrounding lands and waterways.

B. *A Revolution in Transportation*

Advances in transportation—first horse-drawn streetcars, later regional steam railroads and electric trolleys—transformed cities. The "walking" city of the early 1800s was compact, with the wealthy living near the commercial center and the poor occupying basements scattered around town. As new transportation facilities made it possible to commute to work, upper- and middle-class residents moved outward along the streetcar lines to more desirable neighborhoods, while the poor remained behind in subdivided homes abandoned by the affluent. The commercial centers became busy shopping areas easily accessible to all.

C. A Mobile Population

In search of better homes and jobs, the working, middle, and upper classes moved frequently from place to place within the same city and from one metropolis to another.

D. Migrants and Immigrants

In the post–Civil War years thousands of young people, especially women, moved from farms to cities to find employment. Also between 1860 and 1890 some 10 million Northern European immigrants, mostly German, English, and Irish, settled in East Coast and midwestern cities. In the late nineteenth century, these "old immigrants" were joined by the "new immigrants" from Southern and Eastern Europe—Italians, Slavs, Greeks, and Jews–as well as Armenians from the Middle East. Faster and cheaper steamship travel facilitated the immigrants' arrival. By 1890 the foreign-born and their children accounted for four-fifths of the population of Greater New York. Most who disembarked on the East Coast came through the immigration reception centers at Castle Garden (1855–1891) or Ellis Island (1892 on) in New York. German and Scandinavian newcomers, bringing a little capital with them, tended to migrate to midwestern cities and to farms on the prairies beyond. Italians and Irish, usually without cash, took the first jobs they found in eastern cities.

E. Adjusting to an Urban Society

To ease their adjustment, immigrants clustered together in ethnic neighborhoods where they could speak their native language, buy their traditional foods, and celebrate traditional holidays with compatriots and even persons from the same village or district. Though rich in cultural, social, and institutional life, these ethnic enclaves were horribly overcrowded and provided miserable slum housing. The various immigrant groups improved their social and economic status at different rates. The Irish came in such great numbers that they were able to dominate the Democratic party and Catholic church leadership in New York and Boston, where they accounted for 16 percent and 17 percent of the population, respectively. Nationality groups that had high rates of remigration, such as Italians and Chinese, experienced slower upward mobility and assimilation. By the end of the nineteenth century, resentment of the newcomers, from whatever country, was growing.

F. Slums and Ghettos

Neighborhoods deteriorated into slums as landlords packed more and more people into their buildings. The poorer the residents, the greater the crowding and the faster the area's decline. Ethnic slum neighborhoods became ghettos when discrimination and law kept members of the minority group, whether racial or immigrant, from obtaining housing elsewhere, even if they had the money to do so. For example, black ghettos grew in Chicago and Philadelphia, Mexican in Los Angeles, and Chinese in San Francisco. In slums and ghettos, disease, death, and crime rates soared. Middle-class Americans, even reformers who wanted to clean up the slums, tended to blame the deplorable conditions on the residents rather than the socioeconomic forces that oppressed minorities.

G. Fashionable Avenues and Suburbs

In contrast to the slums, grand millionaires' mansions lined Fifth Avenue in New York, Commonwealth Avenue in Boston, Lake Shore Drive in Chicago, and fashionable boulevards in other cities. The wealthy and the middle class also moved to newer, more desirable suburbs on the edges of the old, compact cities. Thus, American cities became increasingly segregated along class as well as ethnic and racial lines.

III. The Urban Challenge

A. Policing the City

Urbanization inevitably brought increased crime. Many cities established professional police forces in the 1830s and 1840s and authorized them to carry clubs and revolvers in the 1850s. The police sometimes fought with immigrant gangs but generally did not enforce state laws curbing gambling, saloons, prostitution, and Sunday business operations in ethnic neighborhoods where the social customs ran counter to such moralistic legislation. The 1894 Lexow investigation in New York discovered that, in exchange for regular payoffs, officers winked at these activities. At least a portion of the bribes ended up in the hands of political bosses who hired and fired the police. Reformers demanded that appointment and supervision of law-enforcement officers be turned over to nonpartisan police commissioners, which was starting to happen by the 1890s.

B. Governing the City

Urban political machines, headed by powerful political bosses, emerged to govern the unwieldy cities with their many competing interests. The machines awarded contracts and franchises to favored businessmen in return for payoffs and gathered the votes of poor immigrants by providing them with relief, legal help, and city jobs. Some bosses, such as Cincinnati's George B. Cox, were relatively honest, whereas others, such as New York's William Marcy Tweed, were grossly corrupt and greedy. By the late nineteenth century middle- and upper-class good-government reformers ("goo-goos") had begun their drives against the bosses.

C. Battling Poverty

Middle-class reformers also set out to relieve poverty. They often tended to blame the problem on character flaws of the poor and "self-destructive" cultural practices of the immigrants. Therefore, reformers concentrated on moral uplift and Americanization campaigns among the needy. Typical were Robert M. Hartley's New York Association for Improving the Condition of the Poor (AICP) and Charles Loring Brace's New York Children's Aid Society. Hartley's organization sent visitors to slum dwellers' homes to urge sobriety, hard work, and responsibility on them. The AICP also called for pure milk laws, public baths, and improved housing. Brace founded dormitories, reading rooms, and workshops for indigent boys and sent thousands of them to live with and work for families in the Midwest. In addition, the Young Men's and Young Women's Christian associations offered rural young people arriving in the cities temporary housing, recreation, and moral strictures against alcohol and other vices.

D. New Approaches to Social Work

By the 1880s the Salvation Army and Josephine Shaw Lowell's Charity Organization Society (COS) had joined the fight against poverty. Lowell's group preached a tough-minded approach to charity, insisting that the needy must meet the standards of responsibility and morality set by the COS's "friendly visitors" to receive aid. Critics charged, with some justification, that the COS was more interested in "controlling the poor than in alleviating their suffering."

E. The Moral-Purity Campaign

Middle- and upper-class reformers attacked what they considered urban vice. Crusaders such as Anthony Comstock and Charles Parkhurst demanded that city officials close down gambling dens, saloons, and brothels and censor obscene publications. In 1894 the nonpartisan Committee of Seventy elected a New York City mayor committed to moral purification, but within three years the effort failed, and the more tolerant political machine was back in power.

F. The Social Gospel

The Social Gospel movement developed in the 1870s and 1880s among a small group of Protestant clergymen. Founded by Washington Gladden, a Congregational minister, the movement preached that urban poverty was caused in part by actions of the rich and well-born and "that true Christianity commits men and women to fight social injustice head on, wherever it exists." Walter Rauschenbusch, a Baptist pastor in New York's "Hell's Kitchen" slums, made the clearest statement of the movement's philosophy in his 1907 book *Christianity and the Social Crisis*.

G. The Settlement-House Movement

Like the Social Gospel ministers, the settlement-house founders blamed poverty not on the poor but on social and environmental causes. Settlement-house leaders, such as Jane Addams and Ellen Gates Starr, believed that middle-class relief workers must reside among the immigrant masses and learn what services they needed by firsthand experience. At Hull House, for example, Addams and Starr ran a day-care nursery, gave legal and health aid, helped find employment, and offered classes in English and other subjects for their immigrant Chicago neighbors. Settlement-house workers also published studies of the terrible housing and sanitation they encountered, and they lobbied legislators for improved services and corrective laws. By 1895 more than fifty settlement houses in various cities were training a generation of young college students, many of whom would become state and local government officials applying the lessons they had learned.

IV. Reshaping the Urban Environment

A. Parks and Public Spaces

Whereas Social Gospelers and settlement-house workers tried to solve the problems of the urban poor, landscape artists such as Frederick Law Olmsted and architects such as Calvert

Vaux attempted to improve the quality of city life by designing and constructing spacious parks as "tranquil country refuge[s] within the city."

B. Boston's Back Bay

The kind of urban planning and design advocated by Olmsted and many other architects was carried out in Boston's Back Bay development between 1857 and 1900.

C. Rebuilding Chicago

The 1871 Chicago fire that destroyed the city's commercial center gave architects, engineers, and businessmen the chance to pioneer in new urban design as they rebuilt. The greatest innovation developed by Louis Sullivan and others was the skyscraper. It was soon imitated in other cities. The changes in Boston and Chicago and the exhibits at the 1893 Chicago Columbian Exposition stimulated the growth of the city-beautiful movement. Municipal art societies, park associations, and civic-improvement leagues strove to grace their cities with imposing civic buildings; sparkling fountains; outdoor sculptures; and landscaped parks, squares, and roadways. Like the followers of architect Richard Morris Hunt, they believed that attractive urban areas would produce better citizens and reduce social disorder. In the early twentieth century the city-beautiful movement evolved into the new field of city planning.

D. Toward a Metropolitan America

Cities slowly began to develop the centralized administrative structures and managerial tools that their large, diverse populations and great size required. Armed with centralized administrative powers, municipal officials in the late nineteenth century built adequate city-wide sewer and water systems that finally brought an end to the cholera, typhoid, and other epidemics that had plagued urban America. In the course of centralization, many cities incorporated surrounding lands or annexed adjacent municipalities. The joining of Brooklyn, Queens, Staten Island, the Bronx, and Manhattan into Greater New York in 1898 represents the biggest of these consolidations.

V. Conclusion

The unprecedented growth of cities between the time of the Civil War and 1900 forced millions of Americans—old, urban upper and middle classes; newly arrived rural migrants; and old and new immigrants—to make tremendous adjustments. The cities often became arenas for class and ethnic conflict over issues such as temperance, moral uplift, the role of the political machine and boss, and the causes and cures for urban poverty. By 1900, however, new conceptions of the services and responsibilities that municipal government had to undertake to make the metropolis livable were beginning to crystalize. In the coming progressive era, this enlarged vision of government would slowly make its way into national politics.

VOCABULARY

The following terms are used in Chapter 19. To understand the chapter fully, it is important that you know what each of them means.

demographer one who studies vital and social statistics and trends concerning births, deaths, marriages, diseases, and population

exodus a going out; a departure or emigration, usually of a large group of people

compatriots fellow countrymen and countrywomen; persons from the same country

remigration the return of immigrants to their country of origin

ghetto any neighborhood or quarter in which a minority group is required to live by law or discrimination (originally, Jews in Venice, Italy)

patina a film or coloring on a surface—for example, the greenish coloring on old bronze produced by oxidation

tacitly not openly expressed or permitted but understood

symbiosis the living together of two organisms, with each dependent on the other—for example, the fungus and alga that together make up lichen

bombastic high-sounding; inflated (style of speech)

tycoon a businessman who has great wealth and power

IDENTIFICATIONS

After reading Chapter 19, you should be able to identify and explain the historical significance of each of the following:

Jacob Riis, *How the Other Half Lives*

"walking" cities

trolleys

"old immigrants"; and "new immigrants"

Castle Garden and Ellis Island

"dumbbell tenements"

Horatio Alger

political boss, machine, and ward captain

Tammany Hall

"Big Jim" Pendergast

William Marcy Tweed

Thomas Nast

"goo-goos"

Robert M. Hartley and the New York Association for Improving the Condition of the Poor

Charles Loring Brace and the Children's Aid Society

Josiah Strong, *Our Country*

Josephine Shaw Lowell and the Charity Organization Society

Anthony Comstock

Charles Parkhurst

Washington Gladden, Walter Rauschenbusch, and the Social Gospel

Jane Addams and Hull House

Florence Kelley

Frederick Law Olmsted and Calvert Vaux

Boston's Back Bay

city-beautiful movement

SKILL BUILDING: GRAPHS

After looking carefully at the line graph titled "The Changing Face of U.S. Immigration, 1865–1920" on page 608 of the textbook, you should be able to answer the following questions:

1. In which years did overall immigration to the United States exceed 1 million?

2. In which periods did overall immigration to the United States drop significantly? From your knowledge of American history, can you account for this? Were things happening in this country during those periods that might have discouraged immigrants from coming?

3. Where did the so-called old immigrants come from? During which years did this old immigration peak?

4. Where did the new immigrants come from? During which years did the new immigration peak? Did the numbers of new immigrants arriving during their peak years exceed the numbers of old immigrants arriving during their peak period?

5. During which years did Asian immigration to the United States hover close to zero? Can you account for this from your knowledge of American history?

Now look at the line graph "Immigration of Skilled and Unskilled Workers, 1860–1900" on page 611 of your text. Based on this graph, answer the following questions:

1. During the period 1860–1900, did the percentage of unskilled laborers arriving in the United States exceed the percentage of skilled workers? How do you account for this?

2. During the years 1860–1900, what was the overall trend for the proportion of unskilled laborers among immigrants? Based on your knowledge of American history during these years, explain why this trend may have occurred.

3. In the same period, did the proportion of skilled workers entering the United States show an overall trend or merely periodic dips and peaks?

4. Do the dips in percentage of unskilled laborers entering the United States seem to correspond to periods of economic depression in the U.S. economy?

HISTORICAL SOURCES

One historical source the author of this chapter used is letters that persons who immigrated to the United States wrote to friends and family. On pages 608–609 one such letter is quoted. What does the author wish to illustrate with these letters? Thousands of letters and transcripts of oral interviews of immigrants have been collected in archives of immigrant and ethnic history. The newest of these collections is being developed at Ellis Island, where the main building has been restored as an immigration museum.

Look at "A Place in Time: Immigrant Milwaukee in the 1890s." What does this capsule history demonstrate about the causes of conflict between immigrants and native-born city authorities?

The author of Chapter 19 also uses as historical evidence architects' and landscape artists' plans and buildings that were constructed in the late nineteenth century and are still standing. For example, on pages 623–624 the author cites Olmsted's and Vaux's original plan for Central Park; on pages 624–625 the author refers to the layout and major buildings found in Boston's Back Bay section; and on page 626 the Reliance Building, Masonic Temple, and other Chicago skyscrapers are used as evidence. In each case what conclusions does the historian draw about ideas, values, and technology prevalent in nineteenth-century America?

MULTIPLE-CHOICE QUESTIONS

Circle the letter of the item that best completes each statement or answers the question.

1. In the "walking" city of the early nineteenth century,
    a. the rich and poor lived in distinctly different neighborhoods.
    b. the wealthy lived near the commercial center.
    c. the poor lived near downtown, the wealthy at the outer edges of the city.
    d. few people owned their own homes.

2. An electric streetcar system was first developed in
    a. Richmond, Virginia.
    b. Chicago, Illinois.
    c. Denver, Colorado.
    d. New York, New York.

3. Which of the following statements about American cities between 1860 and 1900 is *incorrect?*
    a. Runaway growth of urban population swamped municipal services and facilities.
    b. Terrible housing and sanitary conditions developed in them.
    c. By 1900 the majority of the American people lived in them.
    d. Their neighborhoods became increasingly segregated along class, ethnic, and racial lines.

4. By 1890 the foreign-born and their children made up what portion of New York City's population?
    a. one-half
    b. one-third
    c. two-thirds
    d. four-fifths

5. Which of the following immigrant groups was made up mostly of poor peasants who settled heavily in northeastern cities and had a high rate of remigration?
    a. Germans
    b. Eastern European Jews
    c. Italians
    d. Armenians

6. The urban political machines and their political bosses
    a. were always Democrats, rather than Republicans, in the late nineteenth century.
    b. angered building contractors by having municipal construction done by city employees on a not-for-profit basis.
    c. dispensed city jobs, legal help, and relief to poor immigrants in exchange for their votes.
    d. were often controlled by the native-born, wealthy elite groups who secretly ran them.

7. Which of the following would be most likely to challenge the statement that moral deficiencies of the immigrant poor caused their poverty?
    a. Josephine Shaw Lowell and the Charity Organization Society
    b. William S. Rainsford and the Social Gospel ministers
    c. Josiah Strong in his book *Our Country*
    d. Robert M. Hartley and the Association for Improving the Condition of the Poor

8. Jane Addams and her coworkers at Hull House did all of the following *except*
    a. establish a day-care nursery for the children of working mothers.
    b. pressure Congress to restrict the flow of poor immigrants to the United States.
    c. pressure legislators to enforce sanitation regulations and pass laws protecting the urban poor.
    d. run classes, a laundry, an employment bureau, and recreation programs.

9. Which of the following people were most closely associated with designing parks as tranquil country refuges within the city?
    a. Frederick Law Olmsted and Calvert Vaux
    b. Richard Morris Hunt and John Wellborn Root
    c. Louis Sullivan and Richard Morris Hunt
    d. Thomas Nast and "Big Jim" Pendergast

10. The Lexow investigation found
    a. that the police permitted gamblers, prostitutes, and saloonkeepers to operate unmolested in poor immigrant neighborhoods in exchange for payoffs.
    b. that landlords permitted their dumbbell tenement buildings to become unsanitary, overcrowded firetraps.
    c. that blacks, Italians, Chinese, and other minorities were kept out of middle-class neighborhoods by restrictive real-estate covenants.
    d. that New York's inadequate sewage system contributed to recurrent outbreaks of typhoid and cholera.

SHORT-ANSWER QUESTIONS

1. Explain the reasons for conflict between immigrants and native-born reformers in the late nineteenth century.

2. What did Social Gospel ministers preach?

3. Explain how the approach to and attitudes toward the poor of Jane Addams and Hull House differed from those of Josephine Shaw Lowell and the Charity Organization Society.

4. In what ways did the settlement house movement prepare the way for progressive reform in the early twentieth century?

ESSAY QUESTIONS

1. Discuss the impact of transportation improvements in the nineteenth century on American cities. How did transportation changes affect who came to cities, where people lived in cities and suburbs, and where they worked and shopped?

2. Between 1870 and 1900 nearly 11 million immigrants entered the United States. Discuss who came, why they came, where they settled, how they fared, and the impact they had on urban America.

3. Discuss the rise of the urban political machines and bosses. Why did they emerge? What roles did they play? Who supported them and why? Who fought them and why?

4. Discuss the city-beautiful movement of the late nineteenth century. What was it? Who was behind it? What assumptions about the city and its peoples did it make? What precedents for the future did it create?

5. Discuss the varied responses of nineteenth-century middle-class reformers to urban ethnic diversity, poverty, and crime.

20

Daily Life, Popular Culture, and the Arts, 1860–1900

OUTLINE AND SUMMARY

I. Everyday Life in Flux

A. Rising Standards of Living

The rapid industrialization in the second half of the nineteenth century brought a rising standard of living to millions of Americans. Clothing mass-produced by factory sewing machines allowed great expansion in the wardrobes of the middle and working classes. Kellogg's and Post's breakfast cereals and a host of other commercially prepared foods transformed the national diet. By 1900 urban upper- and middle-class families enjoyed centrally heated homes that had electric lights, telephones, indoor plumbing, mechanical washing machines, and many other conveniences.

B. Bringing New Commodities to Rural and Small-Town America

In the 1870s and 1880s, Aaron Montgomery Ward and Richard Warren Sears published catalogs and established mail-order companies that acquainted rural Americans with urban middle-class fashions and sold, at modest prices, an array of consumer goods. Chain stores, such as F. W. Woolworth's and the A&P, also brought a variety of products to buyers at relatively low prices. While all these goods made life more comfortable for the upper and middle classes and raised their social status, many farm and working-class families could not afford to purchase the same quantity and quality of items, and thus the sense of difference between the haves and the have-nots widened.

C. A Shifting Class Structure

Industrialization and the growth of big business sharpened class distinctions. The number of unskilled workers increased, and a large gap in wages and self-identification opened between them and the skilled craftsmen. The middle class also expanded as national corporations required armies of trained white-collar, professional, and sales personnel. The middle class, with higher incomes and more job security than industrial laborers, achieved a lifestyle that allowed more socializing, planning ahead, buying of expensive possessions, and educating of their children. The rich industrialists and financiers flaunted their worth by building mansions in town and at summer resorts; purchasing racehorses, yachts, and art collections; traveling abroad; and endowing museums. By 1900 the class disparities were striking. Workers (about 44 percent of the population) possessed only 1.5 percent of the national wealth; the middle class (also about 44 percent) possessed 12.5 percent of the wealth; and the upper crust (about 12 percent) owned a whopping 86 percent of the national assets and income.

D. The Changing Family

The level of family income affected family size, life expectancy, infant mortality, and the relationship between parents and children. Overall between 1860 and 1900 Americans lived in nuclear families that had a decreasing birthrate and increasing life expectancy. But the class differences in these matters were substantial. For example, working-class families, needing their children's earnings to survive, had a higher birthrate than upper- and middle-class families. In Buffalo in 1900, laborers averaged 5.7 offspring; business owners and managers, 3.5. The smaller families of the upper and middle classes afforded women some free time and children more attention and education.

E. Working-Class Family Life

Because of their low incomes, working-class black and immigrant families had to rely on the help of children, women, and relatives to make ends meet. Thus the extended kinship network often replaced the nuclear family household. To supplement the breadwinner's earnings, families took in boarders, women took in laundry, and children went to work at ten to twelve years of age. The pooling of many family members' incomes sometimes made it possible for working-class families to buy homes and acquire possessions commonly owned by the middle class.

II. Middle-Class Society and Culture

A. Manners and Morals

The manners and morals of the middle class during much of the nineteenth century were influenced by the Victorian worldview. This outlook held that human society was on an upward course from barbarism to civilization and that progress could be ensured only by strenuous moral effort of the sort exercised by the upper and middle classes. Important virtues, in this view, included sobriety, industriousness, and self-restraint. Workers were told that if they emulated their betters, they would rise to more privileged positions. Victorian morality also stressed the civilizing importance of "culture": fine manners, uplifting literature and art, and classical music. In keeping with this, the wealthy founded and the middle ranks visited a network of cultural institutions, such as the New York Metropolitan Museum of Art and the Boston Museum of Fine Arts, in the 1870s. Displaying proper etiquette, appreciating culture, and exercising moral restraint became badges of status and heightened the visible distinctions between the middle and lower classes.

B. The Cult of Domesticity

Victorian morality assigned a special place to women. Whereas men tended to business and public affairs, women used the domestic sphere to provide the genteel, sensitive, and spiritual influences that moved society toward higher civilization. They decorated their homes as richly and artistically as their means permitted and fostered the family's sense of cultural appreciation. At no time, however, were all middle-class women satisfied with devoting their whole life to this cult of domesticity.

C. Department Stores and Hotels

Innovative entrepreneurs, such as Rowland H. Macy, John Wanamaker, and Marshall Field, developed urban department stores that appealed particularly to the Victorian outlook of the upper and middle echelons. These giant emporiums advertised high-quality goods at low cost and encouraged buyers to believe that owning the right material possessions contributed to civilized living. The department stores were designed to look like palaces, with marble staircases, sparkling chandeliers, and thick carpets, and the deferential sales staff made the upper- and middle-class shoppers feel that their status was being rightfully acknowledged. Grand hotels built in the late nineteenth century, such as New York's Waldorf Astoria and Chicago's Palmer House, also attracted affluent Victorians with "luxury, convenience, and service."

D. The Transformation of Higher Education

Higher education was still restricted to the upper and upper-middle classes. As late as 1900 only 4 percent of youths between eighteen and twenty-one years of age were enrolled in colleges or universities. Indeed, these institutions were seen as the training schools for the future business and professional elites. Wealthy capitalists, such as John D. Rockefeller and Leland Stanford, made large donations to already existing universities or started new ones. With private contributions and state support, more than 150 additional colleges and universities were founded between 1880 and 1900. In this period, the research university was developed and major reforms were instituted in medical and other professional training.

III. Working-Class Leisure in the Immigrant City

A. Streets, Saloons, and Boxing Matches

The neighborhood streets, especially in summer, served as the arena of social life and free entertainment for shop girls, laborers, and poor immigrant families. For workingmen the saloons offered male companionship, reinforcement of group identity, and centers for immigrant politics. One of the favorite spectator sports among workingmen was bare-knuckle prizefighting. In the 1880s and 1890s boxing began to attract a following among upper-class males as well.

B. The Rise of Professional Sports

Americans were the first to turn what had been a children's game into the professional sport of baseball. The earliest teams were the New York Knickerbockers and the Cincinnati Red Stockings. Team owners organized the National League in 1876, and by the 1890s baseball had become big business. It appealed to members of all social groups, particularly workers. Horse racing and boxing contests also drew spectators from all social levels. The most popular sports hero of the nineteenth century was heavyweight boxing champion John L. Sullivan.

C. Vaudeville, Amusement Parks, and Dance Halls

Vaudeville shows, amusement parks like New York's Coney Island, and dance halls were popular with working-class women as well as men.

D. Ragtime

Although the middle class preferred hymns or songs that carried a moral lesson, the masses became fans of ragtime, which originated with black musicians in the saloons and brothels of the South and Midwest. Ragtime's most famous composer, Scott Joplin, introduced this music at the 1893 Chicago Columbia Exposition, and Tin Pan Alley music publishers spread it to a national audience.

IV. Cultures in Conflict

A. The Genteel Tradition and Its Critics

In the 1870s and 1880s a group of upper-class writers and magazine editors, among them Charles Eliot Norton and E. L. Godkin, attempted to set standards for fine writing and art. They insisted that literature must avoid sexual allusions, vulgar slang, disrespect for Christianity, and depressing endings. High-toned journals like *The Century* and the *North American Review* upheld this genteel standard by banishing from their pages authors who violated these rules. Many emerging writers refused to fit into the mold. The works of regionalists like Sarah Orne Jewett, realists like William Dean Howells, and naturalists like Stephen Crane all violated the canons of the genteel tradition in one way or another. Mark Twain's *Adventures of Huckleberry Finn* (1884) and Theodore Dreiser's *Sister Carrie* (1900), among the best novels of the period, were both condemned by proponents of Victorian ideals.

Social scientists such as Thorstein Veblen and W. E. B. Du Bois criticized the business elite and challenged middle-class notions about the link between moral worth and economic standing. The depression and labor unrest of the 1890s further undermined the smug Victorian outlook and its genteel culture.

B. Modernism in Architecture and Painting

Some architects and artists began questioning Victorian ideals of beauty. Modernist architects William Holabird, John Wellborn Root, and Frank Lloyd Wright refused to copy European design. Rather, they looked to their vision of the future for inspiration and argued that a building's form should follow its function. Winslow Homer and Thomas Eakins rejected sentimentality in favor of tough realism in their paintings.

C. From Victorian Lady to New Woman

Although Frances Willard and her Woman's Christian Temperance Union (WCTU) did not openly challenge the cult of domesticity, they broadened the scope of women's social responsibilities. The WCTU, with a membership of 150,000 by 1890, became America's first mass organization of women. Through its crusade against liquor, women gained experience as lobbyists, organizers, and lecturers. Middle- and upper-class club women founded the General Federation of Women's Clubs in 1892 and were getting involved in social welfare projects and tenement reform by the end of the century. As more women pursued higher education—they accounted for more than one-third of all college students in 1900—they developed the self-confidence to break with the Victorian belief in women's separate sphere and went out to compete with men in the public arena. The so-called new woman broke Victorian restraints about dress and exercise, and the most advanced thinkers, such as Charlotte Perkins Gilman, advocated women's economic independence from men through work outside the home. Following Gilman's advice, a growing number of female college graduates entered journalism, social work, education, and other professional careers. However, the new-woman emphasis on economic and social independence and equality had little impact on the lives of working-class women.

D. Public Education as an Arena of Class Conflict

Starting in the 1870s middle-class reformers, such as federal commissioner of education William Torrey Harris, campaigned to expand public schools, bring them under central control, and make attendance mandatory. Harris viewed the public schools as instruments for indoctrinating the masses with middle-class values and outlook. By 1900, as a result of the work of education advocates, thirty-one states had passed laws requiring school attendance for all children from eight to fourteen years of age, the illiteracy rate had dropped significantly, and more than half a million students were attending some five thousand high schools. Centralized urban public-school systems, however, aroused opposition from various quarters. Poor immigrant parents, who needed the wages of their children to survive, objected to laws that kept youngsters in school beyond the elementary level. Catholics disliked the Protestant orientation of the public schools and organized their own parochial systems, and upper-class parents preferred to send their offspring to exclusive, private academies.

V. Conclusion

In the latter part of the nineteenth century, the upper and middle classes, with their genteel Victorian morality and ideals, were dismayed by the raucous, vibrant culture of the working masses. "Respectable" people periodically attempted to suppress "indecent" lower-class enjoyments such as gambling; gathering in dance halls, saloons, and amusement parks; and attending Sunday baseball games and bare-knuckle prizefights. However, Victorian standards of decency were weakening by the 1890s as they came under attack from younger middle-class writers, artists, social scientists, and "new women," as well as the working and immigrant masses. By 1900 the two cultural traditions were reaching an accommodation that blended elements of both. National pastimes became highly commercialized, and the working-class amusements of the nineteenth century evolved into the mass culture of sports spectaculars, movies, and theme parks of modern America.

VOCABULARY

The following terms are used in Chapter 20. To understand the chapter fully, it is important that you know what each of them means.

armoire   a large movable cupboard with doors and shelves used to hold clothing

puddler   a skilled worker who converted pig iron into wrought iron by heating and stirring the molten metal and an oxidizing agent in a reverberatory furnace

nuclear family   a family made up of parents and their minor children (as opposed to *an extended family* or *a kinship network,* which includes grandparents, grown children and their spouses, aunts, uncles, cousins, and so on)

fertility rate   the average number of children born to females between fourteen and forty-five years of age

surrogate   one appointed to act for another; a substitute for another

certitudes   certainties; things you are sure of

effeteness   the condition of having lost vigor or energy; being worn-out or unable to produce

patrician   an aristocrat; aristocratic, noble; befitting an aristocrat or noble

hyperbole   obvious exaggeration for effect

prototype   the original or model from which other things are formed

mores   customs of central importance accepted without question and embodying the fundamental moral views of a group, people, or social class

ethos   dominant assumptions of a people or period; the fundamental spiritual characteristics of a culture

caustic   sarcastic, sharp, biting

platitudes   flat, dull, or trite remarks, especially uttered as if they were fresh and profound

IDENTIFICATIONS

After reading Chapter 20, you should be able to identify and explain the historical significance of each of the following:

John Harvey Kellogg and Charles W. Post

Aaron Montgomery Ward and Richard Warren Sears

F. W. Woolworth

Victorian morality

Henry Ward Beecher

Catharine Beecher, *The American Woman's Home*

cult of domesticity and "the woman's sphere"

Rowland H. Macy, John Wanamaker, and Marshall Field

Charles W. Eliot

Andrew D. White

New York Knickerbockers and Cincinnati Red Stockings

John L. Sullivan

Scott Joplin and ragtime

the new woman

Charles Eliot Norton, Richard Watson Gilder, E. L. Godkin, and genteel culture

Henry James

Mark Twain (Samuel Langhorne Clemens)

Sarah Orne Jewett and the regionalists

Stephen Crane and the naturalists

Theodore Dreiser, *Sister Carrie*

Thorstein Veblen, *The Theory of the Leisure Class*

Frank Lloyd Wright

Winslow Homer, Thomas Eakins, and Albert Pinkham Ryder

Frances Willard and the Woman's Christian Temperance Union

Charlotte Perkins Gilman, *Women and Economics*

"Gibson girls"

Kate Chopin, *The Awakening*

William Torrey Harris

Creoles, Cajuns, Storyville, and Dixieland jazz

HISTORICAL SOURCES

In Chapter 20 the author has used the records of business corporations, among other sources, as historical evidence. For instance, on page 635 a Campbell's soup jingle of the late nineteenth century is quoted. On pages 635–636 Montgomery Ward's and Sears catalogs from the 1890s are described, and a customer's letter to Montgomery Ward's is quoted. How does the historian use this evidence?

In the section on "The Changing Family," the historian turns to data from the federal census. A census has been taken every ten years since the adoption of the Constitution. Originally the census takers simply counted people to facilitate reapportioning of seats in the House of Representatives as population grew and shifted. Recently the census takers have asked many more questions and have gathered much valuable demographic information. Using those data, however, can prove tricky. Why does the author say on page 638 that "historians are cautious in their use of aggregate federal census statistics" from the late nineteenth century? What does the author use the data to illustrate?

Look at "A Place in Time: New Orleans in the 1890s." How does this description of the city's musical culture fit the theme of this chapter about conflicts between middle- and upper-class white genteel culture and working-class and black popular culture? In what ways was New Orleans unique among American cities? In what respects did it mirror the racial and class tensions of the period 1860–1900? In what ways did New Orleans's culture anticipate twentieth-century American trends?

MULTIPLE-CHOICE QUESTIONS

Circle the letter of the item that best completes each statement or answers the question.

1. The overall impact of industrialization on American life in the late nineteenth century was
    a. to reduce the gulf between the standard of living of the rich and the poor.
    b. to make class distinctions less apparent.
    c. to improve the standard of living for many families.
    d. to drive fine-quality goods off the market in favor of mass-produced, shoddy products.

2. Which of the following correctly states income distribution in late-nineteenth-century America?
    a. The middle class was the largest one, controlling more than 50 percent of national wealth.
    b. The working class made up more than 40 percent of the nation but controlled only 1.5 percent of its wealth.
    c. The upper-class elite controlled about 20 percent of the country's wealth.
    d. The wealth was almost evenly divided among classes, with the upper, middle, and working classes each controlling roughly one-third of the national income.

3. Which of the following statements about American families between 1860 and 1900 is correct?
    a. Working-class families generally had fewer children than upper- and middle-class families.
    b. Blacks and immigrants were more likely to live in nuclear families; the upper and middle classes formed extended kinship networks.
    c. Immigrant working-class families expected children to go to work by age ten or twelve, and all members of the family contributed to its support.
    d. Birth control was unknown, and all families continued to have seven or eight children on average.

4. In the late nineteenth century, middle- and upper-class Americans generally frowned on
    a. flaunting their wealth by wearing expensive clothes and lavishly decorating their homes.
    b. women from good families going outside their homes to shop in downtown department stores.
    c. people of good reputation frequenting the grand hotels in cities such as New York, Chicago, and San Francisco.
    d. saloons, vaudeville, and ragtime as immoral, low class, and vulgar.

5. Between 1860 and 1900 all of the following advances in education occurred *except*
   a. the public schools banned physical punishment of children and deemphasized discipline.
   b. the research university developed, and improved training was given to medical and other professional students.
   c. the number of high schools and students attending them rose.
   d. the illiteracy rate fell for persons older than ten years of age.

6. "Prairie-school" houses featuring low silhouettes and rejecting the bulk and clutter of the typical Victorian home were the creation of
   a. John L. Sullivan.
   b. Thomas Eakins.
   c. Andrew D. White.
   d. Frank Lloyd Wright.

7. A member of the working class in the late nineteenth century would have been most likely to read
   a. *The Nation.*
   b. *The Century.*
   c. *Atlantic Monthly.*
   d. *The National Police Gazette.*

8. Who coined the term *conspicuous consumption* to describe the excessive materialism and flaunting of wealth of America's captains of industry?
   a. Mark Twain
   b. Annie MacLean
   c. Thorstein Veblen
   d. W. E. B. Du Bois

9. A good example of naturalism in American fiction is found in
   a. Stephen Crane's *Maggie: A Girl of the Streets.*
   b. Henry James's *The Bostonians.*
   c. Catharine Beecher's *The American Woman's Home.*
   d. Charlotte Perkins Gilman's *Women and Economics.*

10. Compulsory attendance at urban public schools of the late nineteenth century was fought by
    a. Catholic immigrants because of the Protestant orientation of the public schools.
    b. poor working-class families who needed to send youngsters over age ten to work.
    c. upper-class parents who did not want their children mingling with the immigrant masses.
    d. all of the above.

SHORT-ANSWER QUESTIONS

1. Explain the roles of Aaron Montgomery Ward and Richard Warren Sears in marketing products and shaping tastes in rural and small-town America.

2. How did department stores in the period 1860 to 1900 try to appeal to consumers, especially women?

3. Why did Theodore Dreiser's *Sister Carrie* shock guardians of genteel culture in the Victorian age?

4. Describe the changes that took place in American higher education between 1860 and 1900.

5. How did the middle and upper classes in the Victorian period explain why they were more economically successful than the working class?

ESSAY QUESTIONS

1. Discuss the effects of industrialization and the growth of big corporations on the American standard of living and class structure and distinctions in the period 1860–1900.

2. Compare and contrast the patterns and attitudes of immigrant and black working-class families with those of white middle- and upper-class families in the period 1860–1900.

3. Explain the Victorian genteel tradition in the arts. Discuss the writers, painters, architects, and social scientists who broke with it in the late nineteenth century.

4. Discuss the Victorian view of the role of women. How did the so-called new woman of the late nineteenth century challenge the Victorian ideal? Which women were the most affected by the new-woman patterns? Which were least affected by the changes?

5. In the conclusion to Chapter 20, the author writes that in the 1890s, "middle- and upper-class Americans battled against what they deemed 'indecent' lower-class behavior," yet "the . . . frequently denounced working-class culture of the late-nineteenth-century immigrant city can be seen, in retrospect, as nothing less than the fertile seedbed of twentieth-century mass culture." Explain what the author means by this statement, and illustrate your answer with as many specific examples as possible.

21

Politics and Expansion in an Industrializing Age

OUTLINE AND SUMMARY

I. Introduction

From 1877 to 1896 national politics largely ignored the social problems arising from industrialization. This happened in part because the business leaders influential in both political parties preached the doctrine of laissez-faire as far as government regulation was concerned, although they were happy to receive federal subsidies and tariff protection. Rather than tackling substantive issues, politicians spent most of their time fighting over the spoils of office. Meanwhile, agrarian discontent grew and reached a climax in the 1890s with the Populist party and the election of 1896, which was the first election in years to see opposing candidates who truly differed on political-economic policies. In the late 1890s, with domestic problems still unresolved, the nation turned much of its attention to imperialist expansion.

II. Party Politics in an Era of Social and Economic Upheaval

A. *Patterns of Party Strength*

Politics in the period 1870–1900 was a male world, with women neither voting nor holding office. Male voter turnouts were high, and the two political parties—Democratic and Republican—were closely matched in strength. The main Democratic support came from the solid South, states that bordered the South, and recent immigrants in the big cities. The Republicans generally won the votes of rural and small-town New England, Pennsylvania, and the upper Midwest and of native-born businessmen, professionals, and white-collar workers.

B. *The Stakes of Politics*

Tariffs, the currency supply, and benefits for Civil War veterans were the main issues addressed in late-nineteenth-century national politics.

C. The Hayes White House: Virtue Restored

Rutherford B. Hayes's main accomplishments were to restore reasonable honesty to the presidency and to win respect for it after the Grant scandals.

D. Regulating the Money Supply

The nation split on the questions of how much money the government should issue and what should back it. Bankers, creditors, most businessmen, economists, and politicians all believed that, to maintain economic stability and avoid inflation, the money supply must be limited to that which the government could back with its holdings of gold. Debt-ridden southern and western farmers and some manufacturers wanted a larger money supply, including retention of the unbacked Civil War currency (greenbacks), issue of notes backed by silver and gold, and the minting of silver coins. They believed this larger money supply would raise falling farm prices and make it easier to pay off debts. In the 1870s the Greenback party tried to further this program. Even after the party's demise, debtor groups continued to demand a larger money supply and got a little help from the 1890 Sherman Silver Purchase Act.

E. The Spoils System

The spoils system had operated since the days of Andrew Jackson. A group of reformers, including Carl Schurz, E. L. Godkin, and Josephine Shaw Lowell, saw its defects and in 1881 founded the National Civil Service Reform League.

F. Civil-Service Reform

After a crazed job seeker assassinated President James A. Garfield, the civil-service reformers were finally able to convince Congress in 1883 to pass the Pendleton Act. It created a civil-service commission to prepare competitive examinations for federal jobs, and it prohibited politicians from asking government employees for campaign contributions. Gradually it began to raise the honesty and competence of the federal bureaucracy.

III. Politics of Privilege, Politics of Exclusion

A. 1884: Cleveland Victorious

In 1884 the Republicans nominated James G. Blaine, who was tainted by the corruption of the Grant era and was identified with the spoils system. When the Democrats chose Grover Cleveland, who had a reputation for fighting the spoilsmen, a number of Republican civil-service reformers bolted their party to support him. This Mugwump switch helped Cleveland win the presidency.

B. Tariffs and Pensions

Cleveland, a believer in laissez-faire, had little understanding of the social problems caused by industrialization. He did, however, attempt to lower the tariff, arguing that reduced rates would remove a potentially corrupting government surplus of funds, reduce prices for consumers, and slow the growth of trusts. Lower tariffs appealed to farmers and many

Democrats from the West and South but alarmed manufacturers and those Republican politicians who looked out for their interests. Cleveland also angered Civil War veterans when he halted wholesale granting of disability pensions to them.

C. 1888: Big Business and the GAR Strike Back

The tariff became a major issue in the election of 1888. The Democrats renominated Cleveland; the Republicans chose Benjamin Harrison and stood behind high protective tariffs. Industrialists contributed heavily to the Republicans. Although Cleveland received more popular votes than Harrison, he lost in the electoral college. In 1890 the victorious Republicans passed the McKinley Tariff, raising rates to an all-time high. They also rewarded Civil War veterans with generous pensions.

D. Southern and Western Farmers Organize

Farmers believed that the federal government was unresponsive to their needs. Western and southern farmers suffered from falling agricultural prices, a tight money supply, and high interest rates. They were heavily in debt and were overcharged by industrial trusts, grain elevator operators, and railroads. Earlier, farmers had turned to the Grange and the Greenback party to redress their grievances. When these failed, farmers joined the Southern, National Colored Farmers', and Northwestern alliances. The alliances called for tariff reduction, a graduated income tax, public ownership of railroads, and "free silver," among other things. In 1892 the alliances founded the People's or Populist party and wrote a platform based on their program. They also endorsed direct election of senators and other electoral reforms and nominated James B. Weaver for president.

E. African-Americans After Reconstruction

After Reconstruction white Democrats in the South increasingly deprived black southerners of the right to vote. At first the whites used intimidation and terror, but after 1890 they found even more effective means in poll taxes, literacy tests, and grandfather clauses. Southern blacks also were victimized by segregation laws, the convict-lease system, and lynching. Some southern Populists attempted to combat prejudice and encourage white and black farmers to unite against their exploiters, but the southern Democratic elite purposely inflamed racial antagonism to keep poor farmers divided.

The federal government did nothing to protect black rights. The Supreme Court gave its stamp of approval to segregated but equal facilities in *Plessy* v. *Ferguson* (1896). It also upheld poll taxes and literacy tests (1898).

Blacks responded to these abuses in several ways. Some fled the South only to find de facto discrimination in the North. Booker T. Washington advised fellow blacks to accept their second-class status for a time and concentrate on getting ahead economically and educationally. The old abolitionist Frederick Douglass still called on blacks to demand full equality. With the disfranchisement of blacks and the defeat of southern populism, the South became a one-party region, always controlled by the Democrats.

IV. The 1890s: Politics in a Depression Decade

A. 1892: Populists Challenge the Status Quo

In 1892 the Democratic candidate, Grover Cleveland, regained the presidency from the incumbent Republican, Benjamin Harrison. Populist James B. Weaver received more than a million votes, but few of them came from the urban Northeast. The Populists also gained less than one-quarter of the votes of the agricultural South, largely because of the race issue.

B. The Panic of 1893: Capitalism in Crisis

Soon after Cleveland was inaugurated, the nation suffered a financial panic that ushered in a severe depression.

C. The Depression of 1893–1897

During the depression thousands of banks and businesses failed; between 20 percent and 25 percent of the labor force was unemployed; and agricultural prices fell more than 20 percent, completing the ruin of many farmers already in economic difficulty. Hard times increased the appeal of the Populists and spawned strikes and protests. In 1894 Jacob Coxey led a march of the unemployed on Washington to demand a public-works program to create jobs. He was arrested, and the demonstration was broken up. The heightened unrest frightened the middle class.

D. Conservatives Hunker Down

Cleveland, in keeping with laissez-faire doctrine, opposed government help for victims of the depression. His use of force against the Pullman strikers and Coxey's marchers appeared heartless. He angered farmers when, in defense of the gold standard, he induced Congress to repeal the Sherman Silver Purchase Act. Cleveland's actions split his party, as Democrats from agricultural states began to favor free silver. Hard times also led many Americans to question the laissez-faire doctrine.

V. The Watershed Election of 1896

A. 1894: Protest Grows Louder

The voters repudiated Cleveland in the 1894 midterm elections. Congress went Republican, and the vote for Populist candidates climbed more than 40 percent above their 1892 tallies.

B. The Silver Issue

The issue of free silver came to symbolize the deep split between economic classes. Creditors feared that abandonment of a strictly gold standard would cause runaway inflation and ruin. Debt-ridden farmers saw silver as the panacea that would raise farm prices and return prosperity.

C. Silver Advocates Capture the Democratic Party

At the 1896 Democratic convention, western and southern delegates gained control, wrote a platform calling for free silver, and nominated silver advocate William Jennings Bryan. The Republicans nominated William McKinley, who promised to maintain the gold standard and raise the protective tariff. The Populists, though not completely satisfied with the Democratic platform, feared that if they ran their own candidate, they would split the farm vote, ensuring the election of McKinley. The Populists, therefore, endorsed Bryan but nominated one of their own, Tom Watson, for vice president.

D. 1896: Conservatism Triumphant

McKinley received huge campaign contributions from businessmen who feared Bryan. Besides having less money, Bryan was handicapped by the lack of appeal of free silver to factory workers and the urban middle class. They realized that it would probably bring about higher food prices. McKinley won the election, carrying the Northeast, Midwest, and most cities. His party also kept its majority in Congress. As promised, McKinley and the Republicans maintained the gold standard and raised the tariff to an all-time high. These policies aroused little opposition, however, because prosperity returned, more gold became available with new discoveries, and farm prices began to rise. McKinley easily beat Bryan for a second term in the election of 1900. Indeed, the elections of 1894 and 1896 ushered in a long period of Republican dominance in American politics that lasted almost unbroken until the 1930s. The Populist party disintegrated after 1896, but many of the reforms it had advocated were enacted by progressives after 1900.

VI. Expansionist Stirrings and War with Spain

A. Roots of Expansionist Sentiment

In the late nineteenth century the United States showed heightened interest in overseas empire. The example of European nations and Japan, which were seizing colonies in Asia and Africa, stimulated U.S. expansionism. During the depression of 1893–1897 American businessmen and politicians argued that the United States must capture overseas markets to maintain prosperity. Inspired by Alfred T. Mahan's *The Influence of Sea Power upon History*, Republican politicians—including Theodore Roosevelt, Henry Cabot Lodge, and John Hay—claimed that, to be a great power, the United States must build up its navy and obtain far-flung colonies in which to establish fueling stations and bases. Combining religion and racism, Josiah Strong's *Our Country* (1885) told Americans that, as members of the superior Anglo-Saxon race, they were destined to spread Christianity and civilization to "inferior" peoples.

B. Pacific Expansion

Expansionist enthusiasm led the United States to establish a joint protectorate with Germany and Great Britain over the Samoan Islands and to annex Hawaii in 1898.

C. Crisis over Cuba

The Cubans revolted against Spanish rule in 1895, and the Spanish authorities brutally attempted to suppress the rebellion. Public opinion in the United States turned against the Spanish as William Randolph Hearst's *Journal* and Joseph Pulitzer's *World,* using yellow-journalistic sensationalism, featured daily accounts of atrocities. President McKinley did not want to intervene, but he sent the battleship *Maine* to Havana to protect the lives and property of Americans on the island. On February 15, 1898, an explosion on the *Maine* killed 266 of its crewmen. The yellow press immediately accused the Spanish of blowing up the ship, and the public demanded revenge. Bending to popular pressure, McKinley asked Congress to declare war on Spain, which it did in April 1898. It also passed the Teller Amendment proclaiming that the United States had no designs on Cuba and would leave the island as soon as its independence was ensured.

D. The Spanish-American War

The fighting against Spain lasted less than four months. On orders from Assistant Secretary of the Navy Theodore Roosevelt, Admiral George Dewey attacked the Spanish fleet in the Philippines and American troops took Manila. By July 1898 the Spanish were driven from Cuba. The defeated Spanish recognized Cuba's independence and ceded to the United States the Philippines, Puerto Rico, and Guam.

VII. Deepening Imperialist Ventures: The Philippines, China, Panama

A. The Platt Amendment

Contrary to the Teller Amendment, the United States occupied Cuba from 1898 to 1902, then withdrew its forces only after Cuba agreed to the conditions set forth in the 1901 Platt Amendment. This amendment limited Cuba's sovereignty by, among other things, reserving to the United States the right to intervene in Cuba and to maintain a naval base there. Although the Platt Amendment was abrogated in 1934, the United States still retains the base at Guantanamo Bay in Cuba.

B. Guerrilla War in the Philippines

President McKinley was persuaded that the United States should keep the Philippines by the arguments of the expansionists and the desire of businessmen to use the islands as a way of penetrating nearby Chinese markets. That American decision led to a war against Filipino independence fighters. To crush the guerrilla resistance of the Filipinos, the United States used brutal tactics and lost ten times as many soldiers as it had in the Spanish-American War. The United States ruled the Philippines until July 4, 1946, when it finally granted the country its independence.

C. Critics of Empire

Some Americans were horrified by their nation's actions in the Philippines. Among these people were civil-service reformers Carl Schurz and E. L. Godkin, agricultural spokesmen such as William Jennings Bryan, settlement-house founder Jane Addams, and writers and intellectuals such as Mark Twain and William James. They founded the Anti-Imperialist

League, which pointed out that imposing American rule on other peoples by military force violated the principles of human equality and liberty championed in our own Declaration of Independence.

D. The "Open Door": Competing for the China Market

American businessmen, who dreamed of penetrating the Chinese market, became alarmed at developments there. European powers and Japan were forcing the weak Chinese government to lease that country's ports to them—and then they closed those ports to trade and investment by businessmen of any country but their own. U.S. secretary of state John Hay attempted to aid American business by sending his 1899 Open Door notes to the nations involved, asking them to keep their leased Chinese ports open to trade and investment from all countries on equal terms. He received noncommittal replies. Soon thereafter the United States joined those countries in putting down a Chinese uprising against foreign imperialists known as the Boxer Rebellion. Some nations wanted to use the rebellion as an excuse for carving China up into colonies for themselves. Hay announced U.S. opposition to this plan in his 1900 Open Door notes. He asked all countries to respect the territorial integrity of China and repeated the demand for equal trading and investment opportunities there. The Open Door notes became a cornerstone of U.S. policy in Asia and helped shape this country's response to the Japanese drive to conquer China in the 1930s.

E. The Panama Canal: Hardball U.S. Diplomacy

For commercial and strategic reasons, the United States wanted to build a canal across the Isthmus of Panama. In 1902 the United States negotiated a treaty leasing a canal zone from Colombia, the country that owned the isthmus at the time. However, the Colombian senate, hoping for more money, rejected the treaty. An infuriated President Roosevelt conspired with directors of a bankrupt French company that had been trying earlier to build a canal and hoped to profit from the United States' taking over its land lease. Philippe Bunau-Varilla, an official of the company, fomented revolution in Panama, and Roosevelt sent an American warship in 1903 to see to it that the uprising succeeded. The United States then recognized Panama's independence and negotiated a treaty leasing the land, with Bunau-Varilla appointed to speak for Panama. The canal, a great engineering feat by the U.S. Army, opened in 1914, but the imperialistic methods Roosevelt used to seize the area created lasting ill will toward the United States in Latin America.

VIII. Conclusion

The burst of expansionism in the late nineteenth and early twentieth centuries never fully diverted U.S. attention from domestic issues. The Populist party, though it went down to defeat in 1896, left behind the feeling that government must free itself from business domination and play a more active role in solving the economic and social problems arising from industrialization. After the turn of the century, the progressive movement would build on that new attitude.

VOCABULARY

The following terms are used in Chapter 21. To understand the chapter fully, it is important that you know what each of them means.

disfranchisement   depriving persons of the right to vote

myriad   a great number of persons or things

bureaucracy   the body of officials administering the agencies or bureaus of government or other large organizations; excessive governmental or institutional red tape and routine

pliable   easily influenced

spoils system   the practice whereby the victorious political party rewards its supporters with appointments to government jobs, regardless of their qualifications for the positions

patronage   the control of appointments to public office or of other political favors

agrarian   rural, agricultural

lynch   to kill a person by mob action for some alleged offense without due process of law

caveat   warning or caution

de facto   in fact; in reality (as opposed to de jure: according to law or required by law)

reactionary   extremely conservative; favoring a return to the social or political conditions of a past time

panacea   a remedy for all ills or difficulties; a cure-all

jingoism   an aggressive, bellicose spirit or foreign policy that advocates seizing new territories and/or securing national advantages by use of force

sovereignty   independence; self-government or authority of a nation or state

imperialism   the policy of extending the rule or authority of an empire or nation over foreign countries or of acquiring and holding colonies and dependencies

protectorate   the relationship of a strong state toward a weaker state or territory that it protects and partly controls

subjugate   to conquer; to bring under complete control

territorial integrity   condition of a country being whole, entire, and self-governing rather than broken up into the colonies of other countries

IDENTIFICATIONS

After reading Chapter 21, you should be able to identify and explain the historical significance of each of the following:

Rutherford B. Hayes

greenbacks and the Greenback party

Carl Schurz, E. L. Godkin, Josephine Shaw Lowell, and the Civil Service Reform League

James B. Weaver

Pendleton Civil Service Act

Grover Cleveland

Mugwumps

Southern, Northwestern, and National Colored Farmers' alliances

Tom Watson, Mary E. Lease, and the Populist party

poll tax, literacy test, and grandfather clause

Plessy v. *Ferguson*

Booker T. Washington

Jacob Coxey

free silver

William Jennings Bryan

William McKinley

Alfred T. Mahan, *The Influence of Sea Power upon History*

Josiah Strong, *Our Country*

Henry Cabot Lodge

Liliuokalani versus Sanford B. Dole

William Randolph Hearst, the *Journal*, and yellow journalism

Joseph Pulitzer and the *World*

Teller Amendment versus Platt Amendment

Emilio Aguinaldo

Anti-Imperialist League

John Hay and the Open Door policy

Boxer Rebellion

Philippe Bunau-Varilla and the Hay–Bunau-Varilla Treaty

SKILL BUILDING: MAPS

1. On the map of Asia and the Pacific, locate each of the following. Explain the significance of each on late-nineteenth-century and early-twentieth-century U.S. foreign policy.

   Samoa

   Hawaiian Islands, Honolulu, Pearl Harbor

   Philippines, Manila Bay, Manila, Luzon

   Guam

   China, Manchuria, Beijing (Peking)

   Japan

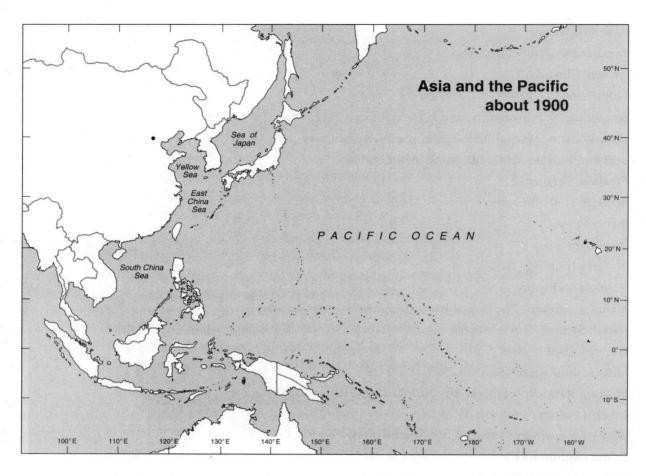

2. On the map on page 275 of the Caribbean and Central and South America, locate the following. Explain the significance of each on late-nineteenth-century and early-twentieth-century U.S. foreign policy.

Cuba, Havana, Santiago de Cuba, Guantanamo

Puerto Rico

Colombia

Panama Canal Zone

Panama

Nicaragua

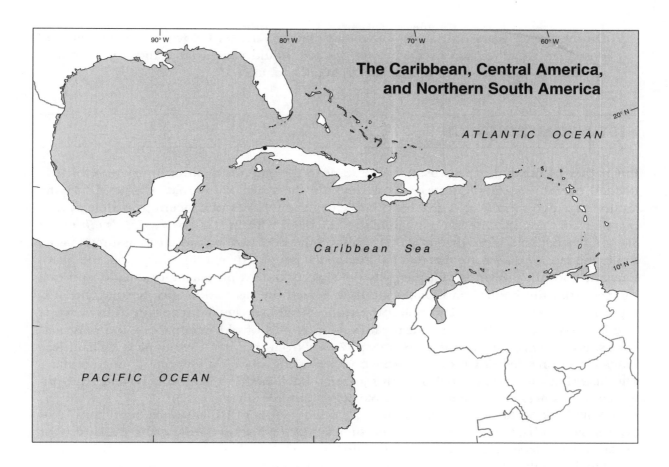

SKILL BUILDING: TABLES

Look at the election tables in Chapter 21. What can you conclude about the relative strength of the two major parties between 1880 and 1892? What had happened to the balance between them by 1900? After reading the chapter, can you explain the reasons for the change? In what election did the candidate with the greater popular vote lose the election? Can you explain how this is possible and could happen again?

Look at the line graph titled "Consumer Prices and Farm-Product Prices, 1865–1913" on page 675 of the text. After studying this graph you should be able to answer the following questions:

1. Was the period 1875–1897 one of overall economic inflation or deflation?

2. During that period, which generally dropped lower: total cost of living for consumers or prices of farm products?

3. During which years did farmers' incomes fall the farthest below their expenditures? Based on what you have read in this chapter, would you say that those years corresponded to the periods of greatest agrarian political unrest?

HISTORICAL SOURCES

In Chapter 21 the author tells us that Americans in the late nineteenth century were bitterly divided over the money question. How does the historian know that? On page 683 the author cites two sources that give historians clues about issues of concern to people at various times in the past. One is a book published in 1894, William H. Harvey's *Coin's Financial School*. Since it sold more than 400,000 copies in the next two years, we can assume that its topic, the money question, interested a great many people. By reading this book, the historian can find out the kinds of arguments the silver standard propagandists made, and one can see from the book's emotional tone how heated the discussion was. Second, the text reproduces a pro–gold standard political cartoon. What message did it convey to its viewers? The historian can find such political cartoons in copies of old newspapers, journals, and books. For example, a cartoon in *Harper's Weekly* from the year 1896 depicts William Jennings Bryan pressing down on the brow of a protesting laborer a fifty-cent "bunco dollar." The historian can certainly tell how this journal, published in the Northeast and read primarily by business and professional people, felt about free silver.

Now look at the sections in Chapter 21 titled "Roots of Expansionist Sentiment" and "Crisis over Cuba." Does the author cite similar historical sources to explain the desire for expansion and feelings of anger against Spain?

Finally, look at "A Place in Time: Chicago in the 1890s." How does this capsule history of Chicago and its Columbian Exposition illustrate the economic, social, and political impact of rapid industrialization on Americans at the time?

MULTIPLE-CHOICE QUESTIONS

Circle the letter of the item that best completes each statement or answers the question.

1. The Pendleton Act provided for
   a. civil-service reform.
   b. using silver as well as gold to back paper currency.
   c. separate but equal facilities for blacks and whites.
   d. higher protective tariff rates.

2. Which of the following was *not* a goal of the Populist party?
   a. having government take over and run the railroads
   b. increasing the money supply
   c. raising the protective tariff
   d. having the people elect U. S. senators instead of state legislatures choosing them

3. Which of the following results of the Spanish-American War aroused the greatest controversy in the United States?
    a. payment of $20 million to Spain
    b. acquisition of the Philippine Islands
    c. removing the Spanish from Cuba
    d. annexation of Puerto Rico

4. American imperialists argued that U.S. participation in the race for colonies would do all of the following *except*
    a. cause lower taxes in the United States.
    b. provide bases for the U.S. Navy.
    c. provide the United States with new markets.
    d. bring civilization to backward peoples.

5. The Populist party was launched chiefly by leaders of the
    a. farmers' alliances.
    b. Grange.
    c. American Federation of Labor.
    d. Progressive party.

6. The free-silver position of the Democrats and Populists in 1896 failed to win much support from urban labor because
    a. it would destroy labor unions.
    b. factory workers were relatively prosperous in the 1890s.
    c. workers liked Grover Cleveland and laissez-faire.
    d. workers feared it would result in higher food prices.

7. The Teller Amendment was later partially repudiated by
    a. the Platt Amendment.
    b. the Hay–Bunau-Varilla Treaty.
    c. *Plessy* v. *Ferguson*.
    d. the Sixteenth Amendment.

8. The yellow journalism of William R. Hearst's *Journal* and Joseph Pulitzer's *World* probably contributed to
    a. Bryan's defeat in 1896.
    b. Cleveland's election in 1884.
    c. the passage of poll taxes, literacy tests, and grandfather clauses.
    d. America's declaration of war on Spain.

9. Which nineteenth-century political figure championed civil-service reform, joined the Mugwump revolt against James G. Blaine, and criticized American imperialism?
    a. Alfred T. Mahan
    b. Benjamin Harrison
    c. Carl Schurz
    d. John Hay

10. In the case of *Plessy* v. *Ferguson,* the U.S. Supreme Court ruled that
    a. poll taxes, literacy tests, and grandfather clauses were unconstitutional devices for undermining the Fifteenth Amendment.
    b. segregated public facilities did not violate the Fourteenth Amendment as long as the separate accommodations were equal.
    c. a federal income tax was unconstitutional.
    d. the convict-lease system violated constitutional guarantees of fair trial and no cruel and unusual punishment.

SHORT-ANSWER QUESTIONS

1. Discuss the causes of agrarian discontent in the period 1870 to 1897.

2. Why did American farmers between the 1870s and 1897 generally favor issuing greenbacks and adopting "free silver"?

3. Discuss the effects of the depression of 1893–1897 on national politics.

4. Why did the Populists decide to endorse the 1896 Democratic presidential candidate, William Jennings Bryan, instead of nominating a member of their own party to run?

5. Explain the relationship the United States established with Cuba after the Spanish-American War.

6. Theodore Roosevelt said, "I took the Canal Zone." Explain how he took it. What were the consequences of his actions for the United States?

ESSAY QUESTIONS

1. Discuss what happened to African-Americans in the post-Reconstruction South. How did the federal government react to these developments? What impact did these developments have on national politics?

2. Write an essay on the rise of populism in the 1890s. How and why was the Populist party founded? What did it hope to accomplish? Why did it fail to become a major party and gain control of the federal government? Did it accomplish anything?

3. Discuss the election of 1896. Who were the candidates? What were the issues? What was the outcome? Why was it an important watershed election?

4. In 1898 the United States declared war on Spain, although there seemed to be little provocation. Why did the majority of Americans and most government leaders favor war?

5. With the annexation of the Philippines, the United States for the first time imposed its rule on a distant people by military force. How can you account for this change in U.S. foreign policy? What pressures and groups led the nation in this imperialistic direction? Were there countergroups trying to prevent this course? If so, why were they unsuccessful?

22

The Progressive Era

OUTLINE AND SUMMARY

I. A Changing American Society and Economy

A. *Immigrant Masses and a New Urban Middle Class*

Cities grew rapidly between 1900 and 1920 as rural Americans and some 17 million immigrants moved into them. Most of the immigrants were fleeing poverty in their native lands. Many of the newcomers huddled in burgeoning urban slums in terrible conditions. Overwhelmed and often corrupt municipal governments failed to provide them with adequate services and public facilities. Settlement-house workers, Social Gospel ministers, and reform journalists had been telling middle-class Americans about the plight of slum dwellers for years; the resulting consciousness of urban poverty helped set the stage for the progressive movement.

The urban middle class, mostly native-born, also was expanding and becoming increasingly self-aware and influential. Especially, college-educated, urban, middle-class women organized social-welfare efforts and revived the feminist movement.

B. *African-Americans in a Racist Age*

In 1900 two-thirds of the 10 million black Americans were still in the rural South, mostly living as sharecroppers. To escape from poverty, disfranchisement, Jim Crow laws, and violence, blacks began migrating to cities and to the North. In the North they encountered de facto segregation and discrimination. Under these difficult circumstances, blacks developed their own communities, culture, and music.

C. *Corporate Boardrooms, Factory Floors*

Domination of the economy by corporate giants accelerated in the first years of the twentieth century. The real wages of industrial laborers rose after 1900 but were still so inadequate that in many families the mothers and children had to go to work to make ends meet. In 1910 at least 1.6 million youngsters between ten and fifteen years of age worked full-time. Industrial laborers spent on average nine and a half hours a day in mills and shops that were often hazardous to their health and safety, as demonstrated by the Triangle Shirtwaist fire. Employers, inspired by efficiency experts such as Frederick W. Taylor, tried to get still more work out of their employees.

D. Workers Organize; Socialism Advances

To improve their lot, workers kept trying to unionize. However, their right to strike was frequently curtailed by conservative court decisions such as *Danbury Hatters*, and employers often hired recent immigrants as scabs when employees struck. Because of these obstacles, the AFL craft unions grew primarily in the skilled trades, leaving most factory workers unorganized. Two unions attempted to help semiskilled and unskilled workers: the International Ladies' Garment Workers' Union, which led successful strikes in the needle trades, and the Industrial Workers of the World (IWW). The IWW signed up western miners, lumberjacks, and migratory farm workers and won a major strike in 1912 in the textile mills of Lawrence, Massachusetts. Unlike the American Federation of Labor, the IWW preached revolution to overthrow capitalism.

The Socialist Party of America, which hoped to end capitalism through the ballot box rather than revolution, also was gaining followers. When party leader Eugene Debs ran for president in 1912, he received 900,000 votes. The same rising discontent that won support for the IWW and the Socialists also opened the way for the progressive movement.

II. The Progressive Movement Takes Shape

A. Progressivism: An Overview

The reform movement known as progressivism arose in response to the problems spawned by industrialization. Progressivism and the earlier populist movement shared the belief that government must become involved in ameliorating these problems, but populism was primarily a farmers' movement; progressivism's main strength lay in the urban middle class. The progressive movement also won important support from urban and immigrant workers, and even some backing from business leaders.

Most progressives accepted the capitalist system; they merely wanted to reform the worst abuses that had developed under it. There was never one unified movement, but many different groups of reformers. Some preached regulation of big business; others concentrated on passing laws to protect workers. Still others thought that the way to solve social ills was to outlaw liquor and prostitution or restrict immigration. Progressives generally attempted to be "scientific" in their approach, backing their demands for change with scholarly studies of deplorable conditions to be remedied.

B. Intellectuals Lay the Groundwork

Many intellectuals criticized laissez-faire and called for an activist government that would regulate business practices and protect the economically vulnerable. These intellectuals included economist Thorstein Veblen, historians Charles and Mary Beard, and journalist Herbert Croly. William James's pragmatic philosophy also undermined fixed dogma about laissez-faire.

C. New Ideas About Education and the Law

New educational and legal ideas paved the way for the progressive movement. John Dewey preached that schools must foster in students respect for the values of democracy and cooperation. Supreme Court justice Oliver Wendell Holmes, Jr., attacked conservative judges for being guided entirely by legal precedent. He insisted that the "law must evolve as society changes."

D. Novelists and Journalists Spread the Word

Muckracking journalists and novelists played an important role in stimulating the progressive movement by exposing to middle-class Americans political corruption and corporate wrongdoing. Muckraking journalists included Lincoln Steffens, who wrote about urban political machines and bosses, and Ida Tarbell, who revealed the cutthroat competitive practices of Standard Oil Company. Magazines such as *McClure's* and *Collier's* specialized in muckraking articles. Novelists Frank Norris in *The Octopus* and Theodore Dreiser in *The Financier* also told tales of business abuses and political corruption. Meanwhile, "Ashcan School" artists and photographers such as Lewis Hine, depicted the harsh world of the immigrants and factory workers.

E. Reforming the Political Process

The earliest signs of the progressive movement appeared in cities where municipal reformers battled corrupt political machines and elected activist mayors dedicated to change. Reform mayors such as Hazen Pingree of Detroit and Tom Johnson of Cleveland generally brought honesty to municipal government, provided city dwellers with improved municipal services and facilities, and forced transportation and utility companies to lower rates and pay their fair share of taxes. Other municipal reformers experimented with commission and city-manager forms of government.

The reform efforts soon moved up to state government. Progressives attempted to democratize politics by establishing secret balloting, the direct primary, the initiative, the referendum, and recall and by helping to enact the Seventeenth Amendment, which provided for popular election of U.S. senators. In practice these measures fell short of producing the democratic results that their progressive authors had hoped for.

F. Protecting Workers, Beautifying the City

Under progressive influence, state governments enacted important social measures: maximum number of hours per workday for female employees, such as Oregon's ten-hour law; factory safety codes, such as the one enacted in New York after the Triangle Shirtwaist fire; workers' compensation acts; bans on child labor; and housing codes. Progressive reformers also began to beautify cities with more parks and playgrounds, broad boulevards, and impressive municipal buildings.

G. Corporate Regulation

States moved to regulate big business, too. The pioneer was Wisconsin, under Governor Robert La Follette. Between 1901 and 1906 he convinced the legislature to introduce the direct primary, create a state railroad commission, increase corporate taxes, and limit business contributions to political campaigns, among other reforms. These progressive measures and La Follette's method of relying on the expertise of academics at the state university became known as the "Wisconsin Idea."

III. Progressivism and Social Control: The Movement's Coercive Dimension

A. Moral Control in the Cities

Some reformers tried to guard morality by inducing cities to censor movies and outlaw gambling and prostitution.

B. Battling Alcohol and Drugs

Prohibition became the biggest moral crusade of the Progressive Era. Due to the efforts of the Anti-Saloon League, the Woman's Christian Temperance Union, and various church groups Congress in 1918 passed the Eighteenth Amendment, which outlawed the manufacture, sale, and shipment of alcoholic beverages. Progressives also enacted the earliest laws regulating the then-widespread use of such addictive drugs as morphine, heroin, and cocaine.

C. Immigration Restriction

Some people believed that immigrants caused poverty and immorality. In 1894 Senator Henry Cabot Lodge and other prominent Bostonians founded the Immigration Restriction League. In 1917, over President Wilson's veto, Congress excluded illiterate immigrants.

D. Eugenics: Scientific Bigotry

Eugenicists claimed that humans and society could be improved by controlled breeding. Inspired by their ideas, a few states passed laws during the Progressive Era allowing forced sterilization of criminals and sex offenders. Pseudo-scientific racism was spewd by some so-called progressive writers, such as Madison Grant in *The Passing of the Great Race* (1916).

E. Racism and Progressivism

Racism in American society reached a peak during these years. Many progressives either ignored racial discrimination or were themselves racists. Southern progressives such as James K. Vardaman combined advocacy of economic and political reform with vicious attacks on blacks. Woodrow Wilson, during his presidency, condoned segregation and discrimination practiced by the federal government. On the other hand, white progressives such as Mary White Ovington helped found the National Association for the Advancement of Colored People (NAACP).

IV. Blacks and Women Organize

A. Controversy Among African-Americans

Booker T. Washington, America's best-known black leader between 1890 and 1915, advised blacks to concentrate on economic advancement through vocational education and, for the time being, accept the South's Jim Crow and disfranchisement laws. Northern black intellectuals and professionals—William Monroe Trotter, Ida Wells-Barnett, and W. E. B. Du Bois—urged blacks to fight for economic, political, and educational equality.

B. The Founding of the NAACP

In 1905 Du Bois and other black critics of Washington formed the Niagara Movement. In 1909 Du Bois and other members of the Niagara Movement joined with white progressives in organizing the NAACP, which rejected Washington's accommodationist advice and began the long fight for racial justice.

C. Revival of the Woman-Suffrage Movement

A new group of feminists emerged to revitalize the women's movement. Carrie Chapman Catt, who became president of the National American Woman Suffrage Association in 1900, led her members in lobbying, distributing literature, and demonstrating. They convinced a number of states to grant women the vote. Impatient with the pace of change, however, Alice Paul organized the Woman's party to bring direct pressure on the federal government. She and her followers picketed the White House and went on a hunger strike. Congress finally passed the Nineteenth Amendment in 1919, and by 1920 it was ratified.

D. Breaking Out of the "Woman's Sphere"

Feminists challenged the assumption that the only proper roles for women were those of wife, mother, and homemaker. Women like Florence Kelley, Margaret Sanger, and Alice Hamilton led the progressive drives to abolish child labor, protect the health of workers and consumers, and establish day-care centers and birth-control clinics.

V. National Progressivism—Phase I: Roosevelt and Taft

A. Roosevelt's Path to the White House

Theodore Roosevelt, who entered the White House in 1901 after an anarchist assassinated William McKinley, became America's first progressive president. A believer in strong executive leadership, Roosevelt enlarged the powers of the presidency, turning the office into both an effective public forum and the center of legislative initiative.

B. Labor Disputes and Corporate Regulation

Unlike earlier presidents who used troops to break strikes, Roosevelt, in the coal miners' strike of 1902, induced management and the United Mine Workers Union to submit the dispute to arbitration by a commission that he appointed. The commission granted the miners increased pay and reduced hours.

Roosevelt did not want to attack big business, but he preached that corporate giants must obey the law and serve the public interest. When he believed that firms like the Northern Securities Company had violated the Sherman Anti-Trust Act, he prosecuted them. Despite his trust-busting, he stayed on good terms with big business, which contributed heavily to his 1904 campaign. In that election he easily won a second term over the conservative Democrat Alton B. Parker. In 1906 Roosevelt strengthened corporate regulation when he signed the Hepburn Act, which gave the Interstate Commerce Commission (ICC) the power to set maximum railroad rates and examine railroads' financial records.

C. Consumer Protection and Racial Issues

Responding to public concern generated by Upton Sinclair's *The Jungle,* Roosevelt persuaded Congress to pass the Pure Food and Drug Act and the Meat Inspection Act. On racial matters, Roosevelt's record is much worse. Especially unjust was his summary discharge of a black regiment in the Brownsville, Texas incident.

D. The Conservation Movement

Roosevelt made his most enduring reforms in conservation. Years of exploitation for private gain had damaged and depleted America's natural environment. By the 1890s land use had become a political issue, pitting business interests, preservationists, and conservationists against each other. While entrepreneurs wanted to continue unrestricted development for private enrichment, preservationists such as John Muir and the Sierra Club wished to save large wilderness tracts for their beauty and spiritual worth. Roosevelt's Forest Service chief Gifford Pinchot, father of the conservation movement, sought government scientific management to make the public domain best serve the resource needs of the nation of his day and in the future. Roosevelt used the presidency to popularize both conservation and preservation. He signed the Reclamation Act (1902) and, in cooperation with Pinchot, set aside some 200 million acres of forest and mineral-rich lands for government-managed use rather than for sale to business. Roosevelt approved the Antiquities Act and created new national parks. By 1916 there were thirteen national parks, and Congress, during President Wilson's administration, established the National Park Service to protect and run them.

E. Taft in the White House

With Roosevelt's backing, his secretary of war, William Howard Taft, won the Republican nomination and election as president in 1908 over third-time Democratic nominee William Jennings Bryan. Pledged to continue Roosevelt's square deal, Taft prosecuted more trusts than Roosevelt had, but Taft lacked Roosevelt's activism, flair for publicity, and political skill.

F. A Divided Republican Party

In the fight shaping up between the progressive (Insurgents) and conservative wings of the Republican party, Taft sided with the conservatives. When he signed the tariff-raising Payne-Aldrich bill, backed conservative Speaker of the House Joseph Cannon, and fired conservationist Gifford Pinchot, Taft alienated progressive Republicans. They joined with Theodore Roosevelt, who returned from a trip abroad in 1910, in denouncing the conservatives and campaigning for revived progressive reform.

VI. National Progressivism—Phase II: Woodrow Wilson

A. The Four-Way Election of 1912

In 1912 Theodore Roosevelt challenged Taft for the Republican nomination. When the convention chose Taft, Roosevelt's backers walked out, founded the rival Progressive party, and nominated Roosevelt. The Democrats gave the nod to Woodrow Wilson, reform governor of New Jersey, and the Socialists ran Eugene Debs. Roosevelt campaigned on his New Nationalism program of accepting big business as inevitable but building a powerful, activist fed eral government to regulate the corporate giants. Wilson's New Freedom, on the other hand, rejected big government in Washington and called for return to an economy composed of small, competing enterprises. Roosevelt did well, but the split in Republican ranks gave Wilson and the Democrats control of the White House and Congress.

B. Woodrow Wilson: The Scholar as President

Wilson had been a political science professor and president of Princeton University before becoming New Jersey governor. He could be a skilled and flexible politician, but at other times he was intolerant and self-righteous.

C. Tariff and Banking Reform

Wilson convinced Congress to pass the 1913 Underwood-Simmons Tariff, which reduced import duties, put several items on the free list, and instituted a federal income tax (authorized by the Sixteenth Amendment ratified earlier that year). Also in 1913 he signed the Federal Reserve Act, which kept banking a private enterprise but imposed public regulation over it. The twelve regional Federal Reserve banks were empowered to expand the nation's credit and money supply by issuing Federal Reserve notes under the supervision of the Federal Reserve Board, appointed by the president.

D. Corporate Regulation

Wilson pushed through Congress the Federal Trade Commission law and the Clayton Antitrust Act. The Federal Trade Commission was a federal regulatory agency with the power to uncover unfair methods of business competition and then issue cease and desist orders against their perpetrators. The Clayton Act supplemented the vague and general Sherman Anti-Trust Act by defining and listing specific illegal practices.

E. Labor Legislation and Farm Aid

Wilson endorsed the clause in the Clayton Act exempting union strikes, boycotts, and peaceful picketing from prosecution under the antitrust laws. He signed the Keating-Owen child labor law (later declared unconstitutional), the Adamson Act providing for an eight-hour day for railroad workers, and the Workingmen's Compensation Act for federal employees. Other legislation helped farmers obtain loans at lower interest rates.

F. Progressivism and the Constitution

Wilson nominated to the Supreme Court progressive Jewish attorney Louis Brandeis. Although conservatives and anti-Semites objected, Wilson persuaded the Senate to confirm Brandeis.

G. 1916: Wilson Edges Out Hughes

In 1916 the Democrats renominated Wilson, who ran against Charles Evans Hughes, the candidate of the now reunited Republicans. In a close race Wilson won a second term.

VII. Conclusion

Although some progressive reforms did less good than their backers had hoped, and despite progressivism's repressive and intolerant elements, the movement as a whole left a legacy of government intervention to regulate destructive corporate practices, protect the economically vulnerable, and ameliorate social problems arising from industrialization. It was a precedent on which the New Deal would later build.

VOCABULARY

The following terms are used in Chapter 22. To understand the chapter fully, it is important that you know what each of them means.

pogroms   physical attacks on Russian Jews made by anti-Semitic Russian mobs, often encouraged by the tsarist government

behemoth   huge and powerful institution, person, or beast

capitalism   a system under which the means of production, distribution, and exchange are mostly privately owned and directed

socialism   a system under which the means of production, distribution, and exchange are owned by the community as a whole and administered by the government

pragmatism   the philosophy that truth is not determined by fixed universal laws but by the practical test of what works (it comes from philosopher William James's 1907 book *Pragmatism*)

direct primary   an election in which the registered members of a political party vote on who their party nominees for office should be

initiative   procedure by which a specified number of voters may propose a law and compel a popular vote on its adoption

recall   the right to remove a public official from office by a vote of the people taken upon petition of a specified number of the registered voters

eugenics   the manipulation of reproductive processes to improve the characteristics of a plant or animal species, especially human beings

diatribe   a bitter and violent denunciation

arbitration   the hearing and deciding of a dispute between parties by a person or persons agreed to by the disputing parties

nostrums   patent medicines

workers' compensation law   a law requiring employers to take out an insurance policy on their employees so that if a worker is hurt on the job, the insurance company will pay medical and living expenses until the worker can return to work (in case of the worker's death, the payments are made to his or her dependents)

cease and desist order   an order by a court or government regulatory agency to stop and refrain thereafter from actions that the agency believes are illegal (if the order is complied with, no punitive action is taken)

IDENTIFICATIONS

After reading Chapter 22 you should be able to identify and explain the historical significance of each of the following:

Triangle Shirtwaist fire

International Ladies' Garment Workers' Union

William Haywood and the Industrial Workers of the World

Margaret Sanger and birth control

Eugene Debs and the Socialist Party of America

Jane Addams

Herbert Croly, *The Promise of American Life*, and the *New Republic*

John Dewey

Lincoln Steffens, Ida Tarbell, and the muckrakers

Tom Johnson and the progressive reform mayors

constitutional amendments of the Progressive Era: sixteenth, seventeenth, eighteenth, nineteenth

Robert La Follette

Anti-Saloon League and Woman's Christian Temperance Union

Booker T. Washington in contrast to William Monroe Trotter, Ida Wells-Barnett, W. E. B. Du Bois, and the Niagara Movement

Mary White Ovington, Oswald Garrison Villard, and the NAACP

Carrie Chapman Catt and the National American Woman Suffrage Association

Alice Paul and the Woman's party

Florence Kelley

Theodore Roosevelt and the coal miners' strike of 1902

Northern Securities Company case

Hepburn Act

Pure Food and Drug Act and Meat Inspection Act

Gifford Pinchot and the conservationists

John Muir, the Sierra Club, and the preservationists

Payne-Aldrich Tariff

the Insurgents and Joseph Cannon

Ballinger-Pinchot Affair

New Nationalism and New Freedom

Underwood-Simmons Tariff

Federal Reserve Act, Federal Reserve Board, and Federal Reserve notes

Federal Trade Commission

Clayton Antitrust Act

Louis Brandeis and *Muller* v. *Oregon*

SKILL BUILDING: TABLES

Look at the tables on the elections of 1904 and 1908 in your text. Compare these with the election tables in Chapter 21. What happened to the balance of power between the two major parties between the 1880s and the early 1900s? William Jennings Bryan was the Democratic candidate in the elections of 1896, 1900, and 1908. Using the information in Chapter 21 and the election tables for 1900 and 1908, can you tell in which year he came closest to winning the presidency? Why do you think that was? In many of the elections between 1880 and 1920, the prohibitionists ran a presidential candidate. Judging from the election tables, can you find any evidence that their appeal to the electorate was growing?

Look at the table "Children in the Labor Force, 1880–1930" in your textbook. In what year did the problem of child labor seem to be most severe? Judging from the data in this chart, do you think the progressive movement had any impact on child labor in the United States? Can you offer any other explanations for the percentage differences between 1880 and 1930?

SKILL BUILDING: GRAPHS

Look at the line graph titled "Immigration to the United States, 1870–1930" on page 701 of the text. After studying the graph, you should be able to answer the following questions:

1. During which years did the United States receive the greatest number of immigrants? Was there any year in which more than 1 million persons arrived?

2. During the peak period of immigration, were the majority of newcomers from Western and Northern Europe or from Southern and Eastern Europe?

3. Just from looking at the graph, can you tell what impact the Immigration Act of 1921 had on how many immigrants arrived and where they came from?

4. What were the effects of major economic depressions in the United States (1873–1879, 1893–1897) and of World War I (1914–1918) on immigration to this country?

HISTORICAL SOURCES

If the historian writing about the Progressive Era is to understand why many Americans of the period favored reform, he or she needs to view the problems facing society as citizens living at the time perceived them. In the years 1890–1917 many middle-class people who did not personally experience exploitation learned about it from books, articles, and studies written by reformers. Examples include Florence Kelley's 1905 book *Some Ethical Gains Through Legislation*, dealing with the evils of child labor, and Lincoln Steffens's *The Shame of Cities* (1904), focusing on municipal corruption. Novelists joined in the move to expose social ills, and because they offered plots with adventures and love stories along with their social message, they reached many more readers than Kelley's or Steffens's nonfiction accounts. Muckraking novels of the period include Upton Sinclair's *The Jungle* (1906), Frank

Norris's *The Octopus* (1901), and Theodore Dreiser's *The Financier* (1912). The historian who wants to understand why Americans called for laws to prohibit child labor, protect consumers, regulate railroads and big business, and clean up graft can read these books. While these works make excellent historical sources, can you see any dangers in the historian's reliance on them as the only or main source of information about the period 1890–1917?

Look at "A Place in Time: Hetch Hetchy Valley in 1913." There you will get some sense of the complexity of the issues progressives addressed. The decision to build the dam in the valley pitted two environmentalists, John Muir and Gifford Pinchot, against each other. What position did each take? Why? Historians find the answers to these questions by looking at sources such as the transcripts of the 1913 hearings before the Public Lands Committee of the House of Representatives and the speeches and writings of the two men.

MULTIPLE-CHOICE QUESTIONS

Circle the letter of the item that best completes each statement or answers the question.

1. Theodore Roosevelt's New Nationalism was in part derived from a book written by
   a. Herbert Croly.
   b. Louis Brandeis.
   c. William Jennings Bryan.
   d. Margaret Sanger.

2. The act of Congress that contained a federal income tax provision was
   a. the Hepburn Act.
   b. the Federal Reserve Act.
   c. the Payne-Aldrich Tariff.
   d. the Underwood-Simmons Tariff.

3. "Corporations and combinations have become indispensable in the business world, . . . it is folly to try to prohibit them, but it is also folly to leave them without thorough-going control." This quotation summarizes the position on the big-business question of which politician?
   a. Woodrow Wilson
   b. William McKinley
   c. Theodore Roosevelt
   d. Robert La Follette

4. All of the following were founders of the NAACP *except*
   a. W. E. B. Du Bois.
   b. Booker T. Washington.
   c. Mary White Ovington.
   d. Oswald Garrison Villard.

5. In the coal strike of 1902, Theodore Roosevelt
   a. followed Cleveland's precedent in using federal troops.
   b. refused to intervene.
   c. insisted that labor and management submit the dispute to arbitration.
   d. sided with the employers against the union.

6. The term *muckrakers* refers to
   a. procurers involved in the white slave trade.
   b. journalists and writers who exposed political corruption and corporate wrongdoing.
   c. opponents of Woodrow Wilson.
   d. women who spread mud on the White House grounds to protest being denied the vote.

7. Which of the following was *not* an electoral reform designed to give people a more direct voice in politics and government?
   a. initiative and referendum
   b. Seventeenth Amendment
   c. Eighteenth Amendment
   d. direct primary

8. Which statement about the progressive movement is correct?
   a. Progressives wanted to use the powers of government to restrain big business and protect the economically vulnerable.
   b. Most progressives rejected the capitalist system, preferring one based on cooperation for the good of the whole community.
   c. Like the earlier populist movement, the progressive movement was primarily agrarian based.
   d. Progressives respected civil liberties so highly that they rejected any legislation that dealt with personal morals, such as sexual activities, drinking, and choice of entertainment.

9. Which of the following preached the need for working-class revolution to seize the means of production from the employing class?
   a. Industrial Workers of the World
   b. American Federation of Labor
   c. International Ladies' Garment Workers' Union
   d. Niagara Movement

10. The "Wisconsin Idea" referred to
    a. the new city-manager and commission forms of municipal government.
    b. the attempts of midwestern progressives to limit immigration, stop prostitution, and prohibit sale of liquor.
    c. the municipal ownership of public utilities advocated by Mayor Tom Johnson.
    d. the program of economic and political reforms by state government pioneered by Governor Robert La Follette.

SHORT-ANSWER QUESTIONS

1. Explain the ways in which the populist and progressive reform movements were similar. In what ways were they different?

2. Which groups of people were attracted to the Socialist Party of America and/or the Industrial Workers of the World in the period 1900–1917? Why?

3. Who founded the National Association for the Advancement of Colored People (NAACP)? Why? How did the founders of the NAACP differ in their ideas from Booker T. Washington?

4. What were some of the political and economic-social reforms enacted by state governments under the leadership of progressive governors such as Robert La Follette?

5. Discuss the contributions of Theodore Roosevelt and his U.S. Forest Service chief, Gifford Pinchot, to the conservation movement. Was Roosevelt also a preservationist? Which of his actions indicate he was or was not?

6. Compare and contrast Theodore Roosevelt's New Nationalist platform with Woodrow Wilson's New Freedom.

ESSAY QUESTIONS

1. Discuss the roles played by women in the progressive movement or movements.

2. The author of Chapter 22 states that "on the issue of racial justice," the record of the Progressives was "generally dismal." Do you agree with this statement? Why or why not? (Support your position with as many relevant examples as possible of the actions of various progressives.)

3. In Chapter 22 the author concludes that the "Progressive Era . . . shines forth as a time when American politics seriously began to confront the massive social upheaval wrought by industrialization." But progressivism also "had its repressive, illiberal, and coercive dimensions." Write an essay either agreeing or disagreeing with this assessment. Support your position with as much specific evidence as possible.

4. Explain the reasons for the break between President Taft and the Insurgent (progressive) Republicans. What were the consequences of this break?

5. One historian has written this about progressive reform: "The Roosevelt Era . . . had been a period of beginnings, of a scattering of pioneer legislation. . . . The Wilson Era, building on this foundation, was a period of sweeping achievement." Do you agree with this statement? Why or why not? Support your position with as much specific evidence as possible.

23

World War I

OUTLINE AND SUMMARY

I. Defining America's World Role

A. *The Roosevelt Corollary in Latin America and the Balance of Power in Asia*

Theodore Roosevelt believed that the United States must play an active role in world affairs, protect American interests in Latin America, and preserve the balance of power in Asia. In 1904 he announced the Roosevelt Corollary. It warned European nations not to intervene in the Western Hemisphere to collect debts owed to their citizens. Instead, the United States would act as policeman in Latin America, keeping order there and seeing that finances were handled properly and debts repaid. Citing his corollary, Roosevelt had U.S. officials take over the Dominican Republic's customs service and manage its foreign debt. Roosevelt also mediated an end to the Russo-Japanese War and used his influence to obtain a peace settlement that maintained the balance of power in Asia. Afterward he tried to improve U.S. relations with Japan by negotiating a gentlemen's agreement to limit Japanese immigration and thus cool American prejudice. Discrimination against Japanese immigrants in the western states continued anyway.

B. *Dollar Diplomacy in China and Nicaragua*

Roosevelt's successor, William Howard Taft, concentrated on promoting American commercial interests abroad, a foreign policy referred to as dollar diplomacy. Taft attempted, without much success, to open greater investment opportunities in China for American business. Using the Roosevelt Corollary, Taft sent marines into Nicaragua to protect U.S. investors there and keep in power a government friendly to American business interests. The marines occupied Nicaragua from 1912 until 1933.

C. *Wilson and Latin America*

Despite criticizing Republican expansionism, Democratic president Woodrow Wilson proved just as interventionist in Latin America as Roosevelt and Taft. To keep order and create a favorable climate for American investors, Wilson ordered marines to occupy the Dominican Republic and Haiti. The marines stayed to supervise those governments until 1924 and 1934, respectively. Wilson repeatedly intervened in Mexico during its revolution, trying to bring to power leaders who were liberal, democratic, and friendly to capitalistic enterprise. U.S.

foreign policy in Asia and Latin America between 1900 and 1914 showed that the United States was willing to become involved in foreign affairs to keep order, encourage the kinds of governments the United States approved of, and protect U.S. economic interests. These same tendencies would later pull the country into World War I.

II. War in Europe

A. *The Coming of War*

Colonial rivalries, arms races, aggressive nationalism, suppressed nationalities, a system of rival alliances, and the romantic notion that war brought out the best in men and countries were all underlying causes of World War I in Europe. In 1914 a Serbian nationalist assassinated the heir to the Austrian throne, an event that precipitated the fighting.

B. *The American People's Initial Responses*

As soon as war began in Europe, President Wilson proclaimed U.S. neutrality and asked the American people to be neutral "in thought as well as in action." Most Americans agreed with Wilson that the United States should not fight, but few had neutral feelings. Wilson and the majority of Americans had emotional bonds with England.

C. *The Perils of Neutrality*

Despite his initial proclamation of neutrality, Wilson asked Congress to declare war on Germany in 1917. What accounts for this turnabout? First, Wilson became convinced that, for the United States to shape the postwar settlement, it must participate in the fighting. Second, Wilson's handling of the issue of neutral rights on the high seas pulled the country into a war with Germany. The British violated our rights to trade by mining the North Sea and stopping ships and goods bound for Germany. Wilson's protests were not vigorous enough to prevent the British from ending almost all German-American trade. Germany retaliated with unrestricted submarine warfare. This led to injuries and the deaths of civilians, including Americans, in the sinking of Allied ships such as the *Lusitania*, the *Arabic*, and the *Sussex*. In ever more threatening notes, Wilson warned Germany to stop unrestricted submarine warfare or the United States would break off diplomatic relations. Some Americans—Secretary of State Bryan, the sponsors of the Gore-McLemore Resolution, and the founders of the Woman's Peace party—believed Wilson's abandonment of the "true spirit of neutrality" would pull the country needlessly into the armed conflict. Finally, American citizens between 1914 and 1917 developed a large economic stake in an Allied victory, making neutrality much more difficult. U.S. trade with the Allies increased nearly fourfold, and American investors lent them $2.3 billion to finance these purchases, on which the United States' continued prosperity depended.

D. *Stalemate in the Trenches*

Between 1914 and 1917 the war on the Western Front in Europe degenerated into a bloody stalemate. British propaganda in the United States charged that the Germans were committing atrocities. German counterpropaganda proved ineffective.

E. The Election of 1916

The war was a major issue in the 1916 election. Because the Democrats sensed the American public's desire for peace, Wilson ran for reelection on the slogan, "He kept us out of war." Charles Evans Hughes, the Republican nominee, sometimes called for a tougher stand against Germany and other times criticized Wilson for having been too threatening. Wilson's close victory seemed to indicate that the majority of Americans still hoped to avoid participation in the conflict.

F. The United States Enters the War

Because Germany decided that full use of its submarines would contribute more to its victory than keeping the United States out of the war, it fully unleashed its U-boats on January 31, 1917. In light of his past warnings, Wilson felt he had no alternative but to break off diplomatic relations. During February and March, German U-boats attacked five American ships, and the United States learned of the Zimmermann telegram. On April 2, 1917, Wilson asked Congress to declare war on Germany, which it did after a short, bitter debate. Three important factors produced this declaration: German attacks on American shipping, U.S. economic investment in the Allied cause, and American cultural links to the Allies.

III. Mobilizing at Home, Fighting in France

A. Raising an Army

After declaring war on Germany, Congress passed the Selective Service Act, under which nearly 3 million men were drafted. In addition, more than 11,000 women volunteered for the navy and marines, where they were assigned to noncombat support services.

B. Organizing the Economy for War

To mobilize the economy behind the war effort, the federal government imposed an unprecedented amount of regulation on American business. It did this by creating thousands of special wartime agencies. The most powerful of these, the War Industries Board, allocated scarce materials, established production priorities, and introduced more efficient production practices. The Food Administration encouraged farmers to increase output, while exhorting civilians to conserve food and fiber. The U.S. Railroad Administration consolidated all the privately owned rail lines into one, unified, government-operated system for the duration of the war.

C. With the AEF in France

The American Expeditionary Force (AEF) sent some 2 million soldiers to France in 1917 and 1918. They arrived at a critical time for the Allies. After the Bolsheviks came to power in Russia, that country dropped out of the war, which freed the German armies on the Eastern Front to fight in the west. With these reinforcements Germany launched an offensive in the spring of 1918 that brought its troops within fifty miles of Paris. American soldiers were rushed to the front, where they helped to stop the German advance.

D. Turning the Tide

By July 1918 U.S. troops were participating in the Allied counteroffensive that, through the summer and fall, drove the Germans out of much of France. In the often brutal fighting, soldiers lost their illusions about war being a great adventure. An influenza epidemic that swept Europe and the United States in 1918 added to the suffering and death.

E. African-Americans in the AEF

More than 260,000 blacks were drafted or volunteered for service in World War I. Fifty thousand went to France. The armed forces were riddled with racism. The army assigned African-Americans to segregated regiments and gave them more than their fair share of menial, heavy-labor duties. The navy used blacks only as messboys, and the marines excluded them entirely. Racist civilians provoked clashes with black troops stationed in Houston and other southern cities. Nonetheless, several African-American regiments served with distinction; one received the French Croix de Guerre.

IV. Promoting the War and Suppressing Dissent

A. Advertising the War

Wilson believed that the federal government must promote unanimous support for the war. Secretary of the Treasury William G. McAdoo pioneered in using advertising techniques and propaganda to sell war bonds. With posters, parades, and movie stars as sales promoters, McAdoo was able to sell enough bonds to finance approximately two-thirds of the war costs. The remainder was paid for with increased federal income and other taxes. The main job of popularizing the war fell to George Creel's Committee on Public Information. It created posters, advertisements, news releases, and films and sent seventy-five thousand speakers around the nation.

B. Intellectuals, Cultural Leaders, and Reformers Present Arms

Many progressive reformers, muckrakers, teachers, and religious leaders supported the war, echoing Wilson's assertion that we were in a struggle to spread liberalism, democracy, and other American values.

C. Wartime Intolerance

The Creel committee's propaganda produced a wave of anti-German hysteria and hatred of anyone who questioned America's participation in the war. As fear and intolerance mounted, German-Americans were victimized, and antiwar radicals were verbally and physically attacked.

D. Opponents of the War

Despite all the "patriotic" pressure, some Americans continued to oppose the war. These included some German-Americans and religious pacifists. A minority of women's rights and progressive leaders, such as Jane Addams and Randolph Bourne, pointed out that the war was killing reform and unleashing reaction and intolerance. Many socialists branded the war a crusade to protect capitalists' profits and saw no reason for workers to die to enrich their bosses.

E. Suppressing Dissent by Law

The government attempted to silence these dissenters with the repressive Espionage and Sedition acts. These made it a crime to criticize the war, government, Constitution, or armed forces. Some fifteen hundred people were convicted and jailed; the Socialist Party of America's leader, Eugene Debs, received a ten-year prison term. The Supreme Court upheld the constitutionality of the laws with the "clear and present danger" doctrine.

V. Economic and Social Trends in Wartime America

A. Boom Times in Industry and Agriculture

Stimulated by war, the American economy boomed. The real income of farmers and unskilled workers rose significantly. Thousands of workers streamed into industrial centers to take jobs in war plants. The influx created terrible housing, school, and other shortages in these cities.

B. Blacks Migrate Northward

Reduced immigration and soaring war production created labor shortages in northern industry. From labor recruiters, black-owned newspapers, letters, and word of mouth, southern blacks learned of these new job opportunities. Hoping to escape southern racism and find good jobs, an estimated half a million black people migrated to the North. In northern cities whites resented the black newcomers, who competed for jobs and housing. In places such as East St. Louis, Illinois, race riots broke out.

C. Women and the War

Many women's rights activists hoped that the war would lead to equality for women. During the war thousands of women served in the military and in volunteer organizations. About one million took jobs in industry. Arguing that women should be rewarded for their major contributions to winning the war, the woman-suffrage movement finally got the Nineteenth Amendment added to the Constitution by 1920. Aside from the vote, women lost many of their wartime gains after the armistice. Those holding well-paying jobs in industry generally were replaced by men returning from wartime service.

D. The War and Progressivism

The war strengthened the prohibition movement. The antiliquor forces argued that the "unpatriotic" German-American brewers should be put out of business and that grain used to manufacture whiskey and gin would be better used to feed the armed forces and our allies. In this atmosphere the Eighteenth Amendment, banning the manufacture, transportation, or sale of alcoholic beverages, was ratified by 1919. The war also boosted the Progressive Era antiprostitution campaign and produced a brief flurry of protective labor laws.

VI. Joyous Armistice, Bitter Aftermath

A. Wilson's Fourteen Points

Wilson presented his fourteen-point peace plan in a speech to Congress in January 1918. It included self-determination, impartial adjustment of colonial claims, freedom of the seas, reduced armaments, and a world association of nations, among other proposals. Whether Wilson could get these ideas incorporated in the treaties signed at the end of the war remained to be seen.

B. Armistice

In October 1918 the Kaiser's government asked Wilson for an armistice based on the Fourteen Points. Almost immediately afterward revolutionaries in Germany deposed the Kaiser and proclaimed a republic. Representatives of the new republic signed the armistice with the Allies on November 11, 1918.

C. The Versailles Peace Conference

Wilson personally headed the American delegation to Versailles. He appointed no prominent Republicans to the delegation, a political mistake since a Republican-controlled Senate would have to ratify any treaty signed. At the conference Wilson had to compromise with the Allied leaders, David Lloyd George and Georges Clemençeau, who had no faith in his Fourteen Points. The Treaty of Versailles that they produced contained some of Wilson's points, most importantly the Covenant of the League of Nations, but not all. Overall the treaty was harsh and punitive and aroused resentment and desire for revenge in Germany. Wilson and the Allied leaders also attempted to overthrow the Bolsheviks in Russia and to isolate and weaken that communist-controlled nation.

D. The Fight over the League of Nations

Dismayed at the treaty's punitive features, Wilson concentrated his hopes on the League of Nations part of it. In July 1919 Wilson submitted the Treaty of Versailles to the Senate for ratification. There it ran afoul of Republican reservationists, led by Henry Cabot Lodge, and isolationists. Out of a mixture of partisanship and fear that U.S. participation in the league would embroil the country in future European wars, the Republicans blocked ratification. Had Wilson been willing to accept the modifications (reservations) that Lodge proposed concerning the league, the treaty would have been approved. Wilson, however, refused to compromise his principles any further.

E. Racism and Red Scare

The war-generated intolerance and antiradical hysteria reached a peak in 1919–1920. Lynch mobs killed seventy-six blacks, and race riots broke out in more than twenty-five cities; the bloodiest occurred in Chicago. A rash of postwar strikes and a series of bombing incidents convinced many Americans that the country was on the verge of a communist uprising. To protect against this supposed danger, the Justice Department, under A. Mitchell Palmer, raided the homes and meeting places of suspected radicals and arrested more than four thousand of them, although there was no evidence that they had committed any crime. Aliens suspected of radicalism were deported.

F. The Election of 1920

The election of 1920 came in the midst of the violence and repression. The Democratic nominee, James Cox, was soundly defeated by Republican Warren G. Harding, who appealed to the public with his promise of a return to "normalcy."

VII. Conclusion

World War I brought death to 10 million people worldwide, including 112,000 Americans. The war transformed American society, helped finally to pass the Eighteenth and Nineteenth amendments, and gave the country its first taste of active government regulation of the economy, although the federal supervisory agencies were often run by businessmen friendly to corporate interests. The intolerance and repression that grew during the war, however, arrested further progressive reform.

VOCABULARY

The following terms are used in Chapter 23. To understand the chapter fully, it is important that you know what each of them means.

belligerent   a country at war

contraband   defined in international law as goods that neutrals cannot supply to one belligerent except at the risk of seizure and confiscation by the other; goods imported or exported illegally

liberal   favorable to progress and reform in economic and political affairs and to individual self-expression and liberty; associated with representative government rather than aristocratic, authoritarian, or dictatorial rule

coup   the act of a small group in bringing about a sudden change of government illegally and/or by force

armistice   a truce; a suspension of fighting by agreement of the parties so they can discuss peace terms

dissent   disagreement with the majority opinion and/or that of the authorities, such as the government

sedition   incitement of resistance or rebellion against the government; action or language promoting such resistance

self-determination   the freedom of a people or nationality to decide for itself the form of government it shall have

autonomy   the right of self-government or independence

abdicate   give up power and the right to govern

reparations   compensation in money, material, labor, etc., by a defeated nation for damage done to civilian populations and property during war

mandate or trusteeship   a commission given to one nation by an associated group of nations (such as the League of Nations) to administer the government and affairs of a people in a territory judged not yet ready for self-government and independence

IDENTIFICATIONS

After reading Chapter 23, you should be able to identify and explain the historical significance of each of the following:

Roosevelt Corollary

gentlemen's agreement

dollar diplomacy

General John J. Pershing

U-boats and unrestricted submarine warfare

Lusitania

National Security League and preparedness

Jane Addams, Carrie Chapman Catt, and the Woman's Peace party

Sussex threat and pledge

Zimmermann telegram

Bernard Baruch and the War Industries Board

Herbert Hoover and the Food Administration

William G. McAdoo and the U.S. Railroad Administration

American Expeditionary Force

Vladimir Lenin and the Bolsheviks

George Creel and the Committee on Public Information

Randolph Bourne

Espionage and Sedition acts, 1917, 1918

Eugene Debs

Schenck v. *United States* and the "clear and present danger" doctrine

East St. Louis race riot, 1917; Chicago race riot, 1919

Eighteenth Amendment

Nineteenth Amendment

Wilson's fourteen-point peace plan

Council of Four at Versailles

Treaty of Versailles and Covenant of the League of Nations

Henry Cabot Lodge, reservationists, and irreconcilables

Article 10 of the League Covenant

Red Scare, 1919–1920, and the Palmer raids

SKILL BUILDING: MAPS

1. On the world map on the next page, locate the following places and explain how each of them was connected with U.S. foreign policy between 1900 and 1917:

Dominican Republic	Mexico	China	Japan
Haiti	Manchuria	Korea	Russia
Nicaragua			

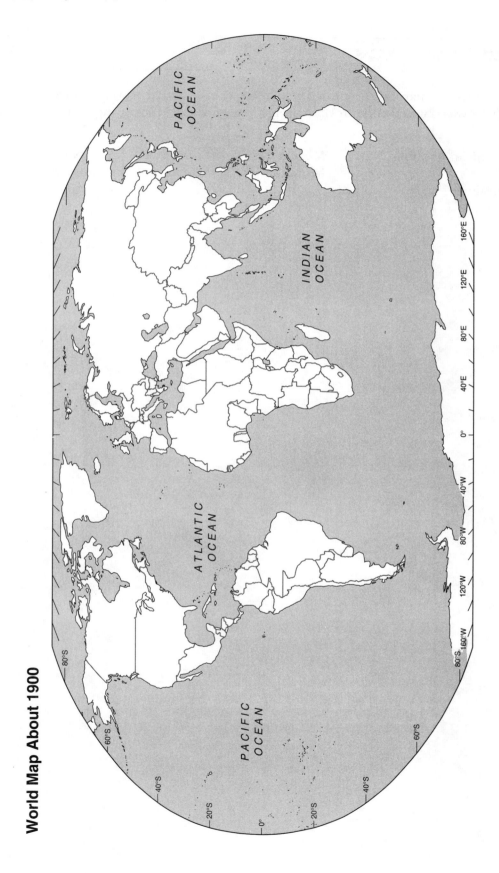

World Map About 1900

2. **On the map of Europe during World War I, (1) indicate the Allied powers, the Central powers, and the neutral countries; (2) indicate the areas and the names of the countries occupied by the Central powers at the time of their greatest success; (3) locate Sarajevo and explain its significance; (4) locate the Marne and Meuse rivers, the Argonne Forest, and Verdun and explain their significance in the war on the Western Front; (5) draw in the Armistice Line of November 11, 1918.**

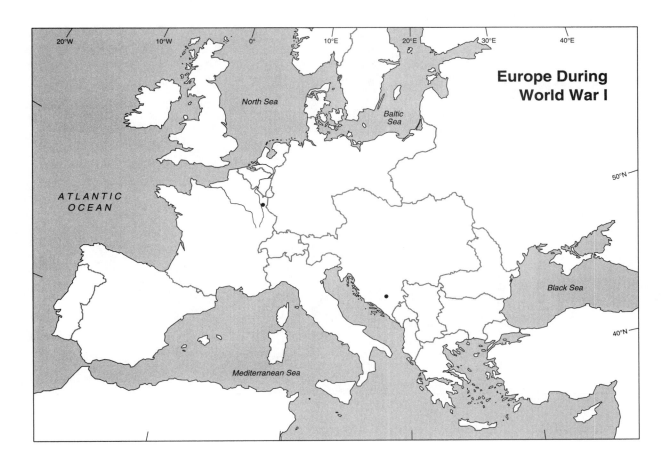

3. On the post–World War I map of Europe, (1) indicate the territories taken from Germany; (2) indicate the territories taken from Russia; (3) indicate the new nations created at the end of the war; (4) show what remained of Austria.

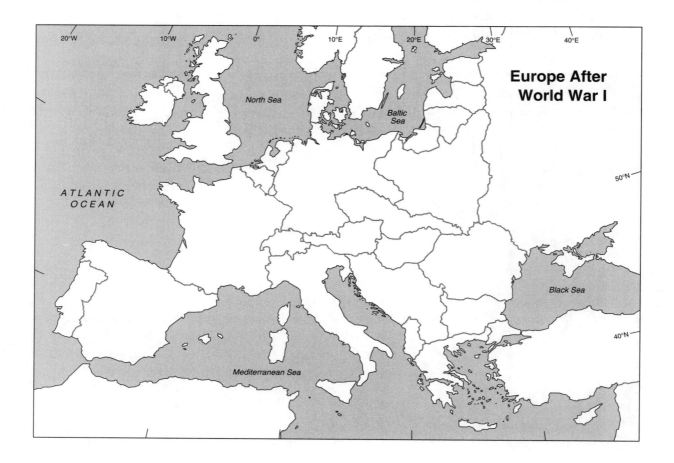

MULTIPLE-CHOICE QUESTIONS

Circle the letter of the item that best completes each statement or answers the question.

1. The Roosevelt Corollary
   a. asserted that the United States had the right to act as policeman in Latin America to keep order and prevent chronic wrongdoing.
   b. was issued to justify the role the United States played in ending the Russo-Japanese War.
   c. reversed that part of the Monroe Doctrine that stated the United States would not intervene in European affairs.
   d. warned the European powers and Japan not to exclude American business interests from China.

2. In the first seventeen years of this century, the United States intervened with military force in all of the following places *except*
   a. Nicaragua.
   b. Mexico.
   c. Jamaica.
   d. Haiti.

3. Secretary of State William Jennings Bryan resigned because
   a. he felt Wilson should have asked for a declaration of war after Germany sank the *Lusitania*.
   b. he believed Wilson's *Lusitania* notes and insistence that Germany stop unrestricted submarine warfare would embroil us in the war.
   c. he wanted Wilson to protest more strongly against British violation of U.S. neutral rights.
   d. he wanted to challenge Wilson for the presidential nomination in 1916.

4. Dollar diplomacy refers to
   a. Woodrow Wilson's allowing U.S. bankers to lend more than $2 billion to the Allies between 1915 and 1917.
   b. William Howard Taft's promotion of U.S. commercial interests in Asia and Latin America.
   c. Theodore Roosevelt's financing of the building of the Panama Canal.
   d. Wall Street's eagerness for the United States to enter World War I.

5. The Zimmermann telegram
   a. pledged that Germany would not sink any more merchant ships without giving warning and saving civilians.
   b. proposed an alliance between Germany and Mexico against the United States; after victory, Mexico would receive New Mexico, Texas, and Arizona.
   c. contained proof that the Germans were committing such atrocities as bayoneting babies.
   d. revealed Germany's designs to conquer and colonize much of Central and South America.

6. The war hastened the approval of two constitutional amendments. These provided for
   a. votes for women and prohibition.
   b. the eight-hour workday and an end to child labor.
   c. equal pay for men and women and votes for black Americans.
   d. direct popular election of U.S. senators and an end to poll taxes.

7. In the case of *Schenck* v. *United States*, the Supreme Court
   a. held that the U.S. Railroad Administration had acted unconstitutionally in taking over privately owned rail lines.
   b. upheld convictions under the Espionage Act on the grounds that free speech could be curtailed when it presented a "clear and present danger" to the country.
   c. ruled that segregated facilities for whites and blacks were acceptable as long as the accommodations were equal.
   d. held that the federal government did *not* have the right to propagandize its own people as George Creel's Committee on Public Information was doing.

8. Which of the following statements is *not* true of the Wilson administration during World War I?
   a. It took over and ran the railroads and imposed greater federal regulation over the economy than ever before in U.S. history.
   b. It set up a federal agency to build public support for the war with news releases, posters, speakers, and other propaganda.
   c. It interned all Japanese-Americans in ten guarded camps until the war was won.
   d. It sold millions of dollars worth of government bonds to Americans through techniques learned from advertising and public relations.

9. The Treaty of Versailles
   a. resembled for the most part Wilson's fourteen-point peace plan.
   b. turned over to Russia large blocks of territory in eastern Europe.
   c. disarmed Germany and stripped her of her colonies.
   d. failed to create an association of nations as Wilson had promised it would.

10. In the two years immediately after World War I, the United States
   a. enjoyed improved relations and cooperation between labor and management.
   b. joined the League of Nations and began to play a larger role in world affairs.
   c. showed a renewed interest in progressive reform and elected an administration promising to carry on Wilson's New Freedom.
   d. experienced heightened racial violence and antiradical hysteria.

SHORT-ANSWER QUESTIONS

1. Who were the candidates and what were the major issues in the election of 1916?

2. Discuss the experiences of African-Americans in the U.S. armed forces during World War I.

3. Discuss the people who opposed U.S. entry into World War I. Who were they? Why did they oppose participation?

4. How did World War I help gain passage and ratification of the Eighteenth and Nineteenth amendments?

5. What caused the Red Scare of 1919–1920? What actions did U.S. Attorney General A. Mitchell Palmer take during the scare?

6. Why can the election of 1920 be seen as a repudiation of President Wilson and all he stood for?

ESSAY QUESTIONS

1. In what ways did U.S. policy in Asia and Latin America between 1900 and 1917 foreshadow U.S. intervention in World War I?

2. In 1914 Woodrow Wilson proclaimed U.S. neutrality and asked the American people to be neutral in thought as well as action. In April 1917 Wilson asked Congress to declare war on Germany. What brought about this turnaround in American policy toward World War I?

3. During World War I how did the U.S. government attempt to mobilize the economy, influence public opinion, and silence all dissent?

4. Discuss the impact of World War I on the home front. Include in your answer the effects of the war on business, labor, agriculture, African-Americans, and women.

5. Woodrow Wilson wanted to draw up a liberal settlement at the end of the war that would ensure peace and democracy for generations thereafter. What prevented the realization of his plans?

24

The 1920s

OUTLINE AND SUMMARY

I. A New Economic Order

A. *A Decade of Prosperity*

Demobilization following World War I disrupted the economy, causing a sharp recession. By 1922 recovery had set in, and for the rest of the decade the economy grew rapidly and prospered. Development of the electrical-appliance (refrigerators, washing machines, vacuum cleaners) and automobile industries contributed to this economic growth and prosperity. Mass production of cars created hundreds of thousands of jobs and stimulated a host of related industries, such as rubber, oil, steel, and highway construction. American business also invested heavily abroad during the 1920s.

B. *New Modes of Producing, Managing, and Selling*

Introduction of the assembly line and other technological advances brought more than a 40 percent increase in productivity between 1919 and 1929. This led to bigger profits and a wave of corporate mergers. By 1929 one hundred corporations controlled almost half the business done in America. Competition also disappeared as corporations joined together in trade associations to fix prices and divide up markets, and networks of chain stores displaced small, independently owned retail stores. Big business successfully boosted sales and profits by introducing installment buying and relying more heavily than ever on advertising. Business influence and values pervaded all areas of American life in the 1920s: big businessmen became the new cultural heroes, politicians vied to serve business, and organized religion tried to copy its selling techniques.

C. *Women in the New Economic Era*

The proportion of women working outside the home stayed at about 24 percent throughout the decade. Working women earned less than men holding similar jobs. The growth of large corporations increased the need for secretaries, typists, and filing clerks, and most of these positions were taken by women. Few women, however, broke into management or the professions, other than the traditionally female ones, such as teaching and nursing.

D. Workers in a Business Age

The 1920s were an unsuccessful time for organized labor. Union membership fell from 5 million in 1920 to 3.4 million in 1929. Management discouraged the growth of unions by intimidation, violence, insistence on the open shop, use of scab labor during strikes, and introduction by some companies of benefits such as stock purchase plans. Although the wages of skilled workers and those with strong unions rose during the decade, the majority of unskilled laborers saw little improvement in pay. Southern, black, Mexican-American, recent immigrant, and female workers clustered at the bottom of the wage scale.

E. Ailing Agriculture

American farmers did well during World War I, but after the armistice, both the European and domestic markets contracted, and prices plunged. Farmers, hard-pressed to repay loans and meet mortgage payments, tried to compensate by growing more. This created surpluses that drove down produce prices further. Members of the farm bloc in Congress attempted to help farmers with the McNary-Haugen bill. It provided for government purchase of surplus produce at a fixed price and resale abroad for whatever it would bring. The bill passed Congress twice, but President Coolidge vetoed it each time. Agriculture remained a depressed sector of the economy throughout the decade.

II. Republicans in Power

A. The Harding and Coolidge Years

A conservative-controlled Republican convention in 1920 nominated Warren G. Harding for president. He then won handily over his Democratic opponent, James M. Cox. The Harding administration was riddled with corruption. Veterans' Bureau chief Charles Forbes stole bureau funds. Attorney General Harry Daugherty and his Justice Department underlings sold influence and immunity from prosecution. Secretary of the Interior Albert Fall leased government oil reserves at Elk Hills, California, and Teapot Dome, Wyoming, to favored businessmen in exchange for bribes. On Harding's death, Coolidge assumed the presidency and corruption died down; however, the probusiness attitudes of the Harding years continued. By twice raising the tariff, the government protected domestic manufacturers from foreign competition. Secretary of the Treasury Andrew Mellon convinced Congress to lower federal taxes for the wealthy. Under Chief Justice William Howard Taft, a Harding appointee, the Supreme Court declared unconstitutional the federal child labor law and the minimum wage act for women workers in Washington, D.C.

B. Foreign Policy in an Isolationist Age

Harding's secretary of state, Charles E. Hughes, called an international naval arms conference in Washington, D.C., in 1921. Out of this conference emerged treaties that imposed a ten-year moratorium on battleship construction and pledged the major powers to respect each other's territorial possessions in the Pacific. Other than calling this conference, the Republican administrations of the 1920s followed an isolationist foreign policy, refusing to join both the League of Nations and the World Court. These administrations also insisted that our World War I allies repay a portion of their war debts to us, then made it difficult for them to do so by curtailing their sales in the United States with high protective tariffs.

C. Progressive Stirrings, Democratic Divisions

Progressive reform sentiment did not completely disappear in the 1920s. A coalition of labor and farm groups in 1924 revived the Progressive party and nominated Robert La Follette for president. A Democratic party badly split between its urban and rural wings nominated an unappealing compromise candidate, John W. Davis. With the economy booming, the Republican incumbent, Calvin Coolidge, won the presidency easily.

D. Women and Politics in the 1920s: A Dream Deferred

Ratification of the Nineteenth Amendment granting women the vote had less impact on politics in the 1920s than many women's rights advocates had predicted. During this period the women's movement splintered: some feminists devoted their efforts to the peace movement; others argued among themselves over backing an equal rights amendment.

III. Mass Society, Mass Culture

A. A Nation of Cities, Consumer Goods, and Automobiles

This was the first decade in which the majority of Americans lived in cities. Throughout the 1920s city life-styles and values spread to more and more of the population. Radio, movies, advertising agencies, and popular magazines, and the messages they carried, all emanated from cities. The new consumer goods were most readily available to city dwellers. New electrical appliances transformed household duties, as did the rise of supermarkets and commercial bakeries. Automobiles had the biggest impact on American culture. Traffic jams, parking problems, mounting accidental deaths, reduced parental supervision of young adults, and the spread of suburbs are examples of the changes brought by cars.

B. Soaring Energy Consumption and a Threatened Environment

The mass production and sales of automobiles and electrical appliances took a heavy toll on the environment and natural resources. Generating enough electricity to power the new appliances consumed millions of tons of coal, barrels of oil, and feet of natural gas, but the most voracious users of gasoline were the millions of automobiles. Not only did the nation waste and heedlessly deplete fossil fuels, but cars, power plants, steel mills, and other industries supplying the ever-growing demand for energy polluted the atmosphere. Cars also made it easier for people to visit and settle in former wilderness areas, which were being paved over and disappearing at an accelerated rate. A few groups protested, but Americans on the whole were indifferent to the environmental threat.

C. Routinized Work, Mass-Produced Pleasure

As assembly-line production made work less fulfilling and time-consuming, Americans turned increasingly to mass-produced entertainment for gratification. Popular magazines, such as *Reader's Digest,* built massive circulations. All over America people listened to the same radio programs and watched the same movies, thus producing a more homogeneous national culture.

D. Fads, Celebrities, and Heroes

The mass communication made possible by radio and film created a series of nationwide fads, heroes, and media events. Examples include the mah-jong craze; sports celebrities like Babe Ruth, Gertrude Ederle, and Jack Dempsey; and the wild acclaim showered on Charles A. Lindbergh for his solo flight across the Atlantic.

IV. Cultural Ferment and Creativity

A. The Jazz Age and the Postwar Crisis of Values

In the so-called Jazz Age, some young people rejected the values of their elders on sexual matters, dress, and decorum. The ideas of Sigmund Freud became popular. Women asserted their freedom by discussing sex openly, wearing makeup, smoking, and shortening their skirts and their hair. This upheaval in manners and morals primarily affected the urban middle class. Most farmers, blacks, industrial workers, and recent immigrants were more concerned with economic survival than experimenting with new life-styles.

B. Alienated Writers

The decade saw the emergence of many talented writers, including Sinclair Lewis, Willa Cather, Ernest Hemingway, and F. Scott Fitzgerald. They were often critical of both the narrow-minded, small-town values of prewar America and the materialistic business culture of the twenties. Some felt so uncomfortable with 1920s America that they spent much of the decade abroad, and yet they cared deeply about finding and creating "an authentic" American culture through their works.

In these same years, the growing black population in northern cities, especially New York, stimulated a flowering of African-American creative activity known as the Harlem Renaissance. All-black stage shows played on Broadway, and African-American writers explored the black experience in poems and novels.

C. Achievements in Architecture, Painting, and Music

American cities in the 1920s were filled with skyscrapers, an architectural trend applauded by many and denounced by others. More than ever, American artists painted the American scene, urban and rural, past and present. Some of the most talented were Thomas Hart Benton, Edward Hopper, John Sloan, and Georgia O'Keeffe. New classical composers appeared, such as Aaron Copland, but the unique contribution of America to the musical world was jazz. In the twenties composers and performers such as George Gershwin, Bessie Smith, Louis Armstrong, and Duke Ellington gained national and international recognition.

D. Advances in Science and Medicine

Americans made strides in many areas of science. Arthur H. Compton won the 1927 Nobel Prize for his studies on X-rays; medical researchers found more effective treatments for diphtheria, whooping cough, measles, and influenza, thus increasing life expectancy. Robert Goddard began his work in rocketry.

V. A Society in Conflict

A. Immigration Restriction

The United States, in 1921, 1924, and 1929, passed restrictive laws that drastically cut the total number of immigrants permitted to enter the country and established quotas for each nationality. Reflecting the fears and intolerance of the time, the laws excluded Chinese and Japanese entirely, and Eastern and Southern Europeans received small quotas. This discriminatory, national-origins quota system remained in American law until 1965. The laws did not curtail immigration from Western Hemisphere countries, which continued to be heavy throughout the 1920s.

B. The Sacco-Vanzetti Case

The Sacco-Vanzetti case further illustrates the intolerance and divisions in society in the 1920s. Nicola Sacco and Bartolomeo Vanzetti were Italian immigrants who were convicted of, and finally executed for, robbery and murder. The evidence was circumstantial, but the prosecution probably prejudiced the jury against them by stressing their ethnic origin and political radicalism. Throughout the decade conservatives opposed the attempts of liberals to win a new trial for the pair.

C. The Ku Klux Klan

Another indication of social conflict and intolerance in the twenties was the rise of the Ku Klux Klan. Preaching hatred toward blacks, Jews, Catholics, immigrants, and the new urban values, the Klan grew to an estimated 5 million members. For a time it exerted real political power in a few states, including Oregon and Indiana. It threatened, intimidated, beat, and murdered those it considered dangerous to a "purified" America.

D. The Garvey Movement

Disillusioned to find the North almost as racist as the South, many poor urban blacks in the 1920s became followers of Marcus Garvey and his Universal Negro Improvement Association (UNIA). Garvey preached black pride, black separatism, and a return to Africa. At its peak the UNIA had eighty thousand members and became the first mass movement among African-Americans.

E. Fundamentalism and the Scopes Trial

A number of states passed laws prohibiting the teaching of any scientific theory that contradicted the account of human origin given in the Bible. When John T. Scopes, a high school biology teacher in Dayton, Tennessee, challenged his state's law, the American Civil Liberties Union hired a team of distinguished lawyers, headed by Clarence Darrow, to defend him. William Jennings Bryan assisted the prosecution. Although Scopes was convicted, the fundamentalist religious position was ridiculed in the courtroom and in the national press.

F. Prohibition

Prohibition split Americans. Its supporters were generally native-born, fundamentalist Protestants, especially those in rural areas. Its opponents included liberals, intellectuals, rebellious youths, and big-city immigrants. Enforcement of prohibition broke down almost immediately because many Americans did not believe in it and organized crime was busy supplying the demand for illegal liquor. Prohibition became a big issue in the 1928 election. Democrat Alfred E. Smith called for its repeal; Republican Herbert Hoover praised it as a "noble experiment."

VI. Hoover at the Helm

A. The Election of 1928

Herbert Hoover won the election by a landslide over Alfred Smith. Many rural, fundamentalist Protestants would not vote for Smith because he was a Catholic and a "wet" and he came from New York City, but the biggest reason for Hoover's victory was economic prosperity and Republican promises that things would get even better.

B. Herbert Hoover's Social Thought

Hoover encouraged voluntary cooperation among corporate leaders to raise wages, plan production and marketing, and standardize products. He believed that kind of self-regulation by business, rather than government intervention, would ensure economic growth and a better life for all. After the depression set in, his clinging to voluntarism and reluctance to use government power would greatly handicap his ability to deal with a sick economy.

VII. Conclusion

In the 1920s Americans tried to adjust to the mass production, mass culture, and urban society that had emerged. The decade's political leadership was conservative and backward-looking. Those who found this new world unfamiliar and threatening often reacted with repression and hate, like the champions of prohibition, the fundamentalists, and the Klansmen. Others embraced the new life-styles made possible by radios, cars, movies, and electrical appliances. The social ferment also produced an outpouring of creative energy: the Harlem Renaissance, jazz, and revitalized American literature.

VOCABULARY

The following terms are used in Chapter 24. To understand the chapter fully, it is important that you know what each of them means.

scabs   workers who take strikers' jobs

isolationist   one who favors a policy of nonparticipation in international affairs

taciturnity   disinclination to speak or be social; being given to few words

suffrage   the vote

materialistic more devoted to accumulating products and possessions than to spiritual needs and considerations

iconoclasm the attacking of others' cherished beliefs and practices

expatriates persons who have withdrawn themselves from residence in their native country

cant insincere statements of goodness or high ideals

eclectic selected from different sources; selecting and using what is considered best from many different styles or systems

nativism the policy of protecting the interests or ways of native inhabitants against those of immigrants; prejudice against or dislike for immigrants

charismatic possessing personal qualities that give an individual influence or authority over large numbers of people

fundamentalism a movement in American Protestantism that preaches that everything in the Bible is literally true and rejects any historical account or scientific theory that differs from biblical statements

speakeasies places where liquor was illegally sold and consumed

anachronistic referring to a thing placed out of its proper time; referring to a hangover from an earlier era

---

IDENTIFICATIONS

After reading Chapter 24, you should be able to identify and explain the historical significance of each of the following:

Henry Ford and *Fordism*

the open shop and the "American Plan"

the farm bloc and the McNary-Haugen bill

Teapot Dome and the other scandals of the Harding administration

Fordney-McCumber (1922) and Smoot-Hawley (1930) tariffs

Andrew Mellon

Charles Evans Hughes and the Washington Naval Arms Conference

Robert La Follette and the Progressive party

Jane Addams and the Women's International League for Peace and Freedom

Alice Paul and the National Woman's party

Oscar DePriest

Charles A. Lindbergh

F. Scott Fitzgerald

Sinclair Lewis

Ernest Hemingway

Willa Cather

Georgia O'Keeffe

Edward Hopper

George Gershwin

Duke Ellington

Harlem Renaissance

Langston Hughes

the Immigration Acts and the national-origins quota system

Sacco and Vanzetti

Marcus Garvey and the Universal Negro Improvement Association

John T. Scopes and the "monkey trial"

Aimee Semple McPherson

Volstead Act, "wets," and "drys"

Alfred E. Smith versus Herbert Hoover

SKILL BUILDING: GRAPHS AND CHARTS

Graphs and charts allow us to convey important historical information and trends in visual shorthand. Look at the graphs and charts in Chapter 24 as examples. First glance at the line graph "Economic Expansion, 1920–1929" on page 772. What does it indicate about industrial production in the 1920s as compared to the prewar years? During which years of the 1920s did the economy go into a short-lived but sharp recession?

Next turn to the pie chart "Women Employed in Professions and Occupations, 1910–1930" on page 775. Did the percentage of employed women in traditionally female occupations (domestic servants, waitresses, beauticians, and so on) change substantially between 1910 and 1930? Did the percentage of employed women working in factories and on farms increase or decrease between 1910 and 1930? Did the percentage of employed women engaged in clerical work increase significantly between 1910 and 1930? What about the percentage in professions?

Next turn to page 783 and look at the line graph "The Automobile Age: Passenger Cars Registered in the United States, 1900–1990." Roughly how many cars were registered in this country in 1910, 1920, 1925, and 1930? Did the number of registered vehicles rise more sharply during the twenties or thirties? How do you account for this?

Finally, look at the table on page 800 dealing with the elections of the 1920s and early 1930s. What does it indicate about American ethnic group voters and the Democratic party? Which was the only ethnic group that did not vote primarily Democratic by 1932? Why do you suppose that was?

HISTORICAL SOURCES

Chapter 24 uses as a source an in-depth community study of Muncie, Indiana, in the 1920s, conducted by two famous sociologists, Robert and Helen Lynd. Their findings, published in

1929 under the title *Middletown,* are referred to on pages 775 and 782–783. What generalizations about American society is the historian making from the findings reported in *Middletown?* Muncie, Indiana, was a medium-sized, midwestern town. Can we be certain that the attitudes, values, and life-styles that the Lynds found there were similar or identical to the ones that prevailed in huge eastern cities such as New York or in small communities in the Far West or Deep South? Does the text claim that a fairly homogeneous national culture emerged in the 1920s?

Look at "A Place in Time: Harlem in the Twenties." Do the attitudes, values, and lifestyles described in this cultural mecca of black America seem at all similar to those that the Lynds found in Muncie, Indiana?

MULTIPLE-CHOICE QUESTIONS

Circle the letter of the item that best completes each statement or answers the question.

1. The decade of the 1920s was the first one in which
   a. farmers drove down agricultural prices by producing a surplus.
   b. the majority of Americans worked in factories rather than on farms.
   c. the majority of Americans lived in cities.
   d. the majority of Americans owned television sets.

2. All of the following contributed to the general prosperity of the 1920s *except*
   a. the development of new consumer-goods industries, especially home electrical appliances.
   b. federal minimum-wage laws that ensured that workers were well paid and thus had additional purchasing power.
   c. the growth of the automobile industry.
   d. a marked increase in productivity due to new technology and industrial techniques, such as the moving assembly line.

3. American foreign policy toward Europe during the 1920s was characterized by
   a. a willingness to forgive and forget the World War I debts owed to the U.S. government by former allies.
   b. a desire to lead and dominate the League of Nations.
   c. isolationism, except for a willingness to enter into a treaty to curtail a naval arms race.
   d. a refusal to participate in the League of Nations but a willingness to join the World Court and abide by its decisions.

4. Which of the following is *not* associated with the Harding administration?
   a. the Teapot Dome scandal
   b. the Washington Naval Arms Conference
   c. probusiness policies such as raising tariff rates
   d. passage of the McNary-Haugen Act to raise farm prices

5. In the election of 1924,

    a. Catholicism and prohibition were the two main issues.

    b. the Democratic nominee, John W. Davis, won by a narrow margin over Republican Calvin Coolidge.

    c. labor, farm, and reform groups revived the Progressive party and ran Robert La Follette for president.

    d. the Democratic party nominated William Jennings Bryan for president for the fourth time.

6. Which of the following was *not* an African-American writer associated with the Harlem Renaissance?

    a. Willa Cather

    b. Langston Hughes

    c. Claude McKay

    d. Jean Toomer

7. The immigration laws passed during the 1920s

    a. favored Eastern and Southern Europeans over Western Europeans.

    b. barred Asian immigration.

    c. barred all Latin Americans from entering the United States.

    d. imposed a limit of 500,000 immigrants each year.

8. Marcus Garvey's Universal Negro Improvement Association

    a. appealed to the small class of black professionals but never to the masses of poor urban blacks.

    b. preached that blacks should remain in the rural South and specialize in farming.

    c. started black-owned business ventures and called for a return to Africa.

    d. gained its main following in the South among sharecroppers.

9. The Sacco-Vanzetti case

    a. pitted fundamentalists against modernists.

    b. indicated that it was difficult for radical immigrants to receive a fair trial in 1920s America.

    c. proved that most Eastern and Southern European immigrants were political radicals.

    d. ended in acquittal for the two Italian immigrants.

10. Which of the following 1920s figures was in many ways a precursor of later television evangelists?

    a. Charles A. Lindbergh

    b. Georgia O'Keeffe

    c. Oscar DePriest

    d. Aimee Semple McPherson

SHORT-ANSWER QUESTIONS

1. Explain why agriculture was economically depressed during the 1920s.

2. What happened to the trade union movement in the 1920s? Why?

3. In what ways did industrial and technological developments in the 1920s increase environmental dangers and the rapid use and waste of natural resources? Was government in the 1920s interested in either conservation or preservation?

4. Explain the economic and social impact of the booming automobile industry on America in the 1920s.

5. How effective was prohibition in reducing excessive drinking? Why wasn't it more successful? What were some of prohibition's socially harmful effects on American society?

6. Discuss Herbert Hoover's social thought. How did his outlook hinder him in fighting the depression that began during his presidency?

ESSAY QUESTIONS

1. What accounts for the economic growth and prosperity of the 1920s? Who benefited most from that prosperity? Who did not share in it and why?

2. Federal policies under presidents Harding and Coolidge reflected the probusiness attitudes of the 1920s. Write an essay discussing and illustrating this statement with specific examples.

3. Discuss the impact of the economic, cultural, and social changes of the 1920s on the lives of American women. Were the changes felt by working-, middle-, and upper-class women?

4. Sharp social conflicts existed in American society in the 1920s. These conflicts produced fear, intolerance, and attempts to "purify" the country by legislation and coercion. Write an essay discussing these conflicts and the attempts of government and private groups to bring back a more traditional and homogeneous America.

5. The 1920s were a time of changing manners and morals and of cultural ferment. Write an essay discussing the changes that took place in popular culture and among artists and intellectuals.

25

Crash, Depression, and New Deal

OUTLINE AND SUMMARY

I. Crash and Depression

A. Black Thursday

In 1928 a wave of wild speculation started. As 9 million Americans played the market in hope of quick profits, they drove stock prices to dangerously inflated levels. Worse yet, they often speculated on borrowed money; that is, they bought on margin. Low taxes for the rich engineered by Secretary of the Treasury Andrew Mellon and the easy-credit policy of the Federal Reserve Board contributed to the speculation. The optimistic buyers ignored warning signs such as the falloff of automobile sales and construction starts. Then, on October 24, 1929, Black Thursday, the speculative bubble burst; stock prices plummeted as panicked shareholders rushed to sell. On the following Tuesday the plunge continued. By mid-November the value of stock had declined by $30 billion. This stock market crash triggered the worst depression in American history.

B. Onset of the Depression

Between 1929 and 1933, the nation sank deeper and deeper into depression. Farm prices declined by 60 percent; more than 5,500 banks failed. Unemployment climbed from 3 percent to 25 percent of the labor force. One of the causes of this depression was maldistribution of wealth. The 40 percent of Americans at the lower end of the economic ladder received only 12 percent of the total national income, whereas most of the wealth generated by technological advances in the 1920s went to the corporate elite. As a result much of the population did not have enough income to keep buying the flow of goods from American factories, and the well-to-do had excess money to speculate with on the stock market. Already by 1929 the automobile, construction, textile, and other industries, with unsold inventories, were forced to cut back and lay off workers. The depressed agricultural sector further weakened the economy. Another cause of the depression was the collapse of European economies under the weight of World War I debt repayments and the unfavorable balance of trade with the United States. This caused our foreign sales to fall sharply.

C. The Depression's Human Toll

As banks failed, depositors lost billions in savings. Thirteen million people lost their jobs; millions of others suffered wage cuts and reduced hours. Everywhere banks foreclosed on farmers and homeowners who could not meet mortgage payments. Hospitals and clinics reported a growing number of malnutrition cases. The suicide rate rose by 30 percent.

D. Hoover's Response

President Herbert Hoover's ideological commitment to private-sector initiative, limited government intervention, and balanced federal budgets severely handicapped him in dealing with the depression. Hoover asked business leaders not to lay off any more workers or impose further wage cuts. Although businessmen initially agreed, they later broke their pledges because they could not sell their products. Hoover preached that private charity and local government must handle relief for the jobless, but private philanthropy and city and county governments were soon overwhelmed by the numbers needing help. Hoover signed legislation creating the Reconstruction Finance Corporation, which was empowered to lend money to failing business corporations, but he held out until July 1932 against using federal funds to assist the unemployed. He spent reluctantly on public works, fearing that too big a program would unbalance the budget. His pronouncements in favor of self-help made him seem indifferent to the suffering of depression victims.

E. Mounting Discontent and Protest

As conditions worsened, protests mounted. Midwestern farmers tried to raise agricultural prices by halting the shipment of food to cities. Destitute veterans marched on Washington demanding immediate cash payment of their bonuses for World War I service. Rather than explain to them why he opposed payment, Hoover ordered the army to remove the "bonus marchers" from the capital. The sight of armed troops expelling peaceful veterans convinced the public of Hoover's callousness.

F. The Election of 1932

The Republicans renominated Hoover, who stuck by his failed antidepression measures. The Democrats nominated Franklin D. Roosevelt. How he would fight the depression was not clear. Nonetheless, the anti-Hoover sentiments of the people carried FDR and the Democrats to lopsided victories in the presidential and congressional elections.

II. The New Deal Takes Shape

A. New Beginnings

The promise of government action and the mood of optimism in FDR's inaugural address lifted people's spirits. The relief, recovery, and reform measures that followed, known as the New Deal, were forged by many contributors. A circle of Roosevelt advisers called the "brain trust" devised broad "programs of federal economic planning." Eleanor Roosevelt and her social-worker and women-reformer friends pushed for legislation to assist the economically disadvantaged and minority groups. Secretary of Agriculture Henry A. Wallace advocated measures to aid hard-pressed farm owners. Old-time progressives, university professors, and able young lawyers joined the Roosevelt administration to contribute ideas and administer new programs.

B. The Hundred Days

Between March 9 and June 16, 1933, the administration introduced and Congress passed an unprecedented volume of legislation. These laws had the overall effect of greatly increasing federal involvement in the economy. The Federal Deposit Insurance Corporation (FDIC) insured bank accounts up to $5,000. The Civilian Conservation Corps (CCC) employed jobless young men on conservation projects. The Home Owners Loan Corporation and the Farm Credit Administration refinanced mortgages and thus saved the homes and farms of millions of Americans. Other important laws imposed regulation on the stock market and established the Tennessee Valley Authority (TVA) and the Public Works Administration (PWA). Washington entered the field of relief with the creation of the Federal Emergency Relief Administration (FERA). The Agricultural Adjustment Act (AAA) and the National Recovery Administration (NRA) aimed at reviving agriculture and business. The former guaranteed parity prices for agricultural produce and paid farmers for not growing crops that were in surplus. The NRA helped business draft and enforce codes to eliminate cutthroat competition, price-cutting, and other ruinous practices in exchange for management promises to bargain with unions chosen by their employees.

C. The NRA Bogs Down

After a brief upturn in the summer of 1933, the economy again slumped, and complaints about the NRA mounted. Management resented government encouragement of unions. Small businesses claimed that the codes helped only the big firms. The NRA bogged down in supervising code making in every possible industry. In 1935 a case challenging the constitutionality of the NRA reached the Supreme Court, and in a unanimous decision the justices struck it down.

D. Troubled Agriculture

Drought and the AAA reduced price-depressing surpluses, and as a consequence overall farm income rose by 50 percent between 1933 and 1937. However, the AAA did nothing for landless farm laborers, and it hurt tenants and sharecroppers. Landlords kicked many tenants and sharecroppers off their property and pocketed the government subsidy checks for withdrawing the land from production. Poor farmers also fell victim to the vast dust storms that rolled over the Upper South and Great Plains, destroying the crops in their paths. Ruined by nature and the AAA, many poor farmers, tenants, and sharecroppers headed for California, where they struggled to survive as migratory farm laborers. Between 1933 and 1935 New Dealers were split between whether the government should concentrate on pulling up the agricultural sector as a whole or on helping the rural poor. It was not until 1935 that legislation aiding farm laborers, tenants, and sharecroppers was passed.

E. Controversy over Relief Strategy

Harold Ickes, the careful PWA administrator, thoroughly checked each project to be underwritten by his agency. As a result the projects eventually built with PWA funds were enduring. In the short run, however, the PWA was slow to get work under way and slow to put money into the hands of the unemployed. Harry Hopkins, the less meticulous head of the FERA, quickly dispensed millions of dollars to the destitute. President Roosevelt, anxious for fast economic recovery, relied more and more heavily on Hopkins, transferring funds from the PWA to Hopkins's FERA and its work projects arm, the Civil Works Administration (CWA). Even after the CWA was terminated in the spring of 1934, Hopkins rather than Ickes dominated federal relief policy-making.

F. The New Deal in Midstream: Popularity and Problems

Although the first phase of FDR's New Deal did not end the depression, the president and his policies gained enthusiastic support from most Americans. This was demonstrated in the 1934 midterm congressional elections when, in contrast to the usual pattern in which the party in power lost seats, the Democrats greatly increased their majorities in the House and Senate.

III. The New Deal Changes Course

A. Introduction

Roosevelt, after receiving overwhelming endorsement from the people in the 1934 elections, took a swing to the left. In 1935 he proposed to Congress a new package of relief and reform measures known as the Second New Deal.

B. Challenges from Right and Left

One reason that FDR launched his Second New Deal was to combat the challenge to his administration from opponents on the political Right and Left. Certain big-business leaders and conservative Democrats and Republicans formed the American Liberty League in 1934. It denounced Roosevelt as a dictator who was leading the country down the path to socialism. Demagogic extremists, such as Charles E. Coughlin, Francis E. Townsend, and Huey Long, also were attacking the New Deal and proposing instead various panaceas for ending the depression. In 1934 and 1935 they were attracting thousands of followers. In addition, FDR embarked on his Second New Deal because the measures passed earlier, while bringing some improvement, had not lifted the economy out of the depression. The frustration with continued hard times showed itself in a wave of strikes, labor unrest, and protests, often led by communists and socialists.

C. The Second New Deal: Expanding Federal Relief

At Roosevelt's request Congress in 1935 passed the Emergency Relief Appropriation Act, granting nearly $5 billion for expanded work-relief programs. The largest part of the money went to the newly created Works Progress Administration (WPA), headed by Harry Hopkins. Between 1935 and 1943 the WPA spent $11 billion and employed more than 8 million people in a variety of construction, clerical, professional, and arts endeavors. Some of the appropriations also went to the National Youth Administration, which helped students support themselves with part-time jobs. Ickes's PWA shared in the money, too, using it for major construction projects. The large amount spent on these work-relief programs caused mounting federal budget deficits. According to British economist John Maynard Keynes, such deficit spending was a positive way to pump funds into the economy and combat the depression. Roosevelt never endorsed Keynesian economics, but he tolerated deficit spending as a short-term necessity to relieve suffering.

D. The Second New Deal: Turning Leftward

The massive relief programs and other laws of the Second New Deal were not intended to please all social classes. They openly aimed at serving the needs of labor and the rural and urban poor. The Resettlement Administration, created in May 1935, resettled and/or made loans to small farmers, tenants, and sharecroppers to turn them into farm owners on productive land. Although the Resettlement Administration aided the rural poor, agriculture as a whole suffered a blow when the Supreme Court in 1936 declared the AAA unconstitutional. The pro-union National Labor Relations (Wagner) Act of July 1935 stimulated the growth of organized labor. It required employers to recognize and bargain with their employees' unions and established the National Labor Relations Board to act as watchdog in labor-management relations. The Social Security Act of 1935 provided for old-age pensions, survivors' benefits for families of deceased workers, unemployment insurance, and aid to dependent mothers and children and the handicapped. Taxes imposed on employers and deductions withheld from employees' salaries financed the old-age and survivors' benefits. The Revenue Act of 1935 (which the wealthy called the "Soak the Rich" law) boosted taxes on corporations and upper-income Americans. These and other Second New Deal laws went a long way toward reducing the appeal of extremist demagogues and saving the capitalist system "by reforming its excesses and addressing some of its less desirable social consequences."

E. The Election of 1936: The New Deal at High Tide

The Republicans nominated Alfred Landon of Kansas to run against Roosevelt, whom the Democrats enthusiastically renominated. Roosevelt swept every state but Maine and Vermont, and the Democrats increased their large majorities in Congress.

F. The New Democratic Coalition

The victories resulted from a new Democratic coalition that had emerged, consisting of the South, urban immigrants, industrial workers, farmers, African-Americans, and women. Black voters were attracted to the Democratic party by Roosevelt's aid to the poor and his stepped-up appointments of blacks to responsible government positions. The Roosevelt administration also made careful efforts to cultivate women's votes.

G. The New Deal and the Environment

The New Deal achieved an impressive record in conservation. The CCC built hiking trails and fire lookout stations and planted thousands of trees. The Departments of Agriculture and the Interior taught farmers soil-conservation practices and stopped overgrazing on public lands. The TVA's dams controlled earth-eroding floods and harnessed the region's resources to serve the needs of its people. Congress created three more national parks, and the president heeded the lobbying of the Wilderness Society, established in 1935, by setting aside more than 7.5 million acres for wildlife refuges. The New Deal did not worry much about problems of atmospheric pollution, overpopulation, and dwindling global resources.

IV. The New Deal Draws to a Close

A. FDR and the Supreme Court

In February 1937 FDR proposed a court-reform bill that would allow the president to appoint a new Supreme Court justice to serve alongside each member of the Court who had reached seventy years of age and would not retire. Roosevelt requested this change because the aging, conservative majority on the Supreme Court had been declaring reform and recovery laws such as the NRA and AAA unconstitutional and seemed likely to invalidate the Social Security and Wagner acts that would soon be brought before it in test cases. Congress killed the president's "court-packing plan" and thereafter defied him on other matters as well. FDR did, however, influence a number of the elderly, conservative judges to modify their views or retire. The Supreme Court upheld the Wagner Act, and between 1937 and 1939 Roosevelt was able to fill four Court vacancies with liberal New Dealers.

B. The Roosevelt Recession

Roosevelt suffered another blow when the economy turned sharply downward in August 1937. The causes of this so-called Roosevelt recession included (1) a reduction in consumer spending power because of social-security deductions and (2) cutbacks, to try to balance the budget, in New Deal work and relief programs. Faced with rising unemployment and slumping industrial output, Roosevelt had to ask Congress for new appropriations to revive and expand the PWA, WPA, and other programs, which restarted economic recovery.

C. The End of the New Deal

In Roosevelt's second term, Congress passed only a few reforms. These included the National Housing Act; the Fair Labor Standards Act; the 1937 Farm Tenancy Act, which replaced the Resettlement Administration with the Farm Security Administration; and a second Agricultural Adjustment Act, similar to the first except for the processors' tax to which the Supreme Court had earlier objected. A coalition of conservative, southern Democrats and Republicans blocked further reform. Roosevelt attempted to break up this anti–New Deal coalition by asking voters to defeat conservatives in the 1938 elections. The people instead elected more conservatives. Thereafter, FDR switched his attention to foreign affairs and proposed no additional domestic reform, and the New Deal ended.

V. Conclusion

The New Deal chalked up impressive accomplishments in relief and reform, although it did not bring about full recovery. That would take World War II. Whereas business interests dominated Washington in the 1920s, in the 1930s government became more responsive to the needs of farmers, organized labor, and other interest groups. The New Deal left behind a permanently expanded and strengthened federal government and presidency.

VOCABULARY

The following terms are used in Chapter 25. To understand the chapter fully, it is important that you know what each of them means.

buying stock on margin   purchasing stock partly with one's own money and partly with money borrowed from a bank or broker specifically for the purpose of buying the stock

gross national product   the market value of the nation's total output of goods and services

foreclosure   the legal action by which a bank repossesses the house or farm of a borrower for failure to keep up regular payments on the mortgage

ideology   the doctrines believed by an individual or a group, often influencing their political and social actions

dark-horse candidate   a little-known or unlikely political figure who unexpectedly wins nomination

pump-priming   government spending (often to the point of creating a budget deficit) for the purpose of stimulating the economy

demagogue   an unprincipled political leader; one who leads people by playing on their prejudices, passions, and fears

panacea   a remedy for all ills; a cure-all

anti-Semitic   prejudiced against or intolerant of Jewish people

deficit spending   government expenditure in excess of its tax receipts and other revenues

collective bargaining   negotiation between employers and union representatives concerning wages, hours, and conditions of work

sacrosanct   sacred; not to be violated

disingenuous   not sincere; lacking in candor or frankness

IDENTIFICATIONS

After reading Chapter 25, you should be able to identify and explain the historical significance of each of the following:

Reconstruction Finance Corporation

bonus marchers

brain trust

Frances Perkins

Harold Ickes and the Public Works Administration

the Hundred Days

Civilian Conservation Corps

Federal Deposit Insurance Corporation

Federal Emergency Relief Act

Harry Hopkins

Tennessee Valley Authority

Agricultural Adjustment Acts, 1933, 1938

National Recovery Administration and Section 7a

Federal Securities Act and the Securities and Exchange Commission

Southern Tenant Farmers' Union

dust bowls and "Okies"

"fireside chats"

Second New Deal

Charles E. Coughlin, Francis E. Townsend, and Huey Long

Works Progress Administration

National Youth Administration

John Maynard Keynes and Keynesian economics

Resettlement and Farm Security administrations

National Labor Relations (Wagner) Act

Social Security Act

Revenue Act of 1935 ("Soak the Rich" law)

Mary McLeod Bethune and the "black cabinet"

Molly Dewson

National Housing Act, 1937

Fair Labor Standards Act, 1938

SKILL BUILDING: MAPS

On the map of the United States on the following page, locate each of the places listed below:

the seven-state region covered by the Tennessee Valley Authority

the areas affected by the dust storms (dust bowls) of the 1930s

Olympic National Park

Shenandoah National Park

Kings Canyon National Park

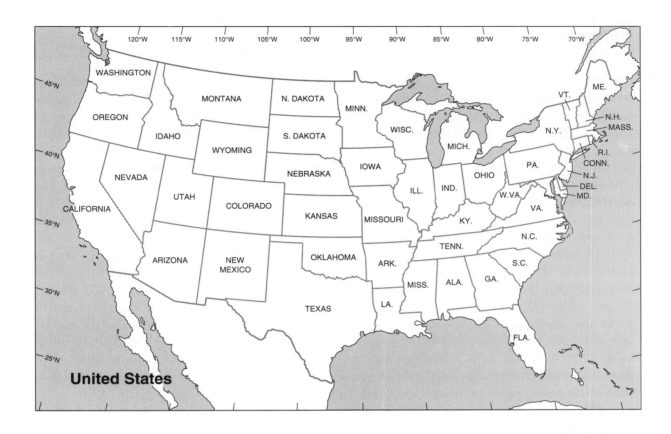

SKILL BUILDING: GRAPHS

Look at the line and bar graphs on page 811, under the title "The Statistics of Hard Times." From these you should be able to learn the answers to many questions about the Great Depression and the New Deal. For example:

1. Judging from the statistics on personal income, unemployment rate, stock prices, and building construction, did the New Deal succeed in reviving the economy to 1929 levels at any point prior to the United States' 1941 entry into World War II?

2. What was the impact of World War II on economic recovery?

3. Judging from all of the statistics shown in the graphs, which was the worst year of the depression?

4. Herbert Hoover, during his presidency, kept predicting that prosperity was just around the corner. Is there anything in these graphs that would support his forecast? The Roosevelt administration claimed that it had made considerable headway in improving the economy by 1939. Do the graphs confirm that assertion?

HISTORICAL SOURCES

The sources of information that historians use to learn about the personalities, feuds, hopes, fears, and intentions of the men and women who wield power in each presidential administration are the memoirs, diaries, and histories those individuals write. Find the places in Chapter 25 that discuss Hugh Johnson, Frances Perkins, Eleanor Roosevelt, Harry Hopkins, and Harold Ickes. Part of what the historian knows about them comes from books that each published: Hugh Johnson, *The Blue Eagle from Egg to Earth*; Frances Perkins, *The Roosevelt I Knew*; Eleanor Roosevelt, *This I Remember*; Harry Hopkins, *Spending to Save*; and *The Secret Diary of Harold L. Ickes*. Why are such books good historical sources? Why is it important that historians check any "facts" they obtain from these memoirs, diaries, and histories against several other sources before relying on them?

On page 832 of the text and in "A Place in Time: Cimarron County, Oklahoma—Heart of the Dust Bowl," the author refers to pictures taken by Dorothea Lange and other New Deal photographers. In the 1930s the Farm Security Administration employed Lange, Walker Evans, Arthur Rothstein, and other talented photographers to compile a visual record of rural America: its people, problems, and poverty. A selection of these photographs can be found in the book *The Years of Bitterness and Pride: FSA Photographs, 1935–1943* (New York, 1975). Find a copy of this volume, and look at photographs 76 and 83 by Rothstein. Both show dust storm–battered Oklahoma in 1936. In what ways do the pictures enhance the verbal descriptions in "A Place in Time"?

Historians suggest that these dust storms were not unavoidable acts of nature; human use and misuse of the land contributed. How? What actions did the New Deal take to try to remedy the environmental damage?

MULTIPLE-CHOICE QUESTIONS

Circle the letter of the item that best completes each statement or answers the question.

1. In 1932 President Hoover used the army to expel which of the following protest groups from Washington, D.C.?
   a. farmers demanding that government support agricultural prices
   b. women demanding equal treatment from relief officials
   c. World War I veterans demanding immediate payment of their bonuses
   d. blacks demanding passage of a federal antilynching law

2. Who hoped to be elected president in 1936 by building a huge following for his "Share Our Wealth" scheme (confiscate the great private fortunes and redistribute the money to the poor)?
   a. Harold Ickes
   b. Henry Wallace
   c. Francis E. Townsend
   d. Huey Long

3. Which of the following best characterizes Herbert Hoover's handling of the depression?
    a. He followed the advice of Secretary of the Treasury Andrew Mellon to do nothing and wait for economic recovery to occur naturally.
    b. His efforts were limited by his fears of unbalancing the federal budget and concentrating too much power and responsibility in Washington.
    c. He refused to have the federal government help failing business corporations.
    d. He initiated vast new programs to employ the jobless, control farm surpluses, and regulate banking and the stock exchange.

4. The leader of Franklin Roosevelt's "black cabinet" was
    a. Hugh Johnson.
    b. Frances Perkins.
    c. Mary McLeod Bethune.
    d. Harold Ickes.

5. Two reforms passed during Roosevelt's second term were the
    a. Fair Labor Standards Act and National Housing Act.
    b. National Industrial Recovery Act and Agricultural Adjustment Act.
    c. Social Security Act and Wagner Act.
    d. SEC and WPA.

6. During the New Deal, which interest group exercised less influence over the federal government than it had in the 1920s?
    a. organized labor
    b. farmers
    c. business
    d. social workers

7. Which federal programs created during the Hundred Days were later declared unconstitutional by the Supreme Court?
    a. NRA and AAA
    b. FDIC and HOLC
    c. FERA and CCC
    d. TVA and PWA

8. Which of the following agencies was created during Hoover's administration to help failing business corporations and continued to be active through the New Deal years?
    a. Federal Emergency Relief Administration
    b. Tennessee Valley Authority
    c. Federal Deposit Insurance Corporation
    d. Reconstruction Finance Corporation

9. John Maynard Keynes's economic theory
    a. suggests that deficit spending by the government can stimulate economic recovery.
    b. was closely followed by Franklin Roosevelt and his New Deal.
    c. stresses the importance of a government's maintaining a balanced budget at all times.
    d. was proved wrong by America's experiences in the 1930s.

10. The "Okies"
    a. founded the American Liberty League.
    (b.) were farmers displaced by dust storms, depression, and the AAA who migrated to California.
    c. were the main followers of Dr. Townsend, who demanded a pension for elderly farmers and laborers.
    d. founded the first union for ranch hands, cowboys, and country-music performers.

SHORT-ANSWER QUESTIONS

1. What caused the huge stock market boom in 1928–1929 and its subsequent crash in October 1929? How did the practice of buying on margin contribute to both boom and bust?

2. Compare the New Deal's attitudes toward urban Democratic political machines and bosses with those of the earlier progressive reformers.

3. Which groups made up the new Democratic coalition that reelected Roosevelt by a landslide in 1936? Why was each group attracted to the New Deal?

4. Discuss the record of the New Deal on conservation and the environment.

5. Describe Roosevelt's court-packing plan. Why did he propose it? Did he win or lose the fight to remake the Supreme Court? Why?

6. What caused the "Roosevelt recession"? What did the New Deal do to combat it?

7. What brought about the end of the New Deal in 1939?

ESSAY QUESTIONS

1. Discuss the causes of the depression of the 1930s.

2. Compare and contrast President Hoover's and President Roosevelt's attempts to deal with the depression and its victims. Why did each president follow his particular course?

3. Discuss how the Roosevelt administration affected the lives of women and blacks. How much progress was made in raising each group to full political and economic equality with white males?

4. One historian has written, "When Franklin D. Roosevelt faced the newly elected Congress in 1935, the result promised to be a fresh outburst of reform and recovery legislation which would surpass even that of the Hundred Days." Explain what movements and events in America in 1934 and 1935 were pushing Congress and Roosevelt toward this new "outburst of reform."

5. Compare and contrast the legislation and programs of the first and second New Deals. In what ways was the second merely a continuation of the first? In what ways did the second represent a leftward shift, a significant change in direction? How successful was each in reviving the economy?

26

American Life in a Decade of Crisis at Home and Abroad

OUTLINE AND SUMMARY

I. The American People in the Depression Decade

A. *The Plight of a People*

The depression imposed tremendous suffering. Even with all the New Deal programs, the unemployment rate never fell much below 14 percent during the thirties. A quarter of all farm families had to accept relief to survive, as did 1 million elderly citizens. The hard times brought both physical and emotional distress to millions. According to one historian, much of the generation that lived through the depression carried with it thereafter an "invisible scar."

B. *Industrial Workers Unionize*

In 1933 fewer than 3 million workers belonged to unions. Management in the steel, automobile, textile, and other mass-production industries had defeated all previous attempts to organize their employees. In the 1930s the combination of hard times and the prolabor attitude of government revived interest in unions. At first the American Federation of Labor, committed to protecting the narrow interests of its skilled craft-union affiliates, failed to grasp the new opportunities. But some of its more activist leaders, including John L. Lewis and Sidney Hillman, in November 1935 established the Committee for Industrial Organization (later renamed the Congress of Industrial Organizations, CIO) and sent hundreds of organizers to the steel, rubber, car, and textile factories to sign up members in industrywide unions. In March 1937 Lewis convinced U.S. Steel to sign a contract recognizing the steelworkers' union and granting pay increases and a forty-hour workweek. When General Motors refused to negotiate, Walter and Victor Reuther and other United Automobile Workers (UAW) officials led sit-down strikes that halted all production for six weeks. President Roosevelt and the governor of Michigan refused to use the army or militia to dislodge the strikers, and the occupiers beat back the attacks of local police. Thus General Motors had no alternative but to sign a contract recognizing the UAW.

Henry Ford and Tom Girdler, leader of Republic and other "Little Steel" companies, refused to deal with unions and fought them with violence, as in the Battle of the Overpass and the Memorial Day Massacre. Even they, however, finally recognized and bargained with unions by 1941. The textile workers of the South; agricultural laborers; domestics; and most women, black, and recent immigrant workers remained unorganized. Nonetheless, the labor movement in the thirties scored a major breakthrough, raising union membership to more than 8 million. Powerful corporations gave in to unionization because of workers' militance, management's fear of labor violence and sabotage, and above all the refusal of the New Dealers to put the power of government on the side of business against strikers.

C. Mixed Blessings for Women

During the depression women workers suffered about a 20 percent unemployment rate; were often displaced by men in teaching, social work, and librarianships; were usually paid less than men; and were often told that if they married, they would be dismissed. Some women workers were helped by unions and by the Fair Labor Standards Act, but many of the occupations in which women predominated were not covered by either. Despite all these disadvantages, the proportion of women, including married women, in the labor force continued to grow.

D. Blacks, Hispanic-Americans, and Native Americans Cope with Hard Times

The depression slowed the movement of rural African-Americans to cities and to the North. In 1940, 77 percent of the 12 million African-Americans still lived in the South. Blacks in agriculture and industry had even higher rates of displacement and unemployment than whites, and they were often denied equal protection of the law, as demonstrated by lynchings and the case of the Scottsboro boys. Blacks organized and protested as best they could.

The depression was equally hard on more than 2 million Hispanics. Many of the Mexican immigrants were migratory farm laborers who competed for jobs with the "Okies" arriving in the Southwest. With a surplus of farm workers, employers and relief officials put pressure on Hispanics to return to Mexico, and half a million did during the 1930s. Those who remained either drifted to the barrios of southwestern cities or worked for miserably low wages on large farms. Mexican-Americans occasionally struck for better pay.

The 170,000 Indians were the poorest of all Americans. By 1933 they had lost to whites two-thirds of the land they had owned in 1887, the year the ill-conceived Dawes Act was passed. John Collier, a reformer, became Roosevelt's commissioner of Indian affairs. He used CCC and WPA labor and money to create jobs and build much-needed facilities on Indian reservations. He also proposed legislation to end the Dawes Act, stop all further sale of Indian lands, grant self-government to the tribes, and encourage revival of Native American culture. After much opposition from both land-hungry whites and some Native Americans, Collier saw part of his program embodied in the 1934 Indian Reorganization Act, which did at least reverse the steady loss of Indian lands. After the New Deal, however, Collier resigned and federal protection of Native Americans evaporated.

E. Family Life and Population Trends

Hard times brought changes in family life and population trends. Marriage rates and birthrates declined, while desertion increased. Population and urban growth slowed. The shift of people westward across the continent, however, continued. If the depression broke up some families, it produced in others greater solidarity and promoted a spirit of cooperation among people. The poor shared what little they had with those even poorer.

II. The American Cultural Scene in the Thirties

A. *The Golden Age of Radio*

Listening to the radio was an extremely popular activity in the 1930s. The comedy of Jack Benny and George Burns and Gracie Allen and the melodrama of the soap operas gave people an escape from bleak economic reality. Mass culture became even more standardized than it had been in the twenties.

B. *The Silver Screen*

Movies, too, were enormously popular. A few documentaries and some dramas dealt with contemporary social problems. But most Hollywood films offered escape from a troubled world. Americans flocked to see gangster movies like *Little Caesar,* musicals like *Gold Diggers of 1933,* and the Marx Brothers comedies. Hollywood films of the thirties presented most characters as stereotypes.

C. *The Literature of the Early Thirties*

Fiction in the early thirties was somber in tone and radically "challenged the fundamental premises of American ideology." James T. Farrell's *Studs Lonigan,* John Dos Passos's *U.S.A.,* and Nathanael West's *Miss Lonelyhearts* are examples. Radical novelists and playwrights such as Jack Conroy, Josephine Herbst, and Clifford Odets often dealt with exploitation of labor and class struggle in their works.

D. *The Later Thirties: The Popular Front and Cultural Nationalism*

Writers and artists in the latter half of the 1930s found much to admire in America's history and its people, though not necessarily in its capitalist economic system. Several things account for this upsurge in cultural nationalism: (1) the rise of aggressive fascism abroad threatened all the democratic and humanitarian values our country claimed to uphold; (2) the communists, between 1935 and 1939, praised New Deal America and advocated a Popular Front of all left-wingers and liberals against fascism: the Loyalists' struggle against Francisco Franco's fascist rebels in the Spanish Civil War (1936–1939) especially awakened American liberals and intellectuals to the fascist menace; (3) the WPA art projects encouraged appreciation of America's heritage. John Steinbeck's *The Grapes of Wrath* and James Agee's and Walker Evans's *Let Us Now Praise Famous Men* paid tribute to the endurance of America's rural poor. Composers Aaron Copland and George Gershwin used American folktales and racial minorities in their works. American jazz and swing blossomed. Regional writers, such as Zora Neal Hurston and William Faulkner, and painters, such as Thomas Hart Benton, depicted their home sections of the nation. American folk art and historical museums and novels became popular.

E. The Age of Streamlining

The look of material objects surrounding Americans in the 1930s began to change as business, hoping to boost sales, adopted the industrial design known as streamlining. Corporate attempts to show the public that capitalism could bring the nation a prosperous, modern, streamlined future reached a high point at the New York World's Fair of 1939.

F. Undercurrents of Apprehension

If Americans felt more positive about their society in the late thirties, they also experienced growing apprehension about the gathering war clouds. That may be why so many people overreacted to Orson Welles's 1938 radio dramatization of *War of the Worlds.*

III. The United States in a Menacing World

A. Introduction

While Americans struggled with the depression at home, aggressive, militaristic fascist regimes came to power in Italy, Germany, and Japan. The United States reacted to these developments abroad "with ambivalence," torn between dislike of fascism and "an even stronger desire for peace."

B. FDR's Nationalism and the Good Neighbor Policy

In his first inaugural address, Roosevelt pledged the United States to be a "good neighbor" in the family of nations. His administration applied this policy in Latin America by supporting the Montevideo declaration that "no state has the right to intervene in the internal or external affairs of another." FDR withdrew U.S. troops from Haiti, reduced American domination over Panama and the Canal Zone, and refrained from using force against left-wing governments in Cuba and Mexico. The administration did, however, apply economic pressure to influence events in those two countries.

C. The Rise of Fascism in Europe and Asia

Benito Mussolini and his Fascist followers took control of Italy in 1922. In 1933 the Nazi leader Adolf Hitler became chancellor of Germany. Preaching racism, aggressive nationalism, and anti-Semitism, Hitler quickly established an absolute dictatorship over Germany, began persecuting the Jews, and embarked on military buildup and conquest. In 1936 his troops reoccupied the Rhineland; in 1938 they annexed Austria. Meanwhile, Mussolini invaded Ethiopia. Germany grabbed the Sudetenland from Czechoslovakia without firing a shot when, in 1938, at the Munich Conference, the British and French agreed to the transfer to appease Hitler. On the other side of the world, Japanese imperialists seized the Chinese province of Manchuria, renaming it Manchukuo, and in 1937 began a war of conquest to take over all of China. In 1936 the three aggressors signed an alliance.

D. The American Mood: No More War

Americans disliked these actions but were determined not to be pulled into another war. The majority in this country now viewed our participation in World War I as a mistake. The revelations of the Nye Committee about the roles played by bankers and weapons suppliers in that war reinforced that belief. In the thirties students held antiwar protests; novelists and playwrights condemned war in their works; and Congress passed the Neutrality Acts, prohibiting the United States from making loans or selling arms to belligerents.

E. Hesitant Response to the Fascist Challenge

Some Americans admired Hitler and Mussolini, or at least found them preferable to communist leaders. Others saw them as comic rather than dangerous figures. Still other Americans from 1933 on warned of the menace that fascism and its leaders posed to freedom and peace. Almost all agreed, however, that the United States should not go to war against them. Roosevelt, whatever his personal sentiments, hesitated to buck this strong antiwar feeling. Aside from refusing to recognize the puppet government that Japan set up in Manchuria and extending modest loans to China, Roosevelt did little against fascist aggression.

F. 1938–1939: The Gathering Storm

In 1939 Hitler seized the remainder of Czechoslovakia, threatened to attack Poland, and signed the Nazi-Soviet Non-Aggression Pact to ensure Soviet neutrality during the planned German invasion of Poland. Meanwhile, Mussolini sent Italian troops into Albania. These events in Europe intensified the debate in the United States about the role this country should play. Though deploring the aggression, some continued to argue against American intervention, recalling that our participation in World War I had killed the progressive reform movement and had led to repression at home. This time, they thought, we should concentrate on saving reform and democracy in the United States.

On the other hand, many Americans grew alarmed and preached that the United States must take a more active role. FDR agreed. After the fascist conquest of Czechoslovakia and Albania, the president sent messages to Hitler and Mussolini asking them to pledge not to invade any other nation. The two dictators responded with ridicule. Roosevelt also asked Congress to appropriate much more money to build up American defenses.

G. America and the Jewish Refugees

Throughout the thirties German persecution of the Jews intensified. In 1935 the Nazis enacted the Nuremberg Laws, stripping German Jews of citizenship and rights. On *Kristallnacht* in 1938 the Nazis unleashed a wave of violence against Jews, attacking them and their homes, synagogues, and businesses. As the outrages and threats increased, tens of thousands of European Jews fled, seeking countries that would admit them. Sixty thousand entered the United States between 1933 and 1938. Among them were distinguished musicians, architects, writers, and scholars who enriched the cultural life of their adopted nation. Such refugee physicists as Leo Szilard and James Franck played key roles in developing the atomic bomb for the United States.

Congress would not amend discriminatory immigration laws, however, to offer a haven to the hundreds of thousands of additional Jews desperately needing a safe home, nor would Roosevelt exert pressure on the lawmakers to do so. The majority of Americans opposed letting in more Jews, apparently because of isolationist, anti-immigrant, and anti-Semitic attitudes. In 1939 the United States even stopped the *St. Louis,* a ship carrying nine hundred Jewish refugees, and forced it to return to Europe. There the countryless refugees were soon murdered by the Nazis.

IV. Conclusion

The thirties opened on the heels of the stock market crash and closed on the brink of war. Between these bleak events, the decade "brought bright moments of political creativity, social advance, and cultural achievement." Millions of industrial workers became unionized. The NAACP and other organizations continued their fight against discrimination, laying the groundwork for later gains. Writers and artists depicted American life, including its rich regional cultures, in their novels, plays, photographs, and paintings. And all the while, in Europe and Asia, fascism, Nazism, and militarism grew more threatening.

VOCABULARY

The following terms are used in Chapter 26. To understand the chapter fully, it is important that you know what each of them means.

militance   aggressiveness, combativeness

urbanization   growth of cities and towns; movement of population from rural areas to cities and towns

barrios   Hispanic urban neighborhoods

repatriation   the bringing or sending back of a person to his or her own country

assimilation   the process of absorbing or incorporating a minority group into the majority culture or society; the process of making the minority resemble or become like the majority

demographic   pertaining to social statistics such as the births, deaths, marriages, movements, growth, and so on, of populations

proletariat   the industrial working class

totalitarian   of or pertaining to a centralized government that attempts to control all institutions in its society and permits no opposition parties or opinions

streamlining   eliminating all extraneous design features in favor of smoothly flowing surfaces (ones that are often teardrop shaped and offer the least resistance in passing through the air)

appeasement   making concessions to pacify, quiet, or satisfy the other party

IDENTIFICATIONS

After reading Chapter 26, you should be able to identify and explain the historical significance of each of the following:

John L. Lewis

Sidney Hillman

Committee for Industrial Organization, later Congress of Industrial Organizations (CIO)

Walter Reuther, the United Automobile Workers, and the sit-downs

Henry Ford, Harry Bennett, and the Battle of the Overpass

Tom Girdler, "Little Steel," and the Memorial Day Massacre

Scottsboro boys

Richard Wright

John Collier and the Indian Reorganization Act, 1934

Pare Lorentz, "The River" and "The Plow That Broke the Plains"

Marx Brothers

Stepin Fetchit   } actor

James T. Farrell, *Studs Lonigan*   pg 849-850

John Dos Passos, *U.S.A.*   - portray money and USA

Nathanael West, *Miss Lonelyhearts*

fascism and Nazism

Popular Front

Francisco Franco, Spanish Loyalists, and the Spanish Civil War

Ernest Hemingway, *For Whom the Bell Tolls*

Nazi-Soviet Pact, 1939

John Steinbeck, *The Grapes of Wrath*

James Agee and Walker Evans, *Let Us Now Praise Famous Men*

Benny Goodman, Count Basie, and Glenn Miller

Zora Neal Hurston, *Their Eyes Were Watching God*

William Faulkner

Good Neighbor policy

Benito Mussolini

Adolf Hitler, *Mein Kampf*

Munich Conference, 1938

Nye Committee hearings

Neutrality Acts

Nuremberg Laws, *Kristallnacht*, and the "final solution"

St. Louis

SKILL BUILDING: MAPS

1. On the map of Europe and North Africa in the 1930s on the following page, locate each of the following and explain its significance in the coming of World War II:

   Spain

   Soviet Union

   Italy

   Germany

   Rhineland

   Ethiopia

   Austria

   Sudetenland

   Munich

   Czechoslovakia

   Albania

   Poland (area occupied by the Soviet Union; area occupied by Germany under the terms of the Nazi-Soviet Pact)

**Europe and
North Africa, 1930s**

2. On the map below of Asia in the 1930s, locate each of the following and explain its significance in the coming of World War II:

Japan

Manchuria (Manchukuo)

China (areas occupied by Japan as of 1939)

Asia in the 1930s

HISTORICAL SOURCES

In Chapter 26 of the text, the author has used, among others, two types of sources that have proved helpful in the study of modern history: oral-history interviews and public-opinion polls. Equipped with tape recorders and/or notepads, historians have interviewed a broad cross section of people, from the famous and powerful to ordinary men and women, who have lived through a variety of experiences and events, such as immigrating to the United States, coping with the depression, and participating in sit-down strikes. Recordings and/or transcripts of some of these interviews have been placed in oral-history archives, such as the one at Columbia University, which are available to scholars. Others have been published in books. One of the best collections of interviews about life in the 1930s is Studs Terkel's *Hard Times*. The recollection of the automobile worker of the 1936–1937 sit-down strike on page 839 comes from that book. You will find other oral-history accounts on pages 838–840, 842, and 845–846. Why has the author used each of these recollections? Although oral-history interviews are an excellent source, they often contain inaccurate information. Why do you suppose that is so?

On pages 842, 857, and 863 the author cites the findings of public-opinion polls. In each case, what is this information meant to show? Social scientists and statisticians first started taking these polls in a formal, "scientific" way in the 1930s. In 1935 George H. Gallup founded the best known of these poll-taking organizations, the American Institute of Public Opinion. Are the findings of public-opinion polls always accurate? Why or why not?

Look at "A Place in Time: The Los Angeles Barrio in the 1930s." This is an example of ethnic history. The field of ethnic and immigrant history has received increased attention from scholars since the 1960s, as we have come to appreciate fully the fact that America has always been composed of a variety of peoples. To comprehend our nation's past, we must study what each of its ethnic groups contributed to and experienced in that past. What does this account of Mexican-Americans in the depression illustrate about the impact of hard times on various groups and on the ways that government officials reacted to depression problems?

MULTIPLE-CHOICE QUESTIONS

Circle the letter of the item that best completes each statement or answers the question.

1. The Scottsboro boys were
   a. black teenagers sentenced to death by an all-white jury for allegedly raping two white women.
   b. one of the most popular swing bands of the 1930s.
   c. the main characters in Clifford Odets's play about labor unrest and a strike, *Waiting for Lefty*.
   d. young, unemployed Mexican-American farm workers who were forced by relief officials to return to Mexico.

2. Commissioner of Indian Affairs John Collier proposed to
   a. encourage Native Americans to leave reservations and seek jobs in the cities.
   b. stop the further sale of Indian lands, grant tribal self-government, and revive Native American cultures.
   c. end segregated schools for Native Americans, enroll their children in white schools, and thus speed up Indian assimilation.
   d. terminate all special government programs and protection for Native Americans because he believed that they kept Indians dependent and demoralized.

3. Which company agreed to recognize and bargain with the union its workers had joined after the workers occupied its plants in a six-week sit-down strike?
   a. Ford Motor Company
   b. Republic Steel
   c. General Motors
   d. U.S. Steel

4. The protagonist in which of these novels goes to Spain to help the Loyalists fight against Franco and fascism?
   a. James T. Farrell's *Studs Lonigan*
   b. Ernest Hemingway's *For Whom the Bell Tolls*
   c. Richard Wright's *Native Son*
   d. William Faulkner's *Absalom, Absalom!*

5. Which of the following did *not* occur during the depression?
   a. Birthrates and marriage rates declined.
   b. Urbanization and population growth slowed.
   c. Immigration into the United States from Europe and Mexico increased greatly.
   d. High school enrollment increased sharply.

6. All of the following were popular pastimes during the depression *except*
   a. going to the movies.
   b. watching television.
   c. listening to the radio.
   d. listening to swing played by the big bands of Benny Goodman, Count Basie, and Glenn Miller.

7. Women in the 1930s were
   a. excluded from the UAW and other industrial unions.
   b. encouraged by Secretary of Labor Frances Perkins and other New Dealers to pursue good jobs and careers along with being wives and mothers.
   c. concentrated in industries where unionization made the least headway.
   d. driven out of the paid labor force almost entirely.

8. Which of the following statements is true about American attitudes in the 1930s?
   a. The majority of Americans believed that married women had as much right to work at gainful employment as married men.
   b. The majority of Americans still disapproved of going to the movies and considered it to be sinful behavior.
   c. The majority of Americans favored liberalizing U.S. immigration laws to admit more Jewish refugees.
   d. The majority of Americans believed that the United States should have stayed out of World War I.

9. All of the following took strong anti-Nazi positions in the 1930s *except*
   a. Ambassador Joseph P. Kennedy.
   b. journalist Dorothy Thompson.
   c. poet Archibald MacLeish.
   d. cultural critic Lewis Mumford.

10. Which of the following helped convince Americans that U.S. participation in World War I was a mistake that should not be repeated by getting involved a second time?
    a. the Ludlow Amendment
    b. Roosevelt's "Quarantine the Aggressors" speech
    c. the Nye Committee hearings
    d. the *St. Louis* incident

SHORT-ANSWER QUESTIONS

1. What was the Good Neighbor Policy, and how closely did the Roosevelt administration adhere to it?

2. What aggressive actions on the international scene did Fascist Italy and militarist Japan take during the 1930s?

3. In what ways did Hitler defy the terms of the Treaty of Versailles and commit acts of aggression between 1933 and 1939?

4. Explain what the Popular Front was. Who was attracted to the idea? When and why did the Popular Front idea collapse?

5. How did British prime minister Neville Chamberlain and French premier Edouard Daladier attempt to appease Hitler at the 1938 Munich Conference? Did President Roosevelt approve of the agreement they made at Munich? Did Munich bring "peace in our time," as Chamberlain predicted?

6. What was the 1939 Nazi-Soviet Pact? How did it open the door to Hitler's invasion of Poland and World War II? How did American liberals react to it?

7. How did the United States respond to Jewish refugees from Nazi Germany? Why?

ESSAY QUESTIONS

1. One social history of the 1930s is titled *The Invisible Scar*. Is this an appropriate title for a book about the depression decade? Why or why not?

2. In 1933 fewer than 3 million workers belonged to unions; by 1941 more than 8 million did. How and why did this "unionization of vast sectors of America's industrial work force" come about? Which workers were still almost totally unorganized in 1941?

3. Discuss the impact of the depression on the lives of women, blacks, Hispanics, and Indians.

4. Discuss American culture in the 1930s. How did popular culture and the fine arts respond to the political and economic events and conditions of the depression decade?

5. Discuss the reactions of the American public and the U.S. government in the 1930s to the rise of aggressive fascist regimes in Italy, Japan, and Germany. How do you explain these reactions?

27

Waging Global War, 1939 – 1945

OUTLINE AND SUMMARY

I. Into the Storm, 1939–1941

A. *Storm in Europe*

World War II began on September 1,1939, when Hitler attacked Poland. Britain and France, committed by treaty to defend Poland, declared war on Germany. Soon after, the United States revised the Neutrality Acts to permit sales of weapons to belligerents on a cash-and-carry basis. Most Americans favored this move as a way to help Britain and France without having to fight. In April 1940 German armies turned on Denmark and Norway; in May they conquered the Netherlands and Belgium; by mid-June France capitulated. The Germans then began terror bombing raids over the cities of England. During this Battle of Britain, Prime Minister Winston Churchill appealed to President Roosevelt for help. The majority of Americans favored stepped-up weapons shipments to bolster Hitler's one remaining opponent, but an articulate minority feared that such aid would weaken U.S. defenses and needlessly pull us into war.

B. *The Election of 1940*

Because of the menacing situation in Europe, Roosevelt decided to run for a third term. His Republican opponent, Wendell L. Willkie, held foreign-policy views similar to Roosevelt's. During the campaign Roosevelt underlined his interventionist position by signing an executive agreement with Winston Churchill to give Britain fifty overage U.S. destroyers in exchange for leases on air and naval bases in British possessions in the Western Hemisphere. In protest, isolationists organized the America First Committee, which preached that we must not give any aid to belligerents or become involved in the struggle against Hitler. However, in apparent support of Roosevelt's actions, the voters elected him to an unprecedented third term.

C. *From Isolation to Intervention*

When FDR learned that Britain was running out of dollars to buy the war supplies she desperately needed, he proposed the Lend-Lease bill. It would permit the president to lend or lease military equipment to any country whose defense he thought vital to American security. Although this would certainly be an unneutral act, the majority of the public favored it, and Congress passed it in March 1941. When Hitler attacked the U.S.S.R. in June 1941, Roosevelt gave lend-lease aid to the Soviets as well as to the British. Unfortunately, the supplies often ended up at the bottom of the Atlantic because of the constant sinkings by German submarines. To prevent such losses the United States began convoying British ships as far as Iceland, tracking German submarines, and notifying the British of their location. These actions inevitably led to conflict between German and American vessels. By the fall of 1941 the two countries were engaged in an undeclared naval war. Meanwhile Roosevelt and Churchill moved closer to an alliance when they met off the coast of Newfoundland in the summer of 1941 and issued the Atlantic Charter. Still, Roosevelt hesitated to ask Congress for a formal declaration of war against Germany.

D. Toward Pearl Harbor

With Europe at war, Japan expanded its aggression from China to the resource-rich British, Dutch, and French colonies in Southeast Asia. Japan's drive to replace Western imperialists and alone dominate the Far East clashed directly with the Open Door policy of the United States. Though not wanting a war, the Roosevelt administration attempted to change Tokyo's course by applying economic pressure. In July 1940 Washington prohibited the sale of aviation gasoline to Japan. When Tokyo occupied northern Indochina and signed the Tripartite Pact with Germany and Italy, Roosevelt placed an embargo on all metals, chemicals, and machine parts. In July 1941, in response to Japan's seizure of the rest of Indochina, Washington froze Japanese assets in the United States, ending all trade. Japanese prime minister Hideki Tojo decided to make a last-ditch effort to persuade Washington to reopen trade and recognize Japan's conquests. If that failed, Japan would attempt to destroy the U.S. Pacific fleet with a surprise attack on Pearl Harbor, leaving the United States too weak to thwart Japan's imperial dreams. Washington knew its refusal would provoke an attack somewhere in the Pacific. Nonetheless, the Roosevelt administration would not yield and sent warnings to all base commanders. On December 7, 1941, the Japanese struck Pearl Harbor, and the next day Congress recognized that a state of war existed with Japan. On the eleventh Japan's two allies, Germany and Italy, declared war on the United States, and we reciprocated.

E. On the Defensive

In the months after Pearl Harbor the United States faced a bleak situation. Nazi submarines prowled off our east coast and took a heavy toll on Allied ships. Hitler's armies had pushed to the outskirts of Leningrad and Moscow and were launching new offensives in the Crimea and Caucasus. Other German armies landed in North Africa and headed toward the vital Suez Canal. Japan followed the raid on Hawaii with conquests of the Philippines, Malaya, Thailand, Hong Kong, Guam, Wake, Singapore, the Dutch East Indies, and most of the island chains in the Western Pacific.

II. America Mobilizes for War

A. Organizing for Victory

To mobilize the economy Roosevelt established hundreds of special wartime agencies, such as the War Production Board, which allocated scarce materials, limited manufacture of civilian goods, and awarded military production contracts. In 1943 FDR appointed James F. Byrnes head of the Office of War Mobilization, which coordinated the efforts of the many government agencies, private industry, and the military. Under this government direction the United States produced more armaments than Germany, Italy, and Japan combined. Cost-plus-fixed-fee contracts guaranteed handsome profits to the giant corporations that received most of the defense contracts. Federal authority and the federal budget grew rapidly, as did the influence of the military and big corporations on American life.

B. A War Economy

Between 1941 and 1945 the U.S. government spent nearly twice as much as it did from 1788 through 1940. Fueled by this expenditure, the economy boomed. During the war farm income doubled, corporate profits climbed by 70 percent, and unemployment vanished as 17 million new jobs were created. Many of the poor moved into the middle class. Most labor leaders gave no-strike pledges, but John L. Lewis led his miners on repeated work stoppages. An increasingly conservative Congress retaliated with the antilabor Smith-Connally Act. To curb inflation the Office of Price Administration imposed price controls and rationing. As a result the cost of living during World War II rose 28 percent, compared to a 62 percent increase during World War I. The government raised the huge sums needed to fight the war with the sale of bonds, which provided half the money, and with steeply increased federal taxes, which provided the rest.

C. Science and the War

The government also employed thousands of scientists in the drive for victory. The secret Manhattan Project to beat the Germans in the race to develop nuclear weapons was the greatest of the government-sponsored scientific endeavors. Led by physicist J. Robert Oppenheimer, the Manhattan Project spent some $2 billion. On July 16, 1945, it catapulted the world into the atomic age when it tested the first nuclear bomb over the New Mexico desert.

D. Propaganda and Politics

To unify Americans and prevent dangerous security leaks, Roosevelt established the Office of War Information and the Office of Censorship. They interfered less with freedom of speech and the press than similar World War I agencies had.

Full employment and prosperity led to a politically conservative trend. More Republicans and conservative Democrats were elected to Congress in 1942. They cut welfare programs, abolished New Deal agencies, and halted any further reforms.

III. War and American Society

A. The New Mobility

More than 15 million Americans left their homes to serve in the armed forces. Another 15 million moved from one location to another for family and economic reasons. Poor whites, blacks, and Chicanos left rural areas to seek jobs in war-production centers in the North and West. Terrible shortages of housing and other facilities developed in these cities, contributing to urban blight and to conflicts between newcomers and older residents. These vast internal migrations also produced a more uniform national culture and broadened the horizons of many.

B. Education and Entertainment

High school enrollment dropped as more teenagers quit to take full-time jobs. On the other hand, the armed forces sent nearly a million people to college campuses for special training. Americans went to the movies to watch films that entertained them. Films often presented the enemy as fiends and the Allies, including the Soviets, in a highly favorable light. The public gobbled up war news from periodicals such as *Life* and from the reports of radio correspondents Edward R. Murrow, Eric Sevareid, and others.

C. Women and the Family

Drawn by high wages, patriotism, and government encouragement, millions of women went to work in defense plants. By 1945 women constituted over one-third of the labor force. They took on such formerly male-dominated work as welding, riveting, operating cranes, and running lathes, although they earned only about 65 percent of what men received in the same fields. More than one-third of the women had children under fourteen years of age. Because there were few day-care centers, youngsters were often left on their own. Juvenile delinquency increased alarmingly. Marriage, birth, and divorce rates also soared. Some 300,000 women joined the armed forces. After 1945 most women left these wartime occupations but the experience gave them a new sense of their own capabilities.

D. African-Americans and the War

During World War II African-Americans demanded that the nation fight racism at home as well as abroad. The NAACP and the Congress of Racial Equality led the struggle for civil rights. To forestall a massive march on Washington organized by A. Philip Randolph, FDR in 1941 signed an executive order prohibiting racial discrimination in hiring and promotion by government agencies and defense contractors. The Fair Employment Practices Commission he created had little power, but wartime labor shortages opened many new jobs to blacks. Roughly 1 million blacks served in the armed forces, generally in segregated outfits commanded by white officers. They experienced other forms of discrimination as well. In civilian life, tensions developed between blacks demanding equality and resistant whites. Race riots erupted in Detroit and dozens of other places. More than 700,000 blacks left the South to settle in cities of the North and West. The move opened up greater opportunities and potential political power for African-Americans.

E. Native Americans, Mexican-Americans, and Jews in Wartime

Twenty-five thousand Native Americans served in the armed forces; another seventy-five thousand left reservations to work in defense industries. With assimilation impeded by prejudice against them, most Native Americans returned to their reservations after the war. Conditions there had deteriorated badly because Congress had slashed appropriations for Indian programs.

Hundreds of thousands of Mexicans entered the United States, legally and illegally, during the war to work on the big farms in the western states. At the same time many Mexican-Americans left migratory farm labor to seek better jobs in cities. In Los Angeles Anglo-American prejudice against Mexicans exploded in the zoot-suit riot. Some 350,000 Mexican-Americans served in the armed forces, and as with African-American and Native American veterans, they emerged from the experience with a heightened consciousness and demands for equality.

Despite America's condemnation of Nazi persecution of the Jews, anti-Semitic attitudes continued in the United States. These attitudes partly explain why this country refused to admit most refugees and was slow to organize other rescue efforts to save European Jews. By 1945 the Nazis had killed 6 million Jews and several million gypsies, Poles, communists, and homosexuals.

F. The Internment of Japanese-Americans

The government's treatment of Japanese-Americans during World War II was the one glaring exception to its otherwise good civil-liberties record. In an atmosphere of hysteria over Pearl Harbor, fear of Japanese invasion of the mainland, and traditional prejudice against Asian-Americans, the government uprooted 112,000 Japanese-Americans living on the West Coast and locked them in internment camps in remote interior regions. Unwilling in wartime to question claims of military necessity, the Supreme Court in 1944 upheld the constitutionality of evacuation. In the 1980s the government finally admitted that its actions had been unjustified, apologized to Japanese-Americans, and agreed to pay compensation to them for the property losses they suffered when they were detained.

IV. The Battlefront, 1942–1944

A. The Allied Drive in Europe

The British and Americans concentrated on beating Hitler first, Japan afterward. Stalin pressed his two allies to launch an invasion of Europe across the English Channel as quickly as possible. Churchill convinced Roosevelt they should postpone this second front and land instead in North Africa, where by May 1943 they had defeated large German and Italian armies. Meanwhile the Soviets turned the tide of battle in the east by winning at Stalingrad, holding out at Leningrad, and attacking the German invaders along a thousand-mile front. Again postponing the cross-channel invasion, the British and Americans captured Sicily and started a slow march up the Italian peninsula. There they encountered stiff opposition from German troops that were rushed in after Mussolini was deposed and the Italian government surrendered. In 1944–1945 the Soviets cleared the Germans out of the U.S.S.R. and pursued them across Eastern Europe. The British and Americans finally landed on the beaches of Normandy in June 1944 and fought their way toward Germany. The Nazis temporarily stopped the Allied drive in the Battle of the Bulge, but by early 1945 the Americans and British had reached the Rhine.

B. The War in the Pacific

The Japanese advances in the Pacific were first halted in the spring and summer of 1942 at the Battles of the Coral Sea and Midway. Thereafter, the U.S. Navy and Army assaulted

Japanese strongholds in the Solomon, Gilbert, Marshall, and Mariana islands. General Douglas MacArthur, earlier driven from the Philippines, retook Manila by 1945, and the U.S. Navy largely destroyed what was left of the Japanese fleet at the Battles of the Philippine Sea and Leyte Gulf. Despite its devastating losses, Japan showed no inclination to surrender.

C. The Grand Alliance

The Grand Alliance of Britain, the U.S.S.R., and the United States was forged out of military necessity, but the three had different goals for the postwar period. Roosevelt wanted to defeat fascism and establish a new world order strong enough to keep the peace, open trade, and protect national self-determination. Churchill hoped to keep the British colonial empire and maintain a balance of power in Europe against the Soviets. Stalin intended to weaken Germany permanently and to protect his country against any future attacks from the west by imposing Soviet domination over Eastern Europe. FDR attempted to reconcile and paper over these differences with personal diplomacy. He held top-level wartime conferences with other Allied leaders at Casablanca, Cairo, and Tehran. At Tehran, the first meeting of Churchill and Roosevelt with Stalin, details of the Normandy invasion were worked out and other military and political problems discussed.

D. The Election of 1944

Roosevelt had to divert his attention from wartime diplomacy long enough to win reelection in 1944. The Democrats nominated him for a fourth term but dropped Vice President Henry Wallace in favor of Harry S Truman. The Republicans nominated Thomas E. Dewey. In November Roosevelt won an unprecedented fourth term by the smallest margin of his career.

V. Triumph and Tragedy, 1945

A. Introduction

Roosevelt, Churchill, and Stalin conferred for the last time at Yalta in February 1945. Since the Red Army occupied most of Eastern Europe at that point and the United States wanted to secure Soviet help in defeating Japan, Roosevelt and Churchill had to make concessions to Stalin. In return for Stalin's promise that the U.S.S.R. would declare war on Japan shortly after Germany's surrender, the Western leaders agreed to Russia's regaining the territory Japan had wrested from it in 1905. Roosevelt and Churchill settled for Stalin's vague promise to allow free elections in Poland and other Eastern European nations. Stalin endorsed plans for the United Nations founding conference in April 1945 and recognized the anticommunist Jiang Jieshi as ruler of China rather than the communist Mao Zedong.

B. The Defeat of Germany

In April 1945 American and Russian troops met at the Elbe River, and Hitler committed suicide. On May 2, Berlin fell to the Soviets, and on May 8, Germany unconditionally surrendered. In the last phase of the fighting, the Allies liberated the German concentration camps, revealing the scope and horror of Nazi-perpetrated genocide. Roosevelt did not live to see V-E Day. On April 12 he died suddenly, bringing Harry S Truman to the presidency.

C. A New President

Truman distrusted the Soviets and soon accused them of breaking their Yalta promise to allow free elections in Poland. Stalin responded angrily and tightened his hold on Eastern Europe. By the time Truman, Churchill, and Stalin met at Potsdam in July, the Grand Alliance had disintegrated so badly that the three could agree on little.

D. The Atomic Bombs

The fighting in the Pacific continued. In 1945, after suffering heavy casualties, the United States captured Iwo Jima and Okinawa. In July the United States successfully tested an atomic bomb at Alamagordo, and Truman and Churchill issued the Potsdam Declaration, calling on Japan to surrender unconditionally or face "prompt and utter destruction." When Japan rejected that warning, Truman ordered use of the nuclear bombs. On August 6 the first fell on Hiroshima; on the eighth the second hit Nagasaki, following which Japan surrendered. Since then historians and others have probed the United States' motives and debated whether it was justified in dropping atomic bombs on Japanese cities.

VI. Conclusion

Fourteen million fighting men and 25 million civilians died in World War II. Vast areas of Europe and Asia lay in ruins. The United States, much changed socially and economically, emerged physically unscathed and militarily powerful. Almost immediately it locked horns with the Soviet Union in a Cold War and a spiraling atomic arms race that threatened global destruction.

VOCABULARY

The following terms are used in Chapter 27. To understand the chapter fully, it is important that you know what each of them means.

blitzkrieg   lightning war; swift waging of war by use of aircraft, tanks, and other powerful weapons, as practiced by Hitler's armies between 1939 and 1941

executive agreement   an agreement made between the president of the United States and the head of a government of another country; it is binding only on the president who makes it but does not require ratification by the Senate as a treaty does

convoying   using destroyers or other armed naval vessels and/or planes to escort and protect cargo ships and troop transports

embargo   a prohibition of commerce by government order

braceros   Mexican farm laborers brought into the United States under contract for seasonal work who are then expected to return to their country

acculturation   the process and result of adopting the cultural traits of another group

the Holocaust   the name given to the systematic effort of the Nazis to annihilate all European Jews

genocide   the planned extermination of a national, racial, or religious group

IDENTIFICATIONS

After reading Chapter 27, you should be able to identify and explain the historical significance of each of the following:

"phony war"

Battle of Britain

Henry L. Stimson

Henry Wallace

Wendell L. Willkie

isolationists and the America First Committee versus the interventionists

lend-lease

Atlantic Charter

Greater East Asia Co-Prosperity Sphere versus the Open Door policy

Tripartite Pact of the Axis powers

Hideki Tojo

Office of Price Administration (OPA)

James F. Byrnes and the Office of War Mobilization

Smith-Connally War Labor Disputes Act

Manhattan Project and J. Robert Oppenheimer

Servicemen's Readjustment Act (GI Bill of Rights)

"Rosie the Riveter"

A. Philip Randolph and the March-on-Washington Movement

Executive Order 8802 and the Fair Employment Practices Commission

pachucos, sailors, and the Los Angeles zoot-suit riot

Korematsu case (1944)

the Declaration of the United Nations

the Second Front

Dwight D. Eisenhower

Operation Torch and Operation Overlord

Battle of the Bulge

Battles of the Coral Sea and Midway

Chester Nimitz

Douglas MacArthur

Jiang Jieshi (Chiang Kai-shek) versus Mao Zedong (Mao Tse-tung)

Tehran and Yalta conferences

Potsdam Conference and Potsdam Declaration

SKILL BUILDING: MAPS

1. On the map of the European theater of war, 1939–1945, on page 360, locate and explain the military and/or political importance of each of the following:

Warsaw and Lublin, Poland

areas overrun by the German offensive between April and June 1940 (Denmark, Norway, Netherlands, Belgium, Luxembourg, France)

English Channel

Dunkirk

Iceland

areas of Eastern Europe and the Soviet Union held by the Germans as of spring 1942

Leningrad

Moscow

Stalingrad

Crimean Peninsula (Yalta)

Caucasus Mountains

North African campaign (Mediterranean Sea, Egypt, Suez Canal, Morocco, Algeria, Tunisia, Libya, Allied landing areas)

Sicily

Casablanca

Cairo

Rome

Eastern European countries occupied by the Soviet Union in 1944–1945 (Romania, Bulgaria, Yugoslavia, Hungary, Czechoslovakia)

Tehran, Iran

Normandy

Paris

Ardennes Forest (Battle of the Bulge)

Rhine River

Berlin

Vienna

Elbe River

European Theater, 1939–1945

ATLANTIC OCEAN

North Sea

Baltic Sea

England

France

Ger.

Spain

Italy

Slavery

Hungary

Yugo

Poland

Russia

Romania

Bulgaria

Greece

Black Sea

Turkey

Syria

Mediterranean Sea

morocco

French North Africa

Libya

Egypt

Red Sea

2. On the map of the Far Eastern theater of war, 1941–1945, which appears on the following page, locate and explain the military and/or political importance of each of the following:

areas attacked and/or occupied by Japan prior to or on December 7, 1941 (Manchuria, parts of China, Indochina, Thailand, Pearl Harbor)

Dutch East Indies

Burma and the Burma Road

Malaya

Philippines (Manila)

Java

Guam

Wake

Gilbert Islands

Battle of the Coral Sea

Battle of Midway

Solomon Islands (Guadalcanal)

Marshall Islands

Mariana Islands

Battle of the Philippine Sea

Leyte Gulf

Iwo Jima

Okinawa

Hiroshima and Nagasaki

Far Eastern Theater, 1939 – 1945

Mongolia

China

Sea of Japan

Japan

East China Sea

Okinawa

Iwo Jima

PACIFIC OCEAN

India

Burma

Thai.

Indo China

Philippine Islands

South China Sea

Mariana

Hawaii

New Guinea

Coral Sea

Australia

Aleutian

HISTORICAL SOURCES

Look at the discussions of the decisions made at the wartime conferences held at Casablanca, Cairo, Tehran (p. 892), Yalta (pp. 893–894), and Potsdam (pp. 894–895). How do historians know what was said and done at these conferences? Surely Roosevelt, Churchill, and Stalin did not announce to the world as they left Tehran that they had agreed to an Allied landing in France in May or June 1944 to coincide with a Soviet offensive on the Eastern Front. The historian learns what secret decisions were made at which diplomatic conferences some years later (the wait can be twenty-five years or more) when the records from those meetings, held in the archives of the U.S. State Department and the foreign-service offices of other countries, are opened to researchers. In the United States in recent decades, historians have been able to shorten the wait occasionally by bringing court cases under the Freedom of Information Act to force government agencies to declassify secret documents. In other instances secret diplomatic deals have been exposed within a few years because the archives of a defeated nation have been captured by the winner and then published. For example, the agreement between Hitler and Stalin in the 1939 Nazi-Soviet Pact to conquer and divide Poland became public knowledge when the United States captured German records in 1945 and quickly published them to embarrass the Soviet Union. What other sources can the historian use to double-check the accuracy of archival records? What additional sources can the historian consult to find out why the participants in these conferences said and agreed to certain things?

Sometimes discovering why governments follow certain courses of action on the domestic scene can be equally challenging to historians. Look at "A Place in Time: Wartime Hawaii." There we learn that the 160,000 Nisei and Issei living in the islands were not interned in camps as those residing in the Pacific coast states were. The army and the president apparently were less worried about the possible security threat from the large Japanese minority in Hawaii, which had suffered a devastating attack, than from the smaller Japanese population in California, Oregon, and Washington, where no hostilities had occurred. How can we explain the difference in attitude?

MULTIPLE-CHOICE QUESTIONS

Circle the letter of the item that best completes each statement or answers the question.

1. Which of the following sequences of events is correct?
   a. United States sends aid to Britain and the Soviet Union; Japan attacks Pearl Harbor; United States declares war on Japan; Germany and Italy declare war on the United States.
   b. United States declares war on Germany; Japan attacks Pearl Harbor; United States declares war on Japan; United States sends aid to Britain and the Soviet Union.
   c. United States declares war on Japan; Japan attacks Pearl Harbor; Germany and Italy declare war on the United States; United States sends aid to Britain and the Soviet Union.
   d. Germany, Italy, and Japan declare war on the United States; Japan attacks Pearl Harbor; United States declares war on the Axis; United States sends aid to Britain and the Soviet Union.

2. Lend-lease
   a. was favored by isolationists as a way to prevent the United States from having to fight in World War II.
   b. favored the Germans because they were considered better credit risks than the British and Soviets.
   c. was extended to both Britain and the Soviet Union to help them defeat the Nazis.
   d. was one of the most unpopular policies of the Roosevelt administration because it was pulling the country into a war the majority of Americans wished to avoid.

3. Which of the following was unique about the presidential elections of 1940 and 1944?
   a. A candidate was elected president for a third term and a fourth.
   b. The Democratic incumbent ran with no real opposition from the Republicans.
   c. The contests were both so close that the winner had to be decided by a House of Representatives vote.
   d. They were the first two elections in which women voted for president.

4. The United States assisted European Jews threatened by Nazi extermination by
   a. admitting millions of Jewish refugees to the United States.
   b. convincing the British to allow millions of refugees into Palestine.
   c. offering the Nazis trucks and other war supplies in exchange for Jewish concentration-camp inmates.
   d. establishing the War Refugee Board.

5. The United States and Britain launched the long-delayed second front with the
   a. capture of Iwo Jima and Okinawa.
   b. landing in North Africa.
   c. landing in Normandy.
   d. seizure of Sicily and southern Italy.

6. The battle that ended the Japanese offensive and forced her to revert to defending what she had earlier occupied was the
   a. Battle of Midway.
   b. Battle of the Bulge.
   c. Battle of the Philippine Sea.
   d. battle for Iwo Jima.

7. The text states that the main reason for United States' use of atomic bombs against Hiroshima and Nagasaki was
   a. the desire to frighten the Soviets into being more reasonable in Eastern Europe.
   b. America's racist attitudes toward Japan.
   c. the hope of ending the war in the Pacific before the Soviet Union had a chance to get into the conflict.
   d. the reliance of American leaders on technology to win the war with the least sacrifice of American lives.

8. Which of the following did *not* occur during World War II?
    a. The federal government imposed wage and price controls and rationing to combat inflation.
    b. The federal government took over many industries and strictly limited the profits of others.
    c. The federal government raised the income tax and introduced the payroll-deduction system to collect it more efficiently.
    d. Farm income soared, unemployment disappeared, and real wages increased.

9. Which of the following happened during World War II?
    a. Marriage, birth, and divorce rates rose rapidly.
    b. Women were denied the right to serve in the armed forces.
    c. High school and college attendance increased greatly because families had the money to keep their youngsters in school.
    d. The majority of preschool-age children were placed in child-care centers as their mothers worked in defense-industry jobs.

10. A. Philip Randolph's call for a massive march on Washington led to
    a. an executive order permitting the military to evacuate and intern Japanese living on the West Coast.
    b. an executive order prohibiting employment discrimination and creating a Fair Employment Practices Commission.
    c. passage of the Smith-Connally Act restricting union strikes and protests.
    d. prosecution of the sailors involved in the zoot-suit riot against the pachucos.

SHORT-ANSWER QUESTIONS

1. What caused the outbreak of war in Europe in September 1939?

2. Discuss the debate between the isolationists and the interventionists between 1939 and 1941 over the role the United States should play in the war in Europe.

3. What was U.S. policy toward Jewish refugees during World War II?

4. Outline the major strategy and campaigns of the United States and its allies in the European war theater between 1942 and 1945.

5. Outline the major strategy and campaigns of the United States in the Asian war theater between 1942 and 1945.

6. Explain the issues discussed, the controversies that arose, and the decisions made at the Tehran conference.

7. Explain the issues discussed, the controversies that arose, and the decisions made at the Yalta conference.

ESSAY QUESTIONS

1. Discuss the conflicts between the United States and Japan that led to the Japanese attack on Pearl Harbor.

2. Discuss the effects of World War II on American business, labor, and government.

3. Discuss the effects of World War II on African-Americans, Mexican-Americans, Native Americans, and Japanese-Americans.

4. Discuss the impact of World War II on American women, marriage, and the family.

5. Discuss the formation of and strains in the Grand Alliance of the United States, Britain, and the Soviet Union during World War II. How was the second-front controversy related to those strains?

6. Why did the United States drop atomic bombs on Hiroshima and Nagasaki? What explanations have been offered? Do you feel the United States' actions were justified? Why or why not?

28

Cold War America, 1945 – 1952

OUTLINE AND SUMMARY

I. The Postwar Political Setting

A. *Introduction*

Harry S Truman, who became president in April 1945, had been a hardworking senator and a supporter of President Roosevelt's programs, though not a "committed New Dealer." Once in the White House, he replaced liberal cabinet members with moderates, but he also urged Congress to continue and expand New Deal reforms. During his presidency Truman had to contend with a revived Republican party, a divided Democratic party, and a Congress resentful of the great powers that had accrued to the executive branch during the Roosevelt years.

B. *Demobilization and Reconversion*

In response to popular demand, the Truman administration rapidly demobilized the armed forces. Predictions of a postwar depression did not come true. Instead, the reconversion years began a quarter-century of expanding prosperity. The money the government gave to veterans for education, homes, and businesses under the GI Bill of Rights stimulated the economy. With most of its industrial rivals weakened by the war, the United States enjoyed a favorable position in world trade. Further, wartime advances in science and technology made possible the growth of whole new industries, such as electronics and synthetic materials. Consumers, who had accumulated some $140 billion in savings between 1941 and 1945, went on a postwar buying spree, grabbing up homes, cars, electrical appliances, and televisions.

C. *Truman's Troubles*

There was little support after World War II for resuming New Deal reform. Congress passed the watered-down Employment Act in 1946 but balked at Truman's other domestic-reform proposals. With the OPA and price controls terminated, inflation soared. Escalating prices led to an unprecedented number of strikes in 1946 as workers demanded higher wages to keep up with the cost of living. Truman wavered between getting tough with strikers and giving in to their demands. Shortages of housing and consumer goods continued as reconverting industries struggled to catch up with consumer purchases. Americans blamed

Truman for inflation, strikes, and shortages, and in November 1946 they elected Republican majorities to Congress for the first time since 1928.

II. Anticommunism and Containment

A. Confrontation and Polarization

After defeating their common enemy Hitler, the United States and the Soviet Union began to argue over Eastern Europe, especially Poland. To secure his nation against future attacks from the west, Stalin insisted that friendly communist governments must be installed on the Soviet borders. While the Red Army occupied these countries, Stalin broke his Yalta promise to allow free elections and saw to it that communist regimes came to power in Poland, Bulgaria, Hungary, and Romania. President Truman would not accept Soviet domination of Eastern Europe because it violated the principles of national self-determination that the United States had espoused in the Atlantic Charter and Yalta Declaration. Further, Truman believed the spread of communism threatened American economic interests in Eastern Europe and elsewhere. Also, he realized that opposition to Soviet intervention would be popular at home with conservatives and voters of Eastern European extraction.

B. The Cold War Begins

Truman's denunciation of Soviet actions induced Stalin to tighten his grip on Eastern Europe. Nonetheless, the president became more convinced that he should "get tough with the Russians," and he received encouragement. George F. Kennan, a State Department expert on the U.S.S.R., advised that the United States should apply "long-term, patient, but firm and vigilant containment of Russian expansive tendencies." Former British prime minister Winston Churchill, in his iron curtain speech, condemned Stalin's behavior, called for an anticommunist alliance of the English-speaking peoples, and cautioned against sharing atomic know-how with the Soviets. Truman followed Churchill's nuclear advice and threatened to use American naval and land forces if Stalin did not withdraw his troops from Iran. In their emerging Cold War, the United States and the Soviet Union would use economic pressure, nuclear threats, propaganda, and subversion against each other, but they would not engage in direct military combat.

C. European Crisis, American Commitment

In March 1947 Truman asked Congress to appropriate millions of dollars to help the Greek and Turkish governments fight communist rebel movements in their countries. The president declared that this was part of a new American commitment to support peoples all over the world who were threatened by Soviet aggression and/or internal communist uprisings. The Republican-controlled Congress endorsed this Truman Doctrine when it voted to appropriate the money in May. Truman and his secretary of state, George C. Marshall, also worried about the situation elsewhere in Europe. Postwar economic collapse was causing impoverished Western Europeans to vote for Communist party candidates. To curtail the appeal of communism, Marshall and Truman proposed massive U.S. assistance to rebuild European economies. Congress appropriated $17 billion for this Marshall Plan. By 1952 that money had revived Western Europe economically. Communist popularity there had waned, and American business boomed with increased sales to now prosperous European customers.

D. Confrontation

In 1947–1948 Stalin broadened his sphere of influence in Eastern Europe as communist regimes took over Hungary and Czechoslovakia. When the United States, Britain, and France announced that they would unite their zones of occupation in Germany into a rearmed West German state, including the Western-occupied parts of Berlin, the Soviets reacted with the Berlin blockade. Stalin prevented all ground movement of goods and people between West Germany and West Berlin. He hoped to halt establishment of the West German republic or at least force the Western powers out of Berlin. Instead Truman instituted the Berlin airlift. In May 1949 Stalin ended his unsuccessful Berlin blockade, and the West German Federal Republic (West Germany), including West Berlin, was established. Also that year the United States joined with ten European nations and Canada in an anticommunist military alliance called the North Atlantic Treaty Organization (NATO). The Soviets responded by establishing the German Democratic Republic (East Germany), developing their atomic bomb, and in 1955 joining with their satellites in the Warsaw Pact military alliance. Thus the two super-powers divided Europe into rival armed camps.

E. The Cold War in Asia

The United States and the U.S.S.R. also contended for economic and military influence in Asia. The United States pulled a rebuilt Japan into its economic orbit, occupied much of Japan's former Pacific island empire, and crushed a communist movement in the Philippines. But American military and economic assistance to Jiang Jieshi did not save his unpopular Nationalist government from overthrow by Mao Zedong. In 1949 communist takeover of China and Soviet testing of an atomic bomb led to hysteria in the United States and a search for disloyal elements at home to blame for these events. Stung by Republican charges that it was responsible, the Truman administration decided to develop the hydrogen bomb and recommended great increases in military spending. The Soviets built hydrogen bombs, too, and the thermonuclear terror increased.

F. The Korean War

In 1945 the U.S.S.R. and the United States liberated Korea from Japanese rule. The Soviets set up a communist-governed People's Democratic Republic of Korea north of the thirty-eighth parallel; the United States helped create the pro-Western Republic of Korea to the south. Eager to reunite Koreans under its rule, the People's Republic invaded the South in 1950. Truman, without consulting Congress, sent American forces under General Douglas MacArthur to South Korea to repel the invasion. The United Nations also dispatched a token army to fight under MacArthur. U.S., U.N., and South Korean troops soon pushed the North Koreans back to the thirty-eighth parallel, but Truman and MacArthur decided to conquer the North and place it in the hands of the South Korean government. When MacArthur's armies neared the Yalu River, the boundary between North Korea and China, Mao Zedong warned that he would not "stand idly by." MacArthur, ignoring the threat, was caught off guard by the thirty-three Chinese divisions that hurled his troops deep into South Korea.

After months of bloody fighting, MacArthur's forces again reached the vicinity of the thirty-eighth parallel. Truman then ordered the general to hold that position while the United States sought to negotiate a settlement. MacArthur protested, swearing that he could achieve total victory if only Truman would allow him to atomic-bomb and blockade China. When the general would not desist, the president removed him from command to uphold the principle of civilian control over the military. By the time the truce talks concluded in 1953, the border between the two Koreas was set in nearly the same place it had been before 1950, and the United States had expended some fifty-four thousand lives and $54 billion. Between 1950 and 1953 defense spending climbed from one-third to two-thirds of the entire federal budget. The United States also began aiding France against an independence revolt in Indochina, and it created an anticommunist military alliance with Australia, New Zealand, and other countries in Asia.

III. The Truman Administration at Home

A. The Eightieth Congress

The Republican-controlled Congress refused to pass further reforms and began to undo the New Deal. Over Truman's veto it passed the Taft-Hartley Act, which was far less favorable to unions than the Wagner Act had been. Truman courted liberal, labor, and Jewish votes for the next election by condemning the reactionary Congress and recognizing the new state of Israel.

B. The Politics of Civil Rights

In 1946 Truman created the President's Committee on Civil Rights to investigate racism and suggest ways to protect minorities. The committee recommended that Congress pass anti-lynching, anti–poll tax, and other civil-rights bills. When Truman encountered strong resistance from southern Democrats, he failed to submit specific proposals to the lawmakers. At the 1948 Democratic National Convention, liberals and urban politicians, who needed the northern black vote, forced the party to adopt a strong civil-rights plank, committing Truman to press for the measures recommended by his civil-rights committee. This platform induced many southern Democrats to found the rival States' Rights Democratic (Dixiecrat) party and nominate South Carolina segregationist J. Strom Thurmond for president.

C. The Election of 1948

The Democrats ran Truman; the Republicans, Governor Thomas E. Dewey. Truman's defeat seemed likely because of the Dixiecrat split and the defection of some left-wing Democrats to Henry A. Wallace, nominee of the new Progressive party. During the campaign Truman secured the northern black vote by issuing executive orders against discrimination in government employment and segregation in the armed forces. With the support of northern blacks and most of the Roosevelt New Deal coalition, Truman scored an unexpected victory. Neither Thurmond nor Wallace had drained off enough Democratic votes to hurt him.

D. *The Fair Deal*

Truman then asked Congress to pass a package of social and economic reforms he called the Fair Deal. The Eighty-first Congress extended several older New Deal programs, such as increasing the minimum wage and social-security benefits and undertaking slum clearance and public-housing construction. But a conservative coalition of southern Democrats and Republicans blocked all civil-rights and most Fair Deal measures. Truman increasingly turned his attention from domestic reform to the Cold War and the Korean War.

IV. The Politics of Anticommunism

A. *Loyalty and Security*

Truman, concerned by Republican accusations that he was not protecting internal security, established the Federal Employee Loyalty Program in March 1947. It provided for checks on all government workers to root out any disloyal personnel. Between 1947 and 1951 more than three thousand persons were fired or forced to resign, often because they had espoused unpopular ideas, not because they had committed unlawful acts.

B. *The Anticommunist Crusade*

The loyalty program stimulated more fear of subversion. Magazines published stories about the "red" menace. Thirty-nine states passed laws requiring their employees to take loyalty oaths. Teachers, union leaders, and public officials hesitated to advocate reform lest they be suspected of being pro-communist. In 1947 the House Un-American Activities Committee (HUAC) began hearings on communist influence. Witnesses who refused to testify about their own and other people's past political activities and views were cited for contempt of Congress and lost their jobs. After HUAC investigated the entertainment industries, Hollywood studios and radio networks blacklisted employees they considered left-wing, and they turned out a wave of anticommunist films and programs. The Truman administration prosecuted the leaders of the Communist party for conspiracy to preach the overthrow of the government, and the Supreme Court upheld the convictions on the grounds that First Amendment freedoms may be restricted to protect national security. All of this ignored the fact that danger from the thirty thousand American Communists was minimal.

C. *Hiss and the Rosenbergs*

In 1950 former State Department official Alger Hiss was convicted of perjury for lying about providing classified documents to the Soviets. This case heightened public alarm, as did the Rosenberg trial. Ethel and Julius Rosenberg were found guilty of conspiracy to commit espionage as part of a spy ring that had stolen atomic secrets for the Soviets. The Rosenbergs insisted they were innocent, but the judge, reflecting anticommunist hysteria, imposed the death sentence. Republicans claimed these cases proved that the Democratic administrations had been honeycombed with communist traitors.

D. *McCarthyism*

Of all Republicans, Senator Joseph McCarthy exploited the theme of communist traitors among the Democrats most blatantly. Without supporting evidence, McCarthy loudly accused Democratic senators, members of the Truman administration, and other public officials of either being or harboring communist agents. He won a following among insecure and/or discontented groups, and he frightened political leaders into rigid anticommunist stances on complex issues that required open minds and discussion. Witnesses suspected of being subversive were cited for contempt of Congress by lawmakers eager to prove their own loyalty. Congress also passed the repressive McCarran Internal Security Act and the McCarran-Walter Immigration and Nationality Act.

E. The Election of 1952

The Democrats nominated Adlai Stevenson for president; the Republicans, the popular military hero Dwight D. Eisenhower. McCarthyist labeling of the Democrats as the party of treason, public frustration over the stalemate in Korea, and Eisenhower's pledge to go to that country to end the war all combined to win the Republicans control of the White House and Capitol Hill.

V. Conclusion

The election of 1952 marked the close of the early postwar era, a time of prosperity and nearly full employment. It was also a period of "bitter partisanship," unsettling nuclear fears, and "suspicion and repression." The civil-rights movement and the involvement in Vietnam that reached full bloom in the 1960s sprouted between 1945 and 1952.

VOCABULARY

The following terms are used in Chapter 28. To understand the chapter fully, it is important that you know what each of them means.

polarization   moving to opposite or contrasting positions

subversion   working to undermine or overthrow existing institutions, such as the government, especially by secret means

intransigence   unwillingness to compromise

insurgent   one who engages in armed resistance to the established government; a rebel or revolutionary

oligarchy   a form of government in which power is vested in a few or in a dominant class or clique; the members of that class or clique

protectorate   country dependent on the authority of another nation; a state under the guidance of a more powerful state

insubordination   refusal to submit to higher authority

coterie   a group of persons who associate closely; a clique or circle

closed shop   a factory or other workplace in which new workers must join the union before they can be employed

fulminations   explosive outbursts of criticism or denunciation

espouse   advocate or embrace, as a cause

scurrilous   grossly or indecently abusive

recalcitrant   not compliant; uncooperative

red herring   something to divert attention

IDENTIFICATIONS

After reading Chapter 28, you should be able to identify and explain the historical significance of each of the following:

GI Bill of Rights (Servicemen's Readjustment Act of 1944)

Bretton Woods Agreement, International Monetary Fund, and World Bank

Employment Act of 1946 and the Council of Economic Advisers

Yalta Declaration of Liberated Europe

George F. Kennan and the containment policy

James F. Byrnes

Winston Churchill's iron curtain speech

Atomic Energy Act and the Atomic Energy Commission

Truman Doctrine

George C. Marshall and the Marshall Plan

Berlin blockade and airlift

North Atlantic Treaty Organization and Warsaw Pact

General Douglas MacArthur

National Security Council and NSC-68

Edward Teller, J. Robert Oppenheimer, and the hydrogen bomb

Taft-Hartley Act

To Secure These Rights

J. Strom Thurmond and the Dixiecrats

Henry A. Wallace and the Progressive party

Thomas E. Dewey

the conservative coalition in Congress

House Un-American Activities Committee

Federal Employee Loyalty Program

Smith Act and *Dennis* v. *United States*

Alger Hiss, Whittaker Chambers, and Richard M. Nixon

Ethel and Julius Rosenberg

Joseph R. McCarthy and McCarthyism

McCarran Internal Security Act

McCarran-Walter Immigration and Nationality Act

Adlai Stevenson

SKILL BUILDING: MAPS

---

1. On the map of Europe on the following page, locate and explain the historical significance, during the period 1945–1952, of each of the following:

   communist-bloc nations of Eastern Europe (Soviet Union, Bulgaria, Hungary, Romania, Albania, Yugoslavia, Poland, and Czechoslovakia)

   Iran

   Black Sea

   Greece and Turkey

   Mediterranean Sea

   Berlin

   German Federal Republic (West Germany)

   German Democratic Republic (East Germany)

   North Atlantic Treaty Organization members in Europe

   Warsaw Pact members

Europe, 1945–1952

2. On the map of Asia that follows, locate and explain the historical significance, during the period 1945–1952, of each of the following:

Japan

Manchuria

People's Democratic Republic of Korea (North Korea)

Republic of Korea (South Korea)

thirty-eighth parallel

Seoul

Yalu River

Philippines

French Indochina (Cambodia, Laos, and Vietnam)

Taiwan (Formosa)

People's Republic of China

Marshall Islands

Asia, 1945-1952

HISTORICAL SOURCES

In Chapter 28 the author has used as historic sources three significant public speeches: (1) Winston Churchill's iron curtain speech delivered at Westminster College in Fulton, Missouri, in March 1946 (p. 907); (2) President Truman's address to a joint session of Congress in March 1947, in which he announced the Truman Doctrine (p. 908); (3) Secretary of State George C. Marshall's commencement address at Harvard University in June 1947, in which he suggested what is now known as the Marshall Plan (pp. 908–909). The historian can find the contents of these speeches in the *Congressional Record* and in newspapers such as the *New York Times,* which published the full text. How does the author use these speeches? What does he learn from them about the thinking that shaped U.S. foreign policy? What do they tell about the origins of the Cold War?

The historian writing about postwar history has available particularly valuable source material in movies and television. Television and motion-picture cameras recorded for millions of viewers the images of "the rumpled" Whittaker Chambers and "the elegant" Alger Hiss (pp. 922–923). Millions watched as the House Un-American Activities Committee questioned film directors, screenwriters, movie stars, and other "friendly" and "unfriendly" witnesses about their political views (p. 922). Today the historian can read the printed transcripts of these hearings and also view the film footage. How does the author use these printed and visual records in Chapter 28? Do visual images from television and movie cameras tell their own story, or must the historian still interpret what he or she sees?

In "A Place in Time: Los Angeles Confronts the Atomic Age," the historian also refers to a scene recorded by television cameras. What is the scene? What does it show about the concerns of Americans in the late 1940s and early 1950s? What role did government play in fanning these fears?

MULTIPLE-CHOICE QUESTIONS

Circle the letter of the item that best completes each statement or answers the question.

1. Who held up a laundry list and claimed, "I have here in my hand a list of 205 names known to the Secretary of State as being members of the Communist party and who nevertheless are still working and shaping policy"?
   a. Richard M. Nixon
   b. George C. Marshall
   c. Joseph R. McCarthy
   d. Whittaker Chambers

2. Which of the following was accomplished during Truman's presidency?
   a. The armed forces were desegregated.
   b. A national health-insurance system was started.
   c. Labor unions were strengthened by government backing for the closed shop.
   d. A federal antilynching law was enacted.

3. In which of these cases did the Supreme Court rule that Congress could curtail freedom of speech to protect national security?
    a. the *Rosenberg* case
    b. the Alger Hiss trial
    c. *Morgan* v. *Virginia*
    d. *Dennis* v. *United States*

4. The term *Fair Deal* refers to
    a. Harry S Truman's domestic social- and economic-reform programs.
    b. Franklin D. Roosevelt's programs to give labor and farmers more lenient treatment by the federal government.
    c. Joseph R. McCarthy's complaints that communist traitors got better treatment from the Democrats than loyal, hard-working ordinary Americans.
    d. none of the above

5. Which of the following people did *not* agree with and encourage Truman's "get tough with Russia" policy in the late 1940s?
    a. Winston Churchill
    b. Henry A. Wallace
    c. George F. Kennan
    d. Senator Arthur Vandenberg

6. Truman was able to stage an upset victory in the election of 1948 because
    a. he gave in to southern wishes and ran on a weak civil-rights platform.
    b. he chose the staunch anticommunist Richard M. Nixon as his running mate.
    c. he re-created the old New Deal coalition and won an even greater percentage of the black vote than Roosevelt had.
    d. he wooed the left wing of the Democratic party with promises to reach an accord with the U.S.S.R. and to drop the Federal Employee Loyalty Program.

7. NSC-68
    a. was rejected by Truman as prohibitively expensive.
    b. called for negotiations with the Soviet Union to reach a verifiable nuclear disarmament treaty.
    c. was a secret Soviet plan to foment a communist uprising in the United States by 1968.
    d. called for a massive U.S. military buildup to counter the U.S.S.R.'s aggressive intentions.

8. In which of these conflicts did American and Soviet troops clash on the battlefield?
    a. the Korean War
    b. the efforts to get supplies to Berlin despite the Russian blockade
    c. the Indochinese war in which Ho Chi Minh's communists tried to oust the French
    d. none of the above

9. Alger Hiss was accused of
   a. giving, in the 1930s, secret State Department documents to an agent working for the Soviet Union.
   b. preaching the overthrow of the U.S. government by force and violence.
   c. helping the Communists come to power in China in 1949 by sending them information on Jiang Jieshi's secret military plans.
   d. opposing American development of the hydrogen bomb in the early 1950s because of his communist sympathies.

10. The Korean War
   a. ended Soviet occupation of the Korean peninsula.
   b. reunited North and South Korea.
   c. set a precedent for U.S. participation in undeclared wars not approved by Congress.
   d. permanently moved the border of South Korea to the Yalu River.

SHORT-ANSWER QUESTIONS

1. Why did the U.S. economy enjoy a boom after World War II rather than slide back into depression?

2. Explain why the president expounded the Truman Doctrine to Congress. What was Truman proposing? Why did Congress go along with the doctrine?

3. Why did the Soviet Union impose the Berlin blockade, and how did President Truman respond to it?

4. Why were the communists able to take over China in 1949? How did some Republicans explain communist success in China?

5. Who supported Senator Joseph McCarthy and McCarthyism, and why?

6. What accounts for the victory of Eisenhower and the other Republicans in the election of 1952?

ESSAY QUESTIONS

1. One historian has argued that President Truman was at least partly responsible for McCarthyism and the popular obsession with communist subversion that gripped the United States in the late 1940s and 1950s. Discuss your reasons for either agreeing or disagreeing with that charge.

2. Another historian observed, "If the Truman years represent an era of progress, however limited, in civil rights [for black Americans], they represent an era of retrogression in civil liberties [free exercise of the rights guaranteed in the First Amendment]." Discuss the statement and support or refute it with specific evidence from Chapter 28.

3. Discuss the origins of the Cold War.

4. What was the containment policy? How did the Truman administration implement it in Europe and Asia?

5. Discuss the differences between President Truman and General Douglas MacArthur on how to conduct the Korean War. Was the president justified in firing the general? Why or why not?

29

America at Midcentury

OUTLINE AND SUMMARY

I. The Eisenhower Presidency

A. *The General as Chief Executive*

Popular as the World War II commander of Allied forces in Western Europe, Dwight Eisenhower became president of the United States in 1953. He exercised executive authority with restraint; seldom took a public, forceful role in lawmaking; and delegated much responsibility to subordinates.

B. *"Dynamic Conservatism"*

Eisenhower called his approach to governing "dynamic conservatism" or "modern Republicanism." He staffed his administration with corporate executives and expected them to run it with business efficiency. He resisted right-wing pleas to dismantle the New and Fair Deals but tried to restrain further growth of federal activities. Eisenhower's pragmatism led him, despite his dislike of unbalanced budgets, to increase federal spending to combat economic recessions in 1953 and 1957. He also signed the Interstate Highway Act of 1956, which authorized the most expensive public-works program in American history. The forty-one thousand miles of national highway speeded the growth of suburbs, decay of central cities, decline of railroads, dependence on cars and trucks, demand for gasoline, and pollution of the air. In 1956 Eisenhower was renominated by the Republicans and again beat his Democratic opponent, Adlai Stevenson.

C. *The Downfall of Joseph McCarthy*

Although Eisenhower hated McCarthy, the president did not speak out against him and his reckless accusations. Senator McCarthy's 1954 televised hearings, during which he accused the army of protecting communist spies, finally led to his downfall. The Senate censured him, and thereafter the media and public officials ignored him. Fears of internal subversion remained, however, as the House Un-American Activities Committee continued its endless hunt for communists. Right-wing groups such as the John Birch Society warned against the "creeping socialism" of Truman and Eisenhower.

D. The Warren Court

Conservatives were especially upset at the liberal direction Supreme Court decisions started to take after 1953, when Earl Warren became chief justice. Not only did the Court reverse the convictions of some Communist party leaders under the Smith Act, but in 1954 in *Brown v. Board of Education*, it ruled that racially segregated schools violated the Fourteenth Amendment. Eisenhower's failure to back the *Brown* decision and his regret at having appointed Warren encouraged southern resistance. White Citizens Councils, the Ku Klux Klan, and congressional signers of the Southern Manifesto all fought school integration.

E. The Laws of the Land

Southern defiance of the *Brown* ruling reached a high point in September 1957 when mobs of angry whites and the Arkansas National Guard, under orders from Governor Orval E. Faubus, blocked the entry of nine African-American students into Little Rock's all-white Central High School. Eisenhower eventually ordered the U.S. Army into Little Rock to enforce federal authority and protect the black students. Resistance elsewhere continued so fiercely that by 1960 fewer than 1 percent of black students in the Deep South attended integrated schools. Still, Eisenhower's use of troops, no matter how reluctant, raised black hopes and won approval from 90 percent of northern whites. Eisenhower also signed the Civil Rights Acts of 1957 and 1960, which did little to protect the right of blacks to vote but did establish a permanent federal civil-rights commission with broad investigative powers.

II. The Cold War Continues

A. Truce in Korea

The Eisenhower administration signed an armistice that ended the fighting in Korea in July 1953. The settlement left Korea divided between communist North and anticommunist South near the same thirty-eighth parallel border that had existed prior to hostilities.

B. Ike and Dulles

Right-wing Republicans were not satisfied with simply containing the spread of communism. To placate them, Eisenhower appointed the aggressive John Foster Dulles secretary of state. Dulles advocated liberating the Eastern European countries from communism and insisted the West should risk war rather than back down in a crisis. Eisenhower ignored Dulles's advice, however, and essentially continued the containment policy.

C. Waging Peace

Eisenhower tried to achieve "peaceful coexistence" with the U.S.S.R. by meeting Soviet leaders at the 1955 Geneva summit conference. The gathering produced no nuclear-arms-control plan, but subsequently the two powers independently stopped their atmospheric atomic tests. Meanwhile, the United States relied increasingly on its nuclear weapons to deter Soviet aggression, and Dulles committed the United States to defending many Third World military dictators against all uprisings.

D. The Clandestine CIA

In its effort to secure anticommunist regimes, the Eisenhower administration relied more and more on covert actions by the Central Intelligence Agency (CIA), led by Allen Dulles. During the 1950s the CIA helped install pro-Western autocratic governments in Iran, the Philippines, and Guatemala.

E. Conflict in Vietnam

The CIA carried on its most extensive secret operations in Vietnam. After the Vietnamese overthrew French rule, the CIA blocked elections to unify the country and pushed into power the dictatorial Ngo Dinh Diem in South Vietnam. Eisenhower claimed Diem had to remain in office to prevent Vietnam's fall to the Communists, which would be followed by Communist takeovers in all of the surrounding countries.

F. Antiwesternism in the Middle East

When England, France, and Israel invaded Egypt in 1956 to reclaim the Suez Canal from Gamal Abdel Nasser, Eisenhower demanded that they withdraw because they had not consulted with the United States in advance. He feared the Suez expedition might lead to a war with the Soviets, who were backing Egypt. After the aborted Suez venture, the president committed the United States to keeping communism out of the Middle East with his 1957 Eisenhower Doctrine, and the United States continued to view Arab nationalism as "communist inspired."

G. Frustrations Abroad

Eisenhower's support for pro-Western dictators led to anti-U.S. demonstrations in Latin America and Japan and hostility from the new revolutionary government led by Fidel Castro in Cuba. The president's hope for improving Soviet-American relations with a 1960 summit conference was dashed when the U.S.S.R. shot down an American U-2 reconnaissance plane that had been spying on Soviet military installations.

H. The Eisenhower Legacy

President Eisenhower ended the fighting in Korea, kept the peace thereafter, and initiated small steps toward relaxing Soviet-American tensions. On the other hand, he speeded up the nuclear-arms race, expanded the Cold War, and gave the CIA the go-ahead to subvert foreign governments that the United States disliked. At home Eisenhower followed a middle-of-the-road course that pleased neither right-wingers nor liberals. Liberals criticized his failure to denounce McCarthy and racism. Conservatives faulted him for not repealing the New and Fair Deals. Eisenhower will be remembered for his farewell warning about the growing influence of the "military-industrial complex" over American society.

III. The Affluent Society

A. Introduction

In the 1950s the United States enjoyed a broad-based, unprecedented level of prosperity. By 1960, 60 percent of American families owned homes and 75 percent had cars. The prosperity was slightly marred by three brief recessions and worry over a mounting national debt.

B. The New Industrial Society

Greatly increased government expenditures partly accounted for the prosperity and the national debt. Some of the federal money financed public-works and other domestic programs, but the majority of it (about 10 percent of the GNP) went into military buildup. The government also underwrote much scientific research, as did large corporations. New technology from this research fueled the growth of industry, made possible increasing automation, and supplied a host of consumer products. The availability of abundant, cheap petroleum also contributed to economic growth and prosperity.

C. The Age of Computers

The development of computers was one of the most important parts of the postwar technological revolution. Starting with the Mark I calculator in 1944, the manufacturing of ever more complex electronic computers became a billion-dollar business, and the devices transformed the nature of many jobs.

D. Concentration and Consolidation in Industry and Agriculture

Technological advances accelerated the long-term trend toward fewer and larger economic enterprises controlling the United States' industry and agriculture. A new middle class of professionals and administrators arose to manage these corporate giants. The big corporate farms increased their yields and profits by heavy use of chemical fertilizers, herbicides, and pesticides. Until the 1962 publication of Rachel Carson's *Silent Spring,* most Americans ignored the dangers of these toxic substances to the environment. Not until the 1960s and 1970s did states and the federal government begin to ban the use of DDT.

E. Blue-Collar Blues

Union membership and power reached its peak in the early 1950s. The AFL and CIO merged into a single federation in 1955 and won for some of the 36 percent of nonagricultural workers who were unionized benefits such as guaranteed annual wages and health-care plans. Thereafter, the union movement declined, as its successes quieted labor militance; the number of blue-collar laborers fell; and the growing portion of workers in public, white-collar, and service employment proved difficult to organize.

F. Prosperity, Suburbanization, and Mobility

Rising purchasing power, expanding credit, and burgeoning advertising stimulated avid consumerism. During the 1950s Americans purchased 58 million cars, which improved mobility but contributed to increased highway fatalities, air pollution, and the movement of whites to the suburbs. Government highway building, loans, and tax credits also made it possible for former city dwellers to purchase homes in suburbia. The construction industry, adopting mass-production techniques, built 13 million new homes, 85 percent of them in suburbs. While millions of poor blacks and Hispanics moved from rural areas into cities, 18 million mostly white, middle-class Americans left, so that by 1960 the suburban population of the United States equaled that of the central cities. People and industry also moved increasingly from the Northeast to the Sun Belt states of the South and West.

IV. Consensus and Conservatism

A. Togetherness and the Baby Boom

In the 1950s Americans married younger and produced more babies than the previous generation had. The increased birthrate and medical advances that cut infant mortality resulted in the largest population growth of any decade in U.S. history.

B. Domesticity

In the midst of this baby boom, educators, psychologists, and the media all delivered the message that women were most contented when they fulfilled their "natural" roles of wife, mother, and homemaker. Women accounted for a smaller percentage of college students than in the 1920s and 1930s, but they did not all leave the workplace. By 1960 almost 40 percent of women held full- or part-time jobs, and of those some 40 percent had school-age children. Most women, however, worked in poorly paid sales and office positions. There was little protest because the organized feminist movement was at a low ebb.

C. Religion and Education

There were signs of renewed interest in religion in the 1950s, such as the popularity of films and books with religious themes, growing church attendance, and the inclusion of the words *under God* in the Pledge of Allegiance. School and college enrollments reached all-time peaks in the 1950s, but much of the education promoted social and psychological adjustment rather than math, science, and other academic subjects.

D. Affirmation and Anxiety: The Culture of the Fifties

American fiction of the fifties slighted social issues in favor of exploring the personal yearnings of alienated characters. The most significant novels tended to be by southern, black, and Jewish writers, such as William Faulkner, Eudora Welty, James Baldwin, and Philip Roth. Hollywood films, portraying Americans as white and middle class, generally "glorified material success and romantic love." Women were usually shown as "cute, cozy helpmates" or sexy "dumb blondes." Moviegoing declined as Americans watched more television.

E. The Message of the Medium

By the early 1960s, 90 percent of all households owned at least one television, and the industry both reflected and influenced the values and perceptions of the nation. Programs catered to the tastes of a mass audience and nurtured consumerism, conformity, complacency, and racial and gender stereotypes. The television image of political candidates often mattered more than what they really said or did.

V. The Other America

A. Poverty and Urban Blight

Few white, middle-class Americans realized that more than one-fifth of their compatriots still lived below the poverty line. The poor included the elderly, tenant farmers, sharecroppers, and migratory agricultural workers. Native Americans, Appalachian whites, blacks, and Hispanics concentrated in city slums. With their tax base shrinking as well-off whites fled to suburbia, cities were unable to provide adequate schools, housing, public transportation, and social services.

B. Blacks' Struggle for Justice

The struggle of southern blacks for social justice entered a new phase of nonviolent, direct action with the 1955 Montgomery bus boycott, sparked by Rosa Parks and led by Martin Luther King, Jr. After their success in Montgomery, King and other black ministers organized the Southern Christian Leadership Conference to continue the campaign against discrimination.

C. The Hispanic-American and Native American Predicament

Hispanics and Indians were among the poorest and most discriminated against minorities in the 1950s. Nearly 1 million Puerto Ricans migrated from the island to northeastern city slums. Mexican-Americans, many of them "undocumented aliens," filled migratory-labor, construction, light manufacturing, and domestic-service jobs in the Southwest and faced the constant threat of deportation. In the fifties the government terminated all special federal services for Indians and encouraged breakup of the reservations. These policies resulted in the transfer of more than 500,000 acres of Indian land to whites and the further impoverishment and demoralization of Native Americans.

VI. Seeds of Disquiet

A. Sputnik

Russia's launching of Sputnik in 1957 shook American confidence and complacency. In a rush to catch up, the United States created the National Aeronautics and Space Administration (NASA), launched its own missiles, and greatly increased federal spending on education, with an emphasis on turning out more engineers, scientists, and mathematicians to put us ahead of the Soviet Union in the Cold War of arms research and development.

B. A Rebellion of Youth

Many teenagers expressed mild cultural rebellion in their manner of dress, choice of film idols, and enthusiasm for rock and roll and its most popular performer, Elvis Presley.

C. Portents of Change

By the late 1950s the first signs of the "youth movement that would explode in the 1960s" could be seen in the emergence of the Beat writers, such as Allen Ginsberg and Jack Kerouac, and in college student protests against the House Un-American Activities Committee, racial segregation, and the nuclear-arms race.

VII. Conclusion

On the whole Americans in the 1950s were conformist and complacent and enjoyed their great economic prosperity. They largely ignored the persistence of poverty and discrimination in their midst as well as the dangerous concentration of power in the military-industrial complex. But by the end of the decade many felt a sense of uneasiness about the arms race, U.S. foreign-policy commitments, and unsettling social and technological changes.

VOCABULARY

The following terms are used in Chapter 29. To understand the chapter fully, it is important that you know what each of them means.

pragmatic   concerned with or guided by the practical consequences of a given action

junta   a small, governing council or committee (often of military leaders)

demur   to take exception to; to object

autocratic   acting like a dictator; exercising absolute, unchecked power

automation   operating or controlling a mechanical process by highly automatic means, such as electronic devices

oligopoly   situation in which a few large companies dominate a whole industry

conglomerates   huge business corporations created by the merger or takeover of many companies in unrelated fields of industry

Jim Crow   practice or policy of racial segregation

mores   customs of central importance accepted without question and embodying the fundamental moral views of a group, people, or social class

IDENTIFICATIONS

After reading Chapter 29, you should be able to identify and explain the historical significance of each of the following:

"dynamic conservatism" or "modern Republicanism"

Interstate Highway Act, 1956

Adlai Stevenson

"new conservatives" or radical right

Earl Warren

Brown v. *Board of Education of Topeka*, 1954

Orval E. Faubus and the Little Rock desegregation fight

Civil Rights Acts of 1957 and 1960

John Foster Dulles and "brinksmanship"

"peaceful coexistence" and the "spirit of Geneva"

Third World

Allen Dulles, the Central Intelligence Agency, and covert action

Ho Chi Minh, the Vietminh, and the National Liberation Front

the "domino theory" in Asia

Ngo Dinh Diem

Gamal Abdel Nasser

Eisenhower Doctrine

military-industrial complex

Rachel Carson, *Silent Spring*

George Meany, Walter Reuther, and the AFL-CIO

Sun Belt

baby boom

Rosa Parks, Martin Luther King, Jr., and the Montgomery bus boycott

Southern Christian Leadership Conference

House Concurrent Resolution 108, termination, and relocation

National Aeronautics and Space Administration (NASA)

Elvis Presley and rock and roll

the Beats

SKILL BUILDING: MAPS

1. On the map of Asia, locate and explain the historical significance of each of the following in U.S. foreign policy at midcentury:

North Korea

South Korea

thirty-eighth parallel

Philippines

North Vietnam

South Vietnam

seventeenth parallel

Thailand

Burma

Indonesia

Asia, 1945-1952

Sea of Japan

Korea

Yellow Sea

East China Sea

PACIFIC OCEAN

China

Burma

NV

Thailand

Cam.

SV

South China Sea

Philippines

Malaya

Coral Sea

INDIAN OCEAN

2. **On the map of the Middle East, locate each of the following and explain its significance in U.S. foreign policy in the 1950s:**

Egypt

Suez Canal

Mediterranean Sea

Gulf of Suez

Israel

Syria

Jordan

Lebanon

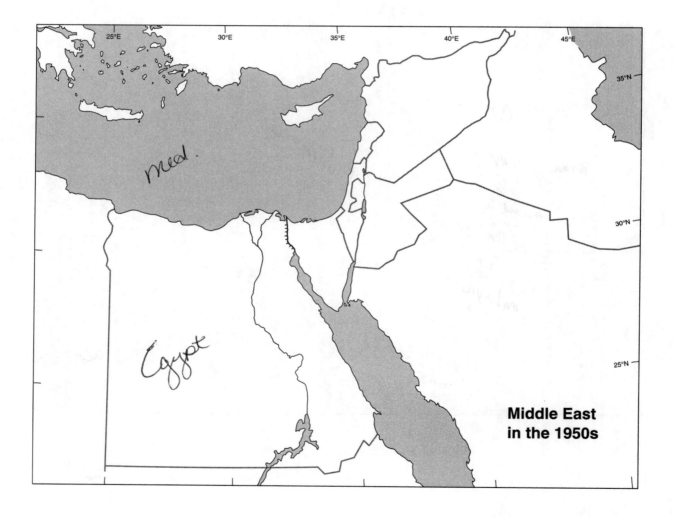

Middle East in the 1950s

SKILL BUILDING: GRAPHS AND CHARTS

Look at the pie charts under the title "Urban, Suburban, and Rural Americans, 1940–1960" on page 945. These charts indicate some of the most significant population shifts in those years. After studying them, you should be able to answer the following questions:

1. Between 1940 and 1960 which area of the United States—cities, suburbs, or rural small towns—declined in its percentage of total population?

2. What happened to the percentage of Americans living in suburbs during that period?

3. Historians tell us that most of the population growth in suburbs came from white, middle-class families moving out of central cities. Yet the pie charts show the central cities containing slightly less than one-third of the population in 1940, 1950, and 1960. Who was moving into the central cities to replace the white middle class migrating to the suburbs?

HISTORICAL SOURCES

In Chapter 29 the author has learned much about the recent past by looking at items of popular culture and entertainment: television programs, Hollywood films, hit songs, most admired movie and rock stars, and the best-selling books of the period. On page 949 the author describes some of the most watched television shows. On pages 947, 948, and 957 the author discusses such 1950s box-office successes as *The Tender Trap, The Robe, Ben Hur, The Wild One,* and *Rebel Without a Cause* and such favorite movie stars as Sandra Dee, Marilyn Monroe, and James Dean. There is a section devoted to Elvis Presley and reference on page 957 to Dick Clark's *American Bandstand.* On pages 946–947 the author discusses the book that sold more copies than any other but the Bible in the 1950s: Benjamin Spock's *Baby and Child Care.* How does the author use each of these examples of popular culture? In each case what does the author claim it shows about American society and values at midcentury? Using the same sources, could you come to different conclusions about 1950s America?

The author also has gathered material from the works of a number of social scientists who described and analyzed post–World War II America. A few examples are John Kenneth Galbraith's *The Affluent Society,* David Riesman's *The Lonely Crowd,* and Michael Harrington's *The Other America.* What are some of the observations about prosperity, poverty, and conformist values that the author draws from these sources?

Look at "A Place in Time: Levittown, U.S.A." This is a capsule history of the post–World War II home-construction industry and one particular company. What does it illustrate about the reasons for the move to the suburbs and the benefits and problems that the population shift has caused?

MULTIPLE-CHOICE QUESTIONS

Circle the letter of the item that best completes each statement or answers the question.

1. President Eisenhower once said "the biggest damn fool mistake I ever made" was
   a. appointing Earl Warren as chief justice of the Supreme Court.
   b. not denouncing Joseph McCarthy and McCarthyism publicly in 1952 and 1953.
   c. appointing John Foster Dulles as secretary of state and allowing him to practice "brinksmanship."
   d. giving the CIA a free hand to conduct covert actions to undermine foreign governments it didn't approve of.

2. Which of the following actions of President Eisenhower pleased the right wing of the Republican party?
   a. his resort to deficit spending to combat downturns in the economy
   b. his signing of the Civil Rights Acts of 1957 and 1960
   c. his appointment of John Foster Dulles as secretary of state
   d. his refusal to abolish the Council of Economic Advisers

3. Which of the following statements about *Brown* v. *Board of Education of Topeka* is correct?
   a. President Dwight Eisenhower praised and gave his full support to enforcing the Supreme Court decision.
   b. The Supreme Court ruled that public schools segregated by race were acceptable if the facilities made available to each race were equal.
   c. The Supreme Court gave the Board of Education of Topeka, Kansas, and other school boards operating segregated school systems one year to integrate them.
   d. The Supreme Court rejected the separate-but-equal doctrine and ruled that racial segregation violates the equal-protection clause of the Fourteenth Amendment.

4. President Eisenhower advanced his domino theory to justify U.S. intervention in the internal affairs of
   a. Guatemala.
   b. Vietnam.
   c. Korea.
   d. Egypt.

5. Which of the following statements about women in the 1950s is correct?
   a. Women generally married later and had fewer children than they had in the 1930s and 1940s.
   b. Women constituted a smaller percentage of college students and received fewer advanced degrees than they had in the 1920s and 1930s.
   c. The proportion of married women who were employed declined.
   d. A greater proportion of women became involved in the feminist movement than ever before.

6. The 1950s government policies of termination and relocation proved disastrous for
    a. Native Americans.
    b. African-Americans.
    c. Mexican-Americans.
    d. Puerto Ricans.

7. Which of these statements about literature in the 1950s is correct?
    a. Novelists were primarily concerned with societal problems, such as poverty, racism, and labor exploitation.
    b. Almost no literature of lasting value was written during this complacent, conformist decade.
    c. Most literature celebrated America's good life of cars, televisions, and suburban homes.
    d. Southern, black, and Jewish writers produced much of the decade's most outstanding literature.

8. Which did *not* occur in the 1950s?
    a. The total number of farms declined as large-scale agribusinesses increasingly dominated farming.
    b. Fewer than 1 percent of American businesses earned more than half of all corporate profits.
    c. The portion of the labor force belonging to unions increased from roughly one-quarter to almost one-half.
    d. More than half of the federal budget each year went to finance military preparedness.

9. About what portion of the American people lived in poverty during the prosperous 1950s?
    a. one-third
    b. one-fifth
    c. one-half
    d. one-tenth

10. The Beats were
    a. a popular rock group in the 1950s.
    b. an anticommunist, paramilitary organization.
    c. a group of nonconformist writers who rejected the materialism and conformity of American society.
    d. CIA agents specially trained to carry out covert actions in Third World countries.

SHORT-ANSWER QUESTIONS

1. What brought about the downfall of Joseph McCarthy? Did his eclipse end excessive fears of communist subversion?

2. Explain the roles in U.S. foreign policy of Secretary of State John Foster Dulles and his brother, CIA director Allen Dulles.

3. What did President Eisenhower mean when he warned Americans to be wary of the military-industrial complex?

4. Describe the economic changes that occurred in American agriculture in the 1950s. What impact did those changes have on the environment?

5. Why in the second half of the 1950s did union membership and influence decline?

6. Describe at least three major demographic changes that occurred in America in the 1950s. What social and political impact would these developments have on the nation?

7. What were the reasons for growing urban blight in the prosperous America of the 1950s?

8. What were the effects on American life of Russia's launching of *Sputnik*?

ESSAY QUESTIONS

1. "Balance and moderation . . . characterized Eisenhower's domestic record. But his middle-of-the-road policies pleased neither liberals nor conservatives." Write an essay either agreeing or disagreeing with this assessment. Back up what you say with as many specific facts as possible.

2. Discuss the Eisenhower legacy in foreign policy. How successful was he in keeping the peace and easing tensions with the Soviets? In what ways did his policies expand the Cold War and accelerate the nuclear-arms race?

3. "A booming, broad-based prosperity made the 1950s a period of economic abundance without historical parallel." Explain the developments and circumstances that produced the prosperity and abundance. What role did government policies play in encouraging economic activity?

4. The section of Chapter 29 dealing with American society and culture in the 1950s is titled "Consensus and Conservatism." Is this an apt title? Discuss major trends in American family life, religion, education, the arts, and entertainment during the fifties to illustrate why this is or is not an appropriate title.

5. Discuss "the other America." What does the term refer to? Which groups made up the other America in the 1950s? Why were they shut out of the unprecedented economic prosperity of that decade?

30

The Turbulent Sixties

OUTLINE AND SUMMARY

I. Introduction

Starting in February 1960, in Greensboro, North Carolina, a wave of sit-ins to desegregate lunch counters and other public places swept through the South. The courage of the black students who initiated these demonstrations emboldened their elders and energized the struggle for racial equality. It also broke the conservative complacency of the 1950s, paving the way for crusading authors like Michael Harrington, Ralph Nader, and Betty Friedan to arouse the nation to the plight of the poor, the dangers to the consumer, and the pervasive sexism. The rhetoric of John Kennedy's New Frontier and Lyndon Johnson's Great Society attracted young, progressive Americans with their promise of an end to these wrongs. But assassinations of key leaders, widespread racial strife, and escalation of the war in Vietnam produced a white, conservative backlash and curtailed social reform. The decade closed in discord and disillusionment.

II. The New Frontier, 1960–1963

A. *The Election of 1960*

Richard M. Nixon, the Republican presidential nominee, identified himself with the still popular Eisenhower and his "middle way," although liberals never forgot Nixon's McCarthyist background. John F. Kennedy, the lesser-known Democratic candidate, challenged his opponent to a series of televised debates. The four debates enhanced the popularity of the telegenic Kennedy and marked the beginning of television's domination in American presidential politics. Kennedy won in the closest contest since 1888.

B. *"To Get America Moving Again"*

Unlike Eisenhower, whose cabinet was top-heavy with businessmen, Kennedy surrounded himself with technocrats and academics. He appointed his closest confidant and adviser, his brother Robert Kennedy, as attorney general. The president gave his administration a cultural tone by inviting artists and writers to the White House, and he used television to broaden his popular appeal. Knowing little of his personal weaknesses, Americans responded warmly to JFK's carefully crafted public image.

C. Kennedy's Domestic Record

Despite Kennedy's call for a New Frontier, he pushed little reform legislation through Congress. Rather than press the fight with Congress, the president concentrated on promoting economic growth through increased military spending and tax incentives to business. At the time of Kennedy's assassination, the economy was indeed booming, but corporate profits had risen faster than personal income, spending on social welfare lagged, and thanks to Rachel Carson's *Silent Spring* and other warnings, Americans were beginning to worry about the polluted environment. In response Congress passed the 1963 Clean Air Act.

D. Kennedy and Civil Rights

Kennedy initially sought to avoid the civil-rights issue because he knew it would divide the Democratic party. The intensity of protests against segregation and the answering fury of southern racists, however, forced the president's hand. Kennedy finally sent federal marshals into the South after white mobs in Anniston, Birmingham, and Montgomery, Alabama, savagely attacked Congress of Racial Equality (CORE) freedom riders who were defying the unconstitutional segregation imposed on interstate travelers. It took still more freedom rides to convince the president that the Interstate Commerce Commission would have to enforce the Supreme Court ruling against segregated interstate transportation. Racist violence also eventually brought Kennedy to dispatch federal troops to the University of Mississippi campus to protect James Meredith, the first black student enrolled there.

E. The African-American Revolution

To expose the viciousness of southern racists and compel Kennedy to act, Martin Luther King, Jr., in 1963 led marches, sit-ins, and pray-ins in Birmingham, Alabama. Police chief Eugene "Bull" Conner, in front of television cameras, sent his police with electric cattle prods, high-pressure water hoses, and attack dogs against the peaceful demonstrators. The televised brutality aroused international indignation and prompted Kennedy, behind the scenes, to convince Birmingham's leaders that they must desegregate stores and upgrade black employees. The concessions won in Birmingham encouraged "Freedom Now!" protests in hundreds of other southern towns and cities. Kennedy began to realize that if the federal government did not commit the nation to "peaceful and constructive" reform of race relations, blacks in their frustration might follow leaders who preached the need for violence. Therefore, the president quickly forced segregationist governor George Wallace to allow two black students to enter the University of Alabama, and in June 1963 Kennedy proposed a broad civil-rights bill. On August 28, 1963, Martin Luther King, Jr., addressed a throng of 250,000 who had marched on Washington to persuade Congress to pass the measure. Unfortunately, the legislation remained bottled up on Capitol Hill, and southern white terrorism continued.

III. New Frontiers Abroad, 1960–1963

A. Introduction

Kennedy tripled overall nuclear capabilities; increased conventional weapons strength; formed the Green Berets to fight pro-communist guerrilla movements; and augmented economic and technical assistance to Third World countries with the Agency for International Development, the Food for Peace program, the Alliance for Progress, and the Peace Corps.

B. Cold War Activism

Kennedy approved a plan formulated under Eisenhower to help anticommunist Cuban exiles in the United States who wanted to invade the island and overthrow Fidel Castro. The Bay of Pigs landing failed miserably, but Kennedy persisted in backing plots to assassinate or depose Castro. Kennedy also took a tough line with the U.S.S.R. in defense of Western occupation rights in Berlin. Unable to dislodge U.S. forces from West Berlin, the Soviets walled it off from their zone.

C. To the Brink of Nuclear War

In October 1962 the Soviet Union and the United States came to the verge of nuclear war over the Cuban missile crisis. Kennedy and U.S.S.R. premier Nikita Khrushchev stepped back from the brink at almost the last moment with an agreement that the Soviets would remove the rockets they had installed in Cuba in exchange for Kennedy's promise not to invade that country. After this brush with disaster, the United States and the Soviet Union moved toward détente, a determination on both sides to avoid direct, armed conflict in settling their differences. A "hot line" was installed between the White House and the Kremlin to facilitate communication. The two powers signed a treaty banning atomic tests in the atmosphere and the oceans. But the nuclear- and conventional-arms races escalated, and the rivalry for influence over the Third World widened.

D. Kennedy and Indochina

In July 1962 Kennedy accepted a compromise that restored a neutralist premier to power in Laos but left communist influence in the countryside intact. Determined to give no further ground to communism in Indochina, the president sent ever more military advisers to South Vietnam to aid in the struggle against the National Liberation Front, or Vietcong. Nonetheless, successive American-backed regimes seemed incapable of winning popular support. By the time of Kennedy's assassination, it was becoming clear that the United States would either have to send in many more combat troops or seek a compromise settlement with the pro-communist Vietcong. We do not know which course Kennedy would have taken had he lived.

E. The Thousand-Day Presidency

On November 22, 1963, in Dallas, Texas, Lee Harvey Oswald shot President Kennedy to death, bringing Vice President Lyndon Baines Johnson to the Oval Office. Kennedy passed on to his successor a mixed legacy. The slain leader had favored social revolution in Latin America but had not promoted it sufficiently with funds. He had compromised in Laos but intensified U.S. entanglement in Vietnam. While praising disarmament and détente, he had pushed a massive arms buildup. In domestic matters also the New Frontier proved more promise than accomplishment. Congress had not acted on the majority of Kennedy's reform proposals, and his administration spent more on missiles and the space race than it did on human welfare. His idealistic rhetoric aroused the hopes of reformers, the poor, and African-

Americans, but he also left behind a hopeless entanglement in Vietnam that would make the fulfillment of rising domestic expectations next to impossible.

IV. The Great Society

A. Toward the Great Society

Johnson urged Congress to approve Kennedy's tax-cut and civil-rights proposals as a memorial to the fallen president. In February 1964 taxes were sliced by $10 billion, and the resulting increase in consumer spending and employment brought in more revenue, thus reducing the federal deficit. The 1964 Civil Rights Act outlawed segregation in public facilities; strengthened federal powers to combat racial disfranchisement and school segregation; and created the Equal Employment Opportunity Commission to intervene in cases of job discrimination based on race, religion, national origin, or gender. Inspired by Michael Harrington's *The Other America*, Johnson and Congress declared war on poverty with the Economic Opportunity Act of 1964, which founded the Office of Economic Opportunity, the Job Corps, VISTA, Head Start, and the Community Action Program. As the 1964 election approached, Johnson said his purpose with these measures and more to come was to create the Great Society, free from poverty and racial injustice.

B. The Election of 1964

The Democrats nominated President Johnson. Conservatives thoroughly disliked his Great Society promise of more federal spending on domestic welfare. Southern segregationists and some white industrial workers resented Johnson's backing of the civil-rights movement. At the Republican convention, these forces and other right-wing elements gained control, nominating ultraconservative Senator Barry Goldwater of Arizona. Goldwater, repudiating moderate Republicanism, advocated ending the graduated income tax, the Tennessee Valley Authority, and ''compulsory'' social security. He hinted that he might use nuclear weapons against Cuba and North Vietnam to bring them into line with U.S. wishes. Johnson won a landslide victory and brought with him huge Democratic majorities on Capitol Hill. The stage seemed to be set for completing the liberal agenda.

C. Triumphant Liberalism

During 1965 Johnson sent to Congress a steady stream of social-welfare and reform proposals and got most of them enacted. These included Medicare and Medicaid, federal assistance to education, the Voting Rights Act, a liberalized immigration law, the establishment of the Departments of Transportation and Housing and Urban Development and funding of major programs for them to run, creation of the National Endowments for the Arts and the Humanities, additions to and protection of the national parks, and tougher antipollution and highway beautification measures. But by 1966 the president's attention and more and more of the nation's resources were diverted from building the Great Society to fighting the war in Vietnam. The dashed hopes of liberals, blacks, and the poor produced urban race riots and anger at LBJ. The riots, in turn, alienated white, middle-class Americans. Democratic losses in the 1966 congressional elections reflected the disappointment and ended most reform efforts.

D. The Warren Court in the Sixties

With Johnson's appointment of Abe Fortas and Thurgood Marshall, the first black justice, to the Supreme Court, the already liberal Warren Court became even more liberal. In the 1960s it handed down decisions banning prayer in public schools, limiting press and film censorship, and requiring equal-size election districts and due process for persons accused of crimes. Liberals applauded. Conservatives railed that the judges were legislating instead of interpreting the law; they were undermining law and order.

V. The Changing Struggle for Equality, 1964–1968

A. The Voting Rights Act of 1965

In 1964 the Student Nonviolent Coordinating Committee (SNCC) and CORE organized the Mississippi Freedom Summer Project, sending thousands of college-student volunteers into the South to run freedom schools and register blacks to vote. Their efforts were stymied by the violence of the Ku Klux Klan and local police officials. To dramatize the problem of continuing disfranchisement, Martin Luther King, Jr., organized mass demonstrations in Selma, Alabama. When a national television audience saw Sheriff Jim Clark and his troopers viciously attack peaceful protestors, the public demanded federal action. President Johnson urged Congress to pass a voting-rights law. The resulting Voting Rights Act of 1965 authorized federal examiners to register qualified voters and suspend discriminatory literacy tests. Poll taxes were abolished by Supreme Court decision and the ratification of the Twenty-third Amendment. For the first time since Reconstruction, African-Americans, through the ballot box, came to have significant power in southern politics.

B. The Long, Hot Summers

The summers of 1965 through 1968 saw the outbreak of race riots in cities around the country, causing some $200 million worth of property damage, seven thousand injuries, and two hundred deaths. The Kerner Commission, appointed by President Johnson to investigate, found the causes of the trouble to be persisting "white racism" that had subjected blacks to poverty, slum housing, poor education, and police brutality. The Kerner report recommended programs to create more jobs and public housing and an end to de facto segregation in northern schools. However, Johnson and Congress, noting the white backlash against further federal assistance to African-Americans, did not act on the proposals.

C. "Black Power"

The Black Power movement, influenced by the teachings of Malcolm X, emerged from the civil-rights campaign in 1966. Its leaders, such as Stokely Carmichael and H. Rap Brown, preached race pride and self-determination, rejected Martin Luther King, Jr.'s nonviolence, and questioned the value of integration.

D. Native American and Chicano Power

The civil-rights and Black Power movements set an example for Native Americans and Mexican-Americans. They began to organize to raise group pride and fight for redress of their grievances, with both nonviolence and threats of force. Native Americans occupied

Alcatraz Island and founded the American Indian Movement (AIM). César Chávez attempted to unionize agricultural laborers in his United Farm Workers, and Chicanos joined such militant societies as the Alianza and La Raza Unida.

E. A Second Feminist Wave

The growing unhappiness of middle-class white women with the 1950s emphasis on maternity and domesticity was articulated by Betty Friedan in *The Feminine Mystique* (1963). Founded in 1966, the National Organization for Women (NOW) grew rapidly and began to lobby for full economic and social equality. Meanwhile younger women, disillusioned by the sexism they had encountered in the civil-rights and peace movements, joined the revived feminist crusade. They established women's liberation consciousness-raising sessions, health collectives, and day-care centers and demonstrated for equal rights and legal abortions.

VI. The Lost Crusade in Vietnam, 1964–1968

A. *The Gulf of Tonkin Resolution*

Johnson, who believed in the domino theory and did not want to give the Republicans grounds for accusing him of being soft on communism, stepped up U.S. involvement in Vietnam. In February 1964 he had the military prepare plans for air attacks on communist North Vietnam, which was supplying the Vietcong with weapons. In August, claiming that North Vietnamese patrol boats had fired on two U.S. destroyers in the Gulf of Tonkin, Johnson persuaded Congress to pass a resolution authorizing the president to "take all necessary measures to . . . prevent further aggression."

B. *Americanization of the War*

In 1965 Johnson started sustained bombing of North Vietnam and by 1968 had dropped three times more tonnage on it than the United States had used against all its enemies in World War II. Nonetheless, Hanoi sent more men and supplies to the Vietcong. Therefore, the president took the fateful step of ordering American combat troops to South Vietnam. Some 485,000 draftees were fighting there by 1967, thus Americanizing the war. Still victory eluded us, and the Joint Chiefs of Staff called for a larger U.S. force.

C. *Opposition to the War*

The Vietnam War polarized the United States as no event since the Civil War had done. Mounting numbers of college students and faculty, intellectuals, clergymen, and liberal Democrats resisted the draft, conducted teach-ins, spoke out, and demonstrated against this escalation. They denounced U.S. meddling in an internal struggle in Indochina. They pointed out that the more than $20 billion that this nation was spending annually on the war was draining almost all revenue from Great Society programs and that the draftees sent to fight and die were primarily the poor and disadvantaged. Television coverage of the carnage further eroded support for Johnson's war. On the other hand, "hawks" demanded that the president win a quick and total victory by hitting the Vietnamese with everything we had.

VII. Conclusion

Much was accomplished in the turbulent sixties. The civil-rights movement and the legislation it induced the federal government to enact ended legally enforced segregation, disfranchisement, and discrimination. Black self-respect was bolstered by the effort, and other formerly suppressed groups—Chicanos, Native Americans, and women—took courage to fight for equality. Johnson's Great Society reforms, at their peak in his first two years in the White House, moved this country toward more equality and justice, but before most of the programs accomplished much, they were undermined by the escalating Vietnam War. In 1966 the federal government was spending more money monthly on that struggle than it put yearly into the war on poverty. Frustrated African-Americans and college-age youths turned to violence to hasten social change but produced instead a conservative backlash against further change.

VOCABULARY

The following terms are used in Chapter 30. To understand the chapter fully, it is important that you know what each of them means.

technocrat   an expert in technical fields and management

filibuster   to prevent a legislative vote by obstructive tactics, especially by making long speeches

monolithic   something made of or resembling a single piece of stone of massive size

immolating   offering a life in sacrifice

consensus   general agreement

cornucopia   an overflowing supply

anathema   a person or thing detested

intimate   hint; to make known indirectly

presaged   foreshadowed, forecasted, predicted

reactionary   someone or something on the far right politically; extremely conservative; favoring a return to conditions of an earlier time

due process   legal proceedings carried out in accordance with established rules and principles

bandolier   a broad belt worn over the shoulder, with small loops to hold cartridges; commonly worn by soldiers and paramilitary groups

ambivalent   having at one and the same time opposite and conflicting feelings about a person or thing

IDENTIFICATIONS

After reading Chapter 30, you should be able to identify and explain the historical significance of each of the following:

Greensboro and other sit-ins, 1960–1961

Michael Harrington, *The Other America*

Ralph Nader

Betty Friedan, *The Feminine Mystique*

Congress of Racial Equality (CORE) and freedom rides

Peace Corps and Alliance for Progress

Bay of Pigs invasion and Cuban missile crisis

Ngo Dinh Diem

National Liberation Front (Vietcong)

New Frontier

Great Society

Economic Opportunity Act (Job Corps, VISTA, Head Start) and war on poverty

Barry Goldwater

Medicare and Medicaid

Immigration Act, 1965

National Endowments for the Arts and the Humanities

Stewart Udall

Baker v. *Carr*

Miranda v. *Arizona*

Civil Rights Act, 1964

Mississippi Freedom Summer Project, 1964

Voting Rights Act, 1965

Kerner Commission and its report

Malcolm X and the Black Muslims

Stokely Carmichael, H. Rap Brown, and Black Power

Huey Newton, Bobby Seale, and the Black Panthers

American Indian Movement (AIM)

César Chávez

Chicanos and Chicanas

National Organization for Women (NOW)

Gulf of Tonkin Resolution

hawks versus doves

SKILL BUILDING: MAPS

On the map of Indochina, locate and explain the importance in U.S. foreign policy of each of the following:

Laos
North Vietnam
South Vietnam
Saigon
Gulf of Tonkin
Hanoi
Danang

Indochina

SKILL BUILDING: CHARTS

Look at the figures in the chart on the election of 1964 in your textbook. How do the election results compare with the outcome in 1960? Can you explain the reasons for the great differences between the two elections?

HISTORICAL SOURCES

Chapter 30 takes advantage of a source that is available to the historian studying the recent past—interviews with eyewitnesses to and participants in the events discussed. Such observations are sprinkled throughout this chapter. What does the author use these quotes to illustrate? In addition, the historian studying the recent past can draw on television coverage and recordings as well as written accounts of significant demonstrations and speeches. Look at "A Place in Time: Washington, D.C., in 1963." In that description of the massive march on Washington at which Martin Luther King, Jr., made his famous "I Have a Dream" speech, what elements could the historian have learned from watching films and listening to recordings of the event? What parts of this capsule history could not be gathered simply by watching and listening? Where do you suppose the author got the information about the event and what came before and after that would not be evident from films and recordings?

MULTIPLE-CHOICE QUESTIONS

Circle the letter of the item that best completes each statement or answers the question.

1. The U.S. Supreme Court during the tenure of Chief Justice Earl Warren made all of the following rulings *except*
   a. requiring states to provide a lawyer at public expense for indigent defendants charged with a felony.
   b. outlawing racial segregation in public schools even if the separate facilities were equal.
   c. overturning the World War II legislation that allowed the government to intern Japanese-Americans.
   d. requiring police to tell a suspect of his or her constitutional rights to remain silent and have a lawyer present during questioning.

2. The Bay of Pigs invasion was
   a. a U.S.-backed attempt by anti-Castro forces to land in Cuba and overthrow the regime there.
   b. the first landing of U.S. marines in South Vietnam and the start of Americanization of that conflict.
   c. the name that southerners applied to the invasion of their region by northern college students and civil-rights activists in the summer of 1964.
   d. an attempt made by the West to supply East Berlin with food after the communists erected the Berlin Wall.

3. The purpose of the 1964 Freedom Summer Project in Mississippi was
   a. to protest the escalation of the Vietnam War.
   b. to help and encourage blacks to become registered voters.
   c. to force the Interstate Commerce Commission to declare segregated transportation facilities unconstitutional.
   d. to persuade the state legislature to ratify the Equal Rights Amendment.

4. Which of these leaders most closely followed the example of Martin Luther King, Jr., in using religion and nonviolent resistance to battle for social justice?
   a. H. Rap Brown
   b. César Chávez
   c. Malcolm X
   d. George Wallace

5. War was avoided in the Cuban missile crisis when
   a. the United States agreed to remove its missiles from Turkey in exchange for the Soviet Union's taking its missiles out of Cuba.
   b. Kennedy agreed to remove Western troops from East Berlin in exchange for Khrushchev's order to dismantle Soviet missiles in Cuba.
   c. the United States agreed to stop its bombing of North Vietnam in exchange for the Soviet Union's removal of missiles with nuclear warheads from Cuba.
   d. Khrushchev agreed to remove Soviet missiles from Cuba in exchange for Kennedy's pledge not to invade that country.

6. "Hawks" and "doves" divided over the issue of whether
   a. the U.S. government should overthrow the Castro regime in Cuba.
   b. the civil-rights movement should use violent acts to protect black rights or rely on nonviolent means.
   c. the United States should seek total victory in Vietnam or a negotiated settlement.
   d. the Warren Court had gone too far in protecting criminals at the expense of their innocent victims.

7. Belief in the domino theory would most likely lead a person to support
   a. federal intervention in the South to protect freedom riders and other civil-rights activists.
   b. a test-ban treaty with the Soviet Union to prevent further atmospheric and ocean firing of nuclear weapons.
   c. American intervention in the Vietnam War to prevent a Vietcong victory.
   d. appointment of more conservative justices to the Supreme Court to prevent it from falling completely under the influence of Warren liberals.

8. Before his assassination in 1963, John F. Kennedy had succeeded in
   a. stimulating the U.S. economy by increased military spending.
   b. getting through Congress a new immigration law that did away with the discriminatory national-origins quota system.
   c. getting through Congress the most far-reaching voting-rights bill since Reconstruction.
   d. all of the above.

9. The feminist revival in the 1960s was brought about by
   a. continuing employment discrimination.
   b. the publication of Betty Friedan's *The Feminine Mystique*.
   c. the sexism that women activists encountered in the peace and civil-rights movements.
   d. all of the above.

10. During the last two years of Lyndon Johnson's presidency, the majority of public funds went into
    a. Medicare and Medicaid.
    b. the Vietnam War.
    c. Head Start and other federally assisted educational programs.
    d. public housing, the Job Corps, and other public-works and employment programs.

SHORT-ANSWER QUESTIONS

1. Briefly explain the roles played by television in the election of 1960 and in John F. Kennedy's thousand-day presidency.

2. President Kennedy remarked in 1963, "The civil-rights movement should thank God for Bull Connor. He's helped it as much as Abraham Lincoln." Explain the meaning of this statement.

3. How and why did President Kennedy deepen U.S. involvement in Vietnam?

4. Describe four major pieces of legislation or programs that made up President Lyndon B. Johnson's Great Society and war on poverty initiatives.

5. Why in his second term did President Johnson go from electoral triumph to widespread rejection by the American people?

6. According to the Kerner Commission report, what caused the wave of race riots in the late sixties?

7. How did President Johnson convince Congress to pass the Gulf of Tonkin resolution? What did LBJ mean when he compared the resolution to "grandma's nightshirt—it covered everything"?

ESSAY QUESTIONS

1. Discuss the accomplishments and failures of John F. Kennedy's thousand-day presidency.

2. Martin Luther King, Jr., observed that President Johnson's desire to end poverty and provide economic opportunity for all Americans was "shot down on the battlefields of Vietnam." Do you agree with King's statement? Why or why not?

3. Discuss the development of the 1960s civil-rights movement. What were its successes and its frustrations? How and why did the Black Power movement emerge from it?

4. Discuss the 1960s movements to gain opportunity, equality, and power for women, Mexican-Americans, and Native Americans. Who participated in them? Why? What tactics did they use? What did each movement owe to the civil-rights and Black Power movements?

5. Compare and contrast the United States in the 1950s and in the 1960s. How do you account for the great differences between the two decades?

31

A Troubled Journey: From Port Huron to Watergate

OUTLINE AND SUMMARY

I. The Rise and Fall of the Youth Movement

A. Toward a New Left

The founding of Students for a Democratic Society (SDS) in 1962 signaled the end of the campus apathy of the 1950s. Its Port Huron Statement, written by Tom Hayden, criticized American society and called on youth to build a true "participatory democracy." The perceived impersonality and bureaucracy of university administrations, the failings of New Frontier and Great Society liberalism, and above all the Vietnam War brought many followers to the movement. At no time, however, did the SDS speak for the majority of college students, who continued to care more about acquiring a good job, a home, a family, and a new car than about remaking America.

B. From Protest to Resistance

SDS adherents staged sit-ins, rallies, campus takeovers, and other demonstrations to protest racism, the military-industrial complex, and the war. Chanting "Hell, no, we won't go!" they encouraged young men to burn their draft cards and flee to Canada rather than serve in the armed forces. Their March Against Death in Washington, D.C., in 1969 drew some 300,000 participants.

C. The Waning of Student Radicalism

In 1970, when President Richard M. Nixon widened the fighting with an invasion of Cambodia, a new wave of campus unrest spread across the country. At Kent State University in Ohio, National Guardsmen opened fire on demonstrators, killing four, and at Mississippi's Jackson State College, highway patrolmen shot two students to death. Students condemned Nixon and the repressive violence, but many older citizens turned against the protestors, saying they got what they deserved for undercutting the president's foreign policy. Frustrated by its inability to end the war much less remake American society, the SDS began to disintegrate. A handful of former members went underground and engaged in terrorism, giving the government a handy excuse for more crackdowns. Other New Left activists drifted into the environmentalist, consumer, antinuclear, and women's movements. Many middle- and working-class people, alarmed by radicalism, began voting for political conservatives by the late 1960s. Still, the New Left did spur broad antiwar sentiment that eventually forced the Nixon administration to extricate itself from Indochina.

D. The Youth Culture

Besides the minority who engaged in radical politics, many young people in the sixties rebelled against accepted middle-class life-styles. Their "counterculture" rejected competitiveness, the work and success ethic, and responsibility in favor of love, cooperation, freedom, and experimentation with drugs and sex. Hippie men grew long hair and beards; they and young women wore tie-dyed T-shirts, torn jeans, and love beads. Probably half of all college students smoked marijuana, and a minority tried hallucinogens. The decade opened with folk-music concerts, proceeded to acid rock and Beatlemania, and in 1969 climaxed with a rock-music festival at Woodstock, New York. But by the late 1960s, the counterculture dream of an age of peace and harmony was already turning sour as the haunts of the flower children in San Francisco's Haight-Ashbury and New York's East Village attracted muggers, rapists, and dope peddlers.

E. The Sexual Revolution

One part of the counterculture, greater sexual openness and permissiveness, spread well beyond the hippies. The sexual revolution was made possible to a considerable extent by waning fear of unwanted pregnancy. In 1960 the Pill became available, and in 1973 the Supreme Court in *Roe* v. *Wade* declared unconstitutional state laws limiting women's right to an abortion during the first three months after conception. Films and plays became sexually explicit. Adult bookstores and moviehouses and topless bars proliferated. Live-in arrangements, divorces, and premarital and extramarital sex were common. Homosexuals organized the Gay Power movement and demanded acceptance and equal rights for gays. All of this erotic liberation, however, offended possibly a majority of citizens, who saw these developments as undermining moral decency. By the 1970s they responded by voting for politicians who promised to clean up the smut and protect the family. In the 1980s worry about AIDS also revived restraint.

II. 1968: The Politics of Strife

A. The Tet Offensive in Vietnam

On January 31, 1968, the start of Tet, the Vietnamese New Year, the Vietcong and North Vietnamese launched a major offensive, capturing much territory from the South and even staging attacks on the capital, Saigon. U.S. forces eventually repulsed the communists, but the heavy death toll on both sides made growing numbers skeptical about whether we could ever win the conflict at an acceptable cost. By March 1968, 42 percent of Americans described themselves as doves, and many of them looked approvingly upon Minnesota's antiwar senator Eugene McCarthy, who had announced that he would enter the upcoming Democratic primaries to challenge Johnson for the presidential nomination.

B. A Shaken President

After McCarthy did surprisingly well in the New Hampshire primary, a second antiwar candidate entered the race—Robert Kennedy. On March 31, Johnson, finally heeding key Democratic foreign-policy advisers, announced that he was deescalating in Vietnam by halting the bombing in the North. Embittered by the hatred that had developed toward him and doubting his chances against the Kennedy charisma, the president added that he would not seek or accept another term in the White House.

C. Assassinations and Turmoil

On April 4, 1968, James Earl Ray assassinated Martin Luther King, Jr. Infuriated blacks rioted in Chicago, Washington, D.C., and other cities. In the midst of the national turmoil, Vice President Hubert Humphrey entered the Democratic race. Humphrey, with a liberal record on civil-rights and domestic reform, received backing from union leaders, Johnson loyalists, and most party officials, who supported the president's Vietnam policies. McCarthy appealed mainly to affluent, educated liberal doves; Kennedy, to the less privileged and various ethnic and racial minorities, as well as peace advocates. On June 5, just hours after he won the California primary, Robert Kennedy was assassinated by a Palestinian refugee, thus removing the best hope for success of the peace forces. In August the Democrats nominated Humphrey, while in the Chicago streets surrounding the convention hall, Mayor Richard Daley's police clubbed antiwar demonstrators.

D. Conservative Resurgence

Richard Nixon, the Republican candidate, made the most of the unrest by promising he could end civil strife; achieve an honorable peace in Vietnam; crack down on radicals; and uphold law and order for the silent majority of hardworking, tax-paying, patriotic Americans. George Wallace, running as a third-party candidate, also appealed to resentful and fearful blue-collar workers, white racists, and people fed up with the counterculture and radicalism.

Wallace captured nearly 14 percent of the vote; Nixon nosed out Humphrey with just over 43 percent. These results indicated that a new conservative coalition had emerged. Fifty-seven percent of the electorate, including much of the old New Deal constituency, had voted for Nixon and Wallace, politicians who repudiated liberal ideals.

III. Nixon and World Politics

A. Introduction

Nixon and his national security adviser and later secretary of state, Henry Kissinger, believed in realpolitik—that is, making foreign-policy moves pragmatically on the basis of power politics and what would advance the national interest, without reference to morality or ideology. They also shared a liking for diplomatic intrigue, hidden from the public.

B. Vietnamization

Nixon and Kissinger decided that the United States must somehow extricate itself from Vietnam. The 1969 Nixon Doctrine pointed to a new course in Asia: henceforth the United

States would supply economic and military assistance to countries threatened by communist subversion or invasion, but it would expect them to do the fighting. The need to recall American ground forces from Vietnam was overwhelmingly apparent. Their morale and discipline had snapped, desertions mounted, and frustration led some American soldiers to commit atrocities against Vietnamese civilians, as in My Lai. Nixon began removing American troops from Vietnam, but at the same time he sought "peace with honor" by sending Kissinger to hold secret peace talks with the North Vietnamese. In hope of wringing concessions from the North Vietnamese, Nixon also authorized bombing raids over the North and over their supply lines in neutral Cambodia and Laos.

C. LBJ's War Becomes Nixon's War

The raids did not accomplish their purpose. Hanoi stood its ground, and the bombing touched off a civil war in Cambodia between the communist Khmer Rouge and pro-American factions. In 1970 the North Vietnamese increased their infiltration of Cambodia, and Nixon, in turn, ordered a joint U.S.–South Vietnamese invasion of that beleaguered country. Nixon also pushed the South Vietnamese into an attack on Laos to destroy communist bases there. The soldiers of the South were routed, and in April 1972 the North mounted a major offensive against Cambodia and the South. Nixon ordered the military to mine North Vietnam's harbors and step up bombing of its supply bases and cities.

D. America's Longest War Ends

The massive bombing finally broke the deadlock in the negotiations that had begun in 1968. In January 1973 the United States and North Vietnam signed the Paris Accords, ending the fighting between them but leaving South Vietnam's future to be settled by the final battles between North and South. America's longest war had cost us 58,000 dead, 300,000 wounded, and $150 billion. The Vietnamese suffered 2 million casualties, the war had ravaged much of Indochina, and the communist regime that gained control of the once peaceful Cambodia killed 40 percent of its people.

E. Détente

Our withdrawal from the war opened the way for détente with China and the U.S.S.R. The falling-out between the two communist giants also made them receptive to easing tensions with the United States. After two decades in which successive American administrations had refused to recognize the People's Republic of China and had blocked its admission to the United Nations, Kissinger paid a secret visit to Beijing in June 1971, followed by a Nixon trip in February 1972, at which Sino-American relations were normalized. In May the president flew to Moscow and signed agreements with the Soviets on trade, technological cooperation, and arms control, including the SALT I pact limiting antiballistic missiles. These moves not only improved the world outlook for peace but also enhanced Nixon's image in an election year.

F. A Multipolar World

In October 1973 the Middle East was again embroiled in war, as Syria and Egypt attacked Israel. U.S. equipment helped the Israelis to repel the assault and counterattack. In retaliation, the oil-producing Arab states imposed an embargo on shipments of petroleum to the United States and its allies. This led to acute shortages, skyrocketing prices, and rampant inflation in the United States. To ease the fuel crisis and reduce Soviet influence in the Middle East, the Nixon administration tried to cultivate better relations with the Arabs and to mediate between them and Israel. In October 1973 Kissinger began his "shuttle diplomacy," flying from one Mideastern capital to another to negotiate peace settlements. He managed to engineer an Israeli-Egyptian cease-fire, a withdrawal of Israeli forces from Egyptian and Syrian territories captured in 1973, and an end to the oil embargo. His efforts improved U.S. relations with Egypt, which began receiving American aid, but Syria and Palestine Liberation Organization (PLO) hard-liners became even more antagonistic toward Israel and increased terrorist attacks on Israeli and U.S. citizens.

In line with realpolitik, Nixon and Kissinger gave economic and military assistance to any country that they thought important to American financial and strategic interests, especially to countries willing to oppose Soviet influence. This policy often included nations ruled by brutal dictatorships, such as Iran under the shah and the Philippines under Ferdinand Marcos. Nixon also secretly handed the CIA $10 million to help a military junta overthrow Chile's democratically elected Marxist president, Salvador Allende.

IV. Domestic Problems and Divisions

A. Richard Nixon: Man and Politician

Nixon possessed traits that made him a successful political leader—intelligence, energy, and concentration. But his personality contained darker elements, too, that ultimately brought about his downfall. Nixon was almost paranoid in his belief that his enemies, especially the "eastern liberal establishment," were out to get him. Therefore, he must destroy them first.

B. The Nixon Presidency

At first Nixon followed a moderate course, signing into law bills passed by the Democratic Congress that increased social-security benefits, subsidized housing for low- and middle-income families, and created the Environmental Protection Agency and the Occupational Safety and Health Administration. Meanwhile many Americans demonstrated increased ecological concern. Former antiwar and civil-rights activists organized the first Earth Day in April 1970, denounced the "obsession with industrial growth and consumerism" that was despoiling the planet, and called for alternative life-styles and government policies to protect the environment. Conservatives decried the cost to business of additional regulations, as well as the increased expenditures that the administration's proposed welfare reform would entail. Thus, Nixon's Family Assistance Plan, guaranteeing a minimal annual income for all Americans, died in the Senate. Subsequent cuts in federal spending on social services left cities more overwhelmed than ever with the burden of providing for their poor.

C. A Troubled Economy

Nixon inherited a budget deficit and inflation from the Johnson administration. To combat these Nixon cut government expenditures and urged the Federal Reserve Board to drive up interest rates. Rising unemployment and a recession resulted, and inflation persisted. Worried about the political impact of hard times, the president tried Keynesian economics. In

1971 he deliberately proposed an unbalanced federal budget, and subsequently he levied surcharges on imports, allowed the value of the dollar to decline, and imposed wage and price ceilings. These policies stimulated the economy and reduced the trade deficit and inflation sufficiently to help get Nixon reelected in 1972. Afterward he ended price and wage controls, and in 1973 inflation and sluggish economic growth (stagflation) resumed.

D. Law and Order

Nixon signed legislation to strengthen the powers of the police. He also used law-enforcement agencies in legal and illegal ways to harass peace advocates, radicals, and his enemies. The Internal Revenue Service paid special attention to tax returns from people in these categories; the FBI and CIA wiretapped their phones and infiltrated their organizations to foment discord and provoke violence. Nixon established the White House "plumbers" to spy on and discredit his opponents. Daniel Ellsberg, who had turned over to the press the secret Pentagon Papers disclosing government lies about U.S. actions in Vietnam, became the plumbers' first target. They broke into his psychiatrist's office to look for medical records that might put Ellsberg in a poor light, and the Justice Department indicted him for theft and espionage.

E. The Southern Strategy

Nixon wooed whites tired of civil-rights activism, especially southerners. His administration opposed extension of the 1965 Voting Rights Act and school busing as a means to further integration. The president pushed the Supreme Court toward the right by his appointments of Chief Justice Warren Burger and three other conservatives.

F. The Silent Majority Speaks

To build a new Republican majority, Nixon also played the role of defender of the family and traditional values against the Democrats, whom the administration identified as the party of the New Left, hippies, the drug culture, abortion, and disorder.

G. The Election of 1972

When the Democrats nominated liberal senator George McGovern for president, they had little chance of winning. Nonetheless, Nixon and his Committee to Reelect the President (CREEP) decided to use every means possible to destroy the opposition, including having the White House plumbers break into Democratic National Committee headquarters in the Watergate complex to install secret wiretaps on the phones. After the burglars were caught, the administration began its attempt to hide the trail to higher-ups. It succeeded long enough to get Nixon overwhelmingly reelected, although the Democrats retained control of Congress.

V. The Crisis of the Presidency

A. *The Watergate Cover-Up*

In 1973 the cover-up began to unravel. One of the convicted Watergate burglars confessed that White House aides were involved. Then *Washington Post* reporters Carl Bernstein and Bob Woodward wrote a series of articles exposing CREEP's use of illegal campaign contributions to finance "dirty tricks" against the Democrats. In February 1973 the Senate established a special committee to probe alleged election misdeeds. It heard damaging testimony and, learning that Nixon had secretly taped all conversations held in the Oval Office, demanded that the president turn the recordings over to the committee. Meanwhile Nixon, pretending to cooperate in the investigation, appointed a new attorney general, Elliot Richardson, who chose a special Watergate prosecutor, Archibald Cox. When Cox also requested the tapes, Nixon fired Cox and accepted Richardson's resignation. This "Saturday Night Massacre" prompted the House Judiciary Committee to start impeachment proceedings against the president.

B. *A President Disgraced*

The administration was further discredited when Vice President Spiro Agnew resigned after pleading no contest to charges of bribe taking and tax evading. Nixon nominated Gerald Ford to replace Agnew. The president continued to stall on releasing the full, unedited recordings. In July 1974 the Supreme Court ruled that he must do so. The following month he surrendered the subpoenaed tapes, and they revealed that Nixon had personally ordered the Watergate cover-up and had lied about his role for two years. Warned that he would almost certainly be impeached and convicted, Nixon, on August 9, became the first chief executive in American history to resign, bringing Ford into office as the first nonelected president.

VI. Conclusion

Nixon's departure marked the end of a period of rancor and polarization. Troubled by the Vietnam experience, rebellious youths, energy shortages, a declining economy, and failure of the Democrats to deliver on the promises of the Kennedy and Johnson administrations, Americans had lost faith in Washington. Nixon had capitalized on the disillusionment to put together a new majority coalition for the Republicans. Although he promised to unite Americans and defend law and order, Nixon engaged in numerous illegal acts. Nearly fifty administration members would eventually be indicted for fraud, extortion, perjury, and other crimes. The Watergate affair would leave many citizens even more distrustful of government, making it difficult for Nixon's successors to lead the nation effectively.

VOCABULARY

The following terms are used in Chapter 31. To understand the chapter fully, it is important that you know what each of them means.

iconoclast   attacker of cherished beliefs or institutions

alienation   feelings of withdrawal or estrangement from a person, thing, or society

maverick   a dissenter

participatory democracy   a society in which most citizens directly share in governmental decisions by holding office or making policy

napalm and Agent Orange   chemicals used by the United States in Vietnam to burn villages and defoliate forests

ecology   the scientific study of the relations between organisms and their environment; the political and social movement to protect those relations

chauvinism   zealous and belligerent patriotism or devotion to any cause

taboo   a prohibition; something set apart or forbidden

monogamy   marriage of one woman with one man

pubescent   arriving or arrived at puberty

realpolitik   a pragmatic politics (especially as applied to foreign policy) based on advancement of the national interest without concern for ideology or morality

paranoid   displaying the traits of a mental disorder in which one mistakenly believes that others have hostile intentions toward him or her

innuendo   an indirect intimation (or hint) about a person or thing, especially of an unfavorable nature

dossier   a file of documents relating to the same matter, subject, or person

vendetta   a blood feud or private war of revenge

prior restraint   a type of government censorship that stops publication beforehand of materials deemed objectionable on moral, political, military, or other grounds, rather than punishing the publisher or writer after the material is printed

impeachment   the charging of a public official, such as the president, with misconduct in office

---

IDENTIFICATIONS

After reading Chapter 31, you should be able to identify and explain the historical significance of each of the following:

Mario Savio and the Berkeley Free Speech Movement

the New Left and red-diaper babies

Students for a Democratic Society, the Port Huron Statement, and Tom Hayden

Kent State and Jackson State killings

hippies and the counterculture

Woodstock

flower children and Haight-Ashbury

sexual revolution, the Pill, *Roe* v. *Wade*, and the Gay Power movement

Tet offensive

Eugene McCarthy

Robert Kennedy

Hubert Humphrey

George Wallace

Mayor Richard Daley versus the Yippies

Henry Kissinger

Nixon Doctrine

My Lai massacre

SALT I

Palestine Liberation Organization (PLO)

Salvador Allende

Neil Armstrong and Apollo II

Daniel Ellsberg and the Pentagon Papers

Warren Burger

Spiro Agnew

George McGovern

Carl Bernstein and Bob Woodward

the White House "plumbers" and the Watergate break-in and cover-up

Saturday Night Massacre

Senator Sam Ervin

SKILL BUILDING: MAPS

1. On the map of China and Indochina on p. 420, locate and explain the importance in U.S. foreign policy of each of the following:

   South Vietnam

   Saigon

   Danang

   Cambodia (Kampuchea)

   Laos

   North Vietnam

   Hanoi

   Haiphong

   People's Republic of China

   Beijing

   Sino-Soviet border

China and Indochina

2. On the map of the Middle East on the following page, locate and explain the importance in U.S. foreign policy of each of the places below:

Syria

Israel

Golan Heights

Egypt

Sinai Peninsula

West Bank

Jerusalem

Jordan

Saudi Arabia

Iran

HISTORICAL SOURCES

Authors writing social history often use a variety of cultural artifacts as sources. In Chapter 31 these include the messages on the signs carried by demonstrators, slogans and chants (remembered or learned from films and tapes), songs and music popular during the period, clothing of the time, hairstyles (remembered or seen in photographs), and bumper stickers. Find places in the chapter where each of these artifacts is referred to or quoted. In each case why is the historian using that source?

Now look at "A Place in Time: Haight-Ashbury in the Mid-1960s." What cultural artifacts are mentioned in that capsule history to paint a picture of the life-style that briefly prevailed there in the 1960s?

The author of Chapter 31 also uses more formal, traditional historical sources, such as the published reports of congressional investigating committees. For example, on pages 1017–1019 the author discusses the testimony about wrongdoing in the Nixon White House given before Sam Ervin's committee. That information can be found in U.S. Senate, Select Committee on Presidential Campaign Activities, *Final Report,* 93rd Cong., 2d Sess., 1974. On page 1019 the writer summarizes the articles of impeachment against Nixon drawn up by the House Judiciary Committee. The full text of those articles can be read in U.S. Congress, House of Representatives, *Report of the Committee on the Judiciary,* 93rd Cong., 2d Sess., 1974.

MULTIPLE-CHOICE QUESTIONS

Circle the letter of the item that best completes each statement or answers the question.

1. Most of the early SDS and New Left members were
   a. from working-class families.
   b. children of parents who had been radicals and activists in the 1930s and 1940s.
   c. from upper-class families who were unhappy with the declining status of the "eastern liberal establishment."
   d. students who were already active in sororities and fraternities.

2. With regard to China, President Richard Nixon
   a. ordered its harbors mined and its southern cities bombed to stop it from aiding the Vietcong.
   b. traveled to Beijing to normalize relations with its communist government.
   c. cut off all trade with it until it improved its human rights record.
   d. authorized the CIA to finance secret plots to overthrow Mao Zedong.

3. Which of the following are *incorrectly* paired?
   a. Tom Hayden and SDS
   b. Mario Savio and the Free Speech Movement
   c. Carl Bernstein and the Yippies
   d. Timothy Leary and LSD

4. It is estimated that in the 1960s at least half of all American college students
   a. tried marijuana.
   b. burned their draft cards.
   c. became hippies or Yippies.
   d. had to leave their studies for two years to serve in Vietnam.

5. Which of the following facts about the election of 1968 indicates that a new conservative majority had supplanted the long-standing New Deal coalition?
   a. Between them, Nixon and Wallace received a majority of the votes of unskilled and semiskilled workers.
   b. Nixon won 43.4 percent of the popular vote.
   c. The great majority of blacks voted for Hubert Humphrey.
   d. Almost all union leaders supported Hubert Humphrey.

6. Which of the following did U.S. involvement in Vietnam accomplish?
   a. It prevented the communists from taking power in Cambodia.
   b. It saved South Vietnam from falling under the control of communist North Vietnam.
   c. It stimulated the U.S. economy sufficiently to ensure full employment, business growth, and balanced federal budgets.
   d. none of the above

7. "That's one small step for man, one giant leap for mankind." This quote refers to
   a. Nixon's decision to resign from the presidency.
   b. the signing of the Paris Accords ending the U.S. presence in Vietnam.
   c. the peaceful inauguration of Gerald Ford after the long nightmare of Watergate.
   d. astronaut Neil Armstrong's walk on the moon.

8. Nixon established the White House "plumbers" to
   a. persuade Congress to confirm his conservative nominees to the Supreme Court.
   b. guard administration security and discredit the president's enemies.
   c. repair the executive mansion after Congress refused to appropriate funds for the work.
   d. drain support away from school busing as a means of reducing segregation.

9. Which of the following statements about Nixon's relations with the Democratic-controlled Congress is correct?
   a. Nixon vetoed bills creating the Environmental Protection Agency and the Occupational Safety and Health Administration.
   b. Nixon never released to Congress the subpoenaed, unedited tapes of conversations in the Oval Office.
   c. The Senate rejected two of Nixon's Supreme Court nominees.
   d. Congress passed an equal rights amendment, but Nixon vetoed it.

10. Why did John Mitchell, E. Howard Hunt, and G. Gordon Liddy arrange the break-in at the Watergate complex?
    a. to find information about Daniel Ellsberg that would discredit him in the eyes of the peace movement
    b. to destroy the Democratic National Committee's files of potential campaign contributors
    c. to wiretap the telephones of the Democratic National Committee
    d. all of the above

SHORT-ANSWER QUESTIONS

1. What were the students at Kent State University protesting in 1970? What happened there? How did students and liberals react? How did the majority of Americans react?

2. Describe the youth counterculture of the 1960s. What caused it to wane by the 1970s?

3. What was the sexual revolution of the 1960s and 1970s? What caused it? What brought about a backlash against it by the 1980s?

4. Discuss what happened inside and outside the Democratic National Convention in Chicago in August 1968. What effect did these events have on the Democrats' chances for victory in November?

5. Explain what President Nixon meant by the policy of Vietnamization.

6. What were the terms of the 1973 Paris Accords between the United States and North Vietnam?

7. Discuss Henry Kissinger's "shuttle diplomacy" in the Middle East. What did it accomplish?

8. How did the Nixon administration bring about the overthrow of the Allende government in Chile?

ESSAY QUESTIONS

1. Discuss the rise and decline of college-student radicalism in the period 1960–1970. What caused the radicalism? Who became radicalized? What forms did radical protest take? Why did radical protest wane?

2. In 1964 Lyndon Johnson was elected president by a landslide. In 1972 Richard Nixon won an equally decisive victory. Yet each man was driven from office in disgrace. Explain the reasons for each one's electoral triumph and subsequent downfall.

3. Nixon, "who had built his reputation as a hard-line Cold Warrior, initiated a new era of détente with the communist powers." Discuss how and why the president accomplished this.

4. "While claiming to be the defender of law and order, the Nixon administration committed numerous illegal acts." Write an essay agreeing or disagreeing with this statement, and back what you say with as many facts as possible.

5. Some political commentators claimed that "the outcome of Watergate proved that the constitutional system had worked." Others believed that it further eroded trust in government and the ability of presidents to lead effectively. What is your interpretation of the outcome and its impact on the United States?

32

Turning Inward: Society and Politics from Ford to Reagan

OUTLINE AND SUMMARY

I. After the Sixties: Changing Social and Cultural Contours

A. America Turns Inward

The social activism of the sixties diminished or turned to other causes. The environmental movement intensified, with fear about nuclear hazards peaking in 1979 after the near-catastrophe at Three Mile Island. The 1960s student radical gave way to the 1970s and 1980s yuppie (young urban professional), preoccupied with personal health, fulfillment, and "a consumption lifestyle." Americans of all ages watched more hours of television and increasingly tuned in to the proliferating cable channels. They also enjoyed the new electronic gadgets: videocassette recorders, compact discs, and personal computers.

B. The Women's Movement: Gains and Uncertainties

The women's movement continued into the 1970s and 1980s. The National Organization for Women (NOW) had almost fifty thousand members by the mid-1970s, but the Equal Rights Amendment it worked for was not ratified. *Roe* v. *Wade* (1973), establishing women's constitutional right to an abortion, was attacked by the right-to-life movement. The controversy between the right-to-lifers and pro-choicers became one of the most politically divisive issues of the 1980s.

Women continued to enter the labor force in record numbers. Fifty-eight percent were working outside the home in 1992. Women made significant gains in business and the professions, but most of them still worked in gender-segregated, low-paying, low-prestige occupations, and their average earnings lagged behind those of men. The conservative presidential administrations of the 1970s and 1980s often instituted policies harmful to women. In 1972 Nixon vetoed a bill creating a national day-care system for the children of working mothers. In 1976 Congress cut off Medicaid funding for most abortions, and the welfare cuts under Reagan especially hurt the large proportion of single mothers and their children who depended on welfare payments.

The 1970s and 1980s saw later marriages, fewer children per family, and more unwed couples living together. By 1991, the divorce rate was over 50 percent.

C. The Two Worlds of Black America

In the 1970s and 1980s the black middle class grew in size and made significant advances: 46 percent of blacks held white-collar jobs by 1990, and 12 percent of the nation's college students were black. However, the plight of the black underclass worsened if anything. About one-third of blacks were trapped in inner-city slums. There half of all youths dropped out of high school, and 60 percent were unemployed. Cocaine addiction, violence, illegitimacy, and welfare dependency were prevalent.

D. New Patterns of Immigration

Since 1965 immigration to the United States has been heavy. Most of the newcomers have arrived from the Western Hemisphere (45 percent) and Asia (30 percent). Today the fastest-growing ethnic group is Hispanics. As in the past, the majority of the immigrants are fleeing poverty, but many have encountered rough conditions in the United States as well. To stem the tide of illegal immigrants, Congress passed the 1986 Immigration Reform and Control Act.

E. Brightening Prospects for Native Americans

In the late 1960s and 1970s Indian militance brought changes in destructive federal policies. The 1974 Indian Self-Determination Act granted tribes the right to administer government-aid programs and schools on their reservations. Native Americans also have won important court cases, including a 1980 award to the Sioux of $107 million for lands in South Dakota wrongfully taken in the nineteenth century. Although Indian pride and rights are on the rise, Native Americans still struggle with high unemployment, alcoholism, and disease.

F. Sexuality in the Era of AIDS

The trend toward greater sexual permissiveness and acceptance of homosexuals was partially reversed by the outbreak of the AIDS epidemic. By 1994 more than 220,000 Americans had died of the disease, and public-health officials exhorted those who would not abstain from sex to practice safer sex by using condoms.

G. The Evangelical Renaissance

In the religious revival of the 1970s and 1980s, some people joined cults such as the "Moonies." Others attended evangelical Protestant churches and watched and contributed to television preachers. The born-again Christians exerted a conservative political influence, condemning the communist world, abortion, and pornography and demanding prayer in public schools.

II. Years of Malaise: Post-Watergate Politics and Diplomacy

A. The Caretaker Presidency of Gerald Ford

After he became president on August 9, 1974, Gerald R. Ford pardoned Richard Nixon for "any and all crimes" he might have committed. On domestic issues Ford proved more conservative than his predecessor. He vetoed environmental, social-welfare, and federal regulatory bills, but a heavily Democratic Congress overrode him on quite a few. Already troublesome, inflation soared, as prices rose by 12 percent in 1974. Ford responded by cutting government spending and backing the Federal Reserve Board's decision to tighten credit, which it did by raising the discount rate. These anti-inflation moves resulted in a severe recession, with an unemployment rate hovering around 11 percent by 1975. Then Ford proposed tax cuts to stimulate consumer spending. This did not end the economic trouble, however. Particularly hard hit was the U.S. auto industry, as high gasoline prices persuaded millions of consumers to buy smaller, fuel-efficient imports rather than American-made gas-guzzlers.

In foreign policy there was considerable continuity between the Nixon and Ford administrations. Ford kept Nixon's secretary of state, Henry Kissinger, and carried on his predecessor's efforts to improve relations with China and the U.S.S.R. In 1975, Ford, Soviet leader Leonid Brezhnev, and the heads of thirty-one other nations signed the Helsinki Accords, which formalized Europe's post-1945 borders and promised respect for human rights and freedom of travel. The accords also encouraged Soviet dissidents, who were starting to demand democratization in the communist countries. Additionally, Ford's presidency witnessed the final collapse of the South Vietnamese government as the North Vietnamese captured Saigon and soon renamed it Ho Chi Minh City.

B. The Outsider as Insider: President Jimmy Carter

The Republicans nominated Ford for president in 1976. The Democrats ran a former governor of Georgia, Jimmy Carter. In the aftermath of Watergate, Carter appealed to the nation with his promise never to lie to the people and the fact that he was a Washington outsider. Carter, who won in a close race, entered office with no clear political philosophy. In his first year he managed to bring unemployment down by implementing a tax cut and increased public works, but thereafter he showed little inclination to launch social-welfare programs that involved federal spending. Having poor relations with Congress, he failed to get it to enact national health insurance and welfare and tax reforms. He did appoint a significant number of women and minority-group members as federal judges.

In foreign policy, Carter was somewhat more successful than in domestic affairs. He and his secretary of state, Cyrus Vance, tried to combat human rights abuses in foreign countries, including Chile, Ethiopia, and South Africa, and moved to forge friendlier ties with the black peoples of Africa. They successfully completed negotiations on and got ratification of treaties transferring control of the Panama Canal and Canal Zone to the Panamanians by 1999 and completed normalization of relations with the People's Republic of China. Carter's initial conciliatory stance toward the Soviets turned tough when the U.S.S.R. invaded Afghanistan in 1980. The president then adopted a series of anti-Soviet measures inspired by his hard-line national security adviser, Zbigniew Brzezinski.

C. The Middle East: Peace Accords and Hostages

Carter's foremost foreign-policy achievement was to invite Egypt's Anwar el-Sadat and Israel's Menachem Begin to Camp David, Maryland, in September 1978. There, with the president's encouragement, the two hammered out an Israeli-Egyptian understanding which was formalized in a treaty in 1979. The Camp David Accords did not end the Arab-Israeli conflict, as Israel continued to build Jewish settlements in occupied Arab territories, the other Arab states refused to talk to Israel, and an Islamic fundamentalist assassinated Sadat.

Carter's worst foreign-policy nightmare also came from the Middle East in 1980, an election year. After Islamic fundamentals overthrew the United States' ally, the shah of Iran, Carter admitted the cancer-stricken monarch to the United States for treatment. Infuriated Iranians stormed the U.S. embassy in Tehran and took some fifty American hostages. A military rescue attempt failed, and Carter was unable to negotiate their release. Not until Reagan's inauguration did the Iranians let the Americans go.

D. A Sea of Troubles as Carter's Term Ends

Inflation grew steadily worse—13 percent annually in 1979 and 1980—largely because of OPEC's repeated price hikes. The Federal Reserve Board countered with an ever-higher discount rate, making borrowing so expensive that home building and other industry stagnated. Carter, believing the answer to our woes lay in fuel conservation, created the Department of Energy and proposed to Congress legislation that would penalize waste and reward restraint. Capitol Hill passed only a fraction of what he asked. Americans blamed the austerity-preaching president for the economic mess, and his popularity plunged farther when he was unable to free U.S. hostages held in Iran. When the Democrats renominated Carter in 1980, he had no hope of winning.

III. The Reagan Revolution

A. Background of the Revolution

Several things prepared the way for the Reagan revolution. Despite the New Deal and Great Society experiences, the old beliefs in rugged individualism and unregulated free enterprise never disappeared entirely. Decades of Cold War rhetoric left a deep suspicion of the Soviet Union and communism. A New Right cultural conservatism had emerged in reaction to the social turmoil and sexual revolution of the 1960s. Thus groups such as Jerry Falwell's Moral Majority threw their support to right-wing politicians. The shift of population to the traditionally more conservative Sun Belt also set the stage for Ronald Reagan.

B. The Man Behind the Movement

Ronald Reagan, ex-movie actor and General Electric spokesman, former governor of California, and the favorite of conservatives, took the 1980 Republican nomination. In November Reagan swept to victory over Carter and independent candidate John Anderson, and his party gained a majority in the Senate for the first time since 1955. Reagan carried the southern and western states and a majority of the blue-collar vote. Of the old Roosevelt coalition, only blacks remained solidly in the Democratic camp. On the day Reagan was inaugurated, Iran finally released the American captives.

C. Reaganomics

Reagan believed that the way to make the economy prosper was to lift government regulation and taxes off the back of business. In 1981 he persuaded Congress to cut income taxes by 25 percent and make up for the lost revenue with drastic reductions in domestic spending. He also appointed persons who shared his commitment to deregulation to head federal agencies. Secretary of the Interior James Watt opened national forest and wilderness areas to private developers. The secretary of transportation rescinded 1970s regulations for reducing air pollution and making cars safer and more efficient. By 1982 the economy was in a deep recession. The unemployment rate reached 10 percent. Minorities and the inner-city poor suffered severely as social-welfare programs dried up. The nation also experienced enormous foreign-trade deficits. Obsolete plants in the industrial heartland could not meet foreign competition and from 1979 to 1983 laid off 11.5 million workers as they shut down. Farm exports dropped, causing thousands of family-run farms to go under. Because military spending increased rapidly and the sluggish economy resulted in less tax revenue collected, the federal deficit soared. By 1983, with inflation at last licked, the economy began to rebound.

D. The Great Bull Market

The period 1982–1987 witnessed numerous corporate mergers, many insider-trading and other get-rich-quick schemes, and a great bull market that tripled the average price of stocks. Then, on October 19, 1987, the market crashed, with the biggest single-day drop in its history. Unlike 1929, however, a depression did not follow.

E. Reagan Confronts the "Evil Empire"

During his first term Reagan was hostile toward the U.S.S.R., calling it an "evil empire." Claiming that the Soviet and Cuban communists were trying to gain footholds in Central America, the administration supported a military junta in El Salvador in its brutal attempts to suppress left-wing rebellion. It also funded and trained the contras in Nicaragua in their efforts to overthrow the pro-Marxist Sandinista government. When Congress banned further military aid for the contras, the White House secretly raised money from private right-wing groups and foreign governments to continue the arming. The president also dispatched marines to Grenada to topple a radical government.

F. Tragedy and Frustration in the Middle East

Reagan had no success in bringing peace to the Middle East. In 1982 Israel invaded Lebanon to force the Palestine Liberation Organization (PLO) out of its stronghold there. As a result of the raid, the PLO withdrew, but civil war between rival Lebanese Christian and Muslim factions heated up. The president sent two thousand U.S. marines into Lebanon as part of an international peacekeeping force to oversee the orderly exit of the PLO, but in October 1983 a Muslim terrorist attack killed 239 of the Americans. In 1984 Reagan recalled the remaining men.

G. Military Buildup and Antinuclear Protest

Reagan launched the biggest peacetime military buildup in U.S. history. By 1985 the Pentagon's annual budget exceeded $300 billion, almost double what it had been in 1981. Much of the spending went into developing and deploying more nuclear-warhead missiles and other atomic weapons. Alarmed by this buildup, hundreds of thousands of Americans joined the nuclear-freeze movement, seeking a verifiable halt by the superpowers in the manufacture and deployment of nuclear weapons. The 1982 rally of freeze activists and sympathizers in New York City's Central Park drew 800,000, the largest demonstration in U.S. history, and in the fall of that year freeze resolutions passed in nine states. Reagan responded by starting talks with the Soviets on strategic-arms reduction and proposing to build a vast space-based antimissile defense system known as the Strategic Defense Initiative (SDI), nicknamed Star Wars. Opponents of SDI pointed out its prohibitive cost, its technical implausibility, and the great likelihood of its further escalating the arms race.

H. Reagan Reelected

By 1984 Reagan had nearly doubled military spending, aggravated Cold War tensions, produced huge federal-budget and foreign-trade deficits, drastically curtailed social welfare, and weakened government regulatory agencies. The economy had rebounded, however; inflation was almost beaten, and the president was as popular as ever. The Republicans again nominated Reagan and Vice President George Bush in 1984. Walter Mondale, the Democratic candidate for president, ran with Representative Geraldine Ferraro, the first woman to run on the national ticket of a major political party. Reagan won decisively.

IV. Conclusion

In the 1970s and 1980s the United States more than ever had become two societies: millions of young, middle-class Americans concentrated on their psychic well-being and upward socioeconomic mobility, while the poor, minorities, and recent immigrants lived in decaying inner cities plagued by crime, drugs, violence, and inadequate public services. In contrast to the socially conscious New Deal era or the 1960s, the affluent middle class of the 1970s and 1980s ignored the plight of the less fortunate and in 1980 and 1984 voted into the presidency a man who promised to reduce the role of government at home and escalate the nation's anticommunist stance abroad.

VOCABULARY

The following terms are used in Chapter 32. To understand the chapter fully, it is important that you know what each of them means.

yuppie   young urban professional

gentrification   the process whereby middle-class people buy run-down housing in poor inner-city neighborhoods and expensively restore it, resulting in the revival of the area but usually pushing out former residents who can no longer afford to live there

enervated   unnerved, weakened (especially psychologically)

discount rate   the interest rate that the Federal Reserve Board charges banks in the Federal Reserve system for giving them Federal Reserve notes in exchange for promissory notes; when the discount rate is raised, banks have to charge borrowers higher interest

stagflation   a combination of business stagnation and high inflation; the condition that beset the U.S. economy in the late 1970s and early 1980s

euphemistic   substituting a pleasant expression for an unpleasant, harsh, or offensive one; for example, *He passed away* instead of *He died*

insider trading   profiting on the stock market through private knowledge of planned corporate actions

---

IDENTIFICATIONS

After reading Chapter 32, you should be able to identify and explain the historical significance of each of the following:

Sam Walton and discount stores

Three Mile Island

Me Generation

Silicon Valley

Roe v. *Wade*, right-to-life movement, and pro-choice supporters

National Organization for Women (NOW)

Equal Rights Amendment

"feminization of poverty"

Immigration Reform and Control Act, 1986

American Indian Movement (AIM)

Indian Self-Determination Act, 1974

Moonies

Jerry Falwell and the Moral Majority; Pat Robertson and the Christian Coalition

Helsinki Accords

Zbigniew Brzezinski

Camp David Israeli-Egyptian Accords

Iranian hostage crisis

political action committees (PACs)

Reaganomics

Secretary of the Interior James Watt and the Sagebrush Rebellion

Donald Trump and Ivan Boesky

Sandinistas versus contras

Palestine Liberation Organization (PLO)

nuclear-freeze movement

Strategic Defense Initiative (Star Wars)

Sandra Day O'Connor

Walter Mondale and Geraldine Ferraro

SKILL BUILDING: MAPS

1. On the map of North Africa and the Middle East which follows, locate and explain the importance to U.S. foreign policy of each of the following:

   Afghanistan

   Israel

   West Bank

   Egypt

   Port Said

   Syria

   Jordan

   Iran

   Tehran

   Lebanon

   Iraq

2. On the map of the Caribbean and Central America below, locate and explain the importance to U.S. foreign policy of each of the following:

Panama

Panama Canal Zone

El Salvador

Nicaragua

Honduras

Costa Rica

Cuba

Grenada

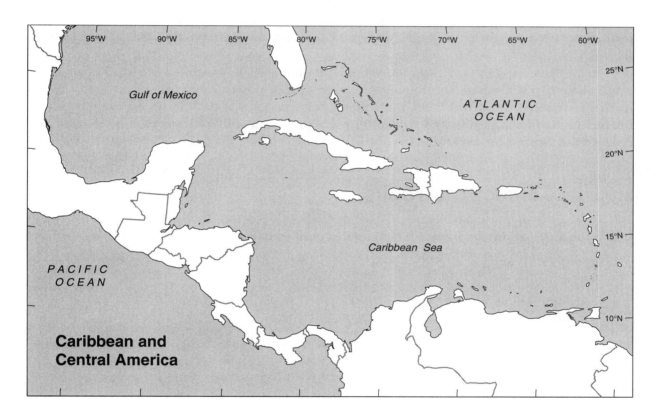

Caribbean and Central America

SKILL BUILDING: GRAPHS

Look at the graphs in Chapter 32. From glancing at the one titled "Changing Demographics," you should be able to answer the following questions:

1. About how many Hispanics lived in the United States in 1992?

2. About how many Asians and Pacific Islanders are there likely to be by 2050?

Now look at the graph "The Election of 1980" and answer the following questions:

1. Was this a close election or a landslide?
2. The losing candidate, Jimmy Carter, won the electoral votes of which states?
3. Did the third-party candidate, John Anderson, carry any state?

HISTORICAL SOURCES

In Chapter 32 the author has used many of the historical sources we have noted earlier, including data from the U.S. Bureau of the Census. For example, many of the chapter's observations about family patterns, women in the work force, conditions of the black underclass, and ethnic make-up of America's population come from census studies. Look at page 1030, where the author makes statements about Hispanics based on Census Bureau estimates. What are these findings? Why can't the historian rely on the accuracy of census figures?

In "A Place in Time: Houston Rides the Economic Roller Coaster" the author again uses local history to illuminate the impact of national and international events on the lives of American citizens. How did OPEC's changing price policies and Middle East conflict affect life in Houston in the 1970s and 1980s? Why was the impact different in Houston than in the cities of the Northeast and Midwest?

MULTIPLE-CHOICE QUESTIONS

Circle the letter of the item that best completes each statement or answers the question.

1. In the 1970s and early 1980s the Federal Reserve Board repeatedly raised the discount rate to
   a. stimulate new-home construction.
   b. encourage borrowing for new-plant construction.
   c. combat inflation.
   d. combat unemployment.

2. The only sector of the Roosevelt New Deal coalition that continued through the 1980s to vote consistently for the Democratic presidential candidate was
   a. blue-collar workers.
   b. farmers.
   c. Irish, Polish, and other ethnic Americans.
   d. blacks.

3. Which of the following happened during Jimmy Carter's presidency?
   a. Treaties transferring control of the Panama Canal and Canal Zone to Panama by 1999 were ratified.
   b. The inflation rate was finally slowed to 6 percent annually.
   c. The United States invaded Grenada to topple an anti-American left-wing regime.
   d. The INF Treaty was negotiated and ratified.

4. Jerry Falwell's Moral Majority and other evangelical Protestant groups
    a. tended to be politically conservative and therefore strongly pro-Reagan.
    b. were concentrated in the South and therefore almost always supported Democratic candidates.
    c. were the strongest supporters of peaceful coexistence with the U.S.S.R. and China.
    d. opposed prayer in public schools and other attempts to disregard the separation of church and state.

5. All of the following happened during Ronald Reagan's first term as president *except*
    a. the most massive military spending in U.S. peacetime history.
    b. runaway inflation.
    c. a drop in U.S. exports of both agricultural and industrial products.
    d. deregulation of many industries.

6. Three Mile Island is associated with
    a. the Star Wars defense system.
    b. a near-disastrous accident at a nuclear-power plant.
    c. gentrification of a run-down area.
    d. the "feminization of poverty."

7. Which of the following statements about women in the 1980s is correct?
    a. The majority held paying jobs outside the home.
    b. They were close to achieving equality of pay with men.
    c. Almost half of the lawyers, doctors, and engineers in this country were women.
    d. They were likely to marry at a younger age and have more children than women in the 1950s.

8. The Reagan administration extended military aid and training to the contras in hope that the contras would overthrow a leftist government in
    a. Afghanistan.
    b. Grenada.
    c. Cuba.
    d. Nicaragua.

9. Which of the following statements about the Camp David Accords is correct?
    a. The signers promised to respect human rights, which gave courage to Soviet dissidents.
    b. They were negotiated by Israel and Lebanon with the help and encouragement of President Reagan.
    c. They were agreed to by Israel's Menachem Begin and Egypt's Anwar el-Sadat and ended the long Arab-Israeli conflict.
    d. Getting Egypt's Sadat and Israel's Begin to negotiate an understanding between their countries was President Carter's greatest foreign-policy achievement.

10. Which of the following statements about the election of 1984 is correct?
    a. The Republicans won control of both the White House and Congress for the first time since the Eisenhower years.
    b. A major political party nominated a woman for vice president for the first time in U.S. history.
    c. An incumbent president was defeated by a candidate claiming to be an honest Washington "outsider."
    d. It was one of the three closest contests in the twentieth century.

SHORT-ANSWER QUESTIONS

1. Describe the new patterns of immigration into the United States that set in after 1965.

2. Which social activist movements of the 1960s continued strongly in the 1970s and 1980s? Why?

3. What was the *Roe* v. *Wade* decision? Why did it prove to be politically divisive throughout the 1980s?

4. In what ways did prospects for Native Americans improve in the late 1960s and 1970s? What significant problems continued to plague American Indians?

5. "Religious faith has always loomed large in American history, but after 1970 it played a more decisive cultural and political role than it had for years." Explain why the author of Chapter 32 makes this statement. Do you agree?

6. What were the troubles that overwhelmed the Carter administration and prevented Carter's reelection?

7. Explain the meaning of the term "Reaganomics."

ESSAY QUESTIONS

1. "The story of black America in the 1970s and 1980s was really two very different stories." Explain what this quotation means using as many facts as possible.

2. Discuss the waxing and waning of détente between the United States and the Soviet Union from the 1970s to 1984. What caused each of the periods of strain and relaxation of tensions?

3. Compare and contrast American society and culture in the 1960s and the 1980s.

4. Discuss the foreign policies of the United States in Africa, Latin America and the Caribbean, and the Middle East under the Ford, Carter, and first Reagan administrations.

5. What is meant by the term "the Reagan Revolution"? According to Chapter 32, what accounted for the appeal of Ronald Reagan and his policies to the American electorate in the 1980s?

33

Beyond the Cold War

OUTLINE AND SUMMARY

I. Problems and Opportunities in Reagan's Second Term

A. *Tax Reform, Budget Deficits, and Trade Gaps*

During Reagan's second term, immigration and tax-reform measures passed, but the legacy of Reaganomics—huge budget and foreign-trade deficits—continued.

B. *Middle East Encore: Talks and Terrorism*

The Middle East remained a thorny problem. In December 1987 the Intifada, a Palestinian uprising against Israel, began, and U.S. efforts to convince Jordan, the Palestinians, and Israel to negotiate failed. The Palestinians and their backers, especially Libya's Colonel Muammar el-Qaddafi, resorted to terrorist attacks against U.S. citizens, including bombing a Pan Am jet in 1988.

C. *The Iran-Contra Scandal*

The Iran-contra affair, the worst scandal of the Reagan administration, also originated in Middle Eastern problems. Robert McFarlane, Oliver North, and other members and staff of the National Security Council in 1985–1986 secretly arranged shipments of U.S. weapons to Iran. Then they diverted money from the sales to the Nicaraguan contras at a time when Congress had forbidden further aid to them. To hide their activities, North shredded incriminating documents requested by investigators. A congressional committee chaired by Senator Daniel Inouye found no evidence that Reagan had known of the scheme but criticized him for his casual style of supervision and disregard for the law, which invited such behavior from subordinates. North and others involved were subsequently tried and convicted. North's conviction was overturned in 1991 on technical grounds.

D. *More Scandals and Embarrassments*

Lesser scandals also marred Reagan's second term. Evidence of bribes and conspiracy in the granting of military contracts surfaced. Reagan's secretary of the interior, James Watt, and attorney general Edwin Meese were accused of influence peddling, which led to the latter's resignation. Despite these and other revelations, the president remained popular.

E. *Reagan's Mission to Moscow*

The U.S.S.R., bedeviled by domestic crises, sought an easing of tensions abroad, which was reflected in its willingness to make concessions in its arms-control talks with the United States. In 1987 the two superpowers negotiated the Intermediate Nuclear Forces (INF) Treaty. It removed twenty-five hundred U.S. and Soviet missiles from Europe and provided for on-site verification inspections. The agreement opened a new era of détente, capped by Reagan's visit to Moscow in May 1988 and the U.S.S.R.'s decision to withdraw its forces from Afghanistan. Ironically, Reagan, the Cold Warrior, denouncer of arms control, and architect of massive military buildup, "seemed destined to be remembered for . . . bettering relations with the Soviets and reducing the risk of global war."

F. *The Election of 1988*

Vice President George Bush captured the Republican nomination, and Massachusetts governor Michael Dukakis beat Jesse Jackson for the top spot on the Democratic ticket. Bush campaigned on Reagan's achievements, tried to distance himself from the Iran-contra scandal, and painted Dukakis as soft on crime and deficient in patriotism. The governor was unable to refute Bush's claims and articulate a strong vision of the United States' future. Both candidates avoided important issues, resorting instead to photo opportunities and televised spot commercials. Bush won 54 percent of the vote, while the Democrats widened their majorities in Congress.

II. The Bush Years: Resolve Abroad, Drift at Home

A. *The Cold War Ends*

Soon after Bush's inauguration, Soviet power collapsed. First the Eastern European countries discarded their U.S.S.R.-backed communist regimes. Then East and West Germany reunited, and the Baltic republics declared their independence from Moscow. With our former Cold War adversary clearly no longer a threat, in 1991 President Bush signed another treaty with Gorbachev reducing each country's strategic nuclear arsenal by 25 percent.

Meanwhile Gorbachev's attempts to revive the Soviet economy by introducing some free enterprise alarmed hard-line Communists, who in August 1991 tried to overthrow him. Boris Yeltsin, president of the Russian Republic, and his followers squelched the coup, outlawed the Communist party, and proclaimed the end of the U.S.S.R. Overwhelmed by the rush of anticommunism and resurgent nationalism, Gorbachev resigned.

President Bush and his secretary of state, James Baker III, reacted cautiously to the events in Eastern Europe. In 1992 Bush proposed economic aid for Russia, and Baker tried to see to it that the nuclear arsenal and know-how of the former Soviet republics did not fall into the wrong hands. The United States further cut back its nuclear stockpiles.

Bush abandoned Reagan's interventions in Nicaragua and El Salvador, and the long civil wars there subsided. However, the United States invaded Panama; toppled its leader, Manuel Noriega; and brought him to Florida to stand trial for drug selling. The United States withdrew support of corrupt Filipino president Ferdinand Marcos and recognized his democratically elected successor, Corazon Aquino.

When the economic sanctions of the United States and other countries against the racist white government of South Africa induced it to release Nelson Mandela and drop most apartheid laws, Bush resumed normal trade. The administration refused to impose trade sanctions on China in retaliation for its brutal suppression of prodemocracy demonstrators. The president traveled to Japan in hopes of persuading that prosperous nation to ease the U.S. trade deficit by buying more U.S. products. Little came of his attempt.

B. Operation Desert Storm

After years of weapons stockpiling, including nuclear and chemical, Saddam Hussein, dictator of Iraq, invaded Kuwait on August 2, 1990. Although the United States had favored Iraq in its earlier war against Iran, President Bush, as well as other world leaders, now saw Hussein as a serious menace. The president, enlisting the support of Congress, the American people, and the United Nations, demanded Iraqi withdrawal from Kuwait. When Hussein did not comply, on January 16, 1991, the United States and other U.N. members began daily bombing raids on Iraqi troops, supply depots, communication centers, and cities. Saddam Hussein retaliated by firing Scud missiles at Israel and Saudi Arabia. The United States tried to intercept these missiles with its Patriot missiles. On February 23, 1991, the U.N. and U.S. ground assault began, and within one hundred hours Kuwait was liberated and Bush declared a cease-fire. U.N. inspectors entered Iraq and began dismantling Hussein's nuclear-weapons plants, but the dictator remained in power, crushing Shiite Muslim and Kurdish uprisings against him.

In the wake of the Persian Gulf War, Bush attempted to reopen Arab-Israeli peace negotiations. In November 1991, Israel, the Palestinians, and various Arab states met for talks, first in Madrid and then Washington. Reaching agreements, however, proved extremely slow and difficult.

C. Domestic Discontents

Bush inherited economic ills stemming from his predecessor's policies. Savings-and-loan associations collapsed. Deregulation of the Reagan years that permitted savings-and-loan associations to extend risky loans and speculate in real-estate and other questionable ventures largely caused these disasters. Because deposits in these institutions were federally insured, making good on the losses cost the American taxpayers billions of dollars.

The huge federal deficit produced by Reagan's tax cuts and enormous military spending grew still larger due to the S&L bailout, Gulf War costs, welfare, and Medicare/Medicaid payments. The 1990 package of new taxes and reduced spending failed to stanch the fiscal bleeding. Then, in 1990, recession hit. Sales, housing starts, and tax revenues fell; unemployment climbed. States dropped social-welfare programs, and more than 2 million additional Americans sank below the poverty line. Those in the middle class, once enthusiastic about Reaganomics, became skeptical, but they still displayed little compassion for the poor.

The economic downturn highlighted deep-seated social maladies. Poverty and anger in inner cities worsened and in April 1992 erupted into rioting in Los Angeles and other places. Public schools languished. In 1989, the *Exxon Valdez* oil spill ruined six hundred acres of pristine Alaskan coastline, and the Environmental Protection Agency (EPA) pronounced the air in more than 100 U.S. cities hazardous to breathe. The Bush administration largely ignored these problems. It continued to favor more oil exploration and drilling in Alaska and undermined international treaties on global warming and mining in Antarctica. Bush did, however, sign the 1990 Federal Clean Air Act, passed by the Democratic-controlled Congress.

D. The Supreme Court Moves Right

To swing the Supreme Court farther to the right, Reagan appointed conservatives Sandra Day O'Connor, the first woman justice; Antonin Scalia; and Anthony Kennedy, as well as elevating William Rehnquist to chief justice to replace the retiring Warren Burger. Bush followed suit, naming two more conservatives, David Souter and Clarence Thomas. The Senate almost rejected the latter because of his questionable judicial qualifications and law professor Anita Hill's charges that he sexually harassed her. As early as 1989, court decisions reflected the new conservative majority. The justices hedged women's abortion rights, narrowed the interpretation of civil-rights laws, and removed some protections for arrested persons. However, in a five-to-four decision, the Court reaffirmed its earlier *Roe* v. *Wade* stand.

E. The Politics of Frustration

Bush's popularity, at a peak after Operation Desert Storm, plunged with the recession. In his 1992 State of the Union message, the president suggested such classic Republican formulas for recovery as middle- and upper-class tax cuts and incentives for business. Democrats denounced his proposals as "politically motivated and inadequate."

In 1992 the Democrats nominated Arkansas Governor Bill Clinton and Senator Al Gore of Tennessee for president and vice-president, respectively. They promised to create jobs, protect the environment, safeguard a woman's right to an abortion, reform welfare, and create a national health-care system. A Republican convention dominated by the right wing renominated Bush and Quayle and denounced abortion, sexual permissiveness, feminism, and other "threats" to family values. Clinton won with 43 percent of the popular vote to Bush's 38 percent. The strong showing of a third-party candidate, billionaire H. Ross Perot, indicated widespread dissatisfaction with both of the major parties. Perot garnered 19 percent of the vote, the most for any independent since Theodore Roosevelt in 1912. The Democrats retained control of Congress, and the number of women and minority members serving on Capitol Hill grew.

III. The Clinton Years: Democratic Disarray, Republican Resurgence

A. Struggling to Shape a Domestic Agenda

In his domestic program, Clinton aimed particularly to please the middle class and blue-collar workers, as well as to advance some of the causes of the 1960s and 1970s, such as feminism. Clinton named many women to cabinet and other top government positions, including Ruth Bader Ginsberg to the Supreme Court and his wife, Hillary Rodham Clinton, to head his Task Force on National Health-Care Reform. The president had only modest success in getting key proposals through Congress. The lawmakers passed the federal spending cuts, tax increases, and the North American Free Trade Agreement with Mexico that Clinton requested but rejected his economic-stimulus package (especially when unemployment fell and new jobs increased in 1993–1994 without any spurt of inflation). The health-care plan eventually unveiled by Clinton's task force fell under such a barrage of lobbying and partisan attacks that by mid-1994 it had lost most of its support. Nor did Congress accept Clinton's ideas for revamping welfare, which both liberals and conservatives disliked, though for different reasons.

By 1994 allegations of sexual and other misconduct and complaints that he was too eager to please and compromise were seriously eroding Clinton's popularity and effectiveness. More ominous to any liberal or even moderate agenda was the expanding influence of the religious right. Pat Robertson's Christian Coalition, through voter registration drives and organizing workshops, had by 1994 gained control of many state Republican parties and local and state governments.

B. The Quest for a Coherent Foreign Policy

Clinton preferred to concentrate on domestic issues, but with the United States left as the only superpower, he had to respond to international crises. The collapse of communism in Eastern and Central Europe unleashed age-old ethnic hatreds. The former Yugoslavia erupted into civil war among Croats, Serbs, and Muslims, and various attempts at settlement by NATO, the United Nations, and the United States got nowhere. The former U.S.S.R. also seemed overwhelmed by economic chaos and national rivalries. Other than offering Russia and Ukraine economic assistance, there was little that Washington could do. Because Bush's humanitarian intervention in Somalia turned sour, Clinton refrained from similar military commitments in Rwanda. He found it more difficult, however, to ignore the brutal junta in Haiti and the Haitian refugees streaming to U.S. shores.

The Arab-Israeli-Palestinian talks begun in the aftermath of the Gulf War finally bore fruit when PLO head Yasir Arafat and Israeli prime minister Yitzhak Rabin signed an agreement at the White House for limited Palestinian self-rule in the Gaza Strip and Jericho. However, Muslim fundamentalist terrorism did not cease. In February 1993, Middle Eastern terrorists bombed the World Trade Center in New York.

In Asia, the Clinton administration followed Bush's lead in pressing Japan to ease the U.S. trade deficit by buying more U.S. goods and in refusing to impose trade sanctions on China for its human-rights abuses.

IV. The 1994 Elections and After: A Sharp Right Turn

In the 1994 mid-term elections, the voters made a sharp rightward turn, electing Republican majorities to both houses of Congress for the first time since 1954. Why did this happen? What did it mean? Some commentators mentioned widespread feelings of frustration among working- and middle-class Americans (perhaps fueled by the stagnation of real income). Others pointed to the organizing and spending of right-wing and special-interest groups, such as the Christian Coalition and the National Rifle Association. Republican politicians, especially Newt Gingrich as Speaker of the House, quickly proposed a "Contract with America," a series of conservative legislative goals. Although the election results seemed to demonstrate a significant ideological shift, it was hard to know if that was so since only 38 percent of eligible voters went to the polls in 1994. The leaders of the Republican-controlled Congress announced their intention to balance the federal budget, cut taxes for middle- and upper-income Americans, increase defense spending, and cut back on various federal welfare programs.

V. A Broader Perspective

A. Economic and Social Trends: Coping with Change

Regardless of who was president and which political party controlled the White House and/or Capitol Hill, certain economic and social trends persisted for several decades. Ever greater numbers of women entered the paid labor force: in 1992, 58 percent of women worked for wages. By the 1990s Americans had a troubling sense that economic opportunities were narrowing and that they were not likely to be better off than their parents. These perceptions rested on various developments. The nation's share of total world output of goods and services dropped from one-third in 1950 to one-fifth by 1990, and more foreigners held ownership in U.S. businesses, banks, and real estate than formerly. The proportion of Americans engaged in relatively high-paying unionized industrial jobs relentlessly shrank, while those having to settle for low-paid, non-union, no-security, no-benefits, service-sector positions grew. Between 1970 and 1990, average family real income barely rose, and that of factory workers declined. Unemployment, even during periods of national prosperity, was alarmingly high for unskilled, poorly educated young people. In the inner cities and among minorities, the problems were magnified. In 1994, Detroit's youths suffered almost a 50 percent jobless rate. Indeed, some commentators claimed that the United States had developed a permanent "outer class" that was "lacking work, uneducated, politically apathetic, [and] socially adrift."

The gap between the black middle and lower classes widened. More African-Americans than ever before graduated from college and held elective office by 1993, but for the one-third of blacks living below the poverty line, conditions worsened. A similar gap separated Hispanics as more of them moved into the middle class and political office, but over a quarter remained impoverished.

The 1990s also saw a pronounced rise in the hate rhetoric and organizing activity of the radical right (religious, cultural, and political).

B. An Imperiled Environment

The past decades witnessed American government's making halting and uncertain efforts to address long-term, worldwide environmental hazards. These included the disposal of radioactive nuclear waste, wildlife- and forest-destroying acid rain, depletion of the protective ozone layer, and global warming.

C. A New World Order?

In recent years we have seen the end of the Cold War and the disintegration of the Soviet Union, events that eased the threats of totalitarianism and nuclear war. However, new trouble spots have erupted around the globe. Complex issues, such as how to handle the disparity in living standards between the industrialized Northern Hemisphere and the impoverished, underdeveloped Southern Hemisphere, face the world. Defining what role the United States should play on the international scene and how it should relate to the United Nations are challenges with which the American people and government must wrestle.

VI. Conclusion

By the 1990s, the United States was increasingly divided into two Americas: the educated, prosperous, professional, and middle classes "thriving in the new service-based economy dominated by computers and . . . interactive communication" and "an outer class stuck in poverty and despair." Rapid social and demographic changes had spawned outbursts of fear and hate. In the years ahead, can America's multicultural society "find the resources to sustain a sense of common national identity or will fragmentation and mistrust prevail"?

VOCABULARY

The following terms are used in Chapter 33. To understand the chapter fully, it is important that you know what each of them means.

patrician   person of high birth; person born into the upper class

market economy   one in which decisions about production, pricing, and distribution are made by private entrepreneurs seeking profits and responding to economic forces such as supply and demand rather than by centralized government planning

commonwealth   a group of sovereign states associated by their own choice and linked by common objectives and interests; for example, the association that exists among Great Britain, Canada, India, and other countries known as the British Commonwealth

apartheid   South Africa's policy of racial separation

trade deficit   a condition that exists when a nation earns less from its exports than it spends on imports

colossus   something or someone of great size, scope, or importance

dichotomy   division into two contrasting groups

Newt Gingrich   Republican leader who proposed a "Contract with America" after the 1994 elections

IDENTIFICATIONS

After reading Chapter 33, you should be able to identify and explain the historical significance of each of the following:

Intifada and Middle East terrorist attacks

the Iran-contra scandal, Robert McFarlane, John Poindexter, and Oliver North

Donald Regan, Edwin Meese, and James Watt

INF Treaty and the Moscow summit

Jesse Jackson and Michael Dukakis

Mikhail Gorbachev and Boris Yeltsin

James Baker III

General Manuel Noriega

Nelson Mandela and the African National Congress

Saddam Hussein

Operation Desert Storm and General Norman Schwarzkopf

S&L bailout

Exxon Valdez

ozone shield

William Rehnquist

Clarence Thomas versus Anita Hill

H. Ross Perot

Ruth Bader Ginsberg

Hillary Rodham Clinton and the Task Force on National Health-Care Reform

gays, the military, and ''Don't ask, don't tell''

North American Free Trade Agreement (NAFTA)

''ethnic cleansing'': Serbs, Croats, and Muslims

Colin Powell

SKILL BUILDING: MAPS

1. On the map of Europe on the next page, locate and explain the historic changes that took place in the late 1980s and 1990s in each of the following:

    Germany

    Berlin

    Estonia

    Latvia

    Lithuania

    Belarus

    the Ukraine

    Poland

    Russian Federation

    states created from the former Yugoslavia

2. On the map of the Middle East and North Africa, which follows, locate and explain the
historic events that occurred in each of the following in the late 1980s and 1990s:

Libya
Egypt
Afghanistan
Israel
West Bank
Jericho
Gaza Strip
Jordan
Syria
Kuwait
Kuwait City
Iraq
Baghdad
Saudi Arabia
Riyadh
Persian Gulf

Middle East and North Africa

MULTIPLE-CHOICE QUESTIONS

Circle the letter of the item that best completes each statement or answers the question.

1. Which of the following statements about the election of 1992 is correct?
   a. The right wing of the Republican party dominated its national convention and wrote its platform.
   b. An independent candidate for the presidency won a larger portion of the vote than any other third-party candidate had since the election of 1912.
   c. Bill Clinton's victory owed much to his success in reviving the New Deal Democratic coalition.
   d. all of the above

2. The only arms-control treaty to provide for destruction of a class of existing weapons and for on-site inspection for compliance is
   a. SALT I.
   b. SALT II.
   c. the Non-Proliferation Treaty.
   d. the INF Treaty.

3. During President Bush's administration, the United States dispatched military forces to
   a. Afghanistan and Iran.
   b. Syria and Egypt.
   c. Panama and the Middle East.
   d. all of the above

4. All of the following events occurred internationally in the late 1980s and early 1990s *except*
   a. Ferdinand Marcos was driven from power in the Philippines.
   b. the Kurds of Iraq successfully defied Saddam Hussein and established an independent state.
   c. Mikhail Gorbachev resigned from office, and the Soviet Union ceased to exist.
   d. East and West Germany reunited, and the Baltic states declared their independence.

5. The collapse of the savings-and-loan industry
   a. was caused by the excessive federal regulation that kept savings-and-loan associations from making profitable investments.
   b. led to the ruin of depositors in those institutions, who lost all they had in their accounts.
   c. triggered a serious depression, much as the 1929 stock market crash did.
   d. worsened the budget deficit because Washington had to spend billions of dollars to repay federally insured depositors.

6. By 1990 what portion of African-Americans lived below the poverty line?
   a. one-half
   b. one-fourth
   c. one-third
   d. one-fifth

7. The *Exxon Valdez* incident involved
   a. an oil spill that fouled the waters off Alaska.
   b. a terrorist attack on an American oil tanker.
   c. an OPEC conspiracy to jack up the price of oil.
   d. Exxon's offering illegal payments to members of Reagan's cabinet to obtain leases to drill for oil in the Alaska wilderness.

8. Which of the following statements about Presidents Reagan and Bush and the Supreme Court is correct?
   a. There were too few resignations from the Supreme Court to give Reagan and Bush a chance to appoint a new majority reflecting their political philosophies.
   b. Because of Reagan's and Bush's political conservatism, they appointed only white males as justices.
   c. Through their appointments to the Supreme Court, Reagan and Bush created a conservative majority that is likely to continue into the twenty-first century.
   d. Despite the fact that their appointees had to be confirmed by the Democratic-controlled Senate, Reagan and Bush won approval for all the justices they nominated.

9. During his first year in office, President Bill Clinton successfully pushed through Congress
   a. a plan for national health-care reform.
   b. the North American Free Trade Agreement (NAFTA) with Mexico.
   c. a budget that provided for a much expanded federal-jobs program and other pump-priming measures to stimulate the economy.
   d. a measure opening opportunities for military service to declared homosexuals.

10. Between 1970 and 1990 the average annual income, adjusted for inflation, of American industrial workers
    a. declined.
    b. nearly doubled.
    c. rose slightly.
    d. increased by 25 percent.

SHORT-ANSWER QUESTIONS

1. Explain the Iran-contra affair.

2. Discuss briefly the record of the Reagan and Bush administrations on environmental issues.

3. What actions did the Bush administration take in Central America (Nicaragua, El Salvador, Panama)? Why did it take those actions in each case?

4. What were the main foreign-policy initiatives of the United States toward Japan and China during the Bush and Clinton administrations?

5. What were President Clinton's suggestions for revamping America's welfare system? Why were they controversial? What happened to them?

6. What has been the political impact of Pat Robertson's Christian Coalition?

7. Discuss the reasons for the decline in union membership and union influence in national politics.

ESSAY QUESTIONS

1. The author of Chapter 33 says of President Reagan, "The vigorous Cold Warrior, denouncer of earlier arms-control treaties, and champion of massive military spending seemed destined to be remembered for his part in bettering relations with the Soviets and reducing the risk of global war." Discuss this statement, using as many specific facts as possible, and offer some possible explanations of this paradox.

2. In 1991 a *New York Times* editorial commented, "George Bush remains mystifyingly incomplete: shrewd and energetic in foreign policy and just the reverse—clumsy and irresolute—at home." Write an essay agreeing or disagreeing with this assessment and explain your reasons with as many specific facts as possible.

3. "Clinton began his presidency in January 1993 with confidence and high energy. But grueling difficulties on both the domestic and foreign-policy fronts quickly propelled his administration into rough waters." Discuss the domestic and foreign policies of the Clinton administration, and explain in what respects it floundered in "rough waters."

4. Discuss the Persian Gulf War. What caused it? Why and how did the United States intervene? How was it fought? What effects did it have on developments in the Middle East and on the U.S. domestic scene?

5. In "A Place in Time: Miami in the 1990s," the author writes, "In this vibrant, garish . . . city, many of the most urgent social issues facing contemporary America emerge in particularly stark fashion." Write an essay identifying those social issues and discussing how they were illustrated in both Miami and the rest of the nation.

EPILOGUE

Looking Ahead—Looking Back

OUTLINE AND SUMMARY

I. Changes and Challenges Ahead

Experts predict that the population of the United States will grow to 310 million by 2080 and that the portion of the population over sixty-five years of age will continue to climb. These demographic trends will challenge American society to find ways to provide for and employ about a third of a billion citizens, and they put great pressure on America's social security and medical-care systems. In the twenty-first century, U.S. society will become increasingly multicultural and nonwhite. It is projected that by 2050 today's minorities (Hispanics, blacks, Asians, and Native Americans) will comprise almost half the nation. The U.S. economy is likely to remain the world's largest for a long while, but it will face escalating competition from the European Common Market and the Pacific Rim countries. The economic and social maladies of America's inner cities will probably persist into the next century despite overall prosperity. In the post–Cold War period, the United States is just starting to feel its way toward a suitable international role for itself.

II. Facing Up to Change

Rather than viewing change as offering positive challenges, some Americans are reacting with fear and hostility toward the country's democratic traditions, government, and cultural and ethnic diversity. These people fail to see the many positive aspects of contemporary national life. Despite its faults, the U.S. educational system is one of the most open and equal in the world. American political thinkers and social scientists are calling attention to thorny economic and social problems and offering creative solutions in a spate of books, such as Robert Reich's *The World of Nations* and Albert Gore's *Earth in the Balance*.

III. Drawing Strength from the Past

Our national past should encourage us in facing today's problems. The U.S. Constitution, written in 1787 for an agrarian population of 4 million, has proved through time to be a wise and flexible instrument that still works in the 1990s for a modern industrial society of 255 million. The federal system allows creative experiments in solving social ills to emanate not just from Washington but also from state and local governments. Since 1787, slowly and sometimes painfully, the American political system has moved from including only propertied white males to embracing all adult citizens. When economic troubles, such as those accompanying the industrial revolution, threatened the welfare of large numbers of people, muckraking journalists exposed the dangers, and government acted to protect society. Although we have sometimes violated our own best traditions, for most of our history and to the present day, our respect for human rights has been a beacon for the rest of the world. With all of these strengths in our heritage, our great challenge is "to pass on to future generations the enduring vision of freedom and common purpose that others have transmitted to us from the past."

VOCABULARY

The following terms are used in the Epilogue. To understand it fully, it is important that you know what each of them means.

quincentennial   five hundredth anniversary

cacophony   harsh noise

cursory   hastily done

franchise   the right to vote

IDENTIFICATIONS

Woodstock festival

D-Day ceremonies

Robert Reich, *The World of Nations*

Albert Gore, *Earth in the Balance*

Vaclav Havel

MULTIPLE-CHOICE QUESTIONS

Circle the letter of the item that best completes each statement or answers the question.

1. Demographers predict that in the twenty-first century, the U.S. population will
   a. grow by some 60 million people.
   b. contain a larger percentage of children than it does in the 1990s.
   c. contain a smaller percentage of elderly people than in 1990.
   d. become more ethnically and racially homogeneous.

2. By the year 2000, America's largest ethnic minority will probably be
   a. blacks.
   b. Asians.
   c. Hispanics.
   d. Indians.

3. By what date did all adult Americans first have the constitutional right to vote regardless of race, gender, or economic standing?
   a. 1877
   b. 1950
   c. 1990
   d. 1920

4. In 1989 Chinese students demonstrating for more freedom in their country used which of the following symbols?
   a. the hammer and sickle
   b. the Statue of Liberty
   c. the swastika
   d. all of the above

SHORT-ANSWER QUESTIONS

1. What are some of the challenges that the United States will face in the twenty-first century because of the demographic trends noted in the Epilogue?

2. What predictions about the U.S. economy does the Epilogue make?

3. The Epilogue states that one source of the U.S. tradition of respect for human rights comes from landmark judicial decisions. From your study of American history, discuss three specific cases.

ESSAY QUESTIONS

1. The British philosopher John Stuart Mill claimed that there is great value in "placing human beings in contact with persons dissimilar to themselves." Such contacts have "always been . . . one of the primary sources of progress." Write an essay either agreeing or disagreeing with Mill, and back up your position with what you have learned from your study of American history.

2. The Epilogue states, "In contemplating the present tangle of problems, Americans . . . feel apprehensive, . . . however, our national experience furnishes reason for encouragement." What in our national experience gives us reason to believe that we will be able to confront and conquer our contemporary problems?

Preparing for the Final Examination: Prologue, Chapters 1 to 16

As you approach the end of part 1 of your American history course, you may well wonder how you are supposed to remember all those facts for the final. Here are some hints for preparing to take that semester exam: (1) do not wait until the night before the test (or even the last couple of days prior to it) to start your studying; (2) review the notes that you have taken on class lectures and assigned readings other than your textbook; (3) review the chapters of this study guide, rereading carefully the Outline and Summary portion of each; (4) as you do steps 2 and 3, look for issues and themes that seem to come up again and again. History, after all, is about change and continuity over time. Therefore, ask yourself as you review what things about American society changed between the colonial period and the end of Reconstruction and why. On the other hand, which things remained essentially constant or recurred periodically throughout those years? The following sample multiple-choice and essay questions are designed to assist you in pulling together all the facts and seeing more clearly the patterns of change and continuity over the first centuries of American history.

MULTIPLE-CHOICE QUESTIONS

Circle the letter of the item that best completes each statement or answers the question.

1. Which of the following ended slavery everywhere in the United States?
    a. Lincoln's Emancipation Proclamation
    b. the Crittenden compromise
    c. the Thirteenth Amendment
    d. the Fifteenth Amendment

2. The statement "We hold these truths to be self-evident, that all men are created equal, that they are endowed by their Creator with certain unalienable rights . . ." is found in
    a. the Declaration of Independence.
    b. the U.S. Constitution.
    c. Lincoln's first inaugural address.
    d. all of the above.

3. Which of the following people is *incorrectly* matched with the reform he or she championed?
   a. Dorothea Dix—more humane treatment of the mentally ill
   b. Elizabeth Cady Stanton—women's rights
   c. Jonathan Edwards—separation of church and state and religious toleration
   d. William Lloyd Garrison—abolition of slavery

4. The convention held at Seneca Falls, New York, in 1848
   a. threatened that New England and New York would secede if peace were not made with England immediately.
   b. launched the feminist movement.
   c. was the first held by a political party to nominate its candidate for president.
   d. launched the abolitionist movement.

5. The forty-ninth parallel became the dividing line between
   a. northern and southern states.
   b. American and British parts of the Oregon Territory.
   c. Kansas and Nebraska.
   d. the Mexican cession and the Louisiana Purchase.

6. The case of *Commonwealth* v. *Hunt* is significant in the long struggle of
   a. labor to win recognition of unions and the right to strike.
   b. women to gain equality in receiving an education.
   c. the federal government to increase its powers at the expense of the states.
   d. the abolitionists to end slavery in Washington, D.C.

7. Which of these statements comes closest to expressing Secretary of the Treasury Alexander Hamilton's views on the proper financial program for the federal government?
   a. A government should be frugal and avoid a standing debt.
   b. The government should repudiate the financial obligations incurred by the Continental Congress.
   c. The federal government should tie the monied classes of the nation to it by selling public securities at attractive rates of interest to them.
   d. The federal government should encourage the states to pay off their debts quickly by giving them matching grants.

8. Which of the following statements about the Era of Good Feelings is *incorrect?*
   a. It was a period of one-party politics.
   b. During these years the Republicans adopted much of the centralizing nationalism of the old Federalists.
   c. Congress passed a protective tariff and chartered a new national bank.
   d. The federal government began an extensive program of federally subsidized transportation improvements.

9. A typical western farmer in the 1830s and 1840s would probably favor all of the following federal policies *except*
   a. federal aid for internal improvements.
   b. renewing the charter of the national bank.
   c. easy land-purchase terms for squatters.
   d. the Indian Removal Act of 1830.

10. The influence of Puritanism was greatest and lasted the longest in
    a. New France.
    b. New England.
    c. New York and Pennsylvania.
    d. Virginia and Maryland.

11. During the colonial and Revolutionary War periods, the crop that most shaped the economy and society of the Upper South was
    a. sugar.
    b. cotton.
    c. tobacco.
    d. wheat.

12. Which of these was a slave uprising?
    a. Bacon's Rebellion
    b. Shays's Rebellion
    c. the Whiskey Rebellion
    d. Nat Turner's rebellion

13. Which of the following statements about slavery in colonial America is correct?
    a. Slavery existed in all thirteen English colonies.
    b. The slave population exceeded the free white population in most of the southern colonies.
    c. British attempts to outlaw slavery in her overseas colonies helped to incite the American Revolution.
    d. The majority of those enslaved were Indians rather than Africans.

14. In the eighteenth century most of the British colonies in America were governed by
    a. the elders of the established church.
    b. a governor, council, and assembly—all elected by the people.
    c. a governor appointed by the crown and an elected assembly dominated by the upper classes.
    d. a proprietor or appointed representatives of the company that had established the colony.

15. Thomas Jefferson was responsible for all of the following *except*
    a. framing the Virginia Statute for Religious Freedom.
    b. drafting the Declaration of Independence.
    c. drafting the U.S. Constitution.
    d. writing the Kentucky resolution.

16. The first systematic statement of the strict versus broad interpretation of the Constitution arose out of the debate over the
    a. tariff.
    b. chartering of a national bank.
    c. barring of slavery from new territory.
    d. purchase of the Louisiana Territory.

17. Which of these describes the Indian policy adopted during the Jacksonian era?
    a. to remove Indians to lands west of the Mississippi River
    b. to establish reservations for Indians in various sections of the country
    c. to force Indians to migrate to territory owned by Mexico
    d. to assimilate the Indians by breaking up the tribes and granting American citizenship to individuals

18. For white males almost all property qualifications for voting had been abolished
    a. by the end of the American Revolution.
    b. with the ratification of the Constitution and the addition of the Bill of Rights.
    c. by 1800, when Jefferson was elected president.
    d. by the Jacksonian era.

19. The right of the federal courts to declare acts of Congress unconstitutional was first exercised in
    a. *Marbury* v. *Madison*.
    b. *McCulloch* v. *Maryland*.
    c. *Dred Scott* v. *Sandford*.
    d. *Ex parte* Milligan.

20. The main purpose of the lyceums of the antebellum period was to
    a. entertain the masses.
    b. diffuse high culture and knowledge to the middle and working classes.
    c. offer vocational training to the working class.
    d. spread evangelical religion.

21. In the 1840s and 1850s many Americans believed that it was the manifest destiny of the United States to
    a. abolish slavery.
    b. become the world's leading industrial power.
    c. build a mighty overseas empire.
    d. spread its borders from coast to coast.

22. By the eve of the Civil War which groups accounted for roughly 50 percent of the population of cities such as New York, Chicago, St. Louis, and San Francisco?
    a. Italians and Eastern European Jews
    b. Irish and Germans
    c. Polish and Chinese
    d. Scandinavians and Hispanics

23. Which of these led directly to the formation of the Republican party?
    a. the Compromise of 1850
    b. the Fugitive Slave Law
    c. the Kansas-Nebraska Act
    d. the *Dred Scott* decision

24. Which of these did Lincoln *oppose* in the first year of the Civil War?
    a. abolishing slavery everywhere in the nation
    b. compensating the owners of freed slaves
    c. colonizing freedmen outside the United States
    d. fighting a war primarily to preserve the Union

25. Many historians believe that Radical Reconstruction was a democratic experiment that failed for all of the following reasons *except*
    a. Congress did not redistribute southern land, and without property the freedmen were too economically vulnerable to hold on to their political rights.
    b. the Republicans were unwilling to continue to use military force to protect blacks and remake southern society.
    c. freedmen failed to understand the responsibilities of citizens and showed little interest in voting and officeholding.
    d. Republicans were willing to abandon the last of the Republican Reconstruction governments in 1877 to secure the election of their presidential candidate, Rutherford B. Hayes.

ESSAY QUESTIONS

1. The antebellum years saw the birth and development of the Federalist, Jeffersonian Republican, Democratic, Whig, and Republican parties. Discuss how and why each of these parties began. Who founded each? To which groups did each one mainly appeal? What led to the demise of the Federalist and Whig parties?

2. Each of the following men was in some way involved in the sectional conflict that eventually led to the Civil War: Thomas Jefferson, John C. Calhoun, Daniel Webster, Henry Clay, and Stephen A. Douglas. Discuss the views and activities of these men regarding the sectional conflict.

3. Trace Abraham Lincoln's position on blacks and slavery from the time of the Lincoln-Douglas debates in 1858 to the time of his assassination in 1865. How and why did he modify his stands?

4. Discuss the causes of the Civil War. Cite as many facts as possible to back up your analysis.

5. Compare and contrast Andrew Jackson's handling of South Carolina's nullification of federal law in 1832 and James Buchanan's handling of that same state's secession in 1860.

6. Explain the causes of the Mexican War and its impact on sectionalism.

7. Ralph Waldo Emerson once wrote, "There is no strong performance without a little fanaticism in the performance." To what extent could this observation be applied to the abolitionists and other antebellum reformers?

8. In 1820, 1833, and 1850 sectional compromises were agreed to and the Union was preserved. What accommodations were made each time, and why did the attempts to reach one more compromise in 1860–1861 fail?

9. If the enduring vision of America is embodied in the Declaration of Independence's statements about equality and universal rights to justice, liberty, and self-fulfillment, how much progress toward those ideals had blacks and women made by 1877? Back up your evaluation with as many specific facts as possible about the status of blacks and women at the end of Reconstruction.

10. In what respects was the Constitution of the United States as written and ratified in 1787 undemocratic? How was the American political system democratized between 1789 and 1877? What undemocratic features remained to be addressed? Give as many specific examples in your answer as possible.

Preparing for the Final Examination: Chapters 16 to 33, and the Epilogue

As you approach the end of your American history course, you may well wonder how you are supposed to remember all those facts for the final. Here are some hints for preparing yourself to take that semester exam. (1) Do not wait until the night before the test (or even the last couple of days prior to it) to start your studying. (2) Review the notes that you have taken on class lectures and assigned readings other than your textbook. (3) Review the chapters of this study guide, rereading carefully the Outline and Summary portion of each. (4) As you follow steps 2 and 3, look for issues and themes that seem to come up again and again. History, after all, is about change and continuity over time. Therefore, ask yourself as you review, "What things about American society have changed between the Reconstruction era and the 1990s and why?" On the other hand, which things have remained essentially constant or recurred periodically throughout all those years?

The sample multiple-choice and essay questions that follow are designed to assist you in pulling together all those facts and seeing more clearly the patterns of change and continuity over the last century or so of American history.

MULTIPLE-CHOICE QUESTIONS

Circle the letter of the item that best completes each statement or answers the question.

1. In which two periods did the federal government make its greatest efforts to protect black Americans by passing civil-rights laws and constitutional amendments?
   a. in the 1920s and 1930s
   b. during the administrations of Ronald Reagan and George Bush
   c. during Reconstruction and the 1960s
   d. during World Wars I and II

2. Which of these was primarily a rural-based reform movement concerned particularly with farmers' economic problems?
   a. the New Frontier
   b. progressivism
   c. populism
   d. the Fair Deal

3. The social worker who established Hull House in Chicago was
   a. Harry Hopkins.
   b. Frances Perkins.
   c. Jane Addams.
   d. Jeannette Rankin.

4. Each of these was a muckraking writer whose book helped to secure passage of federal legislation *except*
   a. John Hay.
   b. Upton Sinclair.
   c. Michael Harrington.
   d. Rachel Carson.

5. Oliver H. Kelly, James B. Weaver, William Jennings Bryan, and Henry Wallace were all associated with promoting the interests of which group?
   a. blacks
   b. Native Americans
   c. organized labor
   d. farmers

6. Which of the following happened to the majority of southern blacks in the years between Reconstruction and 1900?
   a. They were driven out of the South by poverty and discrimination.
   b. They became tenants and sharecroppers on land owned by whites.
   c. They got jobs in factories opening in the Midwest and Far West.
   d. They became independent, landowning small farmers.

7. The administration that ran up the biggest federal budget deficits in U.S. history was that of
   a. Franklin Roosevelt.
   b. Lyndon Johnson.
   c. Ulysses Grant.
   d. Ronald Reagan.

8. All of the following administrations are particularly associated with corruption and wrongdoing in government *except* that of
   a. Ulysses Grant.
   b. Herbert Hoover.
   c. Warren Harding.
   d. Richard Nixon.

9. Which of the wars that the United States fought had the least popular support at home?
    a. Spanish-American War
    b. World War I
    c. World War II
    d. Vietnam War

10. By what year did the majority of the American people live in cities?
    a. 1890
    b. 1920
    c. 1940
    d. 1960

11. In which of these elections was foreign policy *not* an important issue?
    a. 1900
    b. 1916
    c. 1936
    d. 1968

12. After which of these events did women secure the right to vote in national elections?
    a. the Great Depression of the 1930s
    b. passage of the Equal Rights Amendment in the 1970s
    c. passage of the Fourteenth Amendment
    d. World War I

13. In which decade did the United States finally get rid of the discriminatory national-origins quota system in our immigration law?
    a. 1970s
    b. 1960s
    c. 1980s
    d. 1920s

14. The elections of 1912, 1924, and 1948 were similar in what way?
    a. In each one there was a third party calling itself progressive.
    b. In each one the winner received more than 60 percent of the votes.
    c. In each one there was no incumbent running.
    d. Each election was followed immediately by war.

15. Membership in the organized labor movement in the United States increased most rapidly during which decade?
    a. 1890s
    b. 1920s
    c. 1930s
    d. 1970s

16. American armed forces fought against Soviet armies in which of these conflicts?
    a. World War II
    b. Korean War
    c. Vietnam War
    d. none of the above

17. Which of these statements about Native Americans is correct?
    a. Indian tribes lost hundreds of thousands of acres of land to whites under the Dawes Act.
    b. Native Americans resented the Indian Reorganization Act of 1934 because it attempted to suppress Native American culture and force rapid assimilation.
    c. As a result of the termination policy, the great majority of Native Americans live in cities and all reservations have been closed.
    d. none of the above.

18. In which of these periods was the U.S. economy plagued by the highest rates of inflation?
    a. 1875 to 1897
    b. 1900 to World War I
    c. 1920s and 1930s
    d. 1970s and early 1980s

19. All of the following have been used to justify U.S. intervention in Asia *except*
    a. the need to uplift, educate, and teach democracy to backward peoples.
    b. the Good Neighbor policy.
    c. the Open Door policy.
    d. the domino theory.

20. American literature tended to concern itself more with great social and economic questions and less with the emotional state of the individual during which period?
    a. 1930s
    b. 1950s
    c. 1880s
    d. 1970s and 1980s

21. Which of the following happened after both World War I and World War II?
    a. The Senate rejected treaties permitting the United States to join international organizations created to keep the peace.
    b. There was a heightened fear of internal communism and radicalism and greater attempts to suppress them.
    c. There was a postwar depression.
    d. The party in power during the war was defeated in the next presidential election.

22. All of these people were leaders who opposed the United States' participation in a war being fought in their day *except*
    a. Eugene McCarthy.
    b. Jane Addams.
    c. Eugene Debs.
    d. Theodore Roosevelt.

23. Some critics have blamed Franklin D. Roosevelt for giving in to Soviet domination of Eastern Europe at which conference?
    a. Versailles
    b. Potsdam
    c. Yalta
    d. Geneva

24. The treaty granting the United States control over the Panama Canal and Canal Zone was signed and ratified under which president, and the treaty returning control by 1999 to Panama was signed and ratified under which president, respectively?
    a. Theodore Roosevelt and Jimmy Carter
    b. William H. Taft and Richard Nixon
    c. Woodrow Wilson and Lyndon Johnson
    d. William McKinley and Bill Clinton

25. Which of these leaders was the first to gain a mass following among black Americans?
    a. Booker T. Washington
    b. W. E. B. Du Bois
    c. Marcus Garvey
    d. Malcolm X

ESSAY QUESTIONS

1. Compare and contrast the old immigrants (pre-1880s), the new immigrants (1880–1920), and the post–1960 immigrants. Who composed each group? Why did each group come? What characteristics did each display? How did each fare in the United States and why?

2. One history of African-Americans is titled *From Plantation to Ghetto*. Considering the experiences of blacks from Reconstruction to the 1990s, do you think this is an appropriate title? Why or why not? Back up what you say with as many historical and demographic facts as possible.

3. Pretend that you are a filmmaker working on a forty-five-minute documentary about the changing role of women in American society from Reconstruction to 1990. Which persons, events, trends, and laws would you depict in your movie? Why did you make these particular choices?

4. Discuss the impact of World War I, World War II, and the Vietnam War on American society at home. In your answer consider effects on the economy, women, families, minorities, domestic reform, and civil or constitutional liberties.

5. Compare and contrast the Populist, progressive, New Deal, and Great Society reform programs. What do you see as the major achievements of each? What do you think were the most serious failures?

6. Discuss the Latin American policy of the United States from Theodore Roosevelt's corollary to the early 1990s.

7. Trace federal-government policies toward labor and unions from the late nineteenth century to the 1990s. During which periods has the government been most prolabor? During which periods has government been most hostile to unions? How have the changes in government policy affected the labor movement?

8. Initially the majority of the American people did not wish to enter either World War I or World War II. Yet the United States entered both conflicts. Why?

9. From the late nineteenth century to the present progressives-liberals and conservatives have argued over the proper role of the federal government in the economic and social life of the nation. Explain the positions of each side and the rationales for their positions. Discuss concrete examples of legislation, federal programs, and Supreme Court decisions, from the 1890s to the 1990s, that have followed the philosophy of each political camp.

10. Discuss the origins of the Cold War and its impact on U.S. domestic and foreign policy since 1945. When and why did the Cold War end?

11. How do you define the American dream? Based on your definition, during which period between the 1870s and the 1990s has American society come closest to fulfilling your vision? Explain your choice by discussing as many facts about that period as possible.

12. Discuss the preservation, conservation, and environmental movements in the United States from the late nineteenth to the late twentieth centuries. What environmental issues have these movements addressed at various periods? What obstacles and opposition have the movements faced? What do you consider the greatest achievements, if any, of these movements? (In your answer consider the roles played by such individuals as John Muir, Gifford Pinchot, Theodore Roosevelt, Franklin Roosevelt, Rachel Carson, and Albert Gore.)

Answers to Multiple-Choice Questions

Prologue

1. d
2. c
3. b
4. d
5. c
6. b
7. a
8. d
9. a
10. c

Chapter 1

1. c
2. c
3. b
4. c
5. b
6. a
7. c
8. d
9. c
10. a

Chapter 2

1. a
2. c
3. d
4. b
5. c
6. d
7. a
8. a
9. b
10. c

Chapter 3

1. b
2. c
3. a
4. d
5. c
6. a
7. d
8. b
9. d
10. b

Chapter 4

1. b
2. c
3. d
4. a
5. c
6. d
7. c
8. a
9. b
10. a

Chapter 5

1. a
2. c
3. b
4. a
5. c
6. d
7. c
8. b
9. d
10. c

Chapter 6

1. a
2. b
3. d
4. c
5. b
6. d
7. c
8. a
9. c
10. d

Chapter 7

1. d
2. c
3. c
4. a
5. a
6. d
7. b
8. c
9. b
10. b

Chapter 8	**Chapter 11**	**Chapter 14**	**Chapter 17**
1. b	1. b	1. d	1. c
2. a	2. a	2. a	2. b
3. c	3. d	3. b	3. d
4. b	4. b	4. c	4. b
5. c	5. c	5. a	5. d
6. d	6. c	6. d	6. c
7. b	7. b	7. a	7. a
8. c	8. c	8. c	8. d
9. a	9. b	9. d	9. c
10. d	10. a	10. b	10. d

Chapter 9	**Chapter 12**	**Chapter 15**	**Chapter 18**
1. c	1. c	1. c	1. b
2. b	2. d	2. a	2. a
3. d	3. a	3. b	3. d
4. a	4. b	4. c	4. c
5. b	5. c	5. d	5. a
6. d	6. a	6. a	6. a
7. c	7. a	7. c	7. c
8. c	8. a	8. a	8. d
9. a	9. c	9. b	9. b
10. c	10. c	10. a	10. a

Chapter 10	**Chapter 13**	**Chapter 16**	**Chapter 19**
1. a	1. c	1. c	1. b
2. c	2. b	2. b	2. a
3. d	3. a	3. d	3. c
4. a	4. b	4. a	4. d
5. c	5. d	5. c	5. c
6. d	6. b	6. b	6. c
7. c	7. a	7. b	7. b
8. c	8. a	8. c	8. b
9. a	9. b	9. a	9. a
10. b	10. d	10. a	10. a

Chapter 20	**Chapter 23**	**Chapter 26**	**Chapter 29**
1. c	1. a	1. a	1. a
2. b	2. c	2. b	2. c
3. c	3. b	3. c	3. d
4. d	4. b	4. b	4. b
5. a	5. b	5. c	5. b
6. d	6. a	6. b	6. a
7. d	7. b	7. c	7. d
8. c	8. c	8. d	8. c
9. a	9. c	9. a	9. b
10. d	10. d	10. c	10. c

Chapter 21	**Chapter 24**	**Chapter 27**	**Chapter 30**
1. a	1. c	1. a	1. c
2. c	2. b	2. c	2. a
3. b	3. c	3. a	3. b
4. a	4. d	4. d	4. b
5. a	5. c	5. c	5. d
6. d	6. a	6. a	6. c
7. a	7. b	7. d	7. c
8. d	8. c	8. b	8. a
9. c	9. b	9. a	9. d
10. b	10. d	10. b	10. b

Chapter 22	**Chapter 25**	**Chapter 28**	**Chapter 31**
1. a	1. c	1. c	1. b
2. d	2. d	2. a	2. b
3. c	3. b	3. d	3. c
4. b	4. c	4. a	4. a
5. c	5. a	5. b	5. a
6. b	6. c	6. c	6. d
7. c	7. a	7. d	7. d
8. a	8. d	8. d	8. b
9. a	9. a	9. a	9. c
10. d	10. b	10. c	10. c

Chapter 32

1. c
2. d
3. a
4. a
5. b
6. b
7. a
8. d
9. d
10. b

Chapter 33

1. d
2. d
3. c
4. b
5. d
6. c
7. a
8. c
9. b
10. a

Epilogue

1. a
2. c
3. d
4. b

Preparing for the Final Examination: Prologue, Chapters 1 to 16

1. c
2. a
3. c
4. b
5. b
6. a
7. c
8. d
9. b
10. b
11. c
12. d
13. a
14. c
15. c
16. b
17. a
18. d
19. a
20. b
21. d
22. b
23. c
24. a
25. c

Preparing for the Final Examination: Chapters 16 to 33, and the Epilogue

1. c
2. c
3. c
4. a
5. d
6. b
7. d
8. b
9. d
10. b
11. c
12. d
13. b
14. a
15. c
16. d
17. a
18. d
19. b
20. a
21. b
22. d
23. c
24. a
25. c